Domestic Plants and Animals:
The Egyptian Origins

To Conrad, Mary and Margaret with thanks

Domestic Plants and Animals:
The Egyptian Origins

Douglas J. Brewer
Department of Anthropology &
Museum of Natural History
University of Illinois

Donald B. Redford
Near Eastern Studies Department
University of Toronto

Susan Redford
Akhenaten Temple Project
University of Toronto

OXBOW | books
Oxford & Philadelphia

This edition published in the United Kingdom in 2024 by
OXBOW BOOKS
81 St Clements, Oxford OX4 1AW

and in the United States by
OXBOW BOOKS
1950 Lawrence Road, Havertown, PA 19083

Paperback Edition: ISBN 979-8-88857-079-1
Digital Edition: ISBN 979-8-88857-080-7 (epub)

First published in 1994 by Aris & Phillips Ltd

Oxbow Books is grateful to the Petrie Museum for their collaboration in bringing out these new editions

Printed in the United Kingdom by CMP Digital Print Solutions

For a complete list of Oxbow titles, please contact:

UNITED KINGDOM
Oxbow Books
Telephone (0)1226 734350
Email: oxbow@oxbowbooks.com
www.oxbowbooks.com

UNITED STATES OF AMERICA
Oxbow Books
Telephone (610) 853-9131, Fax (610) 853-9146
Email: queries@casemateacademic.com
www.casemateacademic.com/oxbow

Oxbow Books is part of the Casemate Group

Front cover: Ploughing scene from the tomb of Sennedjem, Thebes, *c.* 1200 BC (image in the public domain, courtesy of The Yorck Project (2002); copyright Zenodot Verlagsgesellschaft mbH licensed under the GNU Free Documentation License.)

CONTENTS

List of Tables

List of Figures

SOURCES OF FIGURES

1.1 after Hassan, fig. 17.8 drawn by S. Holland. **1.2** after Butzer 1976, fig., 10; Hassan 1984b, fig. 3; Brewer 1991, fig. 4., drawn by S. Debarr. **2.1.** after Wenke 1991 and Wenke and Brewer 1993. Drawn by S. Debarr. **2.2.** after Millet 1990, fig. 2. Drawn by S. Holland. **2.3.** photo by D. Brewer. **2.4.** after Vandier 1978 fig. 15, Tomb of Ti Saqqara Dyn. V Drawn by I. Samson. **2.5.** photo by D. Brewer. **2.6.** photo by D. Brewer. **2.7.** photo by D. Brewer. **2.8.** photo by D. Brewer. **2.9.** photo by D. Brewer. **2.10.** Photo by D. Brewer. **2.11.** photo by D. Brewer. **2.12** photo by D. Brewer. **3.1.** after Harlan and Zohary 1966; Harlan 1977; Zohary and Hopf 1988; redrawn by T. Sagrillo. **3.2.** After Zohary and Hopf, figs 3, 8; redrawn by T. Sagrillo. **3.3.** Photo by D. Brewer. **3.4.** after Dauma and Goyon 1939, pl.. LXVI; redrawn by I. Samson. **3.5.** photo by D. Brewer. **3.6.** photo by D. Brewer. **4.1.** photo courtesy of the Metropolitan Museum of Art. **4.2.** photo by D. Brewer. **4.3.** after Davies, Beni Hasan I, pl. XIII; redrawn by T. Sagrillo. **4.4.** photo by D. Brewer. **4.5.** photo by D. Brewer. **4.6.** photo by D. Brewer. **4.7.** after Newberry, Beni Hasan II, pl. XIII; redrawn by T. Sagrillo. **4.8.** after Newberry, Beni Hasan I, pl XXXIX and Hall, fig. 8; redrawn by T. Sagrillo. **4.9.** reprinted courtesy of Egyptian Exploration Society. **4.10.** photo by D. Brewer. **4.11.** photo courtesy of the Metropolitan Museum of Art, Gift of Norbet Schimmel, 1981. **5.1.** reproduced from Quibel and Green 1902, pl. LXXVI; courtesy of Egyptian Research Account. **5.2.** photo reproduced courtesy of the Metropolitan Museum of Art. **5.3.** photo by D. Brewer. **5.4.** after Hepper 1990, p. 58; redrawn by T. Sagrillo. **5.5.** photo by D. Brewer. **5.6.** photo by D. Brewer. **5.7.** after Harlan 1986, fig. 2; redrawn by T. Sagrillo. **5.8.** photo by D. Brewer. **5.9.** photo by D. Brewer. **5.10.** drawn by T. Sagrillo. **5.11.** photo by D. Brewer. **5.12.** after Erman 1971, p. 256; redrawn by T. Sagrillo. **5.13.** after Manniche 1989, p. 86; Mekhitarian 1954, p. 79; redrawn by T. Sagrillo. **5.14.** photo by D. Brewer. **5.15.** photo by D. Brewer. **6.1.** photo by D. Brewer. **6.2.** photo by D. Brewer. **6.3.** photo by D. Brewer. **6.4.** photo by D. Brewer. **6.5.** photo by D. Brewer. **7.1** after Zuener 1963, fig. 8; redrawn by I. Samson. **7.2.** reproduced from Winker 1938, frontispiece; courtesy of Egyptian Exploration Society. **7.3.** photo by D. Brewer. **7.4.** photo by D. Brewer. **7.5.** photo by D. Brewer. **7.6.** photo by D. Brewer. **7.7.** photo by D. Brewer. **7.8.** photo by D. Brewer. **7.9.** photo by D. Brewer. **7.10.** after Darby et al. 1977, fig. 3.19 and Wilkinson, 1838,. fig. 349; redrawn by T. Sagrillo. **7.11.** photo by D. Brewer. **7.12.** photo by D. Brewer. **7.13.** photo by D. Brewer. **7.14.** photo by D. Brewer. **7.15.** photo by D. Brewer. **7.16.** after Newberry 1893, fig., XIII; redrawn by. I. Samson. **8.1.** photo reprinted courtesy of petrie, 1953. **8.2.** photo by D. Brewer. **8.3.** photo by D. Brewer. **8.4.** photo by D. Brewer. **8.5.** after Todd p. 102, redrawn by T. Sagrillo. **8.6.** after Todd, p. 103, redrawn by T. Sagrillo. **8.7.** after Todd, p. 106, redrawn by T. Sagrillo. **8.8** photo by D. Brewer. **8.9.** photo by D. Brewer. **8.10.** after Zuener 1963 fig. 4; redrawn by I. Samson. **8.11** photo by D. B. Redford. **8.12.** reproduced from Winkler 1938, p. XXIII; courtesy of Egyptian Exploration Society. **8.13.** reproduced from Quibel and Green 1902, pl LXXVI, courtesy Egyptian Research Account. **8.14.** photo by D. Brewer. **8.15.** after Newberry, 1893, pl. XX; redrawn by I. Samson.. **9.1.** photo by D. Brewer. **9.2.** photo by D. Brewer. **9.3.** photo by D. Brewer. **9.4.** courtesy of Aris and Phillips. **9.5** photo by D. Brewer. **9.6.** courtesy of Aris and Phillips. **9.7.** photo by D. Brewer. **9.8** photo by D. Brewer. **9.9** courtesy of Aris and Phillips. **9.10.** after Kueny 1950, fig. 1; redrawn by I. Samson. **9.11.** after Kueny 1950, fig. 2-3; redrawn by I. Samson.

Acknowledgements

We wish to express our thanks to the University of Illinois Research Board and office of the Dean, Liberal Arts and Sciences, University of Illinois Travel Fund for the financial support of this project and to the Egyptian Antiquities Organization for permission to photograph the many tomb scenes required for this volume. Egyptian antiquities inspector Mr. Mohammed abd Rahman and Director Mr. Yahia Eid were very helpful, providing valuable assistance while working in the many mastabas of Saqqara. We are also indebted to the Canadian Institute in Egypt and its Cairo Director Mr. Edwin C. Brock for logistical support. The British Museum, London, the Egyptian Museum, Cairo, the Metropolitan Museum of Art, New York, and the Egyptian Exploration Society provided the subjects for several illustrations. Mindy James, Sharon Gunneson, Wilma Wetterstrom and Carol Yokell read earlier versions of the manuscript and provided important editorial comments. Sheryl Debarr, Immanuel Samson and Troy Sagrillo deserve special thanks for donating their time and artistic skills to the many illustrations presented in this volume.

PREFACE TO THE 2024 EDITION

In the 1970s, a much-anticipated new series of publications illustrated objects and themes related to the excavations of the archaeologist William Matthew Flinders Petrie (1853–1942) in Egypt, and aspects of the collection of University College London's Petrie Museum of Egyptian and Sudanese Archaeology. A young couple setting up in business in the early 1970s, Aris and Phillips published these works, written by members of the UCL Egyptology Department, in their *Modern Egyptology* series. Building on Petrie's own observations, the authors of these volumes aimed to complete the great task of publishing the Petrie Museum of Egyptian and Sudanese Archaeology's vast collection, and to present some of the research that Petrie himself was not able to address in his own published works during his lifetime. As the current Curator of the Petrie Museum, it is a great privilege for me to support Oxbow Books in their mission to republish the series, which remains a key source of information for all those interested in object-based approaches to the study of the ancient world.

The Petrie Museum, part of University College London (UCL), is home to one of the largest and most significant collections of Egyptian and Sudanese archaeology in the world. Free to visit, this extraordinary collection tells stories about the lives of ordinary people who lived along the Nile Valley thousands of years ago. Originally set up as a teaching collection, the Petrie Museum comprises over 80,000 objects housed together with an internationally important archaeological archive. It is a collection of world firsts and 'oldests': the oldest woven garment; the oldest worked iron objects; the first known depiction of loom weaving; the oldest known written document about women's health; the earliest veterinary treatise; the oldest will on paper. The Museum has Designated Status from Arts Council England, meaning that it is considered to have outstanding resonance and national cultural significance. The collection has a substantial, visible international reputation for research, supporting hundreds of researchers every year, both remotely and in person.

The Petrie Museum is named after Flinders Petrie, who was appointed in 1892 as the first Professor of Egyptian Archaeology and Philology in the UK at UCL. Over three-quarters of the material in the Museum comes from excavations directed or funded by Petrie, or from purchases he made for university teaching. In 1880 at the age of 26, Petrie travelled to Egypt to survey the Great Pyramid. For the next five decades he was at the forefront of the development of archaeology in Egypt and later in Palestine, and his detailed methodological approach continues to shape the discipline today.

Petrie worked at more sites, with greater speed, than any modern archaeologist: seeing his life as a mission of rescue archaeology, Petrie aimed to retrieve as much information as possible from sites that were shrinking dramatically in size as Egypt modernised during the late 19th and early 20th centuries. He published a large part, but not all, of the finds from his excavations in his illustrated typological volumes, arranged according to object types and themes. Today, much of the Petrie Museum's collection is displayed and stored in a way which reflects these publications: for example, several storage cupboards are dedicated to the material illustrated in the 'Objects of Daily Use' volume, and objects in the drawers are arranged according to the order of the published plates. This offers a unique opportunity for researchers to engage with Petrie's typological and methodical approach to archaeology, as well as with the history of museum collections.

The first catalogue to be published in the *Modern Egyptology* series was *Amarna: City of Akhenaten and Nefertiti* in 1972 by Julia Samson, Petrie Museum Honorary Research Assistant. As official publishers to the UCL Egyptology Department the series went on to produce facsimile reprints of eight of Flinders Petrie's most important site reports and many of his object catalogues, originally published through the British School of Archaeology in Egypt. The substantial annual royalties from these reprints were paid into the 'Petrie Fund' at the time, which provided special grants to students in financial need.

In many ways, the new reprints of this classic series can be seen as the latest layer in a vast 'publication stratigraphy' of the thousands of finds from Flinders Petrie's excavations, which now live in museum collections around the world. On reading these volumes, I hope that readers will also be inspired to learn more about the Petrie Museum collection and its fascinating history.

Dr Anna Garnett
Petrie Museum of Egyptian and
Sudanese Archaeology, University College London
January 2023

PUBLISHER'S PREFACE

Oxbow Books is pleased to present this title in our *Classics in Egyptology* series. This series of facsimile re-issues is comprised of two sub-series. The first consists of 16 typological catalogues produced by W.M. Flinders Petrie based on his massive collection of Egyptian artefacts. Mostly excavated by Petrie during many seasons of campaign in the last years of the 19th and early decades of the 20th century, they now reside in the Petrie Museum at University College London. Published between 1898 and 1937 and long out of print, the catalogues were re-issued in facsimile by publishers Aris and Phillips in the 1970s. These were followed in the next 15 years or so by publication of a number of newly commissioned titles, based on more recent examination of elements of the Petrie Collection by contemporary experts, under the name *Modern Egyptology*. A selection of these additional titles forms the second component of our own series.

The archaeology of Egypt continues to fascinate. Multi-disciplinary investigation and research continues unabated, encompassing methodologies, scientific and data processing techniques, theoretical approaches, and even whole paradigms that were unheard of in the 1970s and undreamt of when Petrie was working in Egypt. Yet all the titles included in this series continue to be invaluable sources of basic data, providing an unparalleled resource that can easily be cross-referenced with the actual materials they describe and discuss. They remain within the Petrie Collection where they may be accessed and re-examined as new research flourishes. As historic documents, the Petrie catalogues stand as exemplars of the craft of typological classification, the backbone of modern archaeology – much of which, though refined by absolute dating and another 100 years of research, still stands the test of time.

A note on presentation

The facsimile titles of Petrie's catalogues re-issued in the 1970s were produced from scans of the original publications. Scanning technology at that time was not of the standard or resolution of today. The scans are no longer available, nor has it been possible to obtain, and in doing so destroy, original copies of the Petrie catalogues. These titles have therefore, of necessity, been rescanned from the 1970s re-issues. Where necessary the pages have been digitally enhanced for clarity of reading and to ensure the good quality of the plates, though inevitably a few are not of the standard we might wish, because of the quality of the previous scan, and occasional blocks of text are not precisely 'straight' or evenly situated on the page. However, some pages in the 1970s re-issues had been inserted in the wrong order and this has been corrected. The originals were produced at a folio size. The pages have been reduced slightly to standard A4 for ease of shelving and because this has the effect of slightly improving the scanned images. In some cases, illustrations were presented to scale and the original scale is given on the plate. There were also no digital files available for titles included in the *Modern Egyptology* series, so these too have been scanned from printed copies.

I

INTRODUCTION

No development has had a greater effect on human history than the introduction of domesticated plants and animals. The period during which domesticated forms became established is referred to as the Neolithic and has been accurately characterized as a revolution. Agriculture, which in its broadest sense includes rearing domestic plants and animals for human use, created the economic base and a need for social interactions that led ultimately to the earliest civilizations. The inception of plant and animal domestication and agriculture arose independently in several regions of the world (e.g., China, the Near East, and Mesoamerica), but the Near East has been considered a cradle of early agriculture, and Egypt the site of the earliest great "civilization." This volume summarizes current knowledge about the origins of Egyptian agriculture and describes the numerous domestic species commonly used by the Ancient Egyptians.[1]

Domestication and What it Entails

The obvious steps in discussing Ancient Egyptian domesticates are defining domestication and trying to determine why and where it originated. Numerous definitions for the term "domestication" exist, and all seem to have avid followers as well as critics. For example, Bökönyi, in his discussion on domesticated animals, offered a classic definition that is used by many researchers today. He stated that "the essence of domestication is the capture and taming of animals of a species with particular behavioral characteristics, their removal from their natural living area and breeding community, and their maintenance under controlled conditions for mutual benefits." Opponents state that although this definition serves its purpose in an archaeological context, it equates the capture and taming of an animal with domestication.[2]

Given such a definition, a wolf pup or lion cub taken into captivity and tamed could be considered a domesticate. Critics point out that there is a distinction between keeping and caring for an animal and its actual domestication. Ducos has attempted to counter this criticism by defining domesticates in anthropological terms and taking into consideration the intent and use of the plant or animal in question. He stated that living organisms are domesticates when they are integrated as objects into the socioeconomic organization of human groups, in the sense that, while living, those plants and animals are objects of ownership, inheritance, exchange, and trade as are other objects in a given society.

Although Ducos' definition does account for most anthropological criteria needed to be considered a "domesticate," the definition is somewhat one-sided in that it omits the biological nature of the domestication process. Botanists also, argue over the essential criteria needed for an inclusive definition of domestication and distinguish between cultivated plants and domesticated plants. To cultivate a plant means to conduct those activities associated with the care of a plant such as tilling, fertilizing, seeding, weeding and watering. Cultivation simply implies human activities; domestication deals with the genetic response to those human activities. A cultivated plant, therefore, can be wild or domesticated.[3]

For the purposes of this volume, the following biologically based definition is offered. It cannot account for all cases (e.g. third-generation zoo animals), but it does demonstrate cultural intent and the necessary interplay between humans and plants or animals.

> A domesticated plant or animal is one whose genetic make-up and thus whose gene pool has been altered to satisfy the needs of humans such that if the plant or animal is placed back into its natural environment, it will be at a selective disadvantage when competing against its wild counterparts.[4]

Basically, the definition states that human actions have genetically altered a group of plants or animals in such a way that they are now dependent on human care for their survival. If returned back into the wild, these animals or plants would most likely perish. Although examples do exist of domesticates returning to their natural habitat, it is interesting to point out that descendants of those animals that survived this transition have taken on the behavior and appearance of their wild counterparts. This demonstrates that domestication does not create a new species, but rather selects for particular traits inherent in the wild species. In domestication the forces of natural selection have, in a sense, been superseded by human selection. The feral pigs of New

Zealand and the wild mustang of North America provide good examples of this concept. These animals are descendants of domestic breeds, but once freed from human control, trait selection was, once again, natural and the descendants of the surviving animals look more like their wild ancestral counterparts (e.g., the wild boar and horse) than the domesticated form.

Natural selection serves to limit potential variation to a form that best fits the ecological conditions of a given area. Therefore, wild plants or animals taken from a given region look more like their wild counterparts than their domestic forms. Although the same or even a greater degree of similarity can exist in domestic breeds, morphological differences between genetically related domestic forms are of a higher magnitude than is typically encountered in the wild. One only has to think of the different breeds of dogs to see the degree of similarity that can be attained or the variability that can exist. Also, consider the fact that broccoli, brussel sprouts, cabbage, and cauliflower all belong to the same species. Wild forms that differ significantly from the norm are usually culled out by the natural selection process, but those same characteristics may be precisely the ones selected for by humans.[5]

The early morphological changes associated with domestication may not necessarily be a function of conscious human selection. Each plant or animal has its own evolutionary path to follow, and it is entirely possible that some changes may be purely coincidental. What is actually taking place when wild plants or animals are adopted and dominated by humans does not differ from that which occurs in the natural environment. That is, the same evolutionary process of adaptation is involved, but in this case adaptation is for fitness into a "cultural" niche. The cultural niche offers different selective pressures than those that occur in the wild. Thus, different characteristics, which may not have been important in the wild, may prove advantageous in a domestic context. For example, the supply and type of food available to animals held in captivity would differ from those of wild animals because human groups would likely have different seasonal priorities than the captive animals' wild counterparts. Plants also would be subject to different growing cycles as well as a host of new competitors and pests. Organisms that are not able to adapt to the new niche, either because they will not submit to human dominance or cannot adapt to the new selective pressures, are culled out of the breeding population through natural or human-induced attrition. Some individuals may even return to the wild, but those that have a selective advantage for survival in the cultural niche have, evolutionarily speaking, the best chance of passing on their characteristics to the next generation and ensuring the perpetuation of their genotype.[6]

As a rule, the success in subjugating a species and creating a successful domestic form depends on the presence of certain innate characteristics. For example, with one notable exception, all domesticated animals are gregarious and possess in the wild state a discernible social order. The domestic cat is the one obvious exception. This is not to say that all gregarious animals are predisposed to domestication, as failed experiments with hyena and gazelles by the Ancient Egyptians demonstrate, but that those animals that were successfully domesticated held these traits in common. That some degree of affinity for domestication exists in plants also seems evident when you consider that certain plant families such as Gramineae (grasses) and Leguminosae (beans, peas, etc.) have contributed more than 70 economically important forms; other families (e.g., Cyperaceae, Ranunculaceae, Cactaceae, Caryophyllaceae, Portulacaceae, Berberidaceae, Papaveraceae, Saxifragaceae, Geraniaceae, Onagraceae, Apocynaceae, Asclepiadaceae, Plataginaceae, etc.) have produced no important domesticated species at all.[7]

Although domestication is a process rather than an event, certain points along the continuum can be identified as important stages in the growing influence of selective forces for the cultural niche on a given population. In the initial stages of animal domestication the organisms are genetically the same as their wild counterparts, but they have been behaviorally conditioned or tamed to accept the dominant position of humans. Their breeding habits, however, have not been curtailed; the animal often will breed with wild members of the species. The second stage in the process can be marked by the presence of a restricted breeding population. Control, whether intentional or otherwise, has been attained over potential breeding partners by excluding wild members of the species. The second stage is often correlated with morphological changes such as the reduction in body or horn size, changes in color, or a reduction in the chewing apparatus, such as in dogs and cats. Stage three is marked by the beginning of the intentional development of discernible characteristics in the stock. Size management or the suppression of horn growth are examples of early stage three. Advanced stage three would be indicated by the development of breeds with specifically developed morpho-economic characteristics.[8]

It is not as easy to trace the domestication process in plants as in animals. For plants there is no "behavior" to observe. Genetic reproduction remains the only criterion. When a crop is harvested and all the grain obtained is used as food, it is difficult to determine archaeologically if the stands of fruit or grain were wild or domestic. If, however, some of the collected seeds were used as food and some were intentionally planted, it is likely that the stands were cultivated or perhaps domesticated. When a list of known domesticated plants is surveyed, two important similarities stand out as being common across genera. The size of the seed or fruit tends to be large, although not significantly larger than early domesticated forms, and they are easy to collect in the wild.

The main physiological developments during the early stages of plant domestication are not, as one might think, selection for bigger seeds and fruits, but a breakdown of the natural dispersal mechanism and the regulation of germination. Under natural conditions, wild populations of plants maintain themselves spontaneously. When wild stands are harvested, the seeds that escape the harvester produce the next generation and any genetic effect on the wild population is likely negligible. As soon as harvested seeds are planted, the situation changes. Now there are two populations, one wild and totally dependent on nature, the other planted and tended with selective pressures imposed by humans. Any trait that enhances seed recovery is selectively favored in the cultivated environment. Seed retention through unconscious collection of seeds with tougher connective tissues or shatter resistant pods are obviously beneficial to cultivators. Seeds retained by the plant are available for harvest; individual plants that easily disperse their seeds to the natural environment offer little to the next cultivated generation. Also, periods of long seed dormancy, generally a selective advantage to wild forms, is a disadvantage in cultivated species. The cultivator prefers the plant to grow when planted, not lie dormant for a period of time that could extend over several seasons. Changes in maturation schedule to the near-simultaneous ripening of an entire crop, a condition not strongly selected for in many natural environments, is also an extremely valuable trait to human cultivators.

Exploitation of self-pollinating plants, which would enhance the isolation of particular characteristics, would offer an additional advantage in the initial stages of agriculture. Isolation of characteristics is difficult to do if cross-pollination dominates the reproductive cycle. If self-pollination were to predominate, plants with less brittle stems or tougher pods could in a short time dominate a cultivated plot, and the form could easily be isolated and purer stands grown in successive generations. It is not surprising then that the first known domesticated plants in Egypt and those that show the earliest evidence of being economically important were self-pollinating grasses (i.e., wheat and barley) with a tough connective segment between grain and stem (rachis).[9]

Hunters, Gatherers and Early Farmers

Any discussion of the inception of domestication and food production in Egypt must consider the popular misconceptions about the lifestyle of early farmers and hunting-gathering societies. Ethnographic observations of modern hunter-gatherers and groups practicing simple non-mechanized agriculture have shown that many of our Victorian conceptions are incorrect. The traditional view of the life of hunter-gatherers as one involved in a continuous search for food with little leisure time was often contrasted with that of the early farmer, who had plenty to eat and considerable leisure time to devote to arts, crafts, and the development of a more sophisticated and complex society. Leisure time was thought to be a necessary prerequisite for the development of aesthetic and other activities not related to food production.

A more accurate depiction would place the traditional view of nomadic hunter-gatherers and sedentary agriculturalists at end-points along a continuum of cultural adaptations. Some modern hunter-gatherer groups, for example, are known to engage in agricultural activities, and many sedentary agriculturists engage in hunting and gathering. Because hunter-gatherer groups today are limited to a small fraction of the Earth's surface, the current diversity of lifestyles is probably more restricted than in prehistoric times, when hunting and gathering was the dominant system filling all available niches around the world.

Nevertheless, observations about the life of modern hunter-gatherer groups, even those living in harsh arid environments, suggest that life is not a constant struggle and is composed of considerable leisure time. In fact, some researchers have gone so far as to postulate that no groups on earth have more free time than hunter-gatherers. For example, the Hadza women of Tanzania require, on a yearly average, only about two hours a day to gather the necessary foods for their family. Work conducted on the !Kung San of South Africa has shown that food sufficient to feed a family of four for three days could, on the average, be collected by one woman in a six-hour period. Hunting, a traditionally male occupation, was conducted on an irregular basis, and not out of the need for food, but rather out of personal or group desires. Male and female !Kung San enjoy considerable leisure time and seldom suffer from a lack of food. Other ethnographic accounts of hunter-gatherers depict a similar lifestyle; some of these groups have complicated belief systems as well as displays of artistic and architectural sophistication; characteristics often associated and used to define agriculturally based societies. The Native Americans of the northwest coast of the United States, for example, had enough leisure time to construct large wooden homes with intricate artistic designs that were related to a complex system of beliefs. Some Australian aborigines, although living in an extremely arid environment, possess an equally complex metaphysical system. Hunter-gatherers of the late Paleolithic must certainly have enjoyed periods of leisure as well. The time, skill, and sophistication needed to decorate weapons, tools, and caves with paintings, engravings, and low relief provide ample evidence for this.[10]

In contrast, studies about modern populations involved in non-mechanical agriculture suggest that a total reliance on domestic crops could lead to disaster. Crop yields vary depending on rainfall, pests, and other natural conditions and the stored grain is susceptible to fire, water, pests, and molds. Life in crowded villages is often characterized by unsanitary conditions posing an increased chance for the spread of disease. If crops fail, farmers may have to turn to hunting and gathering to supplement the food supply. To counter these potential hazards many horticultural groups in Amazonia, New Guinea, and elsewhere have adopted a mobile system of agriculture similar in many ways to early Neolithic cultures in Egypt. In these areas, domestic crops serve as only one component of a food procurement system that includes hunting and gathering as well as seasonal relocations to take advantage of other resources. Sedentary agriculture is not feasible in many of these areas because the soil is quickly depleted of the vital nutrients needed to sustain crops. In fact, soil exhaustion was once suggested as a possible cause for the collapse of the Maya civilization in Central America.[11]

The negative effects of a life devoted to farming as opposed to hunting-gathering can be further exemplified by evidence compiled from the study of ancient skeletal remains. Skeletons from Greece and Turkey, for example, show that the average height of hunter-gatherers toward the end of the Ice Age was about 172 cm for men and 162 cm for women. With the adoption of agriculture, average height plummeted to 157 cm for men and 150 cm for women. By classical times, heights were slowly increasing, but to date modern Greeks and Turks have not regained the average height of their ancestors.

An even more graphic example of the effects of switching from a hunter-gatherer diet to one predominantly composed of agricultural products comes from work on Native American remains from the Illinois and Ohio River valleys of the central United States. Near the confluence of the Spoon and Illinois Rivers archaeologists have excavated approximately 800 skeletons. Analysis of these individuals showed that compared to the hunter-gatherers who preceded them, the horticulturalists had nearly a 50 per cent increase in tooth-enamel defects, indicative of malnutrition; a fourfold increase in iron deficiency anemia, evidenced by a bone condition called porotic hyperostosis; a threefold rise in bone lesions, reflecting infectious disease in general; and an increase in degenerative conditions of the spine, probably reflecting a lot of hard physical labor.[12]

Physical effects of the shift to an agriculturally based economy is not well documented in Egypt, but a recent study on the remains of a sample of Archaic and Old Kingdom Egyptians showed that all the Predynastic Egyptians studied suffered from anemia and, with the exception of individuals recovered from elite tombs, all Old Kingdom remains suffered from the same affliction. Such widespread anemia was attributed to poor hygienic conditions, particularly parasitic infestations, characteristic of crowded agricultural communities. A separate study centered in Nubia showed a similar pattern. The development of agriculture there led to nutritional deficiencies that were manifested in the form of slow bone development, anemia, microdefects in dentition, and premature osteoporosis in juveniles and young adult females.

Information available on hunter-gatherers and early agriculturalists exemplified by the few cases presented here should dispel the traditional myth of a hunter-gatherer life always near the brink of starvation and the life of an early agriculturalist as one of leisure. In fact, it may raise the question, why were domesticates developed and adopted in the first place? This is particularly apropos because modern studies on natural productivity have been conducted in some of the very areas where early domesticates are thought to have originated. The gathering of wild einkorn wheat in South Central Anatolia and wild maize in Mexico demonstrates the potential richness of the wild resources available to hunter-gatherers in these areas. On the basis of modern collecting experiments in Mexico, an eleven-day supply of wild maize could be gathered in 3.5 hours. Using only their bare hands, researchers in Turkey collected a little more than one kilogram of edible grain per hour from pure stands of wild einkorn wheat. A 20 per cent increase was noted when a primitive sickle was employed. Additionally, the food value of the wild grain was found to be superior to much of the cultivated grain of today. Moreover, because of the terrain, stands of wild einkorn matured at different rates, allowing a family or group of gatherers to collect grain from numerous locations over a period of several weeks. It was estimated that a small family-size group could harvest in three weeks more grain than they would have eaten in an entire year.[13]

Why, then, did agriculture develop and flourish in an environment as rich as that of the Nile Valley?

Origin of Egyptian Domesticates

Researchers have postulated that changes in the environment, the biological make-up of the animals, or human population (culture) might have produced the needed impetus behind the adoption of domesticates and agriculture in Egypt. It seems impossible, however, to delineate which was the primary cause. Stimuli from each of these spheres no doubt functioned together in this transformation, and the evidence from Egypt appears to support this contention.

The lack or rarity of plant and faunal remains in many early Holocene sites (9800 to 8900 BC) and the difficulty involved in determining whether, on the basis of fragmentary remains, these organisms were domesticated does, however, pose serious problems in attempting to trace the origins of Egyptian agriculture. Criteria composed from three types of data are generally used to identify examples of prehistoric domestication. The first employs physical characteristics of the organisms involved such as size, morphology, and color. The second concerns assessments of the ecological fitness of the plant or animal to the local biotype or the sudden appearance of a new species into an area. Studying the demography, ecology, and biogeography of exploited animal populations often involves comparing sex ratios or mortality and survivorship patterns between recovered archaeological materials and a documented wild population. Artifacts and artistic scenes compose the third source of information.[14]

Unlike the plants and animals of the Levant and Near East, there is no definitive evidence that the wild progenitors that formed the backbone of Egyptian domestic economy (i.e., wheat, barley, sheep, goat; but see entry on cattle) were ever native to the area. Consequently, many scholars believe that paleolithic Egyptians learned the concept of agriculture from their eastern and perhaps western neighbors and that many of the domestic species raised in Egypt originated from these areas. Few scholars, however, have critically evaluated the established concept of a Near East center for agricultural origins. In fact, it could be argued that the Near East agricultural center may be a simple artifact of intensive scholarly research. Traditionally, this area has received so much attention that it is only natural that new discoveries continue to compile at a faster rate than in adjacent areas.

A second, more important factor, however, may lend to the illusion of a Near East agricultural source. Because agricultural systems, like all biological systems, adhere to evolutionary principles, successful systems expand and come to dominate and replace less successful systems. The Near East complex (i.e., barley, wheat, legumes, sheep, goat, and pig) is an example of a very successful system that spread throughout the Mediterranean region, up the Danube and Rhine, and eastward to the Indus Valley. But the success of this complex in Egypt does not automatically imply that when these domestic species were first introduced, they filled a niche unoccupied by other domesticates. It is entirely possible that the Near East complex simply out-competed an already established, but less successful Egyptian system that incorporated indigenous cultivated or proto-domesticated plants/animals. Recent finds at Wadi Kubbaniya of intensive tuber use and in Egypt's Western Desert of possible cultivated sorghum dating to 6,000 BC, lend credence to just such a supposition.[15]

Paleobotanical work in Wadi Kubbaniya has demonstrated that the local inhabitants of the area (ca. 17,000 to 19,000 BP) made extensive use of indigenous tubers and roots for food, in particular nut-grass (*Cyperus rotundus*). Grinding stones once thought to be indicative of seed processing were shown through mass spectrometry to bear the remains of starch and cellulose, indicative of nut-grass tubers, rather than proteins and fats, which would suggest seeds. Although speculative, it could be argued that nut-grass use represents a first step, albeit unconscious, towards Egyptian plant cultivation. Nut-grass tends to thrive in disturbed soils. The digging sticks used to recover the tubers would have stimulated further nut-grass development guaranteeing an equally heavy harvest in the coming year. Nut-grass and Wadi Kubbaniya residents, thus, entered a mutually beneficial relationship long before Near East cultigens entered Egypt.

Farther to the west in what is now an arid desert in the Nabta Playa near the Sudanese border, the remains of several hearths and house sites were excavated by Fred Wendorf and his associates. Within the context of the house sites, ash from cooking pits was collected and found to be rich in plant remains. Plant taxa identified included legumes, grass grains, mustard seeds, *nabk* berries, millet, and sorghum. All the plants recovered from the site represent species that naturally occur in a sub-desert, savanna-type environment, and the seed size and structure corresponded to known wild races. However, preliminary investigation on the lipids in the recovered sorghum grains suggests the possibility of cultivation. Five grains submitted for spectrographic analysis were shown to be more similar to cultivated forms than wild forms. The authors did caution that the finds are preliminary, but they remain important because, although it has been thought that sorghum was domesticated in the African savanna, hard evidence has always been lacking. This lack of evidence has led many to believe that sorghum and millet were secondary domesticates, developed long after wheat, barley, and legumes had become established in Egypt. The evidence of a sub-arid flora in the Nabta Playa at 6,000 BC suggests that a savanna environment extended 600 to 700 km north of its current position. The evidence for extensive use of plants at Wadi Kubbaniya and the similarity of the Nabta sorghum grains to cultivated forms might represent an example of an early transitional step from hunting-gathering to cultivation in North Africa: a step later masked by the introduction of Near Eastern domesticates.[16]

If these preliminary findings are substantiated, current understanding of Egypt's agricultural development will have to be revised. Egypt could no longer be considered a borrower of Near Eastern agricultural technology; Egypt could simply have adopted a more successful crop complex, which resulted in the abandonment of some indigenous cultigens and the continued development of others.

The earliest undisputed record of domesticated plants in Egypt dates to ca. 4,800 to 5,200 BC. It was recovered in archaeological excavations in the Nile Valley and Fayum. A survey of the evidence for domesticated animals in Egypt indicates that the earliest undisputed appearance of cattle and ovicaprids (sheep and goat) dates to about 5,000 BC in Merimde and the Fayum. However, in Egypt's Western Desert two bones believed to represent domestic cattle were recovered in context with materials dated to about 5,500 to 6,000 BC. Bones also believed to be that of domestic *Bos* are associated with cultural materials from Bir Kiseiba and are thought to date to 8,000 BC. The argument for early domestication in the Western Desert is, however, built on ecological criteria rather than on the morphology of the recovered skeletal elements. It was suggested that an environment that supported hare and gazelle, whose elements were also recovered, was too arid to support wild *Bos*. Other indirect evidence in support of the early date for domestic cattle in Egypt is the distinctive rock art depicting harnessed cattle and the reconstructed settlement and subsistence patterns of the ancient Western Desert peoples.[17]

Regardless of the initial date, the adoption of domestication in the Sahara was most probably related to the frequent spatiotemporal variability in rainfall, especially aggravated during periods of severe aridity. Modern studies in the Eastern Sahara have shown that annual rainfall varies considerably from site to site and from year to year. Work conducted by zoologists, archaeologists, and geologists suggests that climatic variability in the early and mid-Holocene was even greater than that which occurs today. Such conditions, it is hypothesized, may have led to serious attempts to manage wild resources. Wild resource management may have begun simply by moving plants and perhaps young captured animals to areas where water was more immediately available. Such an explanation is, however, a simple summary of a complex set of processes.[18]

Evidence from the Fayum suggests that lifestyles of late Paleolithic, Neolithic, and Predynastic peoples of the area were quite similar. In general, a mobile hunting-gathering way of life was maintained throughout these periods, but during the Neolithic domesticated animals and plants were added to the system. That is, domesticates were added to an already broad and diversified, mobile hunter-gatherer lifestyle. These new resources served as additional insurance against an increasingly unpredictable food supply brought on by changing environmental conditions. A complete reliance on domesticates was not practical in this area because of the potential fluctuations in productivity brought on by unpredictable rainfall. Any group that would have fully adopted domesticates in lieu of wild resources would, in the long run, have eventually been forced to abandon such a lifestyle or die of starvation. It, therefore, seems that a balance of wild and domestic resources was best suited to the local environmental conditions and prevailed until the advent of large-scale irrigation during the Middle Kingdom lessened the potential for crop failure.

A mixed strategy such as that outlined for the Fayum is thought to have existed in other areas of the Western Desert as well. Initially, cattle and later ovicaprids were herded and crops planted in those areas where they could be sustained. Groups were not sedentary, but practiced seasonal migration so that they could take advantage of different resources in different areas when they became available. Studies of Egypt's environment suggest, however, that conditions were becoming increasingly more inhospitable during the early to mid-Holocene. Evidence from geologic, climatologic and faunal studies indicates that from ca. 10,000 to 3,000 BC or roughly the time corresponding to the inception of domesticates to the rise of the Egypt's first dynasty, the environment was becoming increasingly more arid. This was accompanied by decreasing Nile floods and increased variability in winter temperature and precipitation. If these assessments are accurate, Egypt's early and mid-Holocene inhabitants were faced with an increasingly less productive (or at least a less predictable) resource base, and undoubtedly some cultural adjustments would have to have been made.

Evidence from the archaeological record supports this scenario. Winter rains were an important feature, affecting the productivity of desert margins and oases, which were used as grazing sites by wild animals and domestic herds. Coinciding with the increasing trend towards aridity, these areas would have become less productive, and cultural groups dependent on the resources of these areas would have had to make adjustments in their settlement/subsistence strategies. The archaeological record provides evidence that during the early to mid-Holocene, the frequency of sites with "Saharan type" artifacts increased dramatically along the Nile. Studies of regional settlement patterns in the Nile flood plain also indicate a corresponding increase in the number and size of sites along the river (ca. 10,000 to 4,500 BC). The associated faunal record demonstrates that a decreasing emphasis was placed on large animals characteristic of more open terrains (e.g., wild cattle, hartebeest, and red-fronted gazelle); an increasingly strong emphasis was placed on Nile resources. Additionally, the type of domesticates known from the Sahara in the early Holocene (ca. 9,800 to 8,900 BP) are the same as those that occur after 5,000 BC in the Nile Valley and Fayum: cattle, ovicaprids, and (perhaps) grain.[19]

Interpreting these different lines of evidence in light of a changing Holocene environment, the increase in the frequency of Neolithic and Predynastic sites near the river may reflect an adjustment towards stabilizing the production of domestic resources and a means to gain more immediate access to the more productive and

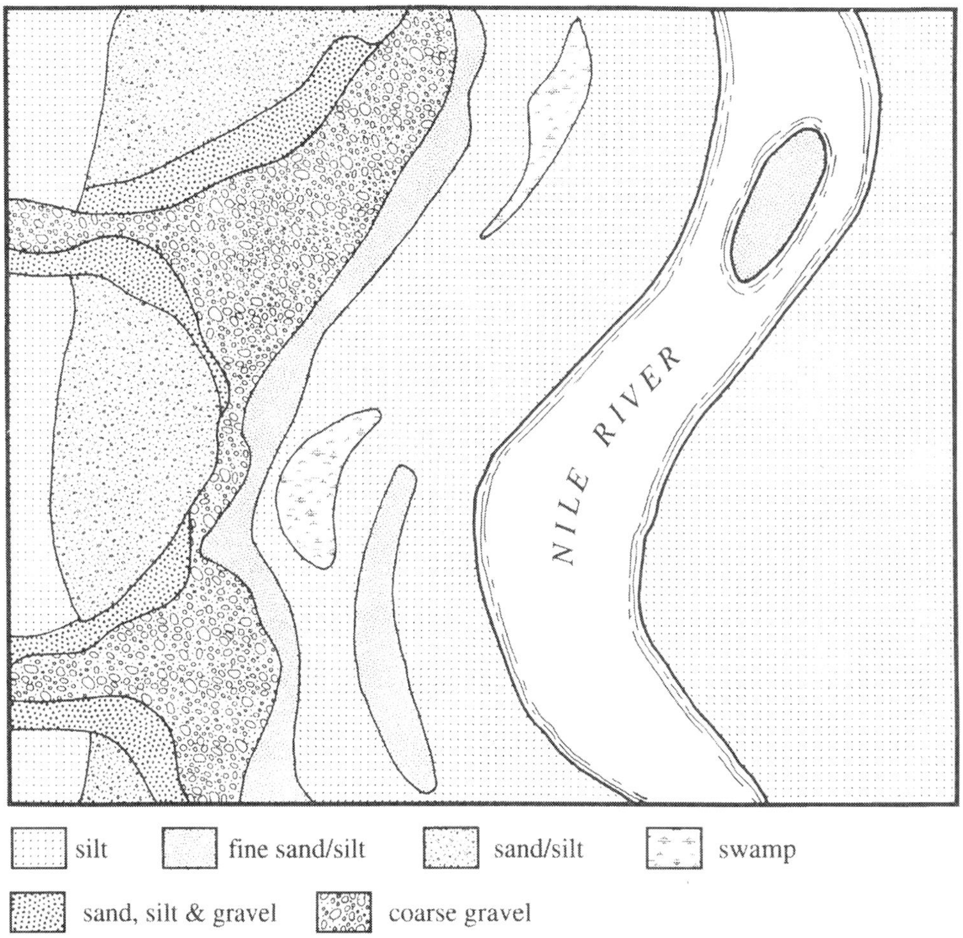

1.1. Geographic zones for a region near Luxor. Preferred settlement areas were the elevated fine sand/silt levees and the sand, silt, and gravel wadi mouths.

stable wild resources offered by the riverine environment. That is, with the loss of desert productivity, Saharan groups migrated to the rich and more stable environment offered by the Nile. The Nile inhabitants initially had no need for domesticates, but as conditions worsened and populations increased, an agrarian lifestyle became selectively advantageous. Although it is difficult to assess the role that any one factor such as environment or population had on the inception of agriculture, population pressure certainly was a catalyst for its evolution. Farming requires more work to produce the same amount of food but overall it can produce larger amounts of food in a given area and thereby feed more people, who in turn, are confined to the area of productivity. Because children are an economic asset to farmers providing an in-house labor force, the size of families tends to be large. More children mean more food is needed, thereby creating the need for more land and labor to cultivate it. The apparent adoption of Saharan domesticates by Nile groups enabled them to produce and store surplus food as is evidenced by the discovery of grain storage facilities at both Merimde and the Fayum. This in turn enabled humans to alter their immediate environment in such a way that restrictions imposed by a mobile hunting and gathering lifestyle became less relevant. Food supplies in the long run became more stable and populations ultimately increased – along with the rate of technological innovation, a corresponding change in social organization, and the need for more food.[20]

The spread of an Egyptian lifestyle based on the production of domesticates most likely followed a pattern governed by the availability of three important geographic criteria. First, settlements were apparently located near the river or major delta branches to facilitate trade and communication. Second, early settlements were concentrated on levees or *geziras* (sand and gravel mounds deposited by pre-Holocene floods) that lay above the normal flood level. Third, land suitable for farming and grazing had to be reasonably close to the settlement area (fig. 1.1).

Agricultural expansion probably first occurred along these preferred geomorphological areas. Once these areas were saturated, less desirable areas began to be occupied and more intensive agricultural methods and possible crop/herd diversification was developed to meet the needs of a rising population. The most obvious improvement to agricultural productivity developed by the Ancient Egyptians was irrigation. Adapting crops and food animals to special conditions through cross-breeding and diversification of domestic species should not, however, be overlooked.

The Prehistoric cultures that evolved from the Egyptian Neolithic, arranged according to sequence dating of ceramics, were from oldest to youngest: Badarian, Amration (Nagada I), and Gerzean (Nagada II) in Upper Egypt and Merimden, Omaric, and Maadian in Lower Egypt (table 1.1). It should be cautioned, however, that this sequence does not represent discrete cultural entities along an evolutionary path of increased complexity; they may very likely have overlapped in time with one another for a short period.[21]

Table 1.1. Chronology of Neolithic and Predynastic Egypt

Date (BC)	Upper Egypt		Lower Egypt
3300-3050	Protodynastic	(Dynasty 0)	Protodynastic
3650-3300	Gerzean	(Nagada II)	Maadian/ Omari B?
3900-3650	Amration	(Nagada I)	Omari A?
4800-4000	Badarian		Merimden/ Fayum A

The subsistence base of these Predynastic peoples can be seen as a more complex outgrowth of the earlier Neolithic system. Cultivated barley, emmer wheat, goats, sheep, cattle, and pigs as well as hunting, fishing, and the collecting of wild plants were still practiced, although emphasis had shifted towards domesticates and sedentism. Predynastic settlements seem to be located in the same areas postulated for the Neolithic: along the Nile Valley and the Nile Delta tributaries, on desert spurs and promontories of abandoned terraces, and dissected pediments overlooking the floodplain. Although it appears no settlements were established in the flood plain itself, it is very likely that many settlements were established on the outer margin of the floodplain, which was rarely affected by the inundation.[22]

As in Neolithic times, the Nile flooding governed Predynastic subsistence activities, resulting in three economic seasons that coincided with inundation, the period of coming-forth (Nile recession) and the period when the land was free of flood waters and dry (fig. 1.2). The importance of agriculture was in producing a high yield of storable foods that could be consumed during the period of lowest overall economic productivity of wild resources – the dry periods and the flood peak. The agricultural economy was also associated with intensive internal trade in various raw materials for decoration and tool-making. It is very likely that grain and perhaps dried fish were exchanged. There is also increasing evidence, through time, of imported goods from distant lands, which not only suggests the presence of a complex economy, but also that vigorous cultural contacts played an increasingly significant role in site location.

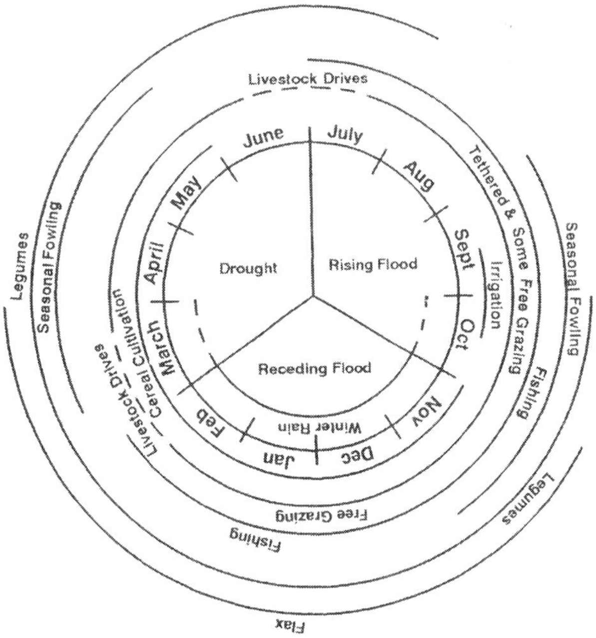

1.2. Annual ecological cycle and probable scheduling of subsistence activities.

Egyptian texts are relatively rich in terms for settlement areas in the valley and adjacent localities and in many ways mimics the sequence in settlement complexity that has been defined archaeologically. Among the earliest symbols are those that appear in the Old Kingdom (Table 1.2). These terms reflect the ecological constraints of the area, reinforcing the notion that geomorphological criteria (such as access to water and protection from floods) were important in establishing early agricultural settlements. Once state-level societies had been established, other terms came into existence reflecting the growing importance of politics, demography, and economics on site location.

One aspect of the late Predynastic and the initial phases of state formation in Egypt seems to have been a shift northward of Egypt's demographic and political center (ca. 3500 BC). Although this shift no doubt was in part due to expanding interactions with Western Asia, the growing importance of Egypt's agriculturally oriented economic base and the Delta's great potential for agricultural productivity must be considered an important aspect of this domestic trend.

Table 1.2. Egyptian lexical terms for settlements in the Nile Valley.

1.  *niwt;* originally a stylized group of round-topped huts surrounded by some kind of circumvallation, the whole indicative of a small agricultural community banding together for protection. Later the word is provisionally translated as "city."

2. 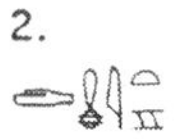 *dmit* "(place of) touching," i.e., a point on the bank of some waterway where vessels can put in, and from which, presumably, goods can be shipped; the later provisional translation is "town."

3.  *i3t*, "mound"; the glyph depicts a hillock out of reach of water on which plants are growing. It is clear that, in the Old Kingdom, a human settlement is hereby denoted: collectively "the mounds of Horus and Seth (Upper and Lower Egypt)" indicates the totality of human settlement in Egypt.

4.  *st*, the "place, seat, abode" of a god. The term refers to the centrality of the cult of the "parochial god", the local town deity of the small farming community.

5.  *wh3yt*, "village, hamlet"; interestingly, the term is clearly a technical application of the word *whyt*, "family, clan, kin-group," and may indicate some kind of grouping according to blood relationship.

6.  *hwt*, usually rendered "mansion" or a similar abode; in fact, the term applies to that kind of rectangular enclosure, surrounded by a tall mud-brick wall with a gate in one corner, which was used to house large numbers of people (workers?), animals(?) or anything else that required protection. In the Old Kingdom it commonly applies to the headquarters of a farm or estate; later to the temenous of a temple.

7.  *inbw*, "walls"; term for a major fortification, approaching the size of a town. The word is part of the original designation of the earliest settlement at Memphis.

8.  *wnt*, a rare word from the earliest period, often applied to the settlement fortifications of Asiatics, and perhaps illustrated by the city wall of Arad in the Negeb.

9.  *bhn*, frequent as the designation of the pylon or fortified gateway of a state temple, but the word is also found applied with accompanying personal name to some kind of rural settlement, perhaps a large villa with surrounding domiciles of dependents.

10.  *sgr*, a term for a fort, often used for surveillance.

11.  *grg(t)*, perhaps literally "foundation," a town founded by someone in the administration with a specific end in mind. The root also means "to equip: for a purpose. In lexical use the term refers to a village, much smaller than *niwt* or *dmi*, inhabited by farmers or hunters.

12.  *(p3) ihw n*, "the barn, cattle shed of (personal name)." An installation for the protection of cattle; occupied also by the herdsman who would sleep with his cattle. Strangers would stop there as well.

13.  *ʿt*, "chamber, house of (personal name)." A very small settlement, probably, like *bhn*, centered upon the dwelling of a single individual.

14. 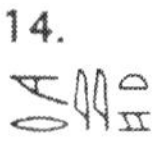 *mryt*, "harbor." This is the standard word for port, both riverine and coastal. It survives in Coptic, *mpw*. Tolls were always levied by the controllers of these installations.

15. 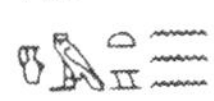 *hnmt*, literally "water-hole, basin," or similar feature. This was the term applied to the waystation which, from the New Kingdom on, dotted the routes of march into Libya and Asia. Reliefs depict a small block house with an adjacent pool of fresh water.

II

SOCIAL ECONOMY

Although Egypt would prosper through trade and conquest, the basis of its economic success would always be its great agricultural productivity. For Egypt, a bountiful harvest meant a thriving economy, and the land could produce mass surpluses of food. The Nile, although it could be a source of much anxiety, was responsible for this legendary bounty. Each year the Nile floods nourished the Egyptian soil, even though droughts may have created shortages in neighboring lands.

> Praise to thee O Nile, who comes forth on the land to make Egypt live! O thou hidden of nature, a darkness even by day, whose following praises him, who moistens the field! Creation of Re to make all animals live, who satiates the desert, a place far from rain (?); beloved of Geb, directing Nepry (the grain god). Lord of fishes, who drives the water fowl downstream ... maker of barley, creator of emmer to make festive the temples ...[23]

Foreigners knew of Egypt's fertility and often made their way to the Nile Valley in search of food and pasture. The well-known biblical account of Jacob serves as one example: "I have heard that there is grain in Egypt; go down and buy grain for us there that we may live and not starve".[24] From all accounts, the Egyptians seemed to tolerate such visitors, although their names were often noted, presumably to monitor their movements.

Demography

The early Nile agriculturalists initially sowed only those lands that were naturally irrigated by the flood waters. Given the natural drainage pattern of the Nile, however, this amounted to only about two-thirds of the potential cultivatable land. Some time during the Predynastic period, the Ancient Egyptians developed a means to control the annual flood waters better, which allowed them to regulate water distribution and extend cultivation beyond the immediate reaches of the flood. Although it is difficult to prioritize the many benefits irrigation offered, the ability to mitigate the effects of variable flood heights by creating a system of reservoirs and canals undoubtedly contributed to the stability of annual crop yields.

Egypt's agricultural potential, combined with an organized system of collection, storage, and redistribution, offered its inhabitants, relative to other contemporary cultures, a dependable food supply in all but the worst of famines. A steady, predictable, and abundant food supply resulted in a demographic expansion through Egypt's Predynastic and Old Kingdom periods. That some sort of geo-political expansion also occurred is supported by the increasing frequency of archaeological sites in Middle Egypt and the Delta from the Predynastic through the Old Kingdom (fig. 2.1). Evidence from several Old Kingdom Delta sites show that the state was increasing its royal holdings in the Delta. Certainly by Dynasties V and VI, as evident from Mendes, powerful nobles had established extensive holdings in the area and textual evidence suggests that Old Kingdom Kom el-Hisn was maintained as a cattle production center to support population or cult centers located elsewhere. Although geographic expansion is not as evident in later periods, population densities undoubtedly continued to rise. Daumas, augmenting fragmentary ancient records with modern data, believed that Dynasty XII Egypt was already densely populated and that the population continued to rise into the Late Period. It has been estimated that Egypt's population may have as much as doubled from the time of Amenophis III to the Saite period (ca. 1400 to 600 BC) and some scholars have estimated that as many as 20 million people might have lived in Egypt by the beginning of the Ptolemaic period.[25]

Although Egypt's fertility undoubtedly led to increases in population growth, demographic expansion and density figures such as those presented above, unfortunately, cannot be supported by hard evidence. A more conservative estimate, based on the amount of cultivatable land and its potential productivity, seems more appropriate. Butzer estimated that during the Predynastic period approximately 16,000 sq km were under cultivation and that this could support some 300,000 inhabitants. In the Old Kingdom, although cultivatable land had not increased markedly, the population rose to 1.5 million. By

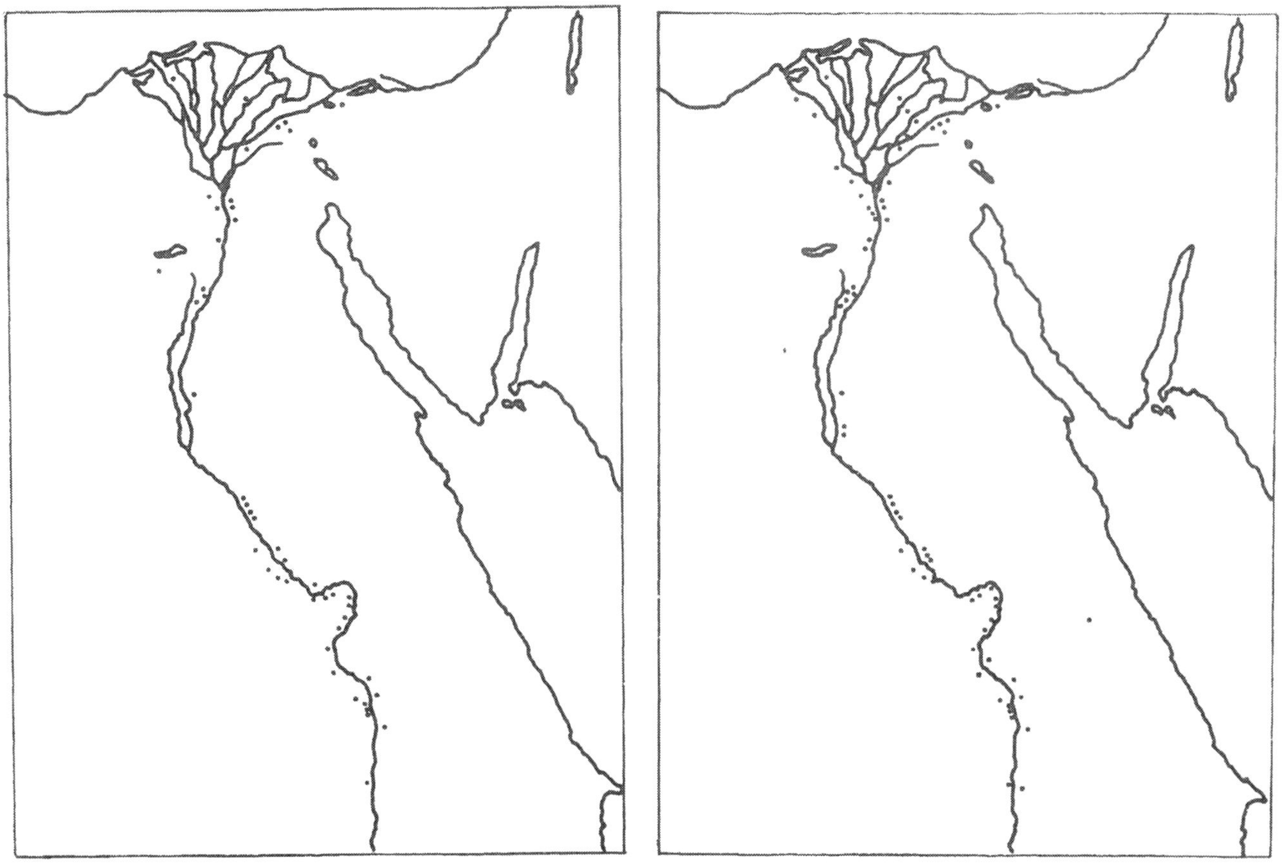

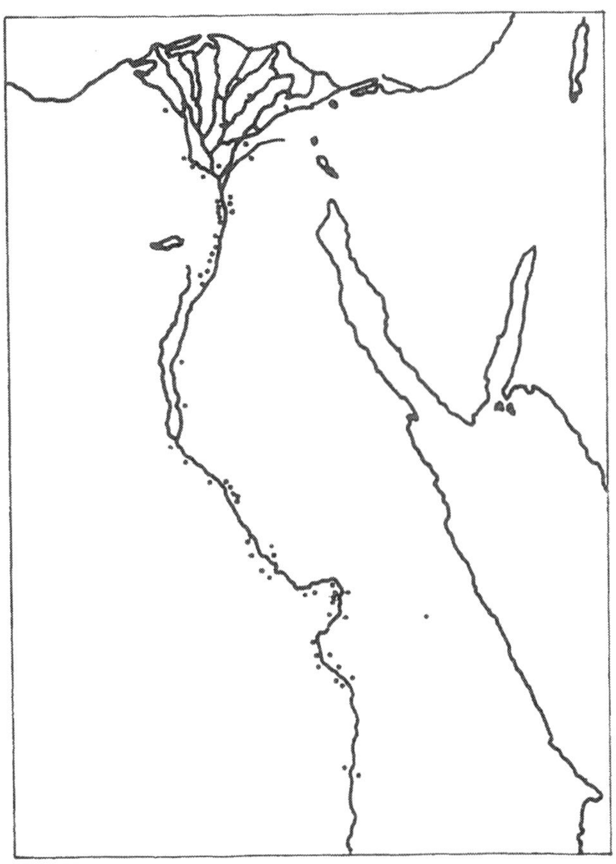

2.1. Important Predynastic (left), Archaic (right) and Old Kingdom (lower) sites of Egypt. Note the northerly shift of site density through time.

New Kingdom times 22,400 sq km were under cultivation, and an estimated 2.9 million people inhabited Egypt. This grew to 4.9 million by 150 BC, when approximately 27,000 sq km were under cultivation.[26]

These figures are considerably lower than those proposed by Daumas and others, but compare favorably with information gleaned from a variety of sources. In the New Kingdom, for example, it is generally agreed that a division of the army totalled about 5000 men. At Kadesh there were four divisions and some household troops, totalling between 20,000 and 25,000 men. These divisions were raised by conscription and as the Papyrus Harris implies, it involved taking one in ten men from temple estates. If these figures are accurate, approximately 250,000 men of military age worked the temples. This would be in general agreement with an estimated New Kingdom population of about three to perhaps five million people.[27]

During the Greco-Roman period, Diodorus estimated the population of Egypt (under Ptolemy Soter) to be about seven million. This figure may have some basis in fact because the Greeks were known to carry out periodic censuses. That a more conservative estimate may be warranted is, however, supported by the census of A.D. 1882, which also estimated the population of Egypt at seven million inhabitants and a 1917 census that estimated 12,752,000 inhabitants. The amount of land under cultivation during these periods was probably somewhere near the pre-dam figure of 23,000 sq km. Thus, given the 18th and 19th century census figures and the productivity of the available cultivatable land, a population estimate in the range of four to five million seems appropriate (if not high), for New Kingdom and Greco-Roman Egypt.[28]

Regardless of the exact figure, as long as the central administrative government maintained control and that control was based on the ideals of *maat*, it appears few went hungry. *Maat* has been variously translated as truthful or righteous. Although its exact translation eludes us, the following passage conveys the essence of the word.

> I was ... one beloved of his father, praised by his mother, loved by all his brethren. I gave bread to the hungry, clothing to the naked, I brought to land him who had no boat ... I was one that said what is good and repeated what is desirable; never did I make any evil accusations to one in authority against any persons, (for) I desired it to go well with me with the great god; and never [did I judge two brothers ...] in such a way as to deprive a son of his father's property.[29]

The quality and diversity of food available to a given individual, of course, differed depending on one's social class. At the top of the social ladder were the King and his immediate family. This was followed in the capital city by court officials, overseers, and the market farmers. In the provinces (nomes) the social elite was made up of the nomarch (the high commissioner of a nome) followed by estate managers and priests. Skilled craftsmen held an important position in society, and if talented, might fall under the patronage of the nomarch or royal family. At the bottom of the social ladder were farm-laborers, herdsmen, fishermen, and others who could neither read nor write and were involved predominantly in manual occupations. The lowest stations among this stratum of society were the farmer, the herdsman, and the fisherman.

A social profile of the Ancient Egyptian population is difficult to reconstruct, but some information is available. For example, a rare glimpse of a small working village in Western Thebes during the Ramesside period was reconstructed from a papyri and archaeological excavations of residential areas. Out of the approximately 1000 people thought to have lived in the town of "Maiunehes," seven house structures were occupied by civil officials, 32 by priests, 12 houses contained scribes, 12 were associated with the military (police and stable masters), 13 with lower officials, 31 structures housed urban craftsmen, and 47 structures were occupied by individuals involved in rural occupations. No occupation could be ascertained for one house structure, and the papyri did not list households of slaves.

Based on this information, nearly one-third of the population was directly involved in agriculture. These figures are, however, misleading because many individuals held more than one job. Two priests, for example, were coppersmiths, and two other priests held civil jobs. One was an inspector, the other, a chief guard. A second text, The Wilbour Papyrus, offers a social profile of farmers that rented land from a temple estate in Middle Egypt during the late New Kingdom. It is interesting to note that only 12 per cent of the land was rented to people we might interpret as intending to work the land themselves. Most of the land was rented to persons of high social status, including official bureaucrats residing in the capital city, who contracted laborers to work the fields. It was also common for individuals in service to the king and his government to maintain a villa and farm in their ancestral nome, which, with the addition of rented land, would offer a generous supplemental income. Thus, although not directly involved in labor activities, the learned and royal class were often "gentlemen" farmers, owning and renting land that others worked.[30]

The king, who was high priest and chief administrator, naturally played a role in agriculture, which was deeply ingrained in the Egyptian system of metaphysics. Agriculture was the gift of Osiris, who was originally a fertility god, but later became equated with Egyptian kingship and was considered the first king of Egypt. As well, he became associated with the

2.2. King Scorpion opening and irrigation canal. Scorpion Mace head, Predynastic.

underworld and ruled over it. Nevertheless, Osiris always maintained an association with agriculture and the king, by performing the necessary rituals, perpetuated the Osiris blessing and assured the prosperity of Egypt. Numerous lines of evidence suggest that the king was also involved in agriculturally related enterprises above and beyond his religious and ceremonial obligation. One of the earliest examples of Egyptian iconography, the scorpion macehead, depicts the king wearing the white crown of Upper Egypt ritually digging or breaking open a canal while his courtiers look on (fig. 2.2). Although the historical significance of the objects has been recently questioned, most scholars tend to agree on the basic interpretation.[31] That King Scorpion chose to commemorate an agricultural act is testimony to the importance of water irrigation and who was ultimately responsibility for it. Later kings would also boast of their accomplishments in the agricultural realm. Menes, the legendary first king of Egypt, was credited with building a canal that drained Memphis. In Dynasty VI an "engineer" named Nekhebu states on his biographical inscription,

> Now His Majesty sent me to lay out a canal for Khemmis of Horus (an area near Buto), and to excavate it. So I excavated it in a space of three seasons (years?), until I returned to the residence with it already filled with water [32]

In Dynasty X Kheti I boasted of a new canal he had constructed to regulate irrigation for a city in Middle Egypt.[33] During the Middle Kingdom, an era known for its weak central administration, nomarchs took special pride in their irrigation achievements; particularly when these constructions mitigated the potential disasters of a low flood while neighboring nomes suffered. Amenemhet, the nomarch of the Oryx nome, during Dynasty XII (reign of Sesostris I, ca.1971 to 1929 BC) recorded his accomplishments in the realm of water regulation among his most important achievements.

> When the years of hunger happened, I then cultivated all the fields of the Oryx nome as far as the southern and the northern boundary,

giving life to its inhabitants and providing its food. No man went hungry in it. I gave to the widow as equally as to her who had a husband. I made no distinction between the great and the small in all I gave. Then came great inundations, bringers of crops and of all things; but I did not exact the arrears of land-tax.[34]

From our modern standpoint, good management leads to prosperity, poor management leads to disaster. That is, when the general administration of Egypt was strong, collection and redistribution networks worked well. When the government was weak, these systems failed and people went hungry. For example, the low Nile floods of Dynasty XVIII are hardly mentioned as "lean times" in the ancient texts because the administration was strong and was supported by numerous military campaigns that brought booty and taxes into Egypt that evidently compensated for any shortages in food production. During the First Intermediate Period, however, when the central government was exceptionally weak, low floods led to food shortages and famine swept the land.[35]

Agriculture and Local Economics

The cost and standard of living for Egyptian agriculturalists are not well-documented. Until the Ptolemaic period, there was no official Egyptian currency. Nevertheless, no financial document written in legal form could dispense with monetary referents. It seems that as early as the Old Kingdom metal was used as a means of fixing and expressing the price of commodities and services. In the New Kingdom, the ratio between gold and silver was 1:2 and 1:100 between silver and copper. Gold depreciated with respect to silver by the middle of Dynasty XVIII to a level of 3:5, but by late Dynasty XIX silver had depreciated to 1:60 (gold to silver) (see table 2.1). These three metals were used as referents in nearly all business transactions, not for actual payment, but rather as a measure of value.

Table 2.1. Relative values of gold, silver and copper.

	gold	silver	copper
Dynasty XII (and/or Hyskos period)	1	2	
Tutmosis III/Amenophis II (Dyn XVIII)	3	5	
Dynasty XVIII		1	96
Ramesses II (Dyn. XIX)		1	104
7th Year of Ramesses IX (Dyn. XX)	1	60	200
17th Year of Ramesses IX	1	2	

The Egyptian economic system was based on bartering, where commodities were exchanged on the basis of values referenced to standardized measures, fixed by the values of these precious metals.[36] To assess a commodity's value it was compared to the weight of gold, silver, or copper expressed in New Kingdom times as a *deben* (91 grams) or its tenth, a *kite*.[37] For example, a piece of land could be worth one *deben* of silver, but would be purchased with a wide assortment of commodities such as linen, livestock, fish, and grain, their net value being equal to one *deben*. An example of the barter and exchange system can be gleaned from the following quote where Isis contracts the services of Anty the ferryman.

I have come to you to ask whether you would ferry me over to the Center Island, because I am carrying the jar of meal for the little boy who for five days up until now has been tending the herds on Center Island, and he is hungry." The ferry man replies: "They told me not to ferry over any woman." Isis then says: "It was on account of Isis that they told you what you (just) said." Anty then states: What will you give me to be ferried over to Center Island?" Isis replies: "I will give you this cake." Thereupon Anty says to her: "What good to me is your cake? When they've told me not to ferry any woman over, shall I ferry you over to Center Island for your cake?" Isis then says to him: "I will give you the gold signet which is on my hand." And he replies: "Give me the gold signet!" [38]

Isis gives it to him and he ferries her to Center Island.

Individuals could purchase farm land in all periods of Ancient Egyptian history, but documents pertaining to the acquisition of land by private parties, although available from the earliest periods, are not numerous. In most cases documents record the conveyance of land, either to a temple or towards the endowment of a mortuary cult. The earliest record for a private transaction dates to Dynasty IV where three *aroures* (about two acres) were sold for a cow. The stated price for the transaction was equivalent to six *shaty* of silver (about 1/2 *deben*: see fn. 15).

Table 2.2. Terms for Egypitan land types

1.  *hrw*, "low-lying land," in contrast to high ground, requiring less cultivation.

2.  *q*ꜣ*yt*, "high ground," Coptic *koie*, "field"; fields not reached by the flood and therefore irrigated artificially.

3.  *nhbw*,"virgin soil, plowland."

4.  *iww m*ꜣ*wt*, "new islands," land newly created by the inundation, which became land of the crown.

5.  *'m't*, "mud flats,"capable of producing grain.

The price of land, of course, depended on its quality. In the days of basin irrigation, the Egyptian *felaheen* (peasant) distinguished between *rei*-fields, which were covered by the flood, and *sharaki*-land, which required irrigation. The Ancient Egyptian made a parallel, but not identical, distinction between what was called *hrw* or low-lying land and *qꜣyt* or high ground. High ground was apparently land that was generally fertile but needed irrigation (table 2.2). Land and commodity prices also fluctuated with the state of the economy. In the Fayum, during Dynasty XVIII, an *aroure* of land (100 X 100 cubits) was worth two silver *shaty* (1/6 of a *deben*). Four hundred years later the same plot of land cost 11 kite (1.1 *deben*). In Dynasty XXI, a period not known for its prosperity, an *aroure* of land next to a canal near Memphis cost only five or six *kite* of silver, upland near Abydos cost one *kite*, and clear common land that was weed infested was priced at 1/2 to 2/5 *kite*. An exhausted, weed-infested piece of land could be purchased for as little as 1/5 or 1/6 *kite* in Dynasty XXII. Comparable shifts in prices can also be noted in other commodities. At the end of Dynasty XVIII a cow could be purchased for eight silver *shaty* and a goat for 1/2 *shaty*. According to Baer, in the New Kingdom, cattle cost up to 130 *deben* of copper, which corresponded to 65 sacks of grain or the yearly income of a skilled craftsman at Deir el Medineh. Under Amenophis IV (Dynasty XVIII), a cow was worth 1/2 *deben* and a bull 2/3 *deben* of silver. Much later, under Chechonq (Dynasty XXV), the price of an ox was 1/5 *deben* and a cow 1 1/8 *deben*.[39]

Based on these prices, land and cattle were probably too expensive for the average peasant farm-laborer to consider. Nevertheless, basic food stuffs were relatively inexpensive throughout the dynastic era. The daily caloric requirements of the peasant farmer and herder were met predominantly through vegetables, bread, beer, fish, and fowl. Higher social classes naturally enjoyed a more diverse menu, which included beef. At the heart of Egyptian economics was the ration system. In the absence of money, people were paid in commodities and presumably bartered the surplus for other items or foodstuffs. In effect, the ration was a "wage" paid for services rendered. Ration lists show wages were calculated in terms of loaves of bread and jugs of beer. The loaves and jugs were measures of value or "units of account" as much as they stood for actual amounts of foodstuffs. A standard basic wage consisted of ten loaves and a measure of beer that could fluctuate between 1/3 to two jugs. This basic wage was thought fit for an ordinary laborer. Ration lists also suggest that as one moved up the social ladder, the distributions increased by multiples of the basic ration. Because important officials received rations too large to physically transfer, common sense would suggest that the ration system must have employed a combination of distributed and notational rations, the latter being, in effect, credit, which as a paper accumulation of unused rations, was exchangeable for other commodities. For example, although rations were issued as loaves of bread and jugs of beer, in the New Kingdom beer was worth approximately 1 *deben* of copper for 50 *hin* (ca. 5 liters) and one loaf of bread cost about 1/5 *deben*. That these were transferable to other commodities seems apparent when we see that vegetables sold for about 1/2 *deben*, and 1 *deben* could buy over a bushel of fish (based on scene of fish for beer at Saqqara). Evidence that rations also changed depending on political and economic circumstances can be seen in the reign of Ptolemy Philadelphus when a 25 per cent drop in the grain rations occurred after his 38th year.[40]

Offering lists, which occur in great number on temple walls, also in part reflect wages. The offerings, which represent only part of the temples income, were divided first between the god and clergy, then among the clergy themselves, who very often were only part-time employees. These individuals entered into contracts with the administrator of the temple, bartering their services for a fraction of the temple offerings; some magnates of the kingdom, however, enjoyed hereditary benefits and received a share of the offerings, but did nothing in exchange for it.

The Egyptian Agriculturalist

Although the Greeks looked upon the life of an Egyptian farmer as one of relative leisure when compared to their own country, to the Egyptians, a farm-laborer's life was not one to be envied. Throughout Egyptian history grain production was the main agricultural activity, and the average peasant farmer was basically a field hand who worked the land of others in exchange for part of the harvest. The tasks of a farm-laborer were considered so menial that prisoners of war were commonly employed as slave labor to carry out farming duties.[41]

If we pull together information from a variety of sources, we can reconstruct a rough outline of how an Egyptian farm operated. First, heredity played an important role in matters concerning the availability of land for cultivation. Not only was title to land passed from one generation to the next, but leasing rights to temple or other government-controlled lands may have been based on heredity as well (e.g., Wilbour Papyrus). The farm itself was thus not a discrete contiguous expanse of land, but rather a composite of plots, owned or rented, that were scattered across the countryside and worked by contracted laborers. One type of land that occurs with increasing frequency as the New Kingdom progresses is *khato*-land of Pharaoh. There is still a degree of uncertainty as to what precisely *khato*-land was. It seems to be land that for some reason, and perhaps only temporarily, lacked an owner or cultivator. In any case, the burden of working the land fell on the local temples, and contemporary literature indicates that this was considered an unwanted burden.[42]

How a crop was divided between owner and cultivator is not clear but some general estimates are available from the New Kingdom and later periods. It seems that during the Saite Period and most likely in the New Kingdom and perhaps earlier, the rent was a pre-assessed quantity (not percentage) of the harvest. Estimates on land productivity based on 19th century and modern yields place these values at about half of an average crop. That is, the owner and cultivator would split the harvest.

The grain yield from any given field was measured annually prior to the harvest for the purposes of taxation. The audit was carried out by a party of government officials that included several scribal assistants. The field was surveyed by means of a premeasured knotted cord that was stretched out over the cultivated area to the boundary stone demarcating the edge of the deeded land (fig. 2.3). From several documents, it appears that about 1/10 of the total harvest was assessed for taxes. This was apparently paid by the land owner. Another ten per cent was saved for seed. In some cases, it is clear that the land owner was responsible for this share; in other examples, the renter/cultivator was clearly responsible for all expenses other than taxes. The laborers working the farm, if not the renter, also had to be paid some portion of the harvest. Additionally, in some instances we see the laborers were offered a gratuity; they were allowed to keep all the produce they could harvest in one day.[43]

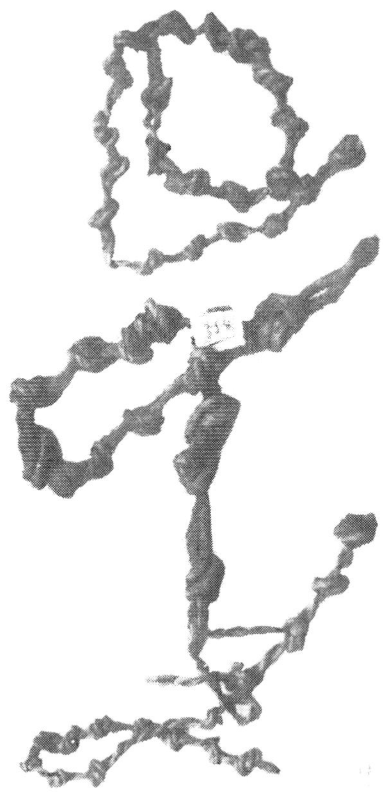

2.3. A knotted surveying rope used in assessing taxes for cultivated land. Egyptian Agricultural Museum, Dokki.

Actual work on the land began as the Nile receded. It was then that proper local management of the irrigation works had to be implemented. This included organizing dyke repairs, dredging the canals, and replacing property boundaries; all of which had to be completed before water could be efficiently directed to the proper fields. It is possible that repairs to irrigation systems might have overlapped with preparation of the fields for planting. Because the ordinary work force in the area was probably not large enough to complete all the tasks, it is presumed statute labor was involved; that is, the raising of labor gangs by decree. The precise details of the means by which the gangs were raised is not known, although it is generally thought that conscription, like irrigation management, was organized and supervised at the local level. That some degree of central control existed, however, is suggested in the duties of the vizier: "It is he who should dispatch regional

2.4. Preparing the land for cultivation. Tomb of Ti, Saqqara, Dynasty V.

officers to construct dikes throughout the whole land." Evidence that compulsory service was not particularly popular can be deduced from court records where punishment for deserters or conscripts that failed to appear for work range from fines to holding family members hostage until the wayward conscript showed for work.[44]

Much of our information regarding agricultural implements and their use is based on scenes in Egyptian tombs. Agricultural scenes date to the Old Kingdom, when the tombs of non-royal persons were first provided with representations of everyday life. As early as Dynasty V a pattern of arrangement evolved that persisted through the New Kingdom and into later times. Although the scenes are culturally biased from the perspective of the upper class, they do provide important insights into agricultural life, albeit ideally constructed so that no detail could jeopardize the posthumous existence of the tomb owner.

The Old Kingdom complex at Saqqara provides some well-preserved examples of standard agricultural themes. The scenes are often balanced in the traditional way by portraying the three seasons of the agricultural year; inundation (*aket*), growing (*peret*), and harvest (*shemu*). In the tomb of Ti six men are shown plowing the fields (figs. 2.4, 2.5). The six men work three plows, shown one behind the other, but, in reality, probably plowed side-by-side. Each plow is drawn by two oxen and is controlled by one farmer pressing down on the handle to keep the share in the ground, while another farmer urges the team on with a staff.[45]

Based on a number of scenes, after the fields were plowed and the seed spread, livestock were used to tread the grain into the ground. In Predynastic and later times, if the farmer was fortunate enough to work a piece of land softened by the annual floods, plowing may not have been necessary.

2.5. A team of men and oxen plowing a field for Ti. Tomb of Ti, Saqqara, Dynasty V.

Rather, the seed was simply spread and a herd of hoofed animals trampled it into the earth. Apparently sheep and possibly goats were used for this task. In New Kingdom times, pigs were also employed.

One aspect of the agricultural cycle that escapes mention in tomb scenes or in texts is weeding the fields prior to plowing and seeding. At least for those lands that remained above the flood waters, weeds would have to be cleared prior to planting. In the central Sudan and elsewhere from North America through Asia, fire is used for this purpose. Setting fire to the fields is beneficial to sowing in several ways: it kills weeds that become established during the fallow period, it works quickly, it is not labor intensive, it returns nutrients to the soil, and if stalks or stubble from the previous harvest still remain on the field, burning destroys pathogens that might reside in crop residue and otherwise might infest seedlings.[46] Burning is an old technique that was very likely practiced in Egyptian agriculture. Why it is not mentioned or featured more frequently is difficult to ascertain. It was undoubtedly a dirty

2.6. (left) An Egyptian plow. New Kingdom, Agriculture Museum, Dokki. 2.7. Egyptian hoes with cross-bracing (centre) and no brace (right). Agriculture Museum, Dokki.

business, and perhaps so common it escapes mention.

The plow in the Dynastic period, based on tomb scenes and actual examples, was a crude wooden implement consisting of two upright handles joined by crosspieces and ending in a curved beam to which a plow share of wood (rarely metal) was attached (fig. 2.6). A wooden crossbar or yoke was fixed to the other end of a long beam that rested upon the oxen's shoulders. By the New Kingdom the yoke was more often attached to a transverse rod fastened to or across the horns of oxen (or the shoulders of other men). Though the design of the typical Egyptian plow was primitive, it was very effective. The plow was needed only to break up the earth, not to turn the soil to one side and leave a furrow as do modern disk plows.

The hoe is similar in design to the plow except that the part corresponding to the share was longer than the handle. Some hoes had the same type of connecting ropes as found on the plow; others were fashioned out of one piece of wood, and no cross-bracing was needed. Hoes of both kinds have been recovered (fig. 2.7). In the New Kingdom hoes often had paddle-shaped blades designed to act both as a useful clod-breaking implement and as a tool for filling baskets (fig. 2.7). In essence, the equivalent of the modern Egyptian *fas*.

Contrary to Herodotus' statement that once the fields had been planted all the Egyptian farmer had to do was wait for the harvest, much work was left to be done, in particular, irrigation. Even the most northerly of the Delta fields needed irrigation water. Crop irrigation was done either by means of opening canals that allowed water to enter the farmer's field or, more often, by hand-carrying water in large earthen jars from canal to field. It was not until the Middle Kingdom that the *shaduf*, a large bucket attached to the end of a pole, was employed. The *sakiye*, a water wheel powered by a draught animal, was unknown in Egypt until the Ptolemaic period.[47]

Scenes of reaping and threshing completed the theme of field labor on tomb walls. Non-mechanized agriculturalists like early agriculturalists cut or pulled their crop plants at harvest time, depending on the soil and the type of crop. If the soil is silty and tends to clod, cutting is generally preferred over pulling. Because the Nile Valley is composed of silty soils, most crops were indeed cut. In the tomb of Sennedjem, a scene shows a team of field hands with sickles harvest the cereal crop by cutting the stalks. Flax, however, is always shown being pulled, which preserved the quality of the fibers (e.g., fig. 4.1).

Egyptians were said to shed tears at the first cutting of the grain. The rite was symbolic of Osiris being lacerated and the workers would chant a dirge called "*maneros*" accompanied by a

2.8. (top) Harvesting the grain for Mereruka. Tomb of Mereruka, Saqqara, Dynasty V. 2.9. (centre) Transporting the grain to the threshing floors. Tomb of Ti, Saqqara, Dynasty V. 2.10. (bottom) Threshing the grain with cattle. Tomb of Ti, Saqqara, Dynasty V.

2.11. A cattle drive "out of the north country". Tomb of Kagemni, Saqqara, Dynasty V.

flute. The last sheaf to be cut was also a moment of celebration. It was commonly considered a young bride and an image was made from it in the shape of a doll and used in harvest festivals. The reaped grain was then hauled off in large baskets carried by donkeys to the threshing floor and the husks were loosened by treading hooved animals over the grain (figs. 2.8; 2.9; 2.10). Prior to storage, the grain was assessed by the scribes of the estate or temple.[48]

Herders

Pastorers were a separate class from agriculturists, but were also held in low esteem because of the prejudices against the physical requirements of their occupation. This attitude did not, however, extend to livestock breeders or those who practiced the veterinary arts. Scenes depicting herdsmen often show them as dirty, unshaven, and dressed in simple, rough clothing, the cloth of which was similar to that covering the backs of cattle. They generally lived in reed structures and ate simple foods.

Herdsmen working an estate were chosen by a foreman on the basis of their skill and personal character. Overseeing the foreman was an appointed official who regulated everything with respect to the livestock, from which field to graze to which stalls to attend. Because everything had to be recorded, the appointed official's duties required filing reports at certain periods with the scribes attached to the foreman's office. Records were compiled through a periodic examination of the cattle prior to their presentation to the owner of the estate.[49]

The life of the herdsman, in contrast to that of the farmer, was not as physically arduous. Scenes depict herdsmen as being fond of their animals and they would often call them by a given name as if they were pets. The herdsmen took great care in providing the animals with proper food, sometimes feeding them by hand and preparing for them medicine or whatever else they required. If, however, some ill fate affected the herd such as disease or failure to instigate a good generation of calves, the herdsman would ultimately be blamed.

The song of a herdsman preserved in a tomb at El-Bersheh gives some insight into their life.

> You have driven oxen along every road. You have trodden the sands, and now your feet tread grass. You are eating tufted plants, and now you are well satisfied, and here is goodness to nourish you.[50]

One unpopular aspect of herding was being away from home for long periods. Several scenes suggest that there were occasions when herds of livestock were driven to the Delta marshes from upland areas to graze and then returned south at a later date. An example of such a cattle drive can be identified from a stela dating to the Hyksos occupation of the Delta. Apparently, a treaty had been entered between the Hyksos overlord Avaris and the vassal Thebaid of Upper Egypt. The importance of Delta pasturage to the maintenance of the herd can perhaps be inferred from the difficulties, no doubt, encountered during these stressful days in Egypt.[51]

> We are at ease in our part of Egypt; Elephantine is strong, and Middle Egypt is with [us] as far as Kusae. The untenanted plots of their land are worked for us, and our cattle are pastured in the Delta fields, while emmer is sent down for our pigs. Our cattle have not been seized.[52]

Cattle drives and Delta pasturing probably coincided with the hot dry season when availability of forage was limited in Upper Egypt. Figure 2.11 records a trip "out of the north country" where the cattle are being driven "upwards." Often associated with such scenes are references or pictorial representations of water crossings. Because the Nile proper was much too large and wide for livestock to cross successfully on their own, these waterways probably represent canals or Deltaic branches of the Nile.

Agriculture and the Afterlife

The predictability of the Nile and the bounty it brought to Egypt had further implications in the afterlife. On the basis of passages from the *Book of the Dead*, the upper class Egyptian who had never toiled in the field and more than anyone thought he or she most likely to enjoy the riches of life after death, ironically faced questions of an agricultural nature in the time of judgment. In the presence of Osiris and his 42 assessors, the deceased was asked, along with questions relating to moral laxity and religious observance, questions reflecting agricultural impropriety. The deceased was expected to respond in the negative

> ... not have I desolated plowed lands, not have I made inroads on fields of other people, not have I driven away the cattle which were upon their pastures, not have I turned back water at its season, not have I cut a cutting (rerouted) in water running,...[53]

After a successful judgment the Egyptian was expected to spend time in the Field of Reeds (Peace), which was visualized as another worldly Egypt, watered by another Nile. From descriptions it is easy to perceive the Field of Reeds as a Delta-type environment where the land was well watered by numerous tributaries. Here the deceased engaged in activities, such as plowing and harvesting, just as if he or she were a peasant working the land. In this context, however, working the land symbolized sowing the ideal state of eternal prosperity, well-being, and comfort-conditions that existed in Egypt, albeit ephemerally, after a bountiful harvest.[54]

> I know the field of rushes [Reeds] of Re: the wall around it is of bronze, and its emmer is five cubits tall with its ear of one cubit, and its stalk (?) of four cubits. Its emmer is seven cubits, with its ear of two cubits and its stalk (?) of five cubits.[55]

It is interesting to note that in the Field of Reeds the deceased is the cultivator and addresses gods and other entities of a higher standing; in the tomb scenes the deceased is seen in the context of overseeing the cultivators laboring in his fields. Another interesting difference between the *Book of the Dead* and the tomb is that in the religious papyri the deceased is at times obliged to make his/her way in the afterlife alone while in the tomb, the owner is shown surrounded by colleagues, family, servants and all the activities that make earthly existence full and notable.

Even after one had achieved eternal life and was guaranteed well-being for eternity, one might still be called upon to do agricultural labor. Thus, by the Middle Kingdom a surrogate figure, the *shawabti*, was introduced into the tomb and by the New Kingdom, it was standard funerary equipment. The *shawabti* was a small statuette showing the deceased owner as a wrapped mummy. At first they were unencumbered, but in the early to mid-Dynasty XVIII they were shown carrying the tools of the field worker, the hoe and the mattock. In later times these tools were incorporated as part of the figure. Most shabti were inscribed with texts designed to bring the figure to life and work on behalf of the deceased if he or she were called upon to do labor.

> Hail shawabti! If it be decreed that [the deceased] should do any of the work which is to be done in the underworld, let all that standeth in the way be removed from before him; whether it be to plow the field or to fill the channels with water ..., you shall say, I am here when thou callest.[56]

III

EGYPTIAN GRAINS

Grains from grasses provide the largest single source of carbohydrates in the human diet. Grasses are one of the most successful plant forms on the earth today and can be found everywhere plants are able to grow. To date more than 650 genera of grasses and more than 10,000 species have been identified. The reproductive unit of grass is, in strictly botanical terms, not a seed but a fruit; the grain refers to what is left after the floral apparatus has been removed. The grass flower is called a spikelet and each spikelet is connected to the fruit-bearing portion of the stock (the rachis) via thin branches called rachilles. The section of the grass plant that contains the rachis, rachilles, and flower is referred to as the head.

Egyptian Wheats (*Triticum* spp.)

Wheat taxonomy (*Triticum*) has traditionally been based on morphological characteristics. Wheats are variable in appearance; there are more than 17,000 identified forms. Taxonomic controversy has arisen around a number of these identifications: some forms designated as separate species are obviously more closely related than their nomenclature would suggest. More recently, cytogenetic evidence has been used to create a firmer basis for taxonomic classification. Genetic studies have placed wheat into three major groups:

1) The 14-chromosone group or diploid group (i.e., containing twice the 7-chromosome grouping "genome A," or in notational form 2n=14). This group includes wild and cultivated einkorn.

2) The 28-chromosome group or tetraploid group (i.e., containing twice the two 7-chromosome groupings called "genomes A and B" or 2n=28). This group includes wild and cultivated emmer and durum (hard) wheats.

3) The 42-chromosome group or hexaploid group (i.e., containing twice the three 7-chromosome groupings "genomes A,B, and C or D" or 2n=42), whose members belong to the bread wheats.

Diploid and tetraploid wheats have wild and cultivated forms. In contrast, all hexaploid wheats are domesticated cultigens. The diploid wheats have only the A genome and are thought to be the most primitive form. Tetraploids, which posses A and B genomes, arose through natural hybridization between a diploid A-wheat and a closely related diploid B-grass, probably *Aegilops speltoides* or a close relative. The hexaploids with A, B, and C or D genomes are a product of a tetraploid-diploid cross. The diploid is thought to be *Aegilops squarrosa* (*T. tauschii*).

Most modern wheats are hexaploid. Because of the high gluten content of the endosperm, hexaploid wheats are valued for bread making. The sticky gluten protein traps carbon dioxide given off by yeast cells and this allows the bread to "rise." The tetraploid or hard wheats, such as durum, possess little gluten and thus the flour dough is less elastic and better suited for pasta and cakes. There are no economically important diploid wheats employed in modern agriculture.

When the entire wheat grain is utilized, wheat provides a number of essential nutrients. Wheat grains are 60 to 80 per cent carbohydrates, two per cent fat, two per cent minerals (including vitamins E and B complex, and eight to 15 per cent protein, containing all essential amino acids except lysine, tryptophane, and methione.[57]

Origins

The two principal cereals of Egypt were barley and emmer wheat, essentially in that order of importance. From the beginnings of plant domestication, barley appears to have been the primary cereal. Emmer was important in Egypt until Hellenistic times, when it was replaced by introduced durum and hexaploid wheats. Einkorn wheat was never an important or dominant crop.

It is universally assumed that these domesticated cereals were derived from closely related wild forms outside of Egypt. In the case of barley and emmer, the wild races are fairly well-known. Figure 3.1 shows the modern distribution of these cereals. The modern range of the wild forms, coupled with the discovery of the earliest domestic grains in these same areas, has led many researchers to conclude that domestic cereals were originally cultivated in the Jordan Valley, southern Levant, or farther east along the Fertile Crescent. From this node, cereal cultivation spread to Egypt.

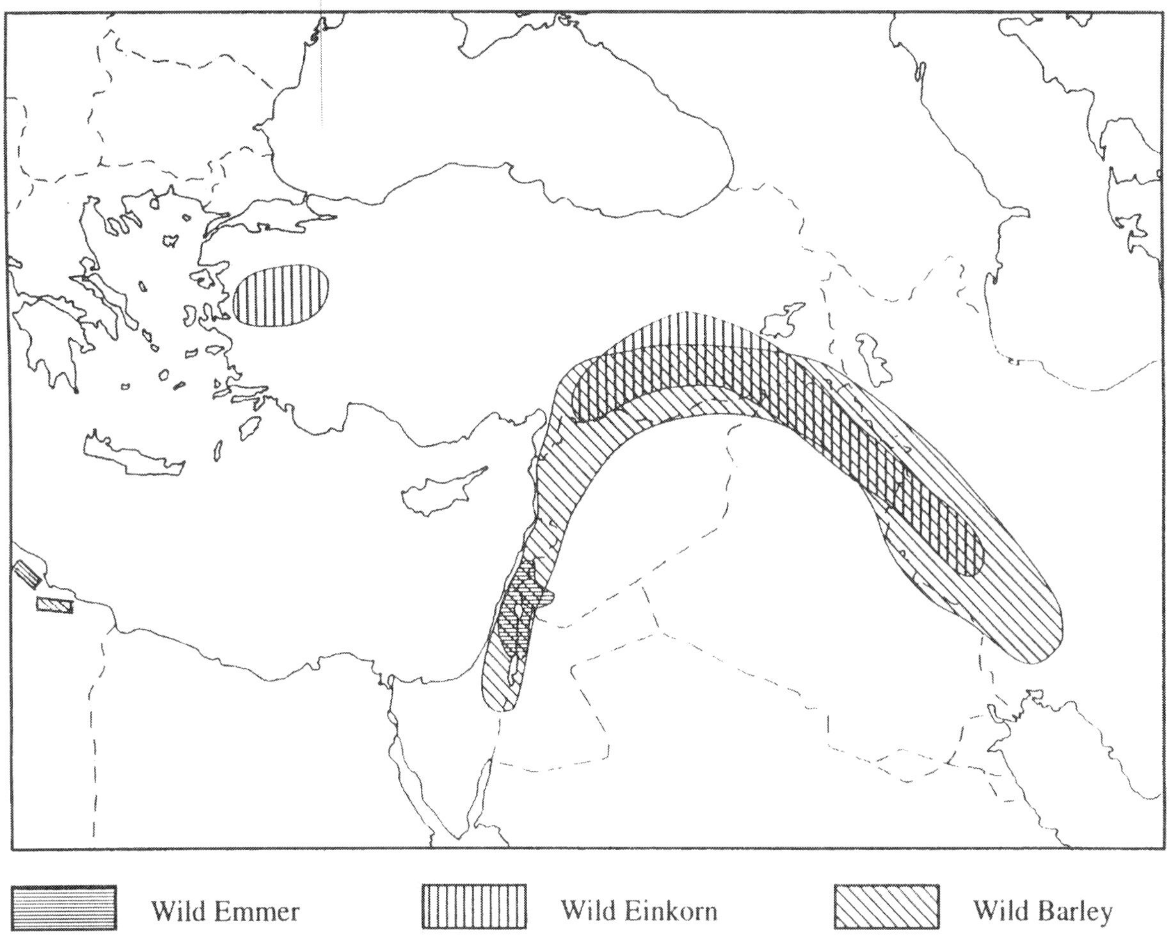

3.1. Distribution of wild einkorn wheat, emmer wheat and barley.

It is important to point out, however, that all three wild cereals show disjunct distributions. To account for this, either recent colonization has taken place or the ranges of these cereals were at one time continuous.[58]

On the basis of geologic, climatologic and faunal evidence, North Africa and the Near East has undergone detectable changes in the environment during the Holocene (ca. 8000 BC to present), and these changes were of a magnitude significant enough to affect plant and animal distributions. Sediment studies suggest that seasonal winter rains once fell on the Eastern Sahara during the early to mid-Holocene, and archaeologists working in the Eastern Sahara have found numerous sites (e.g., Nabta, Bir Kiseiba, Fayum) associated with shallow ephemeral lakes and fauna indicative of a more mesic climate. Given these conditions, it is likely that the wild progenitors of wheat and barley had different and perhaps wider distributions than today. Evidence based on the recovery of wild wheat supports this contention. Wild einkorn, for example, has been found in the pre-pottery Neolithic levels at Jericho, but today the nearest stands are some 100 to 150 km to the north. If these shifts in distribution are a result of a changing environment, as independent lines of evidence seem to indicate, moister, cooler conditions must have prevailed over much of Egypt during the early to mid-Holocene. If this is true, wild barely, which has a wider environmental tolerance than either emmer or einkorn wheat, very likely could have extended continuously from the fertile crescent to Cyrenaica where a disjunct population of wild barley has been identified and probably to some extent up the Nile Valley. The point being that the modern distribution of wild grain does not necessarily reflect distributions at the time of initial domestication. Perhaps, at least for barley, some evidence for indigenous domestication might still be found in Egypt.[59]

It is now certain that plants were an important dietary staple in Egypt by the Upper Paleolithic. In Egyptian Nubia numerous grinding stones and flint blades edged with a lustrous sheen indicative of cutting silica grasses have been recovered.[60] The deposits from which the flint blades were taken dated from 14,550 to 12,000 BP. Thus far more than two dozen species of plants have been identified from several early Upper Egyptian sites. Interestingly, although flint blades bearing a sheen were reported, the dominant plant foods seemed to be roots and tubers, in particular, nut-grass (*Cyperus rotundus*). Strong evidence for cereal grains does not occur before 8000 BP, when millet and sorghum were apparently being collected in the Nabta Playa.[61]

By 7000 BC, grains of domesticated varieties of barley, einkorn, and emmer appear in the Levant and Near East. However, the earliest undisputed date for cultivated grain in Egypt occurs almost 2500 years later, from Neolithic sites in the Fayum and Merimde. The Fayum sites range in age from 5200 to 4100 BC. As stated in chapter one, these sites are thought to have been seasonally occupied. Grain in the Fayum was stored in underground silos located on higher elevations, presumably as protection from ground water. The silos were lined with coiled basketry made of wheat straw and contained barley and emmer wheat.[62]

The site of Merimde on the western edge of the Delta represents a more permanent settlement than those in the Fayum. The site covers about 24 hectares and on the basis of radiocarbon dates taken from upper and lower stratigraphic levels, was occupied for about 1000 years (ca. 5000 to 4100 BC). The Merimde residents lived in round or oval structures two-three meters in diameter. These shelters probably consisted of wooden frames covered with matting. In front of the structures were hearths and storage pits lined with Nile mud. In levels representing the final phase of occupation, the excavators identified semi-subterranean oval structures, which were thought to be communal storage areas. As in the Fayum, both wheat and barley were recovered from basket-lined pit silos.[63]

In the preliminary report on the excavations at El-Omari, an uncarbonized spike of wheat identified as einkorn (*Triticum monococcum*) was recovered. The specimen was apparently submitted to a number of specialists, all of whom agreed with the identification. A separate cache of grain recovered from the underground gallery near the north enclosure wall of the Step Pyramid complex at Saqqara was examined by Täckholm. Emmer wheat and barley were identified as the main component of the sample, but among the wheat grains was einkorn wheat. Einkorn was again identified with grain recovered from Ichete's tomb at Saqqara. Åberg later substantiated this identification, stating that two distinct species of wheat had been recovered, emmer and einkorn. More recently, however, Helbaek reanalyzed the grains and, on the basis of morphological criteria, showed them all to be emmer wheat. In his view, no substantiated evidence exists for einkorn in Egypt before the Greco-Roman period.[64]

Some have questioned why einkorn wheat was never or only rarely cultivated in Egypt, particularly given that it has a wider tolerance to heat and drought than emmer. The preference for emmer can be readily explained in terms of its evolutionary adaptations. Although einkorn is considerably more resistant to cold, heat, and drought than emmer, it is a low-yielding wheat. Although einkorn can out-produce emmer in mountainous regions or areas characterized by severe climates, in the cultivated fields of the Nile Valley, einkorn's adaptations would render it less productive than emmer. Therefore, emmer, with its higher grain yield would be the cereal of choice and remained the predominant and nearly exclusive wheat of Ancient Egypt until Greco-Roman time, when hexaploid wheats predominated. In Egypt today cultivated emmer remains only as a relic.

Authenticated finds of naked (soft hull, hexaploid) wheat prior to the Greco-Roman period are extremely rare, but a number of examples do exist. The wild and cultivated races of emmer and einkorn are "glume wheats" in that the seeds are firmly enclosed by the glumes (hull around the seed) and rather severe processing is required to free them (see fig. 3.2). Processing can be done in a mortar or by other methods of grinding, as is well-documented in Egyptian tombs and models (fig. 3.3). The glumes of the naked wheats, however, are softer, and the seed falls free upon threshing.

Among the material obtained from two of the Fayum Neolithic granaries Percival identified some charred grains as *Triticum aestivum* (*T. vulgare*) a hexaploid bread wheat. At the middle and late Neolithic sites of Merimde-Beni Salame and El-Omari a number of carbonized grains, identified by Helbaek as club wheat (*T. compactum*), were also found. Further examples of hexaploid wheats have been recovered from Dra' Abu el Naga (Dynasty XII, Thebes), the tomb of Rahotep at Meir (Dynasty XII ?) and at Deir el-Medineh (Dynasty XVIII). Although present at a

3.2. An ear (top left), spikelet (top right) and grain (bottom left) of wild emmer wheat and the rachis segment of durum wheat (bottom right).

number of sites, hexaploid or "naked" wheats always form a very minor portion of the recovered grain, the bulk being emmer and hulled barley. Because so few examples of hexaploid wheat have been recovered, it seems likely that they were not intentionally cultivated, but occurred as a stray or accidental component of the emmer wheat crop. Because they are generally considered to be products of hybridization between domestic (tetraploid) and wild (diploid) forms and, as yet, there is no information substantiating wild forms of wheat in Egypt, they probably developed outside of the Nile Valley and were introduced into Egypt along with emmer wheat.[65]

Barley (*Hordeum* spp.)

Barley is a short season, early maturing grain with a high yield potential. Although barley can tolerate high temperatures as long as the humidity is low, it is considered a cool season crop. Like the wheats, barley includes wild and domestic forms and is predominantly self-pollinating. However, in contrast to wheats, barley constitutes a single cytogenetic stock. For this reason, its evolution under domestication is not as complicated.

All forms of ancient barley are thought to have been derived from the wild form *Hordeum spontaneum*. But in spite of its simple cytology, barley is extremely variable. This has enabled it to be cultivated successfully over a range of agro-ecological conditions from high mountains to desert oases. It is also more salt tolerant than other cereals. Unfortunately, as in the wheats, taxonomists have placed closely related forms of barley into different species. Orlov tried to simplify the taxonomy by lumping all cultivated barley types under one species (*Hordeum vulgare*), pointing out that the different morphological types were all interfertile. His classification, however, was not adopted by the majority of scholars. Thus, botanists frequently regard cultivated barley with two rows of grain as *Hordeum distichum* and six-rowed domesticates as *H. hexastichum*. Irregular forms are often referred to as *H. intermedium* and *H. irregular*.[66]

The close morphological similarities between *H. spontaneum* and cultivated barley are coupled with tight cytogenetic affinities: wild *H. spontinum* forms have the same chromosome number (2n=14) as the cultivated barley, and hybrids between domestic and wild forms are fertile and show regular chromosome pairing. The significant difference between wild and cultivated forms is seed dispersal: cultivated barley has a tough rachis; while in wild barley the rachis is brittle (fig. 3.2).[67]

Ancient Egyptian barley is similar to the barley currently grown in the Nile Valley. Although Jackson claims that two-row barley has been recovered and identified, most finds of Ancient Egyptian barley fall within the group of four-rowed and six-rowed types. Barley is frequently recovered from tombs and settlements of all periods, usually in association with emmer. An entire barley plant was found in the coffin of Amenophis I at Dra' Abu el-Naga (Dynasty XVII), and a necklace of germinated barley was found on the mummy of Kent at Sheikh 'Abd el Qurnah (Dynasty XX). Many reports suggest that naked barley was present in Egypt in Predynastic and Dynastic times. However, there have been no published records documenting these identifications. Examination of the abdominal contents of a large number of individuals from Predynastic Naga ed-Der, Upper Egypt showed that almost every one contained husks of barley, suggesting that even if naked barley were present, it was a minor component.[68]

Because so many examples of germinated barley have been recovered, some sources believe that it served not only as a source of food but also for making beer. Others believe the barley was intentionally germinated exclusively for funerary rites. Loret, for example, describes a hollow pyramid model containing germinated barley and a picture of Osiris. He suggests that the germination of the barley figured in the funeral rites of the month of Khoiak in memory of Osiris' death. During Dynasty XVIII objects known as "Osiris-beds" occur in tombs. An example was found in the treasury of Tutankamun. It was a black oblong box containing a figure of Osiris covered in linen. This "Osiris-bed" was constructed of wood shaped in the form of the god, hollowed out, lined in linen, filled with Nile silt, and planted with barley. It is believed the soil was moistened, allowing the grain to germinate, and the inanimate form became green and living, symbolizing the resurrection of Osiris and the deceased. Other examples of Osiris beds with germinated barley are known: two were found in the tomb of Yuya and Thuyu; (Thebes); another specimen was found in the tomb of Mahirper at Thebes.[69]

Linguistic Evidence

Although wild grain was used in the Paleolithic, and grain has been cultivated since at least the fifth millennium BC, the Egyptian words for the different types of grain remain difficult to decipher. The Egyptians employed a number of different words to designate grain (table 3.1) and several remain vague with respect to their inclusiveness. For example, "grain" or "barley" could be indicated by any of four different terms (table 3.1). However, given the Egyptian ability to discriminate subtle differences between other forms of life, it seems likely that these terms refer to something more than barley in general.[70] It may be that the meaning of these terms in the

Table 3.1 Some common Egyptian names for different grains.

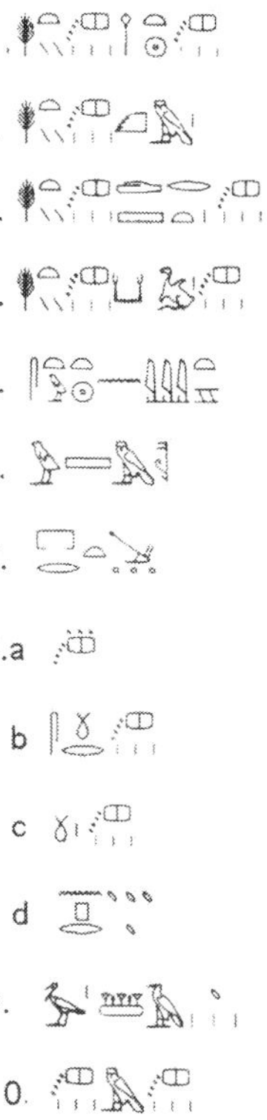

1.	*Bdt ḥdt*	"white emmer"
2.	*bdt kmt*	"black emmer"
3.	*bdt dsrt*	"red emmer"
4.	*bdt kṯ*	"emmer"
5.	*Stwt n sḫt*	"wheat of the field"
6.	*wšm*,	"ear of wheat"
7.	*prt*,	"seed of grain"(?)
8.a	*it*,	"barley or grain in general"
b	*sšrw*,	???
c	*šs*,	??
d	*npr*,	???
9.	*dšı*	"malted barley"
10.	*it m it*	"real barley" (barley as barley)

written language was somehow inferred from context or through time different words came to represent different grains or became less inclusive in their meaning. This is particularly true when cultures and economies expand and establish relationships with other societies. The term "corn" serves as a modern example. In England, corn refers to wheat: in Scotland, oats; and in the United States and Canada, it is used to designate maize (*Zea mays*).

These problems aside, linguistic evidence can often furnish information not available through archaeological pursuits. The Ancient Egyptian word for barley, *it*, initially occurs in Dynasty I and its use continues throughout the Pharaonic period. Expressions denoting "Upper Egyptian barley" and "Lower Egyptian barley" are frequently encountered in ancient texts, but probably refer to the geographical origins of the grain rather than any botanical differences. In modern Egypt, for example: *baladi beheiri* (Lower Egyptian) and *baladi saidi* (Upper Egyptian) are used to designate the geographic origins of wheat.

Beginning in Dynasty XX the saying *it-m-it* (barley as barley) becomes quite common. Two slightly different explanations have been proposed for this term. According to Černý, prices, especially small sums, were often expressed by means of their equivalent value in barley. To avoid confusion when barley was the actual commodity exchanging hands, the term "barley as barley" was employed (i.e., barley in the form of barley). Gardiner, based on Ramasside texts, suggests that *it* referred to grain in general. When it was desired to specify barley as opposed to "grain," the term *it-m-it* was used.[71]

Another common cereal name is *bdt*, later *bty*, which also appears initially in Dynasty I. In a list of cereal names in the Onomasticon of Amenope (Dynasty XX), there appear to be seven different kinds of *bty*, three of which are distinguished by their color (white, black, and red). Emmer does, in fact, vary from white to red or yellow with gradations such as pale red, reddish yellow, amber, and, in some Abyssinian varieties, it can even be a deep purple. Because sorghum, spelt, durum, and einkorn were not cultivated in Egypt during the Dynastic period, *bty* most likely refers to emmer wheat.[72]

During the Old and Middle Kingdoms the leading cereal was barley. Emmer was second, judging from the common expression *it bdt* (barley and emmer). This expression also occurs in the New Kingdom, but the relative importance of the two cereals was reversed. Further evidence of a reversal comes from Dynasty XXV through the Persian period. For example, in the Adoption Stele of Nitokris, dating from the reign of Psammetichus I,

> Three *Khar* of first-class emmer are given to Nitokris from the temple of Re-Atum in Hek'adje nome, ...after it has been offered in the divine presence, everyday and the god has been satisfied therewith ...[73]

The preeminence of emmer is likewise attested in the demotic papyrus from El-Hibeh, known as the "Petition of Peteese," which dates to the reign of Darius I as well as in other demotic papyri from this site.[74]

In a discussion of Ramesside texts relating to the transport and taxation of grain, Gardiner drew attention to the color of the ink used by the scribes in their ledgers. Whenever both black and red ink was used, red ink was employed for *bdt*-wheat and black for *it-m-it* (barley). When both barley and wheat are being referred to as a unit of grain, only red ink is used. So firmly rooted was this habit that whenever this contrast occurs in texts it may be reasonable to infer that the black refers to barley and the red, wheat. Furthermore, because the amounts written in black were both smaller and less frequent, it appears most payments were made with the most abundant cereal, emmer wheat.[75]

Another word denoting some sort of cereal is *swt*. Although it appears to refer to a wheat of some kind, its precise meaning is not clear. It may be a general term for wheat, but this is difficult to substantiate. It was distinct from *it* and *bdt*, because on a stele dated to year eight of Ramesses II, the King brags of his concern for the welfare of his workmen saying: "Upper Egypt continuously conveys for you to Lower Egypt and Lower Egypt conveys for you to Upper Egypt, barley, emmer, *swt*-wheat, salt (?), and legumes in immense quantity." Täckholm believed *swt* denoted naked wheat, but admits that such wheats were relatively unimportant in Egypt until the Greco-Roman period. In a later publication Täckholm suggests that *swt* might refer to einkorn wheat, and Halbaek suggests that *swt* may be a type of emmer wheat that for reasons of poor preservation cannot be distinguished from other common forms.[76]

Another cereal referred to in Old Kingdom tomb scenes is *bsꜣ*. Above some scenes depicting the reaping of barley (?), is the legend "beer for he who cuts the *bsꜣ*." *Bsꜣ* is also mentioned in Old Kingdom tombs in association with bread and beer making. It is not quite certain with which activity the *bsꜣ* is to be connected. From Dynasties III to XII it appears as a label on granaries depicted on funerary monuments. Interestingly, beginning in Dynasty IV the term usually occurs with a palm date. The pairing of *bsꜣ* and dates occurs in four accounts in the Kahun Papyri and in the Moscow Mathematical Papyrus. In two tombs, however, is the world "grinding *bsꜣ*". The verb used, *tiss*, is known only from these examples. Its cognate or derivative, *ts*, "to crush" is used in connection with grain only in the process of beer making. Further evidence that *bsꜣ* was used in beer making is offered by the references mentioned in the Moscow Papyrus, where it is also associated with dates. This association of dates with beer suggests that the fruit was an ingredient of beer.[77]

It is possible that *bsꜣ* could have been an old term for barley, and there are early examples where it appears alongside terms for Upper and Lower Egyptian barley. In a review of Gardiner's discussion of the question, Nims suggests that *bsꜣ* was a word for any grain set aside for beer making and that it might mean malt. In a later article on bread and beer problems of the Moscow Papyrus, Nims cites as additional support for his view, from a study of brewing in Mesopotamia where it is shown that malt was used from the Sumerian period onward and served as a primary food. He suggests that a similar development probably took place in Egypt and cites the presence on a Dynasty II stele of wheat, dates, and *bsꜣ* as an indication of the use of malt as food.[78]

Dried residues from "beer" jars have provided some additional insights concerning ancient brewing ingredients. Beer residues were composed of various cereals including grains of barley and emmer, yeast cells, molds, bacteria, and small proportions of various impurities. That some sort of yeast or leavening agent was known even in Neolithic times seems evident from these studies and from bread recovered from Neolithic Badari, which had a porous texture. The yeast identified from the beer jars was a wild yeast (*Saccharomyces winlocki*), previously unknown.[79]

A detailed description of Egyptian brewing from the fourth century AD shows a marked similarity to the production of *bouza* by the modern *felaheen* (Egyptian peasants). *Bouza* is chiefly made from coarsely ground wheat, barley, and millet. In some parts of the country dates or date juice is added. The grain mash is mixed with water to form a dough and kneaded, and yeast is added. The dough is made into loaves and baked lightly, leaving the enzymes and yeast still active. After baking, the loaves are broken up and put into a vessel with water. Crushed moist wheat that has been exposed to the air is then added. The mixture is then left to ferment. Sometimes a little bouza from an old batch is added as a primer. The final product is then passed through a sieve before being consumed. Ancient Egyptian beer, like modern bouza, is obviously not the clear pale liquid consumed today. Rather, it is a nourishing grog that possesses a slight amount of alcohol that is detectable if too much is consumed.[80]

The similarity between bouza and ancient beer production is quite striking. In the tomb of Ti, a scene depicting bread and beer making provides considerable insight into the production process (fig. 3.4). Tasks common to the making of bread and beer are depicted in the middle register. Grain is first removed from stores, then it is crushed in large mortars (figs. 3.3, 3.4), and ground between two smooth stones. The resulting flour is passed

3.3. Crushing grain with mortar and pestle. Tomb of Ti, Saqqara, Dynasty V.

through a circular sieve (fig. 3.5). In a lower and upper register molds are heated over fires. The bread dough is then mixed, presumably with water, and poured into the heated molds. In some cases a leavening (?) agent may have been used.The final step of bread and beer making involved the ever vigilant accounting of the scribe, whose job it was to assess the *pefsu* or baking value of the bread and beer. The *pefsu* scale was based on the number of loaves or jugs of beer one *hekat* of grain would produce. The higher the value, the smaller the loaves or the weaker the beer. The *pefsu* scale enabled the scribe to calculate equivalences between loaves and jugs of different sizes and strength and thereby established their market value.[81]

Archaeological excavations at Hierakonpolis have uncovered a Predynastic bakery and brewery situated next to each other (fig. 3.6). The integrated scenes from Ti were apparently mimicking the logical physical arrangement of these two integrated activities. An interesting aspect of bread and beer making that remains surprising is that no large grinding mills are known archaeologically, from the literature or from tomb scenes. Even in the New Kingdom, grain was being ground in mortars with pestles and finely ground flour was obtained by grinding grain between stones much as the practice during Neolithic times.[82]

Nevertheless, the fondness of Egyptians for bread and the quantities they produced were so well-known that they were nicknamed Artophagoi or eaters of bread by Herodotus. In the Harris Papyrus (Dynasty XX), 30 different kinds of bread are included in the offering lists for the dead.

3.4. *Beer and bread making scene from the Tomb of Ti, Saqqara, Dynasty V.*

3.5. An ancient sieve. Agricultural Museum, Dokki.

Some bread had to be baked in certain places (even in foreign countries), other types had to be made according to certain prescriptions. Shepherds being away from home for long periods would not have a readily available bakery, but fresh bread was still an important aspect of their life. Flour and water were mixed and kneaded into dough. The dough was then flattened into a large circular shape, which was placed directly on the coals of the fire to bake. The baking bread could be turned with small sticks and a duster was used to remove the ash. The entire process is identical to one used by modern Bedouin herders.[83]

Sorghum and Millet (*Sorghum bicolor/vulgare* and *Panicum* spp./*Pennisetum typhoides*)

Millets and sorghums have a number of characteristics in common. They are all annual, warm weather grasses, they are stimulated into early flowering by shortening of daylight hours, and contain toxic quantities of prussic acid under certain conditions. Although Europeans and North Americans often confuse the two plant groups, morphologically and taxonomically they are quite distinct. The sorghums are all members of one genus (*Sorghum*); millets include several genera. Today the wild progenitor of domestic pearl millet *Pennisetum americanum monodii* is restricted in distribution to the southern margins of the central Saharan highlands where annual rainfall varies between 250 to 800 mm a year. Taking into consideration the rainfall patterns that existed at the end of the last Sahara pluvial phase (5000 to 3000 BC) and the fact that millet is a natural colonizer, the distribution of millets probably extended north into Egypt's Western Desert. *Pennisetum americanum* (pearl millet) has been recently identified growing spontaneously in the Nile Valley and adjacent Western Desert.

It is now known that wild sorghum and millet (genus *Panicum* spp.) were being heavily utilized by the Upper Paleolithic inhabitants of the Nabta Playa as early as 8000 BP. Tests on a sample of the recovered sorghum grains suggest they had stronger similarities to domestic forms than wild ones and that perhaps they represented cultivated forms in the first stages of domestication (see chapter I). If further evidence can be brought to bear on these early tests and the samples are found to be examples of early domestic sorghum, then Egypt's development of early domestic species would further counter the current belief of a single Near Eastern center of domestication.

Although Unger claims to have recognized artistic representations of sorghum (*Sorghum bicolor/vulgare*) (dura) and believes sorghum stems were recovered at Saqqara, this claim could not be substantiated. A scene in the tomb of Kagemni is also thought to depict a form of *Panicum*, but its appearance lacks the definitive characteristics needed to make any solid identification. Täckholm, however, reported that in the museum at Kew is a well-preserved specimen of sorghum recovered by Petrie from El-Lahun. The specimen reportedly was part of a flower garland and thought to date to Dynasty XII.[84] This is the best evidence thus far for the presence of sorghum in Egypt.

One reason why sorghum might have been rare in Egypt is that it is a summer crop, which conflicts with the annual Nile flood and the superior producing winter cereals, wheat and barley. Consequently its development as an indigenous Egyptian domesticate may have been truncated by the introduction from the Near East of higher yielding winter crops.

Barn Grass (*Echinochloa colonum*)

Grains of *Echinochloa colonum* (barn grass) were identified by Netolitzky among the intestinal contents of some Predynastic bodies excavated by Reisner at Naga ed-Der. Judging from the

3.6. The bakery (top) and brewery area (bottom) of Predynastic Hierakonpolis. Insert shows imprint of ancient grain on carbonized residue of a beer vat. Kom el Ahmar, Hierakonpolis

quantity and purity of the grains, Dixon thought it possible that the plant might have been cultivated locally. It is more likely, however, that the grains were harvested from existing wild or weedy stands because no other examples, artistic, textual or archaeological, are known.[85]

Rice (*Oryza sativa*)

In 1752 Count de Caylus gave an account of a large bronze figure of Osiris in his possession. He believes the figure was coated with a thin layer of plaster; intermixed with the plaster as a binder were rice stalks. De Caylus was not alone in his belief that the straws came from the rice plant; some years earlier, in 1739, the figure had also been examined by M. de Bose, who arrived at the same conclusion. Unfortunately, the present location of the statuette is unknown, and it is not possible to date it very closely on the basis of de Caylus' illustration. Apparently, the base, and therefore any inscription that may have existed, was missing. Nevertheless, Daressy was inclined to accept the findings of the two eighteenth-century scholars, but Täckholm believes the identification of rice very unlikely.[86]

This is not to say that the dynastic Egyptians were unaware of its existence. It would appear reasonable to suppose that rice plants may have been known by the inhabitants of the lower Nile Valley, where suitable conditions for growth existed. It is entirely possible that rice could have even been acquired in trade or have been mentioned by travelers visiting Egypt. It is well-known that ceramics, precious stones, and many other commodities traveled to Egypt, so the possibility of trade in a perishable commodity is conceivable. What is clear, on the basis of present evidence, is that rice, whether its existence was known or not, was not cultivated in Pharaonic Egypt. Its likeness does not occur in the tombs, it is not found in inscriptions, it is not mentioned in texts. Additionally, its Coptic name is identical with, and clearly derived from, the Arabic *arouz*. Therefore, rice, most likely, was not cultivated in Egypt until after the Arab conquest.

IV

FIBER AND OIL PLANTS

Egyptian agriculture included plants exploited for their oil and fiber as well as for consumption. Flax appears to be the earliest and best documented oil/fiber crop. Papyrus, a native wild species, was also heavily utilized for its fibrous stalk. Although it may not have been fully domesticated, papyrus appears to have been tended and its growth closely monitored, suggesting that it may have been in the early stages of the domestication process. Several other oil-bearing plants seem to have entered cultivation as weedy forms. As in the cereal grains, the domestication of oil-bearing seed plants altered the seed dispersal mechanisms (with the exception of sesame) so that the release of the seeds was delayed or the seeds were retained by the mother plant. Other changes such as increases in seed size and higher oil yield also occurred. In the fiber-producing plants change was towards longer, straighter fibers.[87]

Fiber Plants

Flax (Linum usitatissimum)

Flax, from the Anglo Saxon *fleax*, is a fibrous grass that provided the Egyptians with linseed oil and the raw material needed for the production of linen, the predominant woven fabric of Dynastic Egypt. Flax fibers are stronger than either cotton or wool and the seeds generally consist of about 40 per cent oil. The seed residue left after oil extraction is high in protein and makes an excellent feed for cattle.

In Ancient Egypt flax was called *shenu*. The same species of flax (*Linum usitatissimum*) was used from Neolithic times through the Dynastic period. The oldest evidence for domesticated flax, like that for barley and wheat, comes from the Levant and southwest Asia. The sites of Jericho (Palestine) and Tell Ramoad (Syria) represent two of the earliest examples of domestic linseeds. The earliest remains of flax in Egypt come from the Neolithic Fayum and Merimde (ca. 4400 BC) and flax seeds have been recovered from Badari (4400 BC).[88]

The word linen is derived from the Greek word for flax, *linon*, and Ancient Egyptian linen varied from being as fine as any produced today, with as many as one hundred threads to the centimeter, to a canvas-like coarse linen and ranged in color from white to golden brown. Color variations as well as texture were related to the maturity of the flax when harvested and how the fibers were processed. Pliny mentions three kinds of flax grown in Egypt: Abestinem, Byssus, and common flax. He says that Byssus was extremely fine and only the rich could afford it. Pliny further mentions four qualities of Egyptian linen cloth: Tanitic, Pelusiac, Butine, and Tentyritic, which probably refer to the four terms used to grade linen: "royal linen," "fine thin cloth," "thin cloth," and "smooth cloth" (ordinary cloth), respectively. Because the names applied to the linens also refer to geographic areas, some of the characteristics attributed to the different grades of linen might have been the result of using different breeds of the plant. Although conjecture, the adaptability of flax to different areas would, over a period of time, likely produce plants with varying qualities of fiber.[89]

The ancestry of cultivated flax is fairly well-established. The genus *Linum* comprises about 200 species spread over the temperate, Mediterranean, and steppe belts of the northern hemisphere. Cultivated flax (*Linum usitatissimum*) is most closely related to wild *L. bienne* (syn. *L. angustifolium*). Both forms have the same chromosome number (2n=30), intercross readily, and are fully interfertile. *Linum bienne* is widely distributed over western Europe, the Mediterranean basin, North Africa, the Near East, and Caucasia. Its distribution in the Near East resembles that of barley in that a disjunct population is also found in Libya. On the basis of a close genetic affiliation and morphology, *L. bienne* is now identified as the wild progenitor of *L. usitatissimum*. As in the cereal crops, the main changes under domestication were a shift to a nondehiscent seed capsule.[90]

Cultivated flax (*L usitatissimum*) is an annual plant, but some wild forms are biennial or perennial; all are predominantly self-pollinating. Flax grown predominantly for their fiber reach 120 cm high, have few branches, and grow best in the temperate regions of the world. Oil varieties are shorter, branched and tend to flourish in warm climates. Egyptian varieties served a dual purpose, producing oil and fiber, and stood intermediate between the tall less-branched and short-branched varieties. Egypt's geographic location and environment, placed midway along a cline stretching from the oil varieties of sub-Saharan Africa to the northern fiber varieties, probably had more to do with establishing this intermediate form than any manipulation by humans.

A valuable characteristic of flax is that it is less exacting in climatic demands than any of the other major cereals or fibrous vegetables grown by the Ancient Egyptians and can quickly adapt to varying conditions of soil and temperature. Flax grows best, however, under moist soil conditions such as well-watered grassy areas, near springs, seepage areas, and marsh land.

The stalk or stem of the flax plant is smooth, erect, slender, and curiously constructed in that the majority of its composition is a pithy core that is hollow when dry. Between the cylindrical woody center and the outer bark, running in symmetrical layers all the way from root to blossom, are the tough flax fibers of raw linen. The "bast" (flax) fibers are the cells that in the living plant carry the sustaining nutrients in solution from the soil. Each fiber is made up of a number of long cylindrical cells, the ends of which are positioned next to similar cells above and below. Linen fabrics can be easily identified because in the prepared fiber, the junction between cells is normally of greater diameter than the cells themselves and under magnification the fibers resemble a jointed grass like bamboo. The pithy core and fibers are encased in a thin outer sheath that, together with the other components of the plant, is firmly bound by a natural gum or pectin. From the main stalk extend alternate, lanceolate, light-green leaves. The stems are crowned by corymbose panicles of small, delicate, blue flowers. When ripe, these flowers are replaced by rough, reddish-brown capsules, approximately the size of peas. Each capsule unit contains small, smooth green seeds, the linseed of modern commerce.[91]

Climate and soil are important factors affecting the quality of the plant and its fibers. Although flax can be grown with varying success on most types of soil (with the exception of sandy, alkaline soils) the best soils in Egypt are the loamy-clay soils of the Delta and, coincidentally, the best climate for flax is also in the Delta, where the cool, humid breeze of the sea is beneficial to the first stages of plant growth (December through March). The Delta's dry spring climate also assures timely plant and seed formation.

On the basis of tomb scenes and classic accounts, the records of 19th century flax cultivation in Egypt can be used as a model for Dynastic times. The preparation of the land first involved plowing the soil at least twice. The farmers then usually divided the field into beds with raised borders to control watering. It was apparently thought best to sow flax after clover or after the land had lain fallow. The best period for planting was the last week in October to mid-November; late sowing had a marked negative effect on productivity and quality of the crop. Flax was harvested from the end of March to early April.[92]

For fine linen, flax stalks were pulled from the ground by their roots while the stem was still green (fig. 4.1).[93] The green stems are soft and free enough from gum to be spun into very fine threads. They can also be bleached white. Flax stems were pulled rather than cut because cutting might stain the inside fibers so that they could not be bleached clean enough to be converted into white cloth. If the stalk was allowed to mature from green to yellow, the gum became nearly insoluble, and the flax fiber was correspondingly coarser. This flax was used to make the strong linen necessary for working clothes. When the stalks were allowed to fully mature, the fiber was too tough to be used for anything but ropes, mats, and the coarse linen needed for sacks and the rough garments of the lower class.

After the stalks had been collected from the field, they were stripped of leaves and blossoms by drawing them through the teeth of a comb-like tool or series of upright forks, a process called rippling. They were then tied in loose bundles to ripen in the sun (fig. 4.2). When this had been completed, the bundles of flax were subjected to steeping (retting) in little square artificial pools of water for about ten days. The long, tedious process was necessary to soften the woody stalk of the flax plant and help remove much of the binding pectin that held the fibers together so that they could be extracted easily. Retting had to be monitored because if more than about 50 per cent of the binding pectin were leached out, the linen fibers would disintegrate into unusable parts. When thoroughly retted and dried in the sun, the

4.1. Harvesting grain and pulling ripened flax (third register). Tomb of Sennedjem, Deir el Medina, Dynasty XIX.

flax stalks were passed through fluted rollers, which quickly broke up all woody matter. The valuable, semi-transparent linen fibers were then recovered.[94]

Scenes from the tombs of Sennedjem, Ti and Beni Hasan mirror the cultivation and preparation sequences of 19th century Egypt. Flax was pulled rather cut (see fig. 4.1), and the stems were rippled and steeped in water (fig. 4.3). The process of steeping the stalks of the flax plant is well-represented in a tomb at Beni Hasan where a man is seen hauling water up a flight of stairs and another is pouring water into the steeping pools (fig. 4.3). After steeping, the stalks were placed in the sun and repeatedly turned over until perfectly dry. After drying, they were beaten by mallets (figs. 4.3, 4.4) on stone slabs. The fibers were separated and cleaned by pulling them through a toothed object made of wood or bone (in later times, iron) that resembled a sort of comb (fig. 4.5). The comb removed the *tow* or loose fibers of flax and also split the fibers to prepare it for spinning into finer sizes of yarn.

Egyptian yarn seems to have all been spun by hand, and the spindle is invariably seen in pictures representing the manufacture of cloth. Egyptian spindles were slender sticks that tapered at the bottom and had a weighted whorl at the top (fig. 4.6). The whorls were made of wood, stone, or ceramic. Flax fibers were initially prepared for spinning by rolling the fibers on a flat surface, most commonly the thigh, to loosen and separate the twisted flax fibers. The individual fibers or *rolog* were then wound on to a rod, a ceramic reel, or spool. The wound ball was placed in a ceramic or wicker basket, the lid of which had small holes through which the flax threads passed smoothly for spinning. Fibers prepared in this manner are usually referred to as roves or rovings.

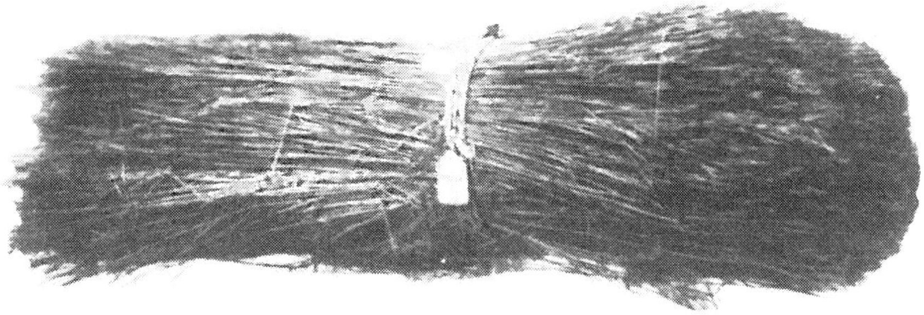

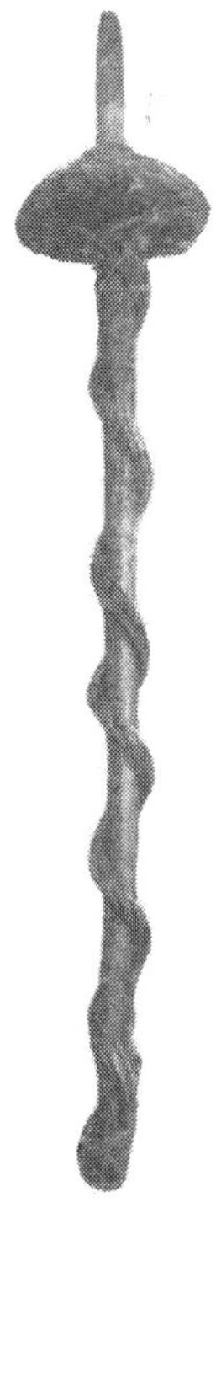

4.2. (top) Ancient Egyptian flax bound after ripening in the sun. Agricultural Museum, Dokki.
4.3. (centre) Steeping the flax stalks to remove the pectin and beating it with a mallet. Tomb of Khenty, Beni Hasan, Dynasty XII.
4.4. (centre rightt) A mallet for beating flax. Agricultural Museum, Dokki.
4.5. (bottom leftt) An ancient flax comb for splitting and separating fibers. Agricultural Musuem, Dokki.
4.6. (bottom right) Egyptian spindle whorl with a wrap of flax thread. British Museum, London.

To create thread, two or more fibers were twisted together, in a direction opposite to that in which they were to be spun. Middle Kingdom reliefs from Beni Hasan depict spinners using different techniques (fig. 4.7). The simplest method, hand spinning, was used for flax fibers. Single roves were guided from the ceramic or wicker vessel by the spinner's fingers onto the suspended spindle, which was rotated by rolling the stick on the thigh. The momentum of the spinning motion was maintained by the whorl, twisting the fibers into a single thread. Another technique also shown in a scene from Beni Hasan shows the rove drawn over a fixed rod and spun by rolling the spindle between the palms of the hand. Spinning with two spindles and multiple roves simultaneously enabled the creation of ply-threads. If the spindle was turning and viewed from above, it would be spinning counter clockwise or Z-spun. If the spindle were turning clockwise, it would be S-spun. It is often stated that Egyptian thread was predominantly Z-spun. Hall believes the logic behind Z-spun thread is that the fibers generally turn in that direction naturally. Although this may be true, it is interesting to point out that while observing many modern Egyptian village spinners, those that spun right-handed tended to create Z-spun thread and those that were left-handed tended to create S-spun thread unless they intentionally wished Z-spun.[95]

Weaving the threads into cloth demands the use of two distinct groups of parallel threads. One set, the warp, is kept under tension during weaving; the second set, normally referred to as the weft, is passed over and under the warp threads at right angles to them. A loom serves to keep the warp threads under tension during weaving. Looms vary considerably in design and function and it is customary, when describing simple looms to refer to them as vertical or horizontal looms, depending on whether the threads of the warp are maintained upright or parallel to the ground.

Egyptian looms were generally variants of a single type of horizontal loom, the beam-tension loom. In such looms the warp threads are held at each end by a beam. The beams can be secured by fastening them to pegs in the ground or supported by a frame. The earliest Egyptian loom was a frameless horizontal ground loom formed by pegs placed in the earth. It is first represented on a Predynastic ceramic dish (now in the Petrie Museum) recovered from a woman's grave at Badari. The horizontal ground loom was used exclusively in Egypt until the end of the Middle Kingdom. It is illustrated in various contemporary tomb scenes at Beni Hasan (fig. 4.8).[96]

The vertical frame loom was introduced by the early New Kingdom. It is very likely that the loom was brought to Egypt by the Hyksos (fig. 4.8). Although its introduction encouraged tapestry weaving, it by no means entirely displaced the horizontal ground loom. The vertical loom can be seen in three Dynasty XVIII Theban tomb paintings, which, although damaged, can be reconstructed to show the component parts. The warp is stretched between two beams and fastened in a rectangular wooden frame by the weaver who sits or squats to work at the loom base.

The manufacture of linen in Egypt from very early times formed one of the principal branches of industry. Weaving was apparently controlled by the state, but was undertaken at a variety of locations, from weaving centers to the home. All Egyptian temples and many estates also seem to have possessed weavers. Linen cloth, under state control, was bartered through professional traders for other commodities. In the royal house, weaving was a particular concern of the harem. Although the women might have taken on some of the delicate work themselves, their prime task was the training, instruction, and supervision of the textile workers.[97] Beyond the state industry, spinning and weaving were also conducted by private citizens who made cloth for personal use and for exchange.

Papyrus (Cyperus papyrus)

The Papyrus plant (fig. 4.9) is one of the most characteristic plants of Ancient Egypt and was used for a variety of purposes. The stalks were intertwined and bundled together to make boats; the inner bark was woven into sail cloth, matting, blankets, and ropes; the lower stock and rhizome were eaten by the Egyptians. Cattle too are known to graze on papyrus. The use most familiar to the modern world, however, is the manufacture of writing paper. The oldest papyrus paper known was found in the tomb of Hemaka, a high official under Udimu (Den), fifth king of Dynasty I (ca. 2890 BC). The next oldest specimen dates to Dynasty V, Abusir and Dynasty VI, Saqqara.[98]

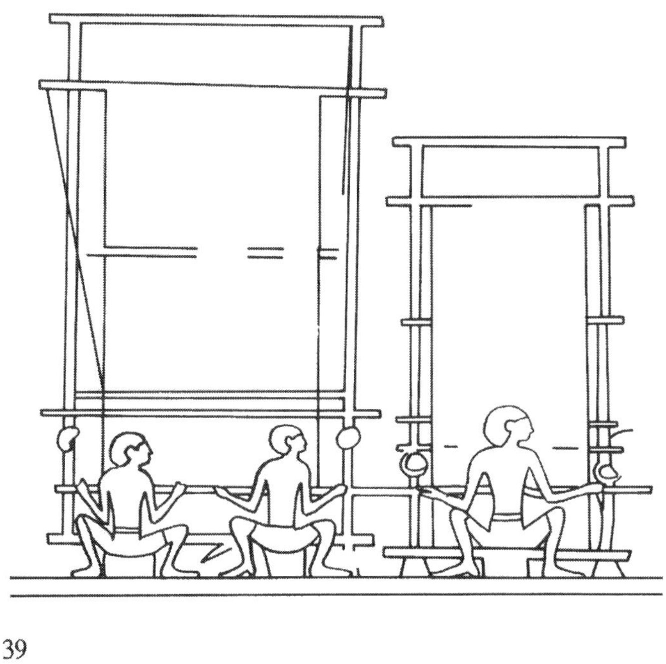

4.7. (top) Egyptian spinners displaying the single rove technique (left), grasping spinning (middle), and spinning with multiple spindles (all). Tomb of Khenty, Beni Hasan, Dynasty XII.
4.8. (bottom) The ground (upper) and vertical (lower) frame loom. Tomb of Khenty, Beni Hasan, Dynasty XII and house of Djehutynefer, Thebes, Dynasty IV.

The status of papyrus as a genetically distinct domesticate is difficult to ascertain. Given the variety of uses papyrus eventually served, from food, to medicines, to paper, and the quantity of raw material needed to supply these demands, its growth was very likely closely monitored and managed. Its use in paper production during Roman times alone would have exhausted natural supples unless some sort of controls were in place. Another point in support of cultivation is that when the Egyptians harvested papyrus, the rhizome was often pulled out along with the stalk. Because seed propagation is not a viable means of reproduction (papyrus reproduces through root-stock propagation), the resource would eventually be exhausted without some sort of conservation or replanting program.

These appeals to practicality lend credence to the notion that papyrus "tending," if not domestication, was undertaken to support the demand for the needed raw material. A successful conservation program needed only to ensure that sufficient rootstocks remained for the next crop, that they be submerged in water, and that the soils were sufficiently moist during the growing season. Extending the crop to new fields could be done simply by dividing the rhizome clumps and replanting them. In fact, such a program may have been in place during the Roman period. The destruction of stands not under Roman control suggests that not only wild papyrus but also cultivated or "tended" forms grew in Egypt as well. Through processes of economic hegemony, cultivated papyrus thrived until the introduction of linen-based paper reduced the need for papyrus to the point that it became economically more feasible to grow other food and cash crops.

Pliny described the manufacture of paper, and modern experiments and production techniques designed for the tourist industry have perpetuated this ancient industry. The part of the papyrus plant used for paper was the stem, which grew above the water line. After pulling or cutting the stalk, the outer rind was removed, and the inner pith was separated into thin strips (ca. 3 to 10 mm). The strips were then laid side-by-side and according to some scholars, organized so as not to overlap. At right angles a second layer was arranged over the first, again side-by-side and not overlapping. Other accounts suggest that the strips should be laid as above on a moist cloth, but in an overlapping pattern with a second cloth laid over the papyrus slices. The next step is to beat the papyrus with a mallet and place the arranged slices in a press. An alternative method is to arrange the strips between moist boards and place a weight on the upper board. Once dry, the papyrus is removed from the cloth or boards as a homogeneous sheet that can be further smoothed by burnishing with a stone or other smooth object.[99]

4.9. Splitting fish next to a thicket of papyrus. Tomb of Rahotep, Meydum, Dynasty IV.

Egypt was the only country in the Ancient world to manufacture papyrus. There was a great demand for it, especially in the prosperous Greco-Roman period when enormous quantities were exported from Alexandria. The famous Alexandria library alone is said to have contained 400,000 papyri. Herodotus states that papyrus was used by the Ionian Greeks, who called it "skins," a name probably derived from the parchment used prior to the introduction of papyrus. In Athens, papyrus was in use as early as the fifth century BC. Evidence for this comes from the purchase of papyrus rolls recorded in an inscription relating to the rebuilding of the Erechteion in 407 BC. Papyrus was also used extensively in ancient Rome where it was required not only for the production of books, but also for domestic purposes and legal documents. So important was papyrus that Rome (ca. 25 BC) attained a monopoly on its production, raising the price to levels that brought criticism from the populace. The revenue from papyrus reached such heights that the proceeds were said to be sufficient to maintain an army.[100]

Apart from its use in making paper and other objects, one overlooked aspect of papyrus has been its potential as animal feed. Papyrus has been shown to be among the most productive plants in terms of biomass per year and is as digestible (30 to 45%) by ruminants as grasses, but is higher in protein. Papyrus is generally not readily available to cattle and other hooved domestic animals because they are not well adapted to foraging in the swampy areas where the plant thrives. But in pre-Roman Egypt, papyrus would have been available to cattle as the Nile reached its lowest levels in spring and it could always be cropped and bundled by herdsmen for feed. In the Middle and New Kingdom when most of the arable land was under cultivation, papyrus would have offered an important supplement to the diet of the vast herds reported to pasture in Egypt. Even in modern sub-Saharan Africa, cattle have been seen grazing on papyrus and it is provided as a supplement to regular fodder.

Today papyrus is rare in Egypt. It is seldom found outside public parks, museum gardens, and areas devoted to the tourist industry. The last recorded sighting of a natural stand of papyrus in the Nile Valley or Delta was in 1820. It still, however, grows in Wadi Natrum and Siwa Oasis and is a common plant in the sud swamps of the Sudan.[101]

The disappearance of papyrus from the Delta and Upper Egypt has been attributed to a number of equally probable causes, including climatic change and human-induced extirpation. Some even believe that it never grew wild in Egypt, but existed only as a cultivated plant.[102] From an historical standpoint this explanation seems unlikely. The innumerable representations of papyrus thickets and swamps in Old Kingdom tombs suggest the plant was a common component of the Nile flora even before it became part of an important industry. The simplest explanation is that human activities resulted in its extirpation from Egypt. In an attempt to gain a monopoly on the production of paper, the Romans were said to have ordered the destruction of all stands of papyrus except those under their control, thereby restricting the distribution of papyrus to tended stands.[103] When linen paper was introduced around 781 AD, the need for papyrus began to decline and by the ninth century AD, papyrus was no longer an essential commodity. The tended stands were abandoned, and the land diverted for use to other more profitable crops.

Papyrus, it seems, could easily be reestablished in Egypt if it were allowed to propagate. Expansion is curtailed, however, because those areas most likely to be colonized were long ago cleared for agriculture. In the Sudan and Egypt, the primary habitat was along the banks of the Nile and its Delta channels; the same land that has been highly prized by agriculturalists since the Neolithic. It is fertile, easily watered, and requires little preparation. These areas also served as pasture for domestic and wild animals. In short, through the years, papyrus habitat has been sacrificed for the cultivation of domestic species.[104]

Oil Plants

4.10. A small oil press, probably for family use. Agricultural Museum, Dokki.

In marketing and the culinary arts, it is common to make a distinction between fats and oils-fats being solid and oils being liquid at room temperature. From a chemical point of view, however, this is an artificial distinction because the basic molecular structures are the same. Therefore, no distinction will be made here. When either the term oil or fat is presented, the other should be inferred.

Most fats have certain nutritional values in common. They are concentrated foods supplying more than twice as many calories as equal weights of proteins or carbohydrates. They, therefore, provide high energy with low bulk. Although current media attention has focused on the negative aspects of "fat" in the diet, it is essential for good nutrition. Fat is required for normal growth and development by providing some essential fatty acids. These are linoleic, linolenic, and arachidonic acids. Tests on animals have shown that deficiencies in linoleic and arachidonic acids resulted in stunted growth, lower reproductive rates, high infant mortality, and poor resistance to infection. Human infants with fat deficient diets suffer from diarrhea, rashes, chafing skin, and reduced growth and weight. Linolenic acid seems to be the most essential of the three for proper health and development and seed oils are an excellent source of this fatty acid.

Egyptians used oil derived from plants for food as well as for lighting and rituals. So important was oil that the state imposed an oil tax on the populace in an attempt to maintain a supply for its own use. Local oil production, however, could not meet the needs of the Egyptians. Oil had to be imported and exacted as tribute from Asia where crops such as sesame and olives were plentiful. Oil was such a valued commodity, it is said that Plato paid for some of the debts he incurred while traveling in Egypt with oil.[105]

The rigid control exerted over oil production and its agricultural support system can be illustrated by the laws enacted by Ptolemy II Philadelphus that created a state monopoly on all aspects of the oil economy. The state determined the quantities and the nomes in which the oil-bearing plants could be grown. Farm contractors (most likely large estate holders) bought the right to sell the oil-bearing plants to legitimate retailers: a legitimacy determined by the state. The retail price and the amount of oil-bearing plants or seeds a given retailer could purchase and sell were also fixed. Additionally, with the exception of temples, only the royal factories could process the plants/seeds for oil. All oil refineries and presses (fig. 4.10) had to be declared to the state, and production itself was limited to certain parts of the year and carried out only under the surveillance of state officials. Even the manufacture of oil presses and mortars was strictly controlled by the government.[106]

Twenty-eight different Egyptian words were used in referring to oils and at least indirectly to oil-bearing plants. Only those plants that were cultivated in Egypt, however, are presented here.

Olive (Olea europaea)

The olive is the most prominent and economically the most important classical fruit tree of the Mediterranean basin. All cultivated species of olive belong to one species *Olea europaea*. It is a relic of the Tertiary flora (6.5 to 1.5 mya) of the Mediterranean and the only species of the genus to survive locally.

The genus *Olea* contains about 35 species distributed all over the world but three species deserve special mention because of their proximity to Egypt. The first is *O. laperrinii*, which has silvery white leaves (lower side) and is native to the Saharan mountains with related species along the Red Sea and Persian Gulf coast. The second species is *O. africana*, which stretches from South Africa to the Egyptian Sudanese border. This species has narrow leaves, golden beneath. A third species, *O. ferruginea*, is native to Iran.

The wild progenitors of the cultivated olive are unknown but it is thought that a cross between two species either *O. africana* or *O. ferruginea* and an ancient proto-*Olea* form (now extinct) might have parented the modern cultigen. The distribution of the extant forms would place the area of origin in the east Mediterranean. From there it spread west to Tunisia and north and east to Europe and Asia Minor. It is mentioned in texts from Ebla dated to about 2500 BC and it is thought that the tree was already extensively cultivated in many parts of the world.

Interestingly, Egypt possesses no native olive trees (at least from Late Paleolithic times); the natural range extends east and west of the Nile Valley. References to olive trees, olives, and olive oil in translations of Egyptian texts must, therefore, be treated with caution. In many cases, the Egyptian words for the moringa tree and ben oil have been incorrectly interpreted as olive oil. The first mention of olives in Egypt is attributed to the Dynasty V King Sahure, who reportedly stated that "olive trees were not to be in profusion in Egypt, whereas in Canaan they abounded." The first finds in Egypt date from Dynasty XVIII (1350 BC), but the tree may not actually have been cultivated in Egypt until later. In fact, the word for olive does not occur until Dynasty XIX, although Davies depicts a fragment of a painted scene from Dynasty XVIII, and an Amarna relief clearly shows an olive branch (fig. 4.11). Interestingly, Hepper reports that olive leaves were recovered from Tutankamun's tomb and he believes that olives were grown locally and were most likely supported through irrigation. Stronger evidence for olives is found in Dynasty XX when Ramesses III is reported to have attempted to plant an olive grove near the temple of the sun-god Re

4.11. A rare depiction of an olive branch from the Amarna period, Dynasty XVIII. Metropolitan Museum of Art, New York.

at Heliopolis. Further evidence includes a leaf from the tomb of Amenhotep II and olive twigs reportedly dated to Dynasty XX or later, identified by Schweinfurth.[107]

Theophrastus said that the olive grew in Upper Egypt and that the oil produced in his day was not inferior to the Greek oil except that it had a less pleasing smell. Strabo, who traveled in Egypt 500 years later, stated that olive trees grew only in Alexandria and the Fayum. Other sources corroborate the reports of these early travelers. Reports state that olive trees were planted in the Fayum around 251 BC, and a 256 BC report mentions young olive trees growing in the Fayum. Olives can still be found in the Fayum and in the Siwa oasis.[108]

It seems that the olive tree never became firmly established in Egypt even after attempts by the Greeks to plant and raise them in the most suitable areas, the Fayum, and Mediterranean coast. Although trees planted in these areas apparently reached maturity, oil production was low. The experiment seems to have been only a minor success at best. This is probably due to the fact that Egypt does not receive enough rainfall to support the needs of the olive tree. Thus, establishing and maintaining an orchard would require considerable irrigation. Olive oil consumption always exceeded production, and the oil was necessarily a major import.

***Sesame* (Sesamum indicum)**

Next to linseed and olive oil, sesame oil was probably the most heavily used by ancient societies and is well-known in modern Egypt. The origins of the sesame plant and its history are, unfortunately, not very clear. There is also considerable difference of opinion among Egyptologists as to whether the sesame and its oil mentioned in the ancient texts was the plant we now know by that name. The Ancient Egyptian word *smsmt* has been wrongly interpreted to mean sesame when it actually may have referred to marijuana (*Cannabis sativa*) or linseed oil. Because so few sesame seeds have actually been recovered in Egypt, it is of particular interest that Petrie reported sesame at Nagada and that a sample from Tutankhamun's tomb was noted as possibly being sesame. If these finds could be taxonomically confirmed, it would account for the earliest examples of sesame in Ancient Egypt.

Sesame is a leafy annual plant that stands about one meter high. The plant produces large pink or white tubular flowers with narrow erect pods about 3 cm long. Contained within the pods are the seeds, which have an exceptionally high oil content (45 to 60%) and the meal is high in protein. Sesame, like the domestic grains, is predominantly a self-pollinating crop, but the frequency of cross-pollination can be high. It is a warm season crop, and unlike flax and other oil seeds, it is well adapted to high temperature and drought but cannot tolerate water-logged soil. It would thus be better suited to Egypt's irrigated areas than land inundated annually.

Sesame seeds contain the lignans sesamin and sesamolin, which are antioxidants that are not in other oils and therefore, sesame oil does not become rancid. In Ancient Egypt the oil of the sesame seed was probably used in unguents and as lamp oil. The workmen at Deir el Medina were thought to include sesame oil in their diet. Sesame oil is not referred to in any of the standard medical texts, possibly because the plant was introduced after the texts had been compiled, but it is mentioned in the Tebtunis Papyri dated to 256 BC and sesame paste, oil, and seeds are mentioned on other late papyri.[109]

Botanical evidence suggests that cultivated sesame originated in either sub-Saharan Africa or the Indian subcontinent where wild forms of the plant still exist. A group of wild and weedy forms native to India and described as *S. orientalis malabaricum* shows the closest morphological, genetic, and photochemical affinities to the domestic plant. Bedigian and Harlan have proposed this to be the progenitor of the cultivated *S. indicum*. If indeed the wild and weedy *S. i. malabaricum* form represents the ancestral form, then domestication of sesame most likely started in India. The oldest record of cultivated *S. indicum* comes from Harappa in the Indus Valley. Although no precise date has been established, the find is thought to date between 2250 and 1750 BC.[110]

From its point of domestication, cultivated sesame spread through Africa and the Near East. In Sumer, sesame is mentioned in the third Ur dynasty (ca. 2350 BC), and archaeological evidence of sesame in Palestine and Syria has also been documented. However, in Mesopotamia there may be a problem in that the word for sesame has also been equated with flax, or simply an oil plant. Although the Mesopotamian world, *samassamu*, does bear a resemblance to the arabic *simsim*, it differs significantly from the coptic *oke* and an Ancient Egyptian word *ake*, which has not been satisfactorily identified, but could be the ancient word for sesame. De Candolle proposed that sesame was introduced into Egypt from Palestine, probably sometime after the Exodus (ca. Dynasty XIX).[111]

Based on ethnographic evidence from northern Nigeria, where sesame is an important crop, harvesting occurs after the leaves have turned yellow and most have dropped off. At this time, the capsules lowest on the plant are ripe and ready to break open. The plants are cut, bundled, and placed against a fence or racks in the field where they are left for about two weeks to dry before threshing. The seed pods shatter during this period of drying. This shattering is enhanced through threshing. In Nigeria, farmers thresh by taking the bundles from the rack, laying them on a piece of cloth, and beating the seed pods with a stick. No experimental figures for seed loss are available, but estimates of 25 to 50 per cent seed loss have been reported by agriculture ministers.[112]

Castor (Ricinus communis)

The castor oil plant (*Ricinus communis*) is indigenous to Africa. It is not a bean, as it is often called, but a spurge. *Ricinus* is Latin for dog tick and the plant was so named because of the seed's resemblance to this canine pest. Although extensively cultivated, it can still be found growing wild on the banks of the Nile and on garbage heaps. There is, however, some disagreement as to whether these or any castor plants can be considered truly wild: their long relationship with humans may have rendered even spontaneously growing plants as feral.

The status of the castor plant in Dynastic times is difficult to ascertain. The origins of castor cultivation is unknown, but Abyssina has been considered by some to be a likely center. Egyptian finds could be examples of introduced plants, wild stands that may have been simply tended, or the seeds could simply have been collected from wild plants. Castor is a perennial plant, although often treated as an annual, and if given the chance can grow as tall as a tree. It has palmate leaves and the seeds are bean-like, oval in shape and glossy black, red, white, or mottled in color. Interestingly, the plant and seeds, which contain ricin, are poisonous. Ricin is probably one of the most toxic naturally-occurring floral poisons. In parts of Africa, for example, mixing castor seed with food is a well-known means of infanticide. The oil is also used to poison cockroaches and rats. In Egypt, castor oil was extracted from the seeds either by roasting and boiling the seeds and then skimming the oil or by grinding the seeds in a mill, putting the mass into a press and then pressing out the oil. Today castor and safflower oil are produced in a similar manner. First, the seeds are crushed using a large round milling stone driven by an ox, camel, or water buffalo. The pulp is then placed into a basket and the basket placed into a depressed area at the base of a screw press. The oil is pressed out by turning the large wooden screw, which further crushes the mash and the extracted oil runs into a small sump. The oil is removed from the sump with a ladle.

In Egypt castor seeds have been found in all periods from Predynastic to Roman times. Brunton commented, however, that seeds found at Badari looked smaller than the cultivated form, suggesting that they might have been wild. The oil was commonly burned in lamps and put to medical uses. Strabo adds that the poor people used the oil for anointing the body.[113] Other possible uses for castor probably included a base for color pigments. Castor oil is well-suited for such use because it dries almost clear, and readily adheres to the surface of such things as metal and smooth stone. It is flexible, which guards against flaking brought on by the stresses of expanding stone caused by daily heating and cooling cycles. The spent hulls or pumace contain too much ricin to be used as feed, but because they contain considerable amounts of nitrogen offer an excellent means to replenish depleted soils. All the major cereals grown in Egypt were nitrogen depleting crops and working castor pumace into the soil could replenished nitrogen.

Safflower (Carthamus tinctorius)

Safflower oil is derived from the seeds of *Carthamus tinctorius* or false saffron. It is a member of the thistle family (Compositae) and is cultivated in Egypt today. Safflower seeds are crushed to produce a bland oil extensively used in salads and cooking. The safflower is an annual herb with yellow flowers. The plant stands about one meter tall, is branched, and all branches terminate in a seed. Safflower is apparently indigenous to the Levant, Persia, and north-west India, although Ethiopia has been considered by some a possible origin for Egypt's cultivated forms. It was introduced into Egypt at least by the New Kingdom, which corresponds to the earliest remains for cultivated safflower. Safflower is frequently mentioned in Ptolemaic texts, but Pliny states that the Egyptians did not consume safflower oil, but used it as a protection against poison stings.[114]

Apart from using the seed for its oil, the Egyptians were apparently fond of the flower as a decorative item, and garlands are often found on mummies. The flowers also made a useful dye. Like castor, safflower oil is an excellent vehicle for mixing pigments and is thought to be superior to linseed oil. The spent husks are high in protein and very likely served as an excellent supplemental food for cattle, sheep and goats. In fact, if still green, cattle and sheep can eat the entire plant without harm from the still soft spines.

From the ancient farmers perspective, safflower had good and bad features. It is not susceptible to bird damage, but is to insects. It is spinous and, therefore, when dry is not favored as food for animals, but the seed pods do not shatter making them easily retrievable. It is well adapted to dry environments and low humidity is essential for a good seed crop and high oil content. Upper Egypt was very likely the major source of safflower in ancient times and today is still a minor crop from Assyut to Aswan. Given the natural requirements of the plant, today's sowing practices in Upper Egypt probably reflect, at least in general, the practices of the Ancient Egyptians. Like today, safflower was probably grown as a border to vegetable and field crops. Occasionally, it may have been grown as a single crop in narrow bands or a solid block. Sowing safflower on the banks of irrigation canals would be an ideal use of otherwise marginal land Safflower, like today, was probably planted in October-November and harvested in April or May.[115]

Linseed (Linum usitatissimum)

The production of flax for its fibers has already been discussed at some length. The seeds of the flax plant, however, also served as an important source of oil. Unlike castor, sesame, and safflower. linseed oil does react readily with oxygen and spoils quickly, giving off a very objectionable odor. However, linseed oil was used for burning in lamps and probably for cooking. It also may have been used as a base for pigments, although castor and safflower are certainly superior pigment bases. Today it is an ingredient of the popular fava bean dish – *ful mudamas*.

Almond (Amygdalus communis)

Almonds were known in Egypt, but they were mostly or totally imported. If grown, they were never produced in quantities sufficient to serve as a source of oil or revenue. This may explain why they are not mentioned in the Revenue Laws. Pliny relates the only literary mention of almond oil, which he states was used in a scent.[116]

Miscellaneous Vegetable Oils

Several oils that were important in Ancient Egypt came from wild indigenous plants. The kernel of the Egyptian balsam tree (*Balanites aegyptiaca*), which at one time was thought to be abundant in Egypt, was used to make balanites oil – an ingredient of a Mendesian scent. Täckholm noted that almost all kernels recovered from archaeological contexts were perforated presumably to get at the oil. The earliest finds date to Dynasty III. Ben oil derived from the nuts of the horseradish tree (*Moringa pterygosperma* and *M. aptera*,) was odorless and sweet. Because it could be kept for long periods without spoiling, it was highly esteemed in perfumery.[117]

Several leafy and tuberous vegetables, which will be dealt with in more detail in separate chapters, also produced oil-bearing seeds that served a variety of purposes. Lettuce, for example, was cultivated in Egypt (especially in Upper Egypt) and was important as much for the oil obtained from the seeds as for the leafy stocks. Pliny states that the radish (*Raphanus sativus*) was held in high esteem because of the large amount of oil that was extracted from it.[118]

V

FRUITS

Fruits constitute an important source of food in Egypt and other countries bordering the Mediterranean Sea. Their long-standing economic contribution is amply reflected in classical traditions. Five of the seven biblical foods were fruits or their derivatives (wine, grapes, figs, dates, olive oil). Olives, grapes, dates, and figs were, and still are, important agricultural products of Egypt and the Middle East. As in most areas of the world, however, the type of fruits grown in Egypt and their economic importance have undergone significant changes through the ages. Some fruits grown today are indigenous, but many were introduced in ancient times and their origins are difficult to identify. The problem is further compounded by the relative lack of evidence and intensive study on the origins of fruit cultivation in general.[119]

Palm Fruits

Date Palm (Phoenix dactylifera)

One of the most obvious fruit groups available to the Egyptians was palm fruit. Three varieties were common in Egypt: the date, the doum fruit, and the argun. Today, Egypt is one of the main producers of dates and it is thought ancient production was also high. The date palm (*Phoenix dactylifera*) is characterized by its slender unbranched trunk (up to 25 m), large leathery feather-like leaves, which in a mature tree can reach three to six meters in length, and the ability to produce basal suckers, which under cultivation are removed and replanted. Date palms start to bear fruits four to five years after planting and reach full production in eight to ten years.[120]

Compared with the other three classic fruit trees (olive, grape, and fig) the date palm requires a much warmer and drier climate. Additionally, a bountiful harvest requires a steady water supply either through irrigation or a high water table. Egypt's Nile Valley is, thus, an ideal area for date cultivation because rainfall is minimal and a steady water supply can be accessed through the Nile. Dates can be grown even in the most northerly areas of Egypt because the trees are salt tolerant and can be grown successfully even when irrigated with brackish water.[121] The date palms in Egypt flower from February through March and produce a "soft" date – a type not usually exported due to the high water content that makes them susceptible to spoilage. Egypt's high temperatures coupled with low air humidity are particularly beneficial to fruit maturation. Under favorable conditions, fruit yield may be as high as 100 kg per tree.[122]

On the basis of archaeological evidence, botanists now think that the date palm (2n=36 chromosomes) was first cultivated in Mesopotamia. The few date pits reported from Egypt, Iran, and Pakistan dating to the sixth and fifth millennia BC, probably represent wild forms. The earliest remains of what seem to be cultivated dates were found in the Ubaidian horizon at Eirdu (ca. 4000 BC). Remains of cultivated dates first appear in Egypt in the Middle Kingdom and by the New Kingdom, dates had become common. It should be pointed out, however, that while excavating an Upper Paleolithic site (Aterian, ca. 14,000 BC) in El-Kharga, Caton-Thompson and Gardner recovered carbonized reed stems and fruit pits of the wild date, *P. reclinata* (originally identified as *P. sylvestris*) and pits of wild dates have been recovered from Nabta. That wild dates have been recovered in a Paleolithic context from Egypt is not altogether unexpected. In the Tertiary (ca. 6.5 to 1.5 mya) the genus *Phoenix* extended well into Europe, but as the climate changed its range became restricted to more southerly areas. Because Egypt is known to have had a less arid climate in the past, wild dates may have existed in some places as relict populations of the once wider distribution. Furthermore, if the recovered pits do represent wild forms, date cultivation may have a much earlier history in North Africa than most scholars now accept.[123]

The cultivated date is closely related to, and interfertile with, a variable cluster of wild and feral dates growing in the southern parts of the Near East. Botanists have identified the cultivated date as a variety of *Phoenix dactylifera*, which represents a group of closely related wild species. These wild varieties are able to hybridize spontaneously with the cultivated clones. Several other wild species of the genus *Phoenix*, distributed over North Africa, Arabia, and southern Asia, also show close genetic affinities with the cultivated date. Prominent among these are the East African forms (*P. reclinata*) and the northeast African palms (*P. atlantica*). These wild dates also seem to hybridize spontaneously with cultivated clones.[124]

The cultivation of the date palm has led to a considerable change in the size and quality of the fruit. In wild dates, the fruit is small with a minimum of pulpy flesh; in cultivated plants, the fruits are larger and contain a considerable amount of sweet pulp. Under cultivation, vegetative propagation is universal. Suckers, which start to appear several years after the setting of the mother plant, are separated from the mother tree and replanted. In fact, this form of cloning is the preferred means of agricultural propagation. Growing trees from seeds is possible, but it produces an equal number of female and male trees and only the female bears fruit.

Egyptian curiosity must have been piqued when date palm cultivation began and only some of the trees bore fruit. Farmers soon learned to clone only female trees to ensure the propagation of fruit-producing trees. To further ensure maximum fruit production, female clones were artificially pollinated. Artificial pollination of date palms is thought to have started as early as 2400 B.C in the Tigris-Euphrates delta. It must have reached Egypt at about the same time, because cultivated dates increase in popularity during the Middle Kingdom.[125]

Dates are very rich in carbohydrates and proteins. The dry flesh of a ripe date is composed of about 75 to 80 per cent sugar (glucose and fructose) and will provide about 1430 calories per pound. Dates are a good source of iron and provide moderate amounts of calcium, copper, magnesium, sulphur, and vitamins A, B1 and B2. A Bedouin proverb declares that a good wife knows how to prepare dates a different way each day of the month. Eaten with milk (a Bedouin concoction), it constitutes a well-balanced form of nourishment.

In ancient times, the fruits were eaten fresh, dried, or fermented into wine. Date wine was consumed, and a "palm wine" was used during the process of mummification to wash the body. Date wine was produced by steeping the dates in water and pressing out the liquid, which was then left to ferment. Dates were also used to sweeten beer. Today, in some places, a liquid extracted from the trunk of the tree is left to ferment and later consumed for its intoxicating properties. Tapping the tree for its sap is known to have been practiced in Assyria and perhaps was the "palm wine" of Ancient Egypt.[126]

Unfortunately, the process of cutting the trunk and bleeding the tree of its sap will eventually result in the tree's death. One means of acquiring sap is to remove the branches from the top of male trees and cut a depression in the stock; a sweet liquid will form in the natural bowl. This method and one in which the tree is tapped near its base is used today in the Western Desert. In tropical Africa the palm sap ferments very quickly through the aid of a natural airborne yeast. In South Africa, for example, the sap has fermented and is consumed within 36 hours of its collection – the alcohol content begins to diminish after this time. Diluted forms of "wine" are also made by adding water and sugar. Such a concoction is ready to be consumed in 50 to 60 hours after collection.

Contrary to modern western views on liquor consumption, consuming about a liter of palm wine every day can be considered a healthy supplement to the peasant diet. A liter of palm wine supples more than 100 per cent of the recommended daily allowance for vitamin C and is also a good source of potassium, riboflavin, lysine, and nicotinic acid. These nutrients would also have served as an important supplement to the starchy diet of Ancient Egypt's peasant class.[127]

The oldest representations of what appears to be the date palm in Egypt appear in the Gerzean period. Objects resembling palm branches are often shown on the bow or stern of boats depicted on Gerzean pottery and in the famous painted tomb at Hierakonpolis (fig. 5.1). Date palms are also depicted in the Archaic period: most notable are a number of excellent representations found in royal tombs at Abydos. The crown depicted on the Narmer palette is thought by some to be made of date palm, but close inspection suggests that papyrus rather than palm branches is depicted.[128]

In Pharaonic times, the date palm served a number of useful purposes, and, consequently, held a special status (fig. 5.2). Not only were the sugar-rich fruits important, but also other parts of the tree. According to Persian and Babylonian passages, there were 360 uses for the date palm. In Egypt palm trunks were used for building, the leaves for matting and basketry, and the fibrous

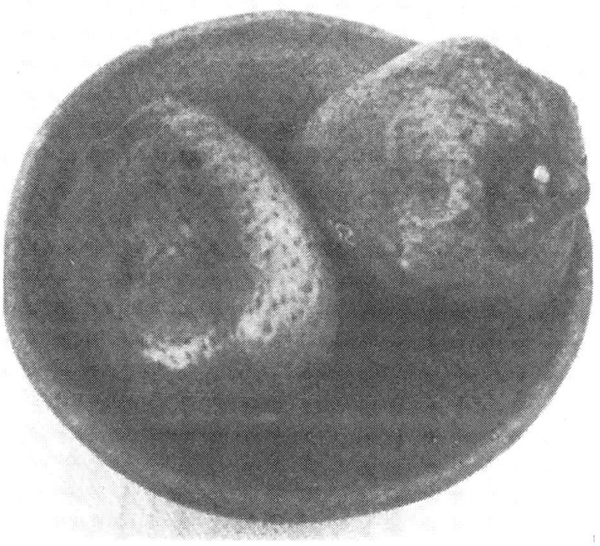

5.1. (top) Late Gerzean boat displaying a palm frond. Painted tomb, Predynastic, Hierakonpolis.
5.2. (centre) A fruit bearing date (left) and doum palm (right) from the Tomb of Sennedjem, Deir el Medina, Dynasty XIX.
5.3. (bottom) The doum fruit. British Museum, London.

bark was used for ropes.[129] The image of the date palm was reproduced on a variety of different materials and carried different meanings. Many representations show a man kneeling and holding palm branches, a symbol of longevity. The date palm was also regarded as a symbol of femininity (the doum palm representing male strength) and it served as a symbol of Upper Egypt. In certain tombs at Deir el Medina the deceased is shown kneeling under the date palm and drinking from the water of a basin or canal to receive the palm's blessings. Because the tree was supposed to grow a palm branch every lunar month, it was also associated with the passage of time and with the span of life. In hieroglyphs, the stripped rib of the palm meant "year," and this sign, which may date as far back as the Dynasty I, associated the palm with the *heb-sed* jubilee of life renewal. Such an association seemed appropriate for the date palm given the tree's ability to reproduce from root stocks and from its ability to survive and reproduce after extensive damage from fire.[130]

***Doum Palm* (Hyphaene thebaica)**

Cultivation of the doum palm appears restricted to Egypt and the neighboring deserts. Because it is not a profit-producing crop, little work has been conducted as to its origins and ancient use. Evidence suggests that the doum palm has been cultivated in Egypt since the Predynastic period: its fibers have been found associated with Dynasty VI tombs, and its leaves and fruits date to the Badarian period. The doum palm is easily identified by its terminal crown of leaves and a repeatedly forked trunk (fig. 5.2). The doum palm, like the date palm, is a dioecious tree. It can reach a height of 20 m with a breadth of about three meters. It is common in Upper Egypt and the desert oases, but relatively rare elsewhere. It is chiefly found around Qena, Aswan, and Kharga, where trees have sprung up from seed. In ancient times it was apparently more widespread. Enneni, a military chief living in Dynasty XVIII Thebes, is said to have had no less than 120 doum palms in his garden and Ramesses III planted doum palms in Heliopolis.[131]

The doum palm flowers in February and March or sometimes as late as April. Unlike the date palm, natural airborne pollination can produce considerable fruit and one male tree can pollinate many females, even when they are located a significant distance away. The doum palm is very sensitive to its environment. This sensitivity is most evident in fruit production. The fruit is smaller when the tree is growing in dry areas such as El Kharga and Kuruk. There the fruits can be so small that they can be mistaken for a different species. When conditions are good, however, the doum palm is quite prolific: each fruit branch bears an average of 40 fruits. The shape of the fruit roughly resembles that of an apple (fig. 5.3). It is spherical with rounded corners and measures about seven to eight centimeters in diameter. The kernel is rectangular, white, and about four centimeters long. Today, the fruits are a popular ingredient in folk remedies.

To prepare the fruit for eating, it is often soaked in water to soften the pulp, which has a sweet, ginger taste. The white, stone-hard kernel is carved into buttons, beads, and items for the tourist trade. It is often referred to as "ivory." In ancient times, cakes were made of the fruits. In the tomb of Rekhmire it is mentioned that 200 doum cakes were offered to the gods.[132] Doum-fruits are frequently found in Egyptian tombs from Prehistoric times onwards. Ramesses III offered 449 and 500 measures of them to Amun-Re at Thebes.[133]

In spite of the ancient accounts regarding the use of the doum fruit, it appears that the tree was valued most as a source of building material. The leaves and bark of the doum palm served many of the same uses as those of the date palm. The quality of the timber, however, is superior. It is stronger, more compact, and heavier than the wood from the date palm. These qualities make it better suited as a raw material for furniture, tools, and stress-bearing beams.

Like most trees of Ancient Egypt, the doum palm held a religious significance. It was considered to be a symbol of male strength. Several representations show the palm being addressed by a man kneeling under the tree. Because the god Thoth could be represented as a baboon, and baboons frequently feed on doum fruits, the doum was Thoth's special tree. Very often, the baboon and Thoth's tree are pictured together. In the Papyrus Sallier, Thoth is even said to resemble a tall doum palm.[134]

Other Palms

A number of exotic palms, possibly introduced, have been reported in the literature (e.g., oil palm, coconut palm, rattan palm), but only the presence of argun palm can be substantiated.

The argun (*Medemia argun*) is a fan palm, like the doum palm, but its stem is unbranched. It was probably never a common tree in Egypt but was, in ancient times, a popular garden tree. The Egyptian argun was most likely a Nubian import, which after a period of acclimatization adjusted to the Upper Egyptian climate. In a list of trees grown in the garden of Enneni (Dynasty XVIII) ten argun palms were said to be cultivated. The fruit has been found in tombs from all periods, the earliest example dating to Dynasty V. The fruit even when fresh, is rather stringy, dry, and relatively tasteless. In Nubia, however, it is buried in the ground for a period of time after which it takes on a sweet taste resembling that of a coconut. Perhaps a similar practice was employed in Pharaonic times to make it a more palatable food.[135] The argun palm is now quite rare in Egypt; it exists only along the old trade road between Nubia and Egypt.[136]

Figs

Two species of figs were cultivated in Egypt, the true or classical fig (*Ficus carica*) and the sycamore fig (*Ficus sycomorus*).

True Fig (Ficus carica)

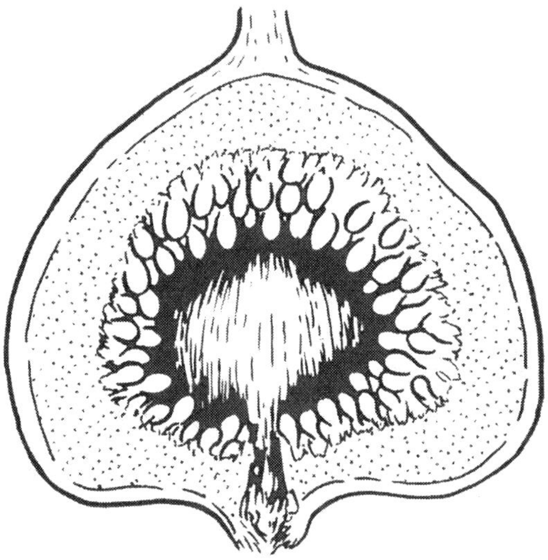

5.4. Syconium of the true fig in cross-section.

The true fig, *Ficus carica*, is one of the classic fruit trees associated with the beginning of horticulture in the Mediterranean basin.[137] The species epithet *carica* refers to an ancient geo-political area in Asia minor. The fig was one of the most important fruits cultivated by the Ancient Egyptians from at least the Middle Kingdom onward. Figs could be consumed fresh in the summer or served as a dried sugar-rich food in the winter. The name *Ficus* comes from the sacred tree *Ficus ruminalis*, which according to Roman legend sheltered the infants Romulus and Remus while they were being cared for by a she-wolf and a woodpecker.

Early fig cultivation was centered in typical Mediterranean environments in close association with olive and grape vines. True figs, like the sycamore, are dioecious and cross-pollinate. In the wild, they depend entirely on sexual reproduction from seed. Under cultivation, their propagation is vegetative. The grower maintains desired qualities by planting cuttings from the mother tree or by grafting the cutting onto another tree. Growing a tree from seeds is less efficient because non-fruit producing males have to be culled and the productivity of individual female trees varies greatly.[138]

The reproductive biology of *Ficus carica*, like that of the sycamore fig, is quite complex and based on a highly specialized symbiotic relationship with a wasp (*Blastophaga psenes*). In natural fruit production, the female tree possesses a syconia, which, like that of the sycamore, is a hollow receptacle that bears numerous minute florets on its inner surface (fig. 5.4). The male tree, in contrast, produces a synconium (or caprafig) that contains male (staminate) and female (pistillate) flowers. The pistillate flowers provide nourishment for wasp larvae. The caprafig of the male tree develops at the same rate as that of the fig wasp. When the female wasp emerges from the caprafig she carries pollen to other fig trees. Some wasps will enter the syconium branch of a female tree through a narrow orifice (ostiole) and become trapped inside. Through their movements, the flowers are pollinated. Because the wasps are unable to insert their eggs inside the long styles of the female flowers, the maturing fig fruits do not contain wasp larvae. Cultivators often assist this symbiotic relationship through a process known as *caprification*. This involves collecting mature male caprafigs and suspending them over female trees. In this way, the wasp is closer to the female fig, which increases its chances of entering and fertilizing the female figs.[139]

The majority of present-day domestic figs are parthenocarpic, i.e., they are able to reproduce large, sweet fruits without the need for fertilization. The resulting fruits are seedless and "waspless," but the tree can only be propagated by cloning. Sometimes the clone is started by placing the start in a melon to help aid root development.

The cultivated fig (diploid 2n=26) of Egypt closely resembles, morphologically, an aggregate of wild and weedy forms widely dispersed over the Mediterranean basin. Botanists regard these figs as the wild progenitor of the cultivated fruit tree and place them within the same species as the cultivated variety. Botanical evidence points to the fertile regions of south Arabia as the center of origin for the domestic form.[140]

5.5. The true fig of Ancient Egypt. Tomb of Nefur, Saqqara, Dynasty V.

Unfortunately, it is very difficult to separate wild from cultivated pips (seeds) and therefore no firm date has been established for the early cultivation of this plant. Pips have been recovered from Neolithic sites in Syria (Tell Aswad, ca. 7800 to 6600 BC) and the prepottery Neolithic of Jericho. In Egypt, very few finds of figs have been reported, and most of the archaeological examples are the sycamore fig. The earliest textual record of the fig comes from the biographical text of a Dynasty III noble, Methen, who had figs planted alongside his house (ca. 2750 BC). Figs are also mentioned in the *Pyramid Texts* and are depicted in tomb scenes of the Old, Middle, and New Kingdom, some of which illustrate monkeys eating and picking fruits and peasants holding baskets. One of the earliest identifiable representations comes from the Old Kingdom tomb of Nefur (fig. 5.5). Deir el Medina is one of the only examples where actual fruits were recovered.[141]

Like the sycamore, the true fig must have been a relatively common fruit. This is suggested by King Ramesses III offering 15,500 measures of figs to the God Amon-Re at Thebes. According to a papyrus dated to around 280 BC, Egypt possessed a summer fig (before the inundation) and a winter fig. This may, however, be a reference to the fact that the fig (more specifically the caprafig or male fig) has the ability to produce three crops a year (winter, spring, and autumn), but the spring crop is the most prolific. Plutarch reported on what seems to be ritual eating of figs and honey during the festival in honor of Hermes (Thoth) on the nineteenth day of the first month. Herodotus relates that figs were among the ingredients with which sacrificial animals were stuffed prior to being burnt. Pliny described a black fig grown in the Delta near Alexandria. Both black and white figs are grown on the Mediterranean coast of Egypt today.[142]

Sycamore Fig (Ficus sycomorus)

The sycamore fig (2n=26), which is sometimes called the Egyptian mulberry, should not be confused with the European or North American mulberry (*Morus* spp.). The sycamore fig is a much taller tree than the true fig, but it produces smaller fruits. The tree has a long life span and can grow to be quite large. The pear-shaped leaves are rough to the touch; they persist throughout the year, except in northerly areas where they are shed in winter. The wild sycamore is restricted to warm climates. In eastern Africa it extends from the Sudan to South Africa and across the Red Sea to Yemen. In these arid areas it can usually be found growing near streams and wadis. Egypt is thought to lie outside the natural range of the sycamore because, unlike the central African forms, it does not grow spontaneously.[143]

The Egyptians appreciated the tree not only for its steady supply of sweet fruits (syconia) but also for its timber, which being a soft wood was often used in the construction of household utensils, sarcophagi, and ornamental boxes. Outside Egypt, the sycamore fig was much less prized, although it was cultivated in the warmer parts of the Levant and, to a lesser extent, in several other locations along the shores of the Mediterranean Sea (e.g., Lebanon, Cyprus, Tunisia).

The cultivation of the sycamore fig (*Ficus sycomorus*) has been almost exclusive to Egypt. There is little doubt among botanists that Egypt was the principal location of its domestic development, but not necessarily its origin. Because Egyptian figs cannot reproduce spontaneously, due to the lack of the proper species of bee needed for pollen transfer and fertilization, the domestic sycamore is thought to have been introduced into Egypt from farther south. There, the appropriate bee exists and the tree reproduces naturally. The archaeological history of the cultivated sycamore extends from the Neolithic, where identifiable remains have been recovered from Omari, through the Dynastic period where the fruits sometimes fill entire baskets, and it is often represented on tomb walls and in relief.[144] Sycamores were apparently so abundant in the Memphite and Latopolite nomes that these areas, located in Lower Egypt and Upper Egypt, respectively, were referred to as "the Land of the Sycamore".[145]

The sycamore was a relatively common tree near private homes. They offered shade and a ready supply of fruit, which is said to have been a source of food for the poor. The biblical note regarding the disastrous effect of inclement weather (caused by God), which destroyed the sycamores with frost reflects the importance of the fruit and the tree. The status that the Ancient Egyptians assigned to the sycamore is further reflected in their mythology. One of the titles of Hathor was "Lady of the Sycamore," and the number of representations of both Hathor and Nut as sycamores receiving offerings or suckling the king are further testimony of its influence. Even the Egyptian word for sycamore tree came to represent "tree" in general. The sycamore was also perceived as a "trysting" tree, a place for lovers to meet. Even today, Egyptian women with marital problems will linger under a sycamore tree.[146]

As in other members of the genus *Ficus*, reproduction in the wild depends on cross-fertilization, aided through a symbiotic relationship with a wasp (*Ceratosolen arabicus*),

5.6. (top) The Egyptian sycamore. Tomb of Nefur, Saqqara, Dynasty V.
5.7. (bottom) Reproduction of a sycamore tree from a bass-relief of a Theban monument. Note the gashed fruit in this scene as well as that pictured in figure 5.6.

and successful germination of the seed. Reproduction of cultivated sycamores is based on clonal propagation (rooting of cut twigs), and fruit production can occur without pollination. (Some clones can set fruit without fertilization [parthenocarpic]). In non-parthenocarpic plants, fruit maturation is artificially induced by gashing the surface of the young fruit. Theophrastus commented that the fruit could not ripen unless it was scraped with an iron claw and, after being scraped, it would ripen in three to four days. This is an old practice in Egypt and can be seen on depictions of fruit dating as early as the Old Kingdom.[147]

The fruit of the sycamore develops in clusters around the trunk and branches. Technically, each fruit is called a *syconium* and like the true fig, possesses an internal cavity, lined with tiny florets, and a hole at the top of the fruit (fig. 5.4). In wild sycamores, the hole offers an entrance for the pollinating wasp, which after leaving a male *syconium*, crawls around inside the female fruit, laying eggs in some of the florets and pollinating others. After five weeks, the young wasps hatch, the wingless males first, followed by the winged females with whom they mate before the latter leave the cavity via holes eaten in the top of the fruit by the males. The whole life cycle of the sycamore is adapted to that of the insect; the fruit ripens at the same time that the insects hatch. Unfortunately, the presence of dead male wasps and larvae inside the fruit makes them somewhat unpalatable.[148]

In Egypt the process differs slightly, because the sycamore hosts the wrong species of wasp and natural fertilization is not possible. The bee *Sycophaga sycamori* does not transplant pollen. In fact, the wasps leave the synconium before the male flower even opens. It, however, does lay eggs in the developing female fruits. Egyptian sycamore figs, therefore, do not produce seeds, but do produce a lot of bee larvae. Shortly after being deposited, the eggs hatch and the larvae begin to develop. A second species of wasp (*Apocrypta longitarsus*) then lays its eggs in the same fruit. These larvae grow faster and "out eat" the *Sycophaga* larvae, causing most to die. To avoid fruit destruction by bee larvae, ancient sycamore growers used to gash each of the fruits while they were still young. Cutting the exterior of the fruit quickens the ripening stage of the fruit from weeks to a few days. By hastening the ripening, the wasp eggs do not have time to hatch (figs. 5.6, 5.7).[149]

The Grape Vine (Vitis vinifera)

The grape vine, together with the olive, fig, and date palm compose the oldest group of cultivated fruit trees developed in the Mediterranean basin. The grape vine is a climbing shrub with no distinct trunk. It thrives in a Mediterranean-type environment, but is able to tolerate cooler and more humid conditions than the palm, olive, or fig tree. This tolerance allows it to extend northward beyond the Mediterranean basin into central Europe and Asia. Today more than 8000 varieties of grapes have been identified and all can be fermented and most can be dried.

The cultivated grape (*Vitis vinifera*) is closely related to an aggregate of wild and feral forms distributed from the Atlantic coast to the western Himalayas. *Vinifera* grapes require long warm to hot dry summers and cool winters for proper fruit development. They are primarily forest climbers and wild forms seem to prefer the climatically mild forest area south of the Caspian Sea and along the southern and eastern coast of the Black Sea. Wild vines are also abundant in the cooler mesic northern fringes of Northwest Africa. Scattered colonies of wild grapes do occur in more xeric areas of the Near East, but are usually confined to the vicinity of springs and streams.[150]

Vitis vinifera is the sole Mediterranean representative of the genus *Vitis*. It, like all members of the genus, is a perennial woody climber with coiled tendrils. All known members of the genus *Vitis* have the same chromosome count (2n=38) and can be easily crossed and produce fully fertile offspring. The degree of interfertility and the frequency of crossing has blurred the various racial boundaries to the extent that it is difficult to pinpoint the origin of the cultivated grape. Botanists formally regarded the wild Mediterranean grape as an independent species (*V. sylvestris*), but because it shows a close morphological similarity to, and is interfertile with, the cultivated grape, the wild *V. sylvestris* complex is now regarded as ancestral to the cultivated form and is a subspecies of *V. vinifera.*

The berries of wild *Vitis* were collected long before the plant was domesticated. Carbonized pips (seeds) of grapes and a few grapes themselves have been discovered in prehistoric sites in central and southern Europe. These remains can be recognized as wild by their pips, which are more spherical and generally possess stocks or 'beaks' constricted at the point of attachment to the body of the seed. These morphological differences are, however, not very consistent and cannot be regarded as the sole means of distinguishing between wild and cultivated forms; archaeological provenience plays an important part in their identification.

Olmo believes domestication started when Neolithic pastoralists marked forest trees that supported particularly palatable grapes. These grapes over the years received preferential treatment and were thereby able to propagate at a higher rate than neighboring "less palatable" vines. As agriculture developed and the forests were cleared, vines producing palatable grapes were preserved along the boundary lines and irrigation ditches of fields where they were protected from the herds. The place of origin, Olmo believes, was in Armenia.

The earliest remains of grape seeds from Egypt were found associated with a tomb at El-Omari. Although no detailed studies were conducted, specialists believe these to be wild grapes. Because Egypt lies climatically outside the natural range of *Vitis*, it seems likely that these finds may represent imported grapes or raisins. Evidence for indigenous Egyptian grape cultivation becomes increasingly more abundant from the Archaic to the Old Kingdom. As early as Dynasty I, written records distinctly specify wine and grape vines and a wine jar was recovered from the tomb of King Den of the first Dynasty. Small carbonized pips of grapes have been found in Dynasty I tombs at Abydos and Nagada, and a rich find of wine jars as well as fragments of raisins were discovered in the Step Pyramid at Saqqara (Dynasty III, 2900 BC). By Dynasty V and VI, grape vines and wine production had become common tomb motifs, and records imply that some vineyards produced considerable amounts of wine. One vineyard, for example, is said to have delivered in one year 1200 jars of good wine and 50 jars of medium quality wine.[151]

Domestication brought about considerable change in the reproductive biology of the grape. The most obvious change is a shift in the mode of reproduction from cross-pollenation to the vegetative propagation of clones (by cuttings or grafting). Just as in the sycamore, this allows the cultivator to overcome segregation in the seedlings and fix desired traits. The second conspicuous development is the breakdown of the wild system of sex determination. Wild grapes are dioecius, and their populations contain an equal proportion of males and females. Fruit setting in the wild depends on cross-pollenation. In contrast, nearly all cultivated varieties are self-fertile: the flowers contain pistils and anthers and the hermaphroditic condition ensures self-pollination and fruit setting without the need of male pollen donors.

Traditional Old World viticulture was based on thousands of distinct clones that varied widely in their habit and preferences for soil and climate. In turn, these variations affected the shape, size, color, and sweetness of the fruits and ultimately the quality and taste of ancient wines. But temperature is the most important climatic factor governing the quality of a wine grape. Under favorable (cool) ripening conditions, the grape will retain a high degree of acidity (a low PH), and develop a rich color. These qualities bring out the aroma and flavor of the grapes, which leads directly to the wine's bouquet and taste. Modern table wines of high quality are produced from grapes grown in areas where suitable summer temperatures prevail. Hot weather during the ripening period produces lower acid levels and a sweeter grape, qualities desirable for sherry but not for a dry table wine.

On the basis of an examination of the many colored tomb paintings, some scholars have suggested that different types of Egyptian grapes existed, including white, pink, green, red, and blue varieties and textual evidence suggests different colored wines. Recovered specimens of grapes are, however, all black. It is possible that either established canons or simply the availability of pigments could have dictated what color a representation might take.[152] The color and type of Egyptian wines is, however, less certain. New Kingdom scenes usually show a dark red juice pouring out of the vats, but most grape juices are more or less clear. In the production of red wine the fermentation occurs on the skins, which are kept immersed in the juice to facilitate the extraction of color and aroma. The pigment (an anthocyanin) is in the cells of the skin in all red and most black varieties and is not released until the semipermeability of the cell wall is destroyed by the alcohol produced in the fermentation process. When the color of the fermenting wine is sufficiently dark, the juice is drawn off, and the fermentation completed off the skins. Fermentation, however, can occur quite quickly in hot weather and could possibly have turned Egyptian grape juice red while still in the vat.

In the production of white wine, only the free-run juice is fermented and contact with skins is avoided or limited to a short period to enhance flavor. The first mention of an Egyptian "white wine" comes from the third century AD when a "white and pleasant, fragrant, easily assimilated, thin wine that does not go to the head" is described. *Abesh* wine has also been considered "a white wine" of "fine taste," although the basis of the color designation is unclear. A third type of wine, a black wine, has also been reported.[153]

It is quite possible that these color distinctions may simply have been a reference to the geographical origin of the wine. Although there is evidence that suggests a black wine was a specific type that served a funerary purpose in the Old Kingdom, it may also signify that the wine was indigenous to Egypt – *km.t*, meaning black, was the ancient word for Egypt. As with black wine, red and white wine could also be geographic distinctions. The word red (*dsr*), for example, had many connotations. It referred to the color red when modifying a noun, but meant *desert* if associated with a hill. It does not, however, seem to have been used in its literal sense to describe a wine. One exception may be a "red wine" highly appreciated during the New Kingdom. In fact, in most cases it cannot be determined if references to color are geographic distinctions or descriptions of wine color (e.g., a Delta or even a desert wine as opposed to white Upper Egyptian wine).[154]

A number of Old Middle and New Kingdom scenes depict the Egyptian wine industry. Supplementing these scenes with information gleaned from noncommercial wine making a reasonable reconstruction of the Egyptian process can be inferred. Portuguese wine-making for example provides a good analagy as it is still made in the traditional way and the climatic conditions are not unlike that of Egypt – very hot and dry.

In Ancient Egypt, as in the noncommercial wine regions of Portugal, the vines were grown high off the ground in an attempt to keep the grapes as cool as possible. Figure 5.8 suggests that the wine grapes grew about 1.5 to 2 meters off the ground, which would help in catching any breeze and keep the grapes away from the reflection of the sun's heat. After picking, the harvested grapes were transferred from baskets to the treading vats (of which no example has been recovered). The grapes were then squeezed by treading, as is still done in some European wineries. In some of the Egyptian illustrations, the treaders are shown maintaining their balance by holding on to ropes or to a cross beam. In other scenes the treaders take hold of each other's hips to form a chain. The treaders trampled the grapes accompanied in some cases by music. In Portugal three men are needed to tread the grapes for about nine hours producing on the average about 2000 liters of juice from two tonnes of grapes.

Although it produces an inferior quality wine, the Egyptians squeezed the lees to obtain more juice. In Portugal a wooden press is used, but in Ancient Egypt a cloth bag was employed. One technique shows one end of the bag attached to a support, and the other end fixed to a pole, which was twisted by several men. Another technique shows both ends of the bag tied to separate poles. Two groups of men turned the poles in opposite directions to squeeze the contents of the bag. Between two groups, a person further stretched the cloth bag by pushing the two poles apart (fig. 5.9). The expressed juice was then strained through a cloth into fermentation jars. Scenes seem to suggest that the juice and the lees were separated before fermentation and thus a white or at least a light colored wine would result. It is not known whether the juice produced by treading and that by squeezing was mixed together or fermented separately. Squeezing would have added parts of the skins and seeds to the juice producing an inferior quality wine. The "squeezing" may also have added some color to the wine.

Fermentation of the juice began almost immediately after the treading had stopped. This is due to a wild yeast that occurs naturally on the grape skins. Based again on modern wine-making in hot climates, the fermentations process took only two to four days. Because fermentation is so rapid, the result is a thin, watery and unflavorful wine. This is a common problem in Portugal and must have been typical of Egyptian wines as well. To bring out the flavor of the wine, fermentation needs to be slowed.

facing page

5.8. Picking (above) and treading (middle) grapes for wine. Tomb of Ptahotep, Dynasty V, Saqqara.
5.9. (below) Squeezing the lees. Tomb of Ptahotep, Dynasty V, Saqqara

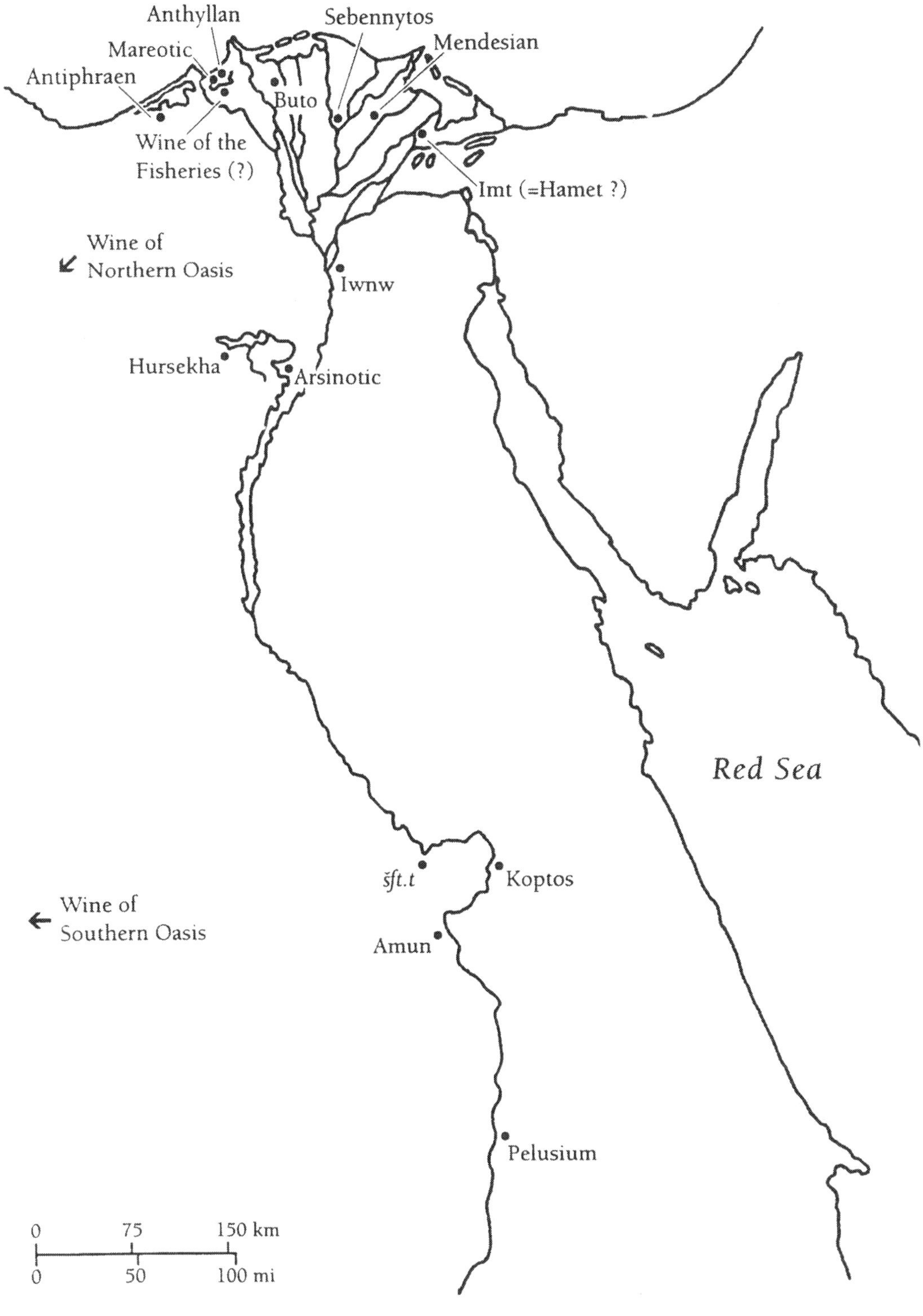

5.10. Approximate location of Egypt's vineyards and wineries

Some uncertainty exists as to the next step in the process. The wine may or may not have been transferred from the original fermenting jar to a second wine jar. This transfer, if it occurred, seems to have been done during the fermentation process or perhaps near its end. Wine vessels were sealed with a cap of straw and clay on which the official stamps were impressed with the year of the king's rule, the district, the name of the wine and, sometimes, the name of the grower. Evidence that fermentation was not complete when the transfer occurred or that no transfer was ever carried out is suggested by the presence, in some cases, of safety holes drilled either in the stopper caps or the necks of the jars. In these safety holes were plugs of straw, wax or clay, which often bore the owner's seal. Because carbon dioxide is a by-product of the fermentation process and is expelled as long as sugar is being converted to alcohol, the stoppers would have been used to allow gasses to escape through manual removal of the plug or they served as a safety valve that would pop if too much gas were to accumulate.

The wine was now ready to drink, but could be "laid down" for a period of time to enhance its flavor. In Portugal the light wine (*vinho verde*) is left to age about six months. Commercial *vinho verde* is aged for two years. One characteristic of the peasant (noncommercial) *vinho verde* wine is that because it is not pasteurized it will undergo a second fermentation if shaken and turn to vinegar. The Roman legionnaires experienced this dilemma in the first few miles of a march and probably explains the wine turned vinegar that was given to Christ during the crucifixion.

The final stage of the wine making process was to taste it and asses its quality. The grade was then indicated on the lids; good, twice good, three times good, sweet and so forth. The final product was decanted or siphoned into small containers for religious or funerary use and larger containers for domestic use. Blending of wines is suggested by scenes showing a servant siphoning wine into a cup from three or more different jars. Because the mixed product is not shown being siphoned into storage jars, it is presumed that blending was carried out just prior to consumption.[155]

An interesting scene from the tomb of Amenemhat, a courtier who served Amenophis III (1405-1367 BC), shows a servant fanning a rack of wine jars. This scene may indicate that the earthen jars were moistened with water and were being cooled for impending consumption or that keeping the wine cool was important in maintaining its quality and flavor, not unlike the cellar storage of modern wines.

Wines in Ancient Egypt, like wines today, were recognized by their vintage, which was often identified by the name of the village, town district, or general geographic region where they were produced. A number of different wine-producing areas can be identified. Although the extent of these regions cannot be defined, their general locality can be located (fig. 5.10). Delta wines were known by several generic names such as "wine of the north country," which was sometimes shortened to "northern wine." As in wine color designations, some evidence suggests that these terms could have different interpretations. For example, "a wine of the north" is listed in the *Pyramid Texts* beside "wine from Buto," suggesting that the former term was not an all-inclusive label for Delta wines.[156]

Upper Egyptian vintages were not as numerous as those of the Delta, but were said to be of excellent quality. Three wines are known from Upper Egypt, and wine was also produced in the oases. Rawlinson stated that Theban wines were known for their lightness and wholesomeness. Interestingly, Theban tombs do not illustrate the technique of "secondary" juice extraction through squeezing a cloth bag, which might account for their lightness.[157]

There has been some debate as to whether the inside of the fermenting jars were coated with an impermeable substance such as resin or bitumen. The size of the wine jars, the enormous amount of wine produced, and the lack of adequate local supplies of either bitumen or resin make this practice seem doubtful. Montet arrived at a similar conclusion on the basis of Strabo's description of Egyptian wine as being "very sweet," and "tends to spoil early." Evidence provided by Lucas seems to confirm this position. He examined wine jars from all periods and found no evidence of coating before the Greek period.[158]

Speculations as to the taste of Egyptian wine compared to modern standards are difficult to provide. Nevertheless, at a very basic level some insights can be gleaned. On the basis of climate,

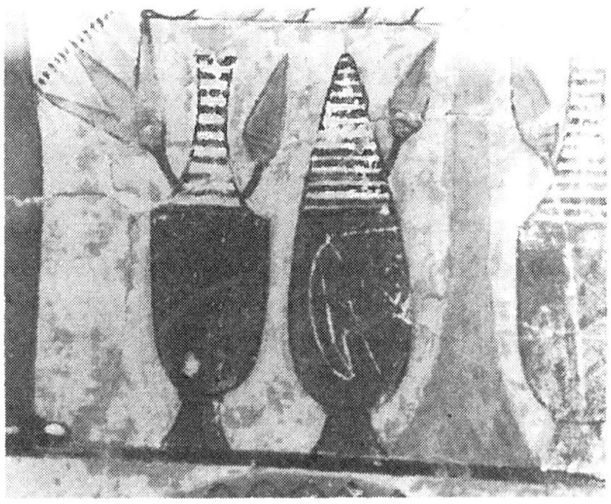

5.11. (left) Banquet wine jars wrapped in the blue lotus. Unknown Theban Tomb, New Kingdom.
5.12. (right) Over indulging in Ancient Egypt. Theban Tomb, New Kingdom.

low acid (sweet) grapes probably predominated the grape crop, producing a sweet rather than dry wine. The process of squeezing the lees and adding that juice with its impurities probably resulted in those wines taking on a rather acrid or bitter taste. Compared to some local modern wines where impurities from seeds and stems are also common, the flavor of the wine is far from palatable. Alcohol content would have varied considerably from area to area and from vintage to vintage, but generally, Egyptian wine would have had a lower alcohol content than modern table wines unless the ancient wine was fortified with more sugar – a process that could have been done if the wine was rebottled and may account for the stoppers in these vessels.

Temperance and Excess. In antiquity wine was principally a source of pleasure. It seems logical that the finer wines remained the drink of the affluent, and that beer and poor vintages were the drink of the populace. In fact, Athenaeus stated that Egyptians were fond of 'drinking' and that those that could not afford wine consumed beer. It has been suggested that the effects (and/or pleasures!) of drinking wine could be enhanced by additives. For example, tomb paintings often depict wine jars wrapped or draped in lotus flowers (fig. 5.11), suggesting that the Egyptians were aware of the narcotic qualities of blue lotus petals when mixed with wine.[159] Also, by steeping mandrake in wine, the Egyptians could concoct a very potent "Mickey Finn." Mandrake possesses known hallucinogenic properties. That overindulgence was in violation of social etiquette can be discerned in some of the texts. The king, a pillar of respect, for example, was supposed to drink only a certain prescribed amount of wine. Although texts as well as the classic writers imply that Egyptians advocated temperance, they do not appear to have been prudish about drinking. Legend tells us that when King Mycerinous found out that he had only a short time to live, he reputably enjoyed life to its fullest. This, of course, included overindulging in wine. He is the first king to be accused of exceeding the limits of propriety through drunkenness. Amasis, an Egyptian king of the Late period, was also considered to be fond of drink to the point of being rebuked by his friends. Some scenes are quite graphic in their depiction of attitudes toward drink. In the tomb of Paheri, an elegant lady is shown presenting her empty cup to a servant and saying ..."give me eighteen measures of wine, behold I should love [to drink] to drunkenness" and several tomb scenes depict the reality of overindulgence (fig. 5.12). It seems Egyptians, like modern party goers, were not spared the negative effects of alcohol.[160]

Apple (*Malus* spp.)

There appears to be some confusion with respect to the presence of apples in Egypt during prehistoric and Pharaonic times. The use of the term "golden apple" to describe oranges, and confusion between the terms used for apricots and apples compounds the problem. Unfortunately, botanical evidence does little to clarify the issue. Although the southern extent of wild apples today reaches no farther than Turkey, textual evidence, albeit scanty, seems to imply that apples were known in Egypt by Dynasty XIX. One reference states that Ramesses II planted *dpht* (apples ?) in his Delta gardens; another says Ramesses III offered 848 baskets of *dpht* to the Nile God.[161]

The earliest solid evidence for apple cultivation occurs near Egypt's Sinai border with the Negev at Kadesh-Barne'a, a Judean outpost dated to around 1000 BC. Because wild apples do not occur in this area, these finds suggest that apples were cultivated in the oasis, and that apple cultivation might have extended into Egypt. Prospero Alpini notes that, by the 16th century, apples were part of the Egyptian diet, and apples do grow in the Nile Valley today, although their size and quality is inferior to European and North American varieties.[162]

Apples and pears have been included for some time in the same genus. Cytogenetic studies, however, have shown that although apples and pears have a number of traits in common, these traits are not due to any recently shared ancestry. Strong evidence for this are the barriers between these fruits, which restrict cross-pollination. Apples, therefore, have been placed under the genus *Malus* and pears in the genus *Pyrus*.

Malus is a genus of 25 to 30 species distributed over the temperate belt of Europe, Asia, and North America. Cultivated apples are closely related and fully interfertile with wild and feral apples. *Malus* spp. shows a marked differentiation into eco-geographical races, some of which have been ranked by taxonomists as independent species. Wild apples reproduce entirely from seed, are self-incompatible (i.e., require cross-fertilization), and are characterized by small fruits (1.5 to 3.0 cm in diameter), which are variable in their shape, color, and taste.

The widespread European wild "crab apple" is usually referred to as *M. sylvestris*. Forms growing in Anatolia, north Iran, and the Caucasus are either regarded as a distinct regional subspecies of *M. sylvestris* (*M. s. orientalis*) or as a separate species (*M. orientalis*). Wild species in Egypt (if they existed) were probably a variant of the *M. sylvestris/orientalis* group.[163]

The domestic apple, *M. pumila* (syn. *M. domestica*), is one of the most important fruit crops of temperate areas. Apples under cultivation are variable. Approximatley 2000 distinct varieties are known, and they vary in fruit size (3 to 12 cm in diameter); color (red, yellow, green); shape; and in the texture and taste of the pulp (sweet to acidic). The majority of present-day cultivars belong to a group of desert apples that bear relatively sweet fruits that can be consumed fresh. "Cooking apples" produce harder and, often, larger fruits. Other varieties such as "cider apples," are selected for their juice. Alcoholic beverages can also be prepared by fermenting ordinary desert apples or wild "crab apples."

Domestic apples thrive in regions where winters are sufficiently cool to provide the trees with the chilling phase necessary to break bud-dormancy. The fruit is a pome, or false fruit, the greater part of which is formed by the receptacle of the flower and not by the ovary. In the core there are five leathery chambers (loculi), each normally containing two seeds. Most apples are fully or at least predominantly self-incompatible, so to set fruit, they have to be pollinated by a different tree. The majority of the cultivars have a diploid (2n=34) chromosome constitution, but numerous clones are triploid (2n=51) and consequently develop only a few seeds in their fruit. Only a few varieties are tetraploid (2n=68).

When grown from seed, cultivated apples segregate widely and most progeny are economically worthless. As in many other fruit trees, successful cultivation depends on vegetative propagation of clones. Because the majority of apples cannot be reproduced from cuttings or suckers, their cultivation depends totally on grafting. Propagation from suckers is possible, but only in a few small-fruited cultivars of western Asia (e.g., the "Hashabi" group in the Near East).

The sum of archaeological evidence suggests that although apples have been extensively collected from the wild, the first signs of apple cultivation appear much later than the establishment of olive, date palm, or grape horticulture. The primary center for the origin of apple cultivation is thought to extend from Asia Minor, through the Caucasus, central Asia, and into Himalayan region.

The art of grafting is apparently a key element to its late development. Because apple cultivation depends almost entirely on this sophisticated method of propagation, successful apple cultivation could only have been practiced after such technology became known. Apples, however, seem to have been known in Egypt. The Harris Papyrus states that carob, pomegranate, and apples were imported into Egypt. Because pomegranate and carob grew in Egypt, it seems likely that apples too might have been grown in limited quantities.[164]

***Carob* (Ceratonia siliqua)**

5.13. A carob tree (?). Tomb of Mena, Thebes, Dynasty XVIII.

There is some uncertainly as to whether the carob tree was cultivated in Egypt, but its ability to grow in poor soils and hot warm climates make it an ideal semi-arid cultigen. Because the pods are flavorful, they are relished by herd animals and carob, therefore, makes excellent fodder. The pods do contain sugar so they are a good source of energy for working animals and are an excellent food for fattening cattle, and are commonly fed to horses, particularly in Arabia. The ground pod, which is not unlike cocoa in taste and texture, is recommend as a healthier alternative and is used in the manufacture of modern beverages. The gum contained in the seeds (carob gum) is used as a demulcent and lubricant. The large pods are rich in protein, starch, and sugar. The locust and wild honey on which John the Baptist subsisted during his trials in the desert and the husks eaten by the prodigal son may well have been carob.[165]

The carob is a tall (ca. 15 m) evergreen tree with large, glossy leaves. Technically, the carob is a legume and is the only surviving species in the genus. Carob is quite drought resistant and does well on non-irrigated lands; the size and quality of the crop is related to the amount of effective rainfall up to an optimum of 58 cm a year. It is questionable whether a profitable crop can be grown in areas with less than 30 cm of rain unless irrigation is practiced. Under optimum conditions as might be experienced in the Delta and along the Mediterranean coast, the carob tree can produce an abundance of fruit. In the Levant, carob trees yield 200 to 250 kg of fruit per tree. In Libya 50 to 75 kg of fruit are commonly produced. Differences in rainfall between these areas account for the discrepancy in productivity. Carob trees in Egypt probably produced substantially more fruit than the Libyan trees and, depending on the availability of water, might approach the productivity of trees in the Levant.

Despite the carob tree's productivity and its potential as food for humans and livestock, there is surprisingly little evidence for it in Egypt. Loret believed that the fruit of the carob tree was known in Egypt from at least Dynasty XII; Newberry identified one pod and six seeds from Dynasty XII Kahun and two pods and several seeds from the Greco-Roman cemetery at Hawara. A simple bow of carob wood from Thebes dating from 1700 BC was presented by Newberry to the Museum of the Royal Botanical Gardens at Kew. In Breasted's translations of Egyptian texts, objects of carob wood are frequently mentioned, but the identifications cannot be regarded as certain.[166]

Manniche believes that carob trees grew in Ancient Egypt and that the pods were used to produce sweet carob beer and medicine where they were ingredients of a vermifuge. The Greek botanist Theophrastus, however, denied the existence of the carob in Egypt "... the fruit is in a pod; some call it the Egyptian fig erroneously; for it does not occur at all in Egypt, but in Syria and Ionia." Nevertheless, a scene from the tomb of Mena, Thebes appears to depict the carob (fig. 5.13). At present, the only carob trees known in modern times are the few examples growing along the Mediterranean coast between Alexandria and Sollum.[167]

***Christ's Thorn* (Ziziphus spina-christi)**

The Christ's thorn, sometimes erroneously referred to as the jujube (*Z. jujuba*), is a spiny evergreen tree that is widely distributed over the savannah areas of east Africa and south Arabia as well as in desert oases and warm, rain-fed territories of the Near East. The tree still grows wild in Upper Egypt and can be found in the Jordan Valley and Lebanon. In its cultivated state it is grown in Egyptian gardens and although its domestic origins are not known, it is a likely Egyptian cultigen. The bush-like tree has alternate stalked oval leaves that are serrated along the outer margin. A pair of very sharp, unequal thorns grow at the base of each leafstalk (except in some cultivated forms). For this reason it was said to have been used for Jesus' crown of thorns. The flowers are pale yellow, small, and inconspicuous. It bears round, yellow, cherry-sized fruits, each of which contains a central stone. The fruits are commonly referred to as *nabk* berries and even today are eaten by Egyptians. The leaf is used by Arabian bedouins to treat dandruff.

Remains of *nabk* berries (*Z. spina-christi*) appear with relative frequency in archaeological context from Predynastic times onward, indicating that the use of the tree predates its cultivated state. It has been discovered in Predynastic tombs, in the tomb of Hemaka (Dynasty I), in the underground galleries of the Zoser complex at Saqqara (Dynasty III), in a Dynasty XII tomb at El Lahun, in a Dynasty XX Theban tomb, at El-Hibeh, and other sites. Numerous whole fruits and seeds mixed with lentils and other fruits were also recovered from Tutankhamun's tomb. The fruits, leaves, and woody parts of the Christ's thorn were widely used in medicines taken internally, in enemas, and applied externally. The wood of the tree is not sufficiently large enough to provide lumber for construction, but it is hard and durable and, therefore, was used to make dowels, which served as cross-tongues for coffins and wooden sarcophagi from Dynasty III through the Roman period.[168]

Persea (Mimusops laurifolia)

Persea is a medium-sized tree (up to 20 m high) with dense foliage and tough leaves. The fruit is about 4 cm long, round with a pointed tip and has four or six sepals. When ripe, the fruit is less than 2 cm in diameter, yellow, and contains a sweet, green, edible pulp enclosing two or three stones. Today, the tree grows wild in Ethiopia, but in ancient times, it grew in Egypt, but whether they were cultivated or wild is difficult to ascertain. Fruits of a species of *Mimusops* have been found

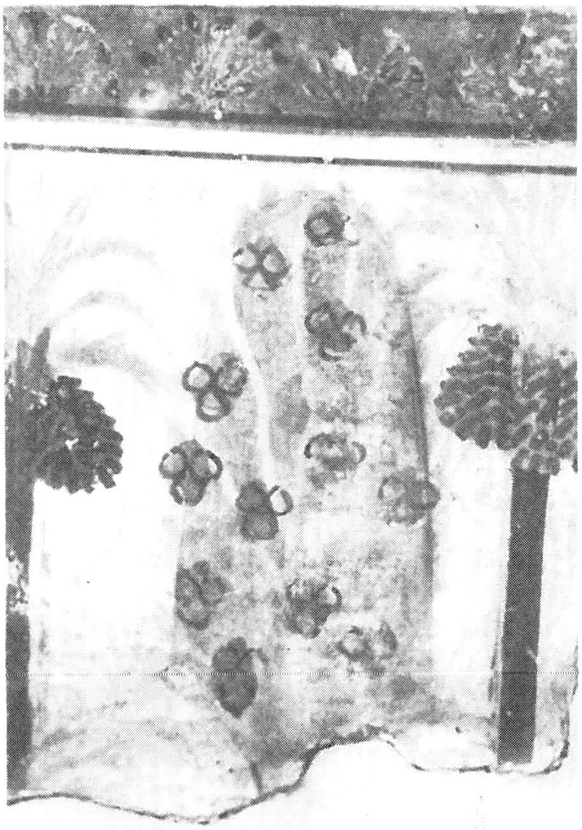

5.14. A persea tree (?). Tomb of Nebamun, Thebes, Dynasty XVIII.

in many tombs; at El Lahun and Gebelein, at Saqqara, and in the tomb of Tutankhamun. Leaves have been identified in New Kingdom mummy garlands (e.g., Ramesses II), where they were folded and stitched into place. Because only fresh leaves could have been used in this fashion, it is likely that trees grew in the immediate area. Further evidence of local persea trees comes from a sample of honey recovered from a Dynasty XIX tomb where the pollen consisted principally of persea and balantes.[169]

The fruit occurs frequently in representations, though it is sometimes difficult to distinguish it from the fruit of the mandrake. (The sepals of the persea are generally shorter than those of the mandrake). One scene in the tomb of Nakht, Thebes, shows persea fruits carried by a young woman. In the Roman period, the tree was apparently dying out in Egypt and cutting it was prohibited by law. By the seventeenth century, it had completely disappeared. Only at the beginning of the present century has it been re-introduced into Egyptian gardens.[170]

The persea tree was regarded as sacred, and kings were often depicted being protected by its foliage or emerging from it (fig. 5.14). It was also related to creation myths because its fruit resembles a heart and its leaf a tongue. Creation was an act of the will (represented by the heart) effected through the utterance of the word (the tongue). Another tradition identified the "cartouche," in which royal names were inscribed, as a persea leaf, because it was on a leaf of this tree that the god Thoth wrote the king's name on his accession to the throne.[171]

Pomegranate (Punica granatum)

5.15. Two pomegranates sitting above a chate melon. Tomb of the steward of Horemhab, Thebes, Dynasty XVIII.

The pomegranate (*Punica granatum*) is a minor crop in traditional Mediterranean horticulture. It is diploid (2n=16,18) with several sterile varieties used in ornamental gardens. It is a deciduous bush (ca. 2 m tall) with conspicuous red flowers. The pomegranate is leafless during the winter, and the rather narrow leathery leaves appear late in the spring. In the fruit-bearing varieties, flowering takes place in the summer, and the scarlet flowers are brilliant and large. As the round fruits develop, the enlarged calyx persists on top. When ripe, the fruit is about the size of an apple (ca. 6 to 12 cm in diameter). The rind, which is leathery and tinged with pink, yellow, and purple, has long been used to make a dye. Inside the fruit are numerous seeds covered with a juicy flesh that can be eaten fresh, or made into a juice. Ancient Egyptians referred to pomegranate juice as *schedou* and it was often fermented into a wine. They also made a dye from the flowers. The rind taken internally was said to combat intestinal worms.

The wild ancestor of the cultivated pomegranate has been identified as *P. granatum*, which grows *en-masse* in the south Caspian belt and in north-eastern Turkey. Domestication brought about an increase in fruit size, and a shift from sexual reproduction to clonal propagation. Desired genotypes are easily maintained by rooting the winter-dormant suckers; cultivated forms set fruit by self-pollination.

The pomegranate seems to belong to the early ensemble of cultivated fruit trees in the Old World. Given the archaeological and pictorial evidence, it is likely that the pomegranate is an imported domesticate to Egypt (fig. 5.15). It is not native to the Levant, so its Egyptian origins must lie farther to the east. It is thought that cultivation originated somewhere in southwest Asia, perhaps Turkey, Syria, or Iran. From there it spread through Palestine and into Egypt. The fact that the first textual and pictorial account occurs at a time when Egypt was in contact with Asia is suggestive of an introduction from the east. Also, the Dynasty XII textual account comes after the Asian (Hyksos) invasion of Egypt, and the pictorial evidence coincides with the return of Thutmose III from his military forays in Asia.[172]

The oldest Egyptian text mentioning this tree was found at Thebes in the tomb of Ani, who lived during the reign of Thutmose I, where it is cited among the trees planted in his funerary park. It is again mentioned in the Papyrus Anastasi IV (1298 to 1235 BC) as part of a preparation for Pharaoh. The pomegranate is likely, therefore, to have been introduced before that period. In fact, Schweinfurth identified it among vegetable remains from Dra' Abu Naga. A pomegranate was also recovered from the tomb of Queen Hatshepsut's butler, Djehuty, (ca. 1470 BC). The first illustration of pomegranates appears in bas-relief on the walls of Thutmose III's temple at Karnak (ca. 1450 BC) along with other plants seen in western Asia during his campaigns.[173]

MELONS, VEGETABLES, AND TUBERS

Compared to cereal grains and fruit seeds, vegetables and tuber crops are highly perishable; their soft parts are seldom preserved in archaeological contexts. Therefore, it is not surprising that few remains of vegetables, tubers, and melons have been recovered from archaeological excavations. As a consequence, their origins are poorly understood.[174] Egypt is the one exception. Numerous noncarbonized remains of vegetables, their seeds, and rind have survived due to the extremely arid environment. Nevertheless, even when evidence seems to point to Egypt as the source of the given cultigen, preservational bias makes it difficult to determine if a find indicates local development or if it is simply a preserved specimen along a lost path of introduction.

Melons (*Cucumis* spp.; *Citrullus* spp.)

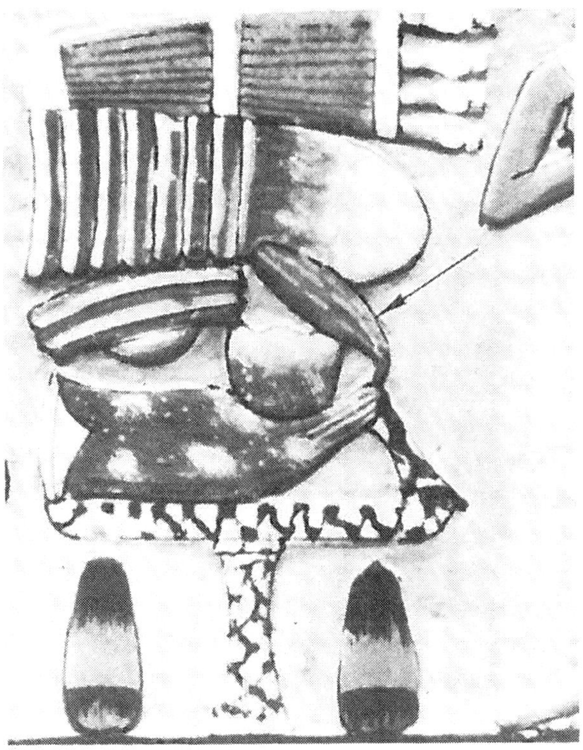

6.1. An Example of a bent chate melon from a Middle kingdom Stele in the Cairo Museum.

The cultivated melon, *Cucumis melo*, contains several economically important variants. All are diploid with a similar chromosome count (2n=24). The most popular are the sweet-fruited and green-fruit varieties. The sweet-fruited varieties – melons, cantaloupes, and muskmelons – were probably brought under cultivation in southwest Asia, or possibly Egypt, at a relatively early date. Green-fruit forms such as the chate melons, are bent fruits that resemble cucumbers and date to at least the Middle Kingdom.

The wild ancestry of both varieties is fairly well established.[175] All domesticated varieties show a close morphological resemblance and full interfertility with a variable group of wild and weedy annual melons distributed over the subtropical and tropical parts of Asia and Africa. The xeric wild type (*C. callosus*), found in Iran, central Asia, and the Near East, is the most closely related to the cultivated melons raised in west Asia and the Mediterranean basin.[176]

Schweinfurth identified material from a tomb at Dra' Abu Naga as melon, but he pointed out that the tomb may have served as a storehouse in recent times. Pictorial evidence seems to indicate that *C. melo* var. *chate* was cultivated as early as the Middle Kingdom (ca. 2040 to 2782 BC) and certainly by the second millennium BC. A clear illustration of a green chate melon (*C. m.* var. *chate*) is presented in figure 6.1. The first literary evidence for melons in Egypt is the Biblical account of the Israelites' passage out of Egypt and their longing for this vegetable. A later reference tells of four large white melons paid as partial settlement of the lease for a vineyard.[177]

The cucumber, *Cucumis sativus*, is not part of the native vegetable ensemble of Egypt or the Near East. Wild forms of *C. sativus* occur only in the Himalayas and adjacent territories east of this mountain belt. *Cucumis sativus* was, therefore, probably first taken into cultivation in northern India and did not arrive in Egypt until relatively late. This may explain why the Ancient Egyptian word for cucumber has yet to be securely identified. Early accounts of the cucumber in Egypt based on pictorial evidence are possibly mistaken identifications of the chate melon, or a product of vernacular English, which refers to *C. m. chate* as a cucumber.[178]

The watermelon, *Citrullus lanatus* (syn. *C. vulgaris*) was cultivated in the Nile Valley by at least Dynasty V and perhaps earlier (fig. 6.2). The

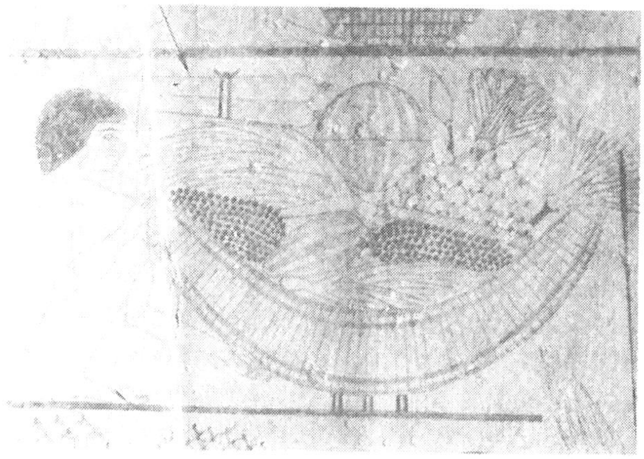

6.2. (left) An example of an Old kingdom domestic(?) watermelon. Tomb of Two brothers, Saqqara, Dynasty V.
6.3. (right) Two leeks presented to Nefur. Tomb of Nefur (alias Bita), Saqqara, Dynasty V.

cultivated watermelon is closely related to, and fully interfertile with, the wild colocynth, *Citrullus colocynthis*. Both are diploid (2n=22) and *C. colocynthis* is the wild progenitor.[179] In its general habit, *C. colocynthis*, closely resembles the cultivated form, but it is a perennial (usually) and bears relatively small (5 to 8 cm) fruits, which have a spongy, intensely bitter pulp. The colocynth is widely distributed over sandy areas in the deserts and semi-deserts of North Africa and west Asia. Its fruits are collected today by desert Bedouin for their medicinal value. They have a strong purgative effect and some desert dwellers say that when a slice of the melon is tied to the heel of the foot, it relieves arthritis pain. The seeds, after special preparation, are also occasionally eaten.[180]

The characteristically small seed of *C. colocynthis* appears in several Egyptian and Near Eastern sites, indicating that the wild form was probably used prior to the domestic variety. The first physical evidence of watermelon comes from Dynasty XII, where seeds as well as leaves were recovered. A large quantity of watermelon seeds were also recovered from Tutankhamun's tomb. Seeds of watermelon, in ancient times, as is true today, were roasted and eaten after the brittle husk was removed. Oil was also extracted from seeds.[181]

Garlic, Leeks, and Onions (*Allium spp.*)

The genus *Allium* represents a popular group of perennial bulbed herbs, which, due to the presence of volatile oils, are best characterized by their odor. There are more than 600 species in the genus with chromosome counts varying from species to species. Throughout Egyptian history *Allium* spp. have been greatly revered and relished, or by certain groups, avoided or forbidden. Despite the occasional ban, *Allium* spp. seems to have been prevalent in Egyptian society as food and offering.[182]

***Leek and Kurrats* (Allium porrum)**

The garden leek and kurrat (2n=32), grouped under the species *Allium porrum* (syn. *A. kurrat*), seem to have ranked among the more popular vegetables of the ancient Near East. The leek is a Mediterranean or Near Eastern form, and its wild progenitor is well-known.[183] The slender kurrats (traditionally called *A. kurrat*) and the more robust leeks (i.e., garden leeks or *A. porrum*) are all closely related to *Allium ampeloprasum*, a wild leek, distributed throughout the Mediterranean basin.

It is apparent from Ancient Egyptian texts as well as from several finds of dried specimens that *A. porrum* was grown in Egypt from at least Dynasty V (fig. 6.3). Täckholm and Drar, however, believe that the European or garden leek was rare in Ancient Egypt, and they attribute all "leek" finds to the kurrat variety. This is supported by analysis of recovered seeds (some in the Dokki museum), which are said to be identifiably different from those of the garden leek. Outside Egypt there are few remains of leeks, but it is known to have been grown in Mesopotamia by the beginning of the second millennium BC, and wild and domestic forms were recovered from mid-Bronze age Jericho.[184]

Leeks are cultivated wholly from seeds, which, in Egypt, can be sown any time from February to July, provided that the seedlings are shaded during the hot months. Two to three kilos of seed, or roughly about 50,000 seedlings, are required to raise one *fedan* (1.038 acres) of leeks. Although the majority of plants ripen in 14 to 16 weeks (from the time of transplanting), a substantial number do not reach full maturity for another four to eight weeks. Consequently, although fresh leeks are available throughout much of the year, it is a labor-intensive crop.[185]

Garlic (Allium sativum)

Garlic, *Allium sativum,* also seems to be an early constituent of the Near East vegetable garden. In contrast to the leek, garlic is maintained by vegetative propagation. Garlic has a number of succulent scales (cloves) joined at the base. These can be separated and planted to form new bulbs. The inflorescence that develops at the top of a stem is about 50 cm high, which is taller than the hollow leaves, but the greenish-white flowers do not produce seeds. Such sterility indicates a plant of long cultivation and adds uncertainty to establishing its ancestry. In fact, botanists do not know the wild ancestor.

Domestic garlic bears the closest morphological resemblance to *Allium longicuspis,* a wild garlic that ranges from central Asia to northern Iran and the southeastern border of Turkey. This species is considered to be the most probable candidate for the ancestor of the cultivated clones. If this is true, garlic was most likely taken into cultivation somewhere on the north-east fringe of the Fertile Crescent or western central Asia.[186]

Wild garlic has been found in Egypt, so it could be argued that Egyptian cultivated garlic might actually have been an indigenous development. Albeit speculative, evidence for the cultivation of garlic, rather than its importation, include finds of long garlic stems carrying leaves and the peduncles of flowers. Garlic with well-preserved leaves was also recovered from Tutankhamun's tomb. It seems that if garlic had been imported, the stems and leaves would have been removed before transporting. Further evidence for local cultivation of garlic is that the Egyptian product is smaller than its European or west Asian counterpart; it often has as many as 45 cloves; its taste is not as strong; and its bulbs are picked three months after planting. Dioscorides also noted that Egyptian garlic had a light purplish hue. These differences were sufficient enough that Sickenberger referred to Egyptian garlic as a distinctive subspecies, *Allium sativum minus.* It is interesting to point out, as Loret had commented earlier in this century, that modern specimens of garlic collected from the Egyptian oases fit the descriptions of the Pharaonic plant.[187] Evidence, albeit "circumstantial," for indigenous development of garlic also comes from the archaeological record where Egypt provides the earliest examples for this *Allium* crop. Several clay models of garlic have been recovered from Predynastic tombs, and well-preserved dry remains of garlic were found in Dynasty XVIII tombs. Outside Egypt such early records are rare.[188]

The Ancient Egyptian name for garlic is debated. Loret stated that it was called *khidjana,* a word found in the Harris Papyrus among a list of offerings presented by Ramesses III and in a demotic papyrus in Leyden. Lefebvre, however, tentatively translated *tꜣn ḥḏw* written in some medical papyri as garlic.[189]

Onion (Allium cepa)

A third member of the genus *Allium, A. cepa,* the common onion, was apparently highly appreciated in Egypt and the Near East. The onion is not a Mediterranean plant. Although its progenitor is not yet convincingly identified, it shows the closest morphological affinity to varieties found in central Asia.[190] Its early appearance in Egypt does, however, suggest an early date for domestication.

An interesting study designed to investigate onion pollination during the dry season in arid Nigeria may have some implications to early Egyptian farming. There insect pollination is carried out mainly by flies. Higher yields were found to occur when onion crops were fertilized with animal dung. In particular, pig dung seemed to promote a high incidence of pollination. Although speculative, onion cultivation in Egypt probably followed closely behind the adoption of domestic cattle, sheep, goat and pig. The dung used as fertilizer also attracted the flies needed for onion pollination. Anyone who has visited Egypt today can certainly vouch for the fact that there is no shortage of flies. Flies in Ancient Egypt were probably just as abundant and putting them to

6.4. Egyptian Onions presented with other produce as an offering to the Tomb owner. Tomb of Ptahotep (above), Tomb of Kagemni (below), Saqqara, Dynasty V.

some good use seems appropriate for such a large workforce. There is little doubt that onion production was exceptionally fruitful in Egypt. Onions are featured in numerous tomb scenes and texts.

The Ancient Egyptian name for onion was *ḥḏw*. Representations of onions appear on the inner walls of the pyramids of Unas (ca. 2423 BC) and Pepi II (ca. 2200 BC), and in nonroyal tombs of both the Old Kingdom and New Kingdom (fig. 6.4). Actual remains of onions, however, date only as far back as Dynasty XVIII; they were recovered from tombs, presumably placed there as offerings, and used in embalming.[191]

Legumes

Nearly 11,000 species of legumes representing 500 genera are recognized, and many are important industrial, medicinal, or food plants. All legumes belong to the family Leguminosae, which is characterized by having a special kind of fruit, a legume, which is a pod that opens along sutures when the seeds are ripe. The importance of legumes as food lies primarily in their high protein content. Most dry legumes contain 20 to 25 per cent protein, which is two to three times the protein value found in most cereals and compares closely to the protein level of lean meat. Legumes are second only to cereals in importance as sources of human food because all parts of the plant, not just the seeds, are rich in protein. Legumes are also valuable for animal forage as well.

Pulses, annual legumes harvested for their seed, were cultivated nearly as early as cereal crops in most regions of the east Mediterranean basin. They were also important because, unlike most flowering plants, which use nitrogen, legumes fix nitrogen through a symbiotic relationship with a root bacterium (*Rhizobium*). These bacteria are able to utilize free atmospheric nitrogen and convert it into nitrates, thus increasing the supply of nitrogenous material available for plants. Because pulses actually add nitrogen to the soil, mixing legume crops with cereals or rotating between cereal and legume crops maintains a higher level of soil fertility. Thus, in addition to offering a dietary balance between protein rich legumes and starchy cereals, the two crops complement each other agriculturally as well.[192]

The agro-economic and dietary roles of cereals and pulses have been appreciated since Neolithic times. Each major agricultural civilization developed not only its staple cereals, but also its characteristic companion legume. Egyptian wheat and barley agriculture, for example, was complemented by lentils.

The available archaeological evidence indicates that lentils and peas were taken into cultivation more or less at the same time as the principal cereals. Their remains are frequently recovered from Neolithic settlements of the Near East Europe, and the Indian subcontinent. The accumulated archaeological data, in fact, suggest that the establishment of food production in the Near East, as well as the rapid spread of this technology to western Asia and Europe was based not only on domestic wheat and barley, but also on the cultivation of legumes.

Like cereals, seed legumes are predominantly self-pollinating, a major asset in domestication. In fact, all of the initial Neolithic domesticates are predominantly self-pollinated, as are their wild progenitors. The major advantages conferred by self-pollination are the establishment of an immediate barrier between wild and cultivated populations and the automatic fixation of desired characteristics. Domestication of the seed legumes shared several adaptive characteristics with grains. First, there is an automatic selection for the retainment of seeds in the pod. In most pulses (e.g., pea, lentil, *Vicia* spp.) seed dispersal in the wild depends on the bursting of the mature pod. The pods of cultivated forms, however, do not burst or at least do not split open as easily: they are harvested and threshed by the cultivator. In the pea and lentil, the change to nondehiscing or slow-splitting pods is a simple genetic event governed by a single recessive gene.

A second conspicuous trend is the change in the dimensions and texture of the seeds. Most cultivated pulses bear considerably larger seeds than their wild progenitors. In some cases, there is a three- or four-fold increase in the volume and the weight of the seed. This increase, it appears, has been a gradual process. The seeds from Neolithic contexts are relatively small and not very different in size from those of their wild relatives. By classic times (in some cases later), however, pulse seeds reached their present dimensions. Another major change concerns the seed coat. The seed coats of wild pulses have a thick, coarse texture, which serves as mechanical protection and delays germination. The smooth, thin seed coats of modern pulses reflect the breakdown of the natural germination process and, as in the cereals, the loss of germination inhibition, which seems to have been an outcome of domestication. The breakdown of germination inhibition is an important factor in maintaining a bountiful crop. For example, in wild lentils only 10 per cent of the seeds will germinate after planting, most germinating in subsequent years. In domestic forms the vast majority of seeds germinate soon after planting.

Finally, in several legumes, domestication brought about striking changes in the external appearance of the plant. The wild relatives of the cultivated pea, grass pea, and the vetches are climbers with tendrils. Under cultivation, however, they evolved stiffer, more robust stems and a reduced dependence on climbing traits, making them better adapted to grow in pure stands in tilled fields.[193]

Lentil (Lens culinaris)

The lentil ranks among the oldest and most appreciated of the cultivated Old World legumes. The slender, annual vetch-like plant grows tendrils that intertwine to form a low tangle about 20 cm high. The minute blue flowers produce flat pods containing two lens-shaped seeds.

The cultivated lentil belongs to the genus *Lens*, a relatively small group of legumes restricted in the wild to the Mediterranean basin and southwest Asia. It is grouped in two integrating clusters based on seed size: (a) small-seeded lentil (subsp. *microsperma*), with small pods and small three to six millimeter diameter seeds; and (b) large-seeded lentils (subsp. *macrosperma*), with larger pods and seeds attaining six to nine millimeters in diameter. As in other pulses, domestication brought about the retention of the seed in the pod (nondehiscence) and a gradual increase in seed size. Large-seeded forms appear later in the archaeological record (ca. first millennium BC) and are regarded as more advanced. In addition to the domestic form, the genus includes four annual, diploid (2n=14), self-pollinated wild species. The cultivated lentil (*Lens culinaris*) shows its closest affinity to *L. orientalis*, a small, wild legume distributed over much of the Near East. In fact, *L. orientalis* looks like a miniature version of the cultivated form, but its pods burst open immediately after maturation.

Lens orientalis grows primarily on shallow, stony soils and gravelly hillsides in open or steppe-like habitats where it forms small, scattered colonies. It also enters disturbed cultivation. In most parts of its distribution, *L. orientalis* is rather inconspicuous or even rare. Chromosomally, the cultivated lentil is fully homologous with the standard *orientalis* race and hybrids between L. *orientalis* lines and *L. culinaris* cultivars are fully fertile.[194] The cultivated crops also show rather close morphological resemblance to *L. nigricans* and *L. ervoides*. Crosses between these wild lentils and the *L. culinaris-orientalis* complex, however, are either incompatible or end in hybrid embryo breakdown, which indicates that *L. nigricans* and *L. ervoides* are genetically quite distinct from the domestic form. Thus, on the basis of botanical and cytogenetic evidence, *L. orientalis* appears to be the most likely wild progenitor of the cultivated lentil.[195]

Cultivated lentils (*Lens culinaris*) manifest a wide range of morphological variation in vegetative and reproductive parts. This is not surprising given the fact that cytogenetic tests have shown that *L. orientalis*, the wild progenitor, is chromosomally quite variable. This variability has led to the evolution of numerous races. All cultivated varieties, however, are diploid (2n=14) and interfertile.

Today, lentils are grown from the Atlantic coast of Spain and Morocco in the west to India in the east. Large quantities are produced in Egypt. In Mediterranean agriculture it is a characteristic companion of wheat and barley. Although yields are low compared to those of cereals (about 50 to 150 kg/ha), lentils stand out as one of the most nutritious legumes. With protein content at about 25 per cent, lentils offer peasant communities an important meat substitute.[196]

Lentils were apparently utilized in the Near East before the establishment of farming villages. Small carbonized seeds of lentil have been rętrieved from pre-farming sites in northern Syria dated between 7500 and 9200 BC (Tell Mureybit, Tell Abu Hureyra). Cultivated lentils seem to be closely associated with wheat and barley agriculture in most of the Near East, and it is possible that they were domesticated together with emmer, einkorn, and barley and should be regarded as one of the original crops of Old World Neolithic agriculture.[197]

Lentils were probably introduced into Egypt at the same time as wheat and barley or shortly thereafter. It is not difficult to determine whether early finds represent cultivated or wild lentils because lentils are not indigenous to Egypt, but determining between indigenous or imported cultivated lentils is nearly impossible. The earliest remains of *Lens* from Egypt come from Neolithic Merimde and Omari. Lentils have also been found in Predynastic Matmar, in the underground stores of Zoser's pyramid, among funeral offerings at Dra 'Abul Naga and Deir el Bahari and at later sites. Pictorial evidence of *Lens* is lacking, but in the tomb of Ramesses III, a servant is shown preparing a meal interpreted as a dish of lentils. Textual evidence, however, is abundant. The "Tale of Wen-amon" relates that Egyptian lentils were bartered for Lebanese cedar wood, and Plutarch indicated that they were offered to Horus the child, son of Isis.[198]

Pea (Pisum sativum)

After lentils, the pea was probably one of the next legumes to be cultivated in the Old World. From its early beginnings, this crop was a close companion of wheat and barley cultivation. Pea, *Pisum sativum*, is well-adapted to warm, Mediterranean and cool, temperate conditions. In peasant communities of the Near East it is an important source of protein. The protein content of the seed is about 22 per cent. Today the pea ranks as the world's second most important pulse. It is grown quite extensively in cool regions such as northern Europe and the northwestern United States. A substantial proportion of the crop is harvested as immature 'green' seed either for direct consumption or for canning and freezing. Mature dry seed was the principal product in classical times.[199]

Pea is diploid (2n=14 chromosomes) and predominantly self-pollinating. As a consequence of self-reproduction, numerous true breeding lines have developed and cultivated peas show a wide range of morphological variation. Difference in the height and habit of the plant (from short field types to tall climbers); the color of the flower (blue, purple to white); the size and form of the seed; the texture and the color of the seed coat and the color of the cotyledons (yellow or green) are common identifiable traits. Hundreds of races are known, and dozens of modern cultivars have been produced by breeders. All of them are interfertile.

As in many other legumes, the conspicuous feature of evolution under domestication is nondehiscence of the pod; the gradual increase of seed size from three to four millimeters to six to eight millimeters in diameter; and the reduction of the relatively thick texture of the seed coat. All are features that result in the breakdown of germination, which is a characteristic of the wild pea.[200]

The cultivated pea belongs to a small genus, *Pisum*, restricted in the wild to the Mediterranean basin and the Near East. On the combined basis of morphology, ecology, and cytology, botanists recently revised the classification of peas. They now recognize only two species, *P. sativum* and *P. fulvum*. The lack of protein differentiation and the low number of biological species within this genus have also led many botanists to believe that *Pisum* is a young genus.[201]

The *P. sativum* crop complex contains the cultivated peas and the wild races closely related to the domestic form. All forms within the complex readily cross with one another and the hybrids are fully or almost fully fertile. All have a similar chromosome structure except for a single reciprocal translocation found in some wild forms and in a few cultivated varieties. *Pisum fulvum*, on the other hand, is a distinct east-Mediterranean wild species with characteristic yellow-brownish flowers and chromosomes that are considerably divergent from those present in *P. sativum*. The two species are reproductively well-isolated in nature, and their hybrids are semi-sterile.

The wild form of *P. sativum* can be divided into two main types. The first type is a tall form previously called *P. elatius*. It is a Mediterranean climber that thrives in the relatively mesic parts of the region. Occasionally *P. elatius* will colonize hedges and terraces bordering cultivation. The second wild type is a shorter, more xeric breed formally named *P. humile*. It is geographically restricted to the Near East, where it occurs in deciduous oak park-forest belts and in open steppe-like herbaceous vegetation (i.e., the same zone that harbors wild wheat, barley, lentils, and flax). From such primary habitat, *P. humile* peas extend into secondary habitats and occasionally infest cereal cultivation. In general appearance some *P. humile* forms resemble the cultivated legume, differing from it mainly by their rough seed coat and by pods that burst open and disperse the seed soon after maturation. Zohary and Hopf, two foremost investigators of crop origins, believe the *P. humile* form is most likely the wild ancestor to the cultivated pea.

Peas are present in early Neolithic farming villages throughout the Near East. Archaeological evidence establishes the pea as one of the earliest crops in Egyptian agriculture. The earliest examples come from Merimde and from prehistoric Naqada. Peas were found in the cemeteries of Hawara and at Dynasty XII Kahun. Although present since the Neolithic, compared to wheat, barley, and lentils, the pea was always a minor crop.[202] The ancient name of this plant was identified as *thw3*.[203]

Faba or Broad Bean (Vicia faba)

The faba bean (also fava) (*Vicia faba*) together with lentil, pea, and chickpea, constitute the principal pulses of Old World agriculture. It grows well in warm, dry Mediterranean environments and in the more northerly temperate parts of Europe and Asia.[204] The plant is robust, stands erect, and reaches a height of about one meter. The white flowers produce pods, containing three to six seeds, and are readily threshed. The seeds are large and high in proteins (ca. 20 to 25 per cent). In Egypt, the dry seed of the faba bean provides the principal protein source of the poor. In both Europe and Asia the seed is also regarded as a valuable animal feed (hence the name "horse bean"). Today large quantities of faba are produced in Egypt.

Vicia faba is a diploid plant with 2n=12 chromosomes. In contrast to peas, lentils, and the majority of grain crops, the broad bean is not self-pollinating and early forms depended on the activity of bees for cross-pollination.[205] Under domestication, broad beans have developed a number of different ecological adaptations, resulting in a considerable degree of morphological variation. Conspicuous intraspecific differences such as the shape, color, and size of the seed are displayed in various strains and these variations have served as the principal characteristic for identifying subspecies of faba.

Taxonomists recognize numerous types of *Vicia faba*, but two main subspecies predominate in a discussion of domestic origins. Forms with relatively small, round seeds (6 to 13 mm long) are placed in *V. faba minor*. Forms with medium seed size (ca. 15 to 20 mm long, 12-15 mm wide and five to eight mm thick) are placed in *V. f. major*. Archaeological remains from Egypt that date from the Neolithic period to Roman times fall within the range of *V. f. minor*. The large-seeded broad beans evidently evolved under domestication much later.[206]

The wild ancestor of the cultivated broad bean, *Vicia faba*, has yet to be identified. The cultivated faba shows close morphological similarities to a group of Mediterranean and Near East wild vetches: *V. narbonensis*, *V. serratifolia*, *V. johannis*, *V. galilaea*, and *V. hyaenicyamus*. Taxonomically, all these vetches are closely related to the domestic *V. faba* and one form (*V. galilaea*) bears a striking morphological resemblance. Nevertheless, the domestic form is chromosomally distinct. Extensive cytogenetic tests have revealed that all known wild types contain the same number of chromosomes (2n=14). Moreover, not only is *V. faba* chromosomally unique (2n=12), but it is also reproductively isolated from all known wild members of its genus. This, in essence, rules out all the 2n=14 vetches (*V. narbonensis-galilaea* group) as possible ancestors of the domestic cultigen. Consequently, either a 12-chromosome progenitor, possibly with a very limited geographic range, has eluded discovery, the ancestor of the domestic faba bean is extinct or a unique species has been created under domestication. The latter would be an extremely rare occurrence: only in wheat has domestication created new species.[207]

The earliest remains of faba beans come from the late pre-pottery Neolithic B (6500 to 6000 BC) of Yiftah'el, Israel. Here a cache of about 2600 well-preserved charred beans were discovered. The beans are small (5.5 by 4.7 by 4.0 mm), and distinctly flat. This suggests *Vicia faba* rather than the wild *V. narbonensis* or *V. galilaea*, which have more globular seeds. A small bean tentatively identified as *V. faba equina* has also been recovered from Jericho and dated to about 6000 BC.[208]

Apart from these finds, there is no other evidence of broad beans from Neolithic farming villages of the Near East. By the third millennium BC, however, larger seeds appear in a number of places in the west Mediterranean basin and central Europe. The earliest unquestionable remains from Egypt were recovered from the Sahure funeral temple (Dynasty V). There were also faba beans reported from Hawara and El Lahun.[209]

The sum of evidence for the origin and use of the faba bean in Egypt is inconclusive. When botanical and archaeological evidence from Europe and Asia are viewed together, it seems to indicate that broad beans appear rather suddenly in the Mediterranean basin and in central Europe around the third millennium BC.

The Egyptian name for the faba bean is thought to be *iwryt*, although Keimer believes it to be *pr*. The term, bean meal, which is so commonly encountered in the medical papyri, remains nonspecific and could apply to a number of different species. It is also possible that it might not refer to a bean at all, but a bean-shaped seed such as *Nelumbium speciosum* (the pink lotus).[210]

Chickpea (Cicer arietinum)

There are only a few finds of chickpeas (often referred to as garbanzo beans in the Americas) from Dynastic Egypt. A sample of chickpeas is presented in the Dokki agricultural museum, dated to 1400 BC Deir el-Medineh, and represents the earliest example of this legume in Egypt. Their hieroglyphic sign suggests that they were known in Egypt during the New Kingdom and a few chickpeas were reportedly found mixed with cereals and other grain in the model granary recovered from the tomb of Tutankhamun.[211]

The chickpea is an erect annual about 20 cm high with pinnate leaves and up to eight serrated leaflets. The most common chromosome count is 2n=16. The very small bluish-to-white flowers produce a short, one- or two-seeded pod. The characteristically shaped seeds have given rise to various names such as chickpea, falcon-head, and ram's head. Its species epithet (*aries*) is Latin for ram.

The chickpea contains 20 to 22 per cent protein, which is 80 per cent digestible. The amino acid profile of the protein, like lentils, is such that it complements cereals. In fact a diet of chickpeas and cereals can fully meet the recommended daily allowance for the essential amino acids.

The center of diversity and the suspected origin of the domestic form lies in western Asia, probably in the Causasus region or Asia minor. From there it spread along the Mediterranean coast and to India. The earliest records of the chickpea date to 5450 BC Turkey. The plant may have reached Egypt and the Mediterranean basin by the third millennium BC, but conclusive evidence is lacking. Linguistic evidence provides little information prior to the Greco-Roman period. Keimer called attention to the resemblance of the chickpea to the face of the hawk and suggested that *hr-bik* could only refer to chickpea because no other Egyptian bean possessed that appearance. The only substantive reference to the chickpea comes from 223 BC: a quantity of chickpeas had been purchased from Sosus and another quantity was to be purchased from Naucratis.[212]

Lupine (Lupinus albus/luteus)

There exists some confusion in the Egyptological and related literature regarding the status of the lupine. The white lupine, *Lupinus albus* (syn *L. termis*) has been cultivated in the Mediterranean region since antiquity and is regarded as one of the characteristic pulses of the regions. Yet the use of the seed is complicated by the fact that lupines generally contain bitter alkaloids that are difficult to remove. Domestication of these pulses meant first learning how to remove the bitter alkaloids and then selecting plants with less bitter seeds. Alkaloids are removed by boiling the seeds and then steeping them in water. The white and yellow lupines (*L. albus* and *L. luteus*) are the common lupines found today in Egyptian markets.

The wild progenitor of the cultivated white lupine has been identified as *L. albus*, which evolved from a Balkan wild type known until recently as *L. graecus*. *Lupinus graecus* was originally thought to be a separate species but has been included in the *L. albus* crop complex as *L. a. graecus*. The derived cultivars are interfertile and chromosomally identical (2n=50) with the wild forms native to the Aegean region. Cultivation of *L. albus* (the white lupine) does not, however, appear to have become established in Egypt until classic Greek and Roman times, and identifiable remains are not available until this period.[213]

Although Wilkinson and Maspero report that they recovered lupines from various tombs, no details were given. Täckholm notes that the only species represented in Pharaonic Egypt is *L. digitatus*. This species has been found twice, once at Abusir (Middle Kingdom) and again at Greco-Roman Hawara. Because *Lupinus digitatus* is a wild plant indigenous to Egypt, early references are very likely wild forms.[214]

Much has been written about "bean" taboos, but the identity of the bean(s) has never been ascertained. The first mention of a restriction is found in the teachings attributed to Pythagoras who, as a young man, was trained by Egyptian priests. Pythagoras, it was believed, thought that the taboo was based on the belief that beans were produced from the same matter as humans. Other ancient writers mention a taboo, but they advanced other explanations. Diodorus observed that priests abstained from several foods, including beans, and viewed the avoidance as a manifestation of self-denial. Pliny thought that beans were shunned because they caused sleeplessness and dulled the senses. Wilkinson believed that beans were taboo to the upper class, but, interestingly, not to the peasant. He cited no justification for this other than that the poor had little to lose by breaking religious doctrine, but nobility and the priesthood were under closer religious scrutiny. Royal decrees and records seem to indicate, however, that legumes were appreciated by the populace and agreeable to the gods. On one occasion Ramesses III offered the Nile god 11,998 jars of shelled beans, on another occasion, the Nile god received 2,398 jars.[215]

Fodder Plants (vetches and clovers)

Evidence for the cultivation of fodder plants in ancient times is quite suggestive, although not yet totally conclusive. A variety of seeds from bitter vetch (*Vicia ervilia*), grass pea (*Lathyrus sativus*), and clover (*Trifolium alexandrinum*) has been recovered through archaeological research. Unfortunately, it has been difficult to ascertain whether the recovered plant remains are representative of wild stands or cultivated plots. Bitter vetch has been recorded from Predynastic Naqada; grass pea, from Neolithic Badari; and clover, from Old Kingdom Kom el-Hisn.[216]

Fodder vetch and clovers grew spontaneously in fields left to fallow or may have even been cultivated in certain areas. It was an excellent feed and provided important proteins and amino acids to herd animals, particularly when consumed while fresh and green.

Leafy Vegetables and Tubers

Lettuce (Lactuca sativa)

The lettuce grown in Egypt, *Lactuca sativa*, is characterized by its straight vertical leaves, which may reach one meter in height. This lettuce is known in Britain as Cos lettuce and in the U.S. and France as Romaine lettuce. It is widely eaten

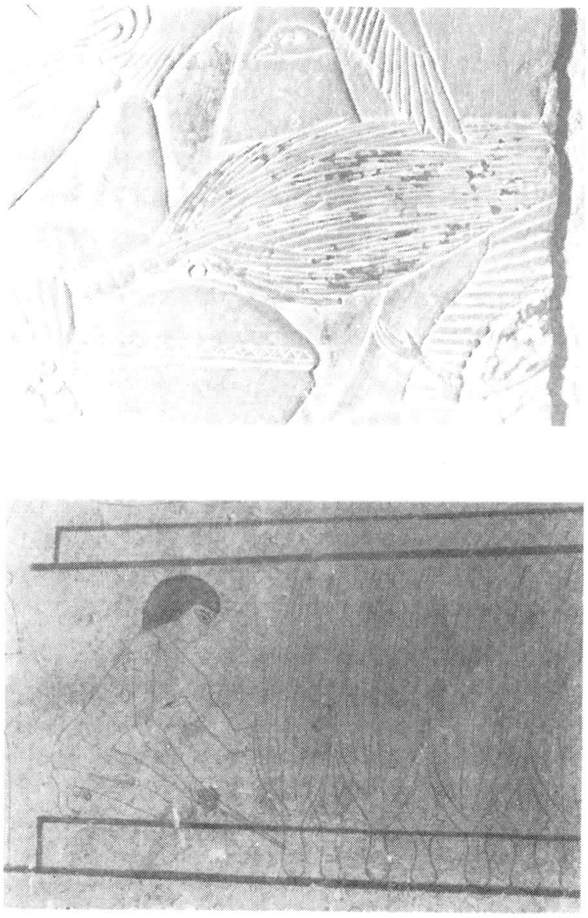

6.5. Lettuce offerings (above) and lettuce cultivation (below) in the Old Kingdom. Tomb of Ti and Nefur, Saqqara, Dynasty V.

in modern Egypt, and an oil is extracted from the seeds.

Lettuce is definitely a west-Asiatic and Mediterranean plant, and its wild ancestor is already well-recognized. The cultivated vegetable shows close affinities to a group of *Lactuca* species centered in western Asia. Its closest wild relative is the weedy *L. serriola. Lactuca serriola* abounds in the Mediterranean basin and the Near East as well as vast areas outside these territories, where it is considered a weed. The wild form is erect, the leaves are blue with spiny processes, the seeds shatter at maturity, and the plant is suffused with latex and is very bitter to the taste.[217]

The exact center of domestic origin is not fully documented but Egypt appears to be among the earliest areas of lettuce cultivation. Illustrations of rosettes of a tall, large leafy vegetable appear in numerous Old Kingdom and Middle Kingdom tombs and monuments (fig. 6.5). Most archaeobotanists agree that these scenes of leafy vegetables depict the garden lettuce of modern Egypt, *Lactuca sativa*. Among the earliest representations are those in the Dynasty V mastabas at Saqqara. Unfortunately, the available illustrated record is not yet complemented in Egypt by dry remains of lettuce leaves or lettuce rosettes, although seeds of lettuce have been reported. Outside Egypt indisputable records of *L. sativa* cultivation appear only in Greek and Roman literature.[218] The important changes incurred through domestication were loss of spines on the leaves, shift to a non-shattering seed head, absence of early flowering, a decrease in bitter latex and an increase in seed size.

In Egypt lettuce was associated early on with Min, the god of vegetation and procreation. A recurring theme is one in which a botanical motif is shown behind the god. The motif is composed of one or several vertical, more or less conical, plants, presumably lettuce, set on a square structure on which the god Min stands. In earlier illustrations the details of the leafage are clearly drawn, and the square base seems to be a schematic rendition of the field on which the plant is growing. After Dynasty XVIII, however, the motif is so stylized that details are obscure. In other illustrations Pharaoh is seen presenting one or two leafy vegetables (lettuce ?) to Min with the associated text clearly stating that the aim of the offering was to have the god perform the act of procreation. Lettuce also appears as an offering in many tombs.[219]

The Egyptian relationship between lettuce, Min, and procreation is not so difficult to understand when mature primitive forms of lettuce are viewed. Such varieties, often bred for their oil, can stand 1.5 m tall and when a leaf stock is broken, it bleeds a milky white juice, a substance no doubt associated with semen. Even today, Egyptian peasants believe one will have many children if plenty of lettuce is eaten.[220]

Loret suggested that the hieroglyphic plant *ibw* referred to lettuce, but this identification did not appear acceptable to Keimer and others. The generally accepted name for the plant is *'bw*. A bread was made from *ibw*. Only *ibw* – not *'bw* – was used medicinally, either internally or externally.[221]

Celery (Apium graveolens)

Celery is a biennial plant with 12 paired chromosomes (2n=22) and stands about 30 to 80 cm high with a bulbous fleshy root and strong-smelling leaves. The leaves are large, broad, pinnately lobed, and borne on thick stalks, which are edible in cultivated plants but are very strongly flavored in wild plants. The flower heads are typical of the parsley family having an umbrella shape and numerous small white flowers. Celery prefer to grow in moist areas, and wild forms grow in Africa, Europe, and the Americas. It has seen use as a tonic, appetizer, and carminative.[222]

The origins of celery are unclear. The only evidence of celery in the Egyptian diet is a short note by Apicius stating that the seeds were incorporated in sauces for grilled fish. The Ancient Egyptian word for celery was *m,tt*. There are four kinds of *m,tt* recorded. Celery is thought to be the northern variety, and parsley the desert variety.[223]

Radish (Raphanus sativus)

The tuberless, large, and small tuber radishes all belong to the same species, *Raphanus sativus*. Three wild species show close similarity to the cultivated forms and to date no single species can be considered the wild progenitor. Some authors have even argued that perhaps all three wild forms (*R. raphanistrum, R. maritimus/landra, R. rostratus*) contributed to the development of the modern cultivated radish.

Apart from two radishes discovered in the Dynasty XII necropolis at El Lahun, that Darby claims Täckholm identified as the leaves and tuber of the radish (var. *aegyptiacus*), no other finds have been reported. Banga's comment that the *R. niger* variety of radish was depicted on the inner walls of the pyramids could also not be substantiated, although the *R. niger* type of radish would be the likely form to be grown in Ancient Egypt due to its tolerance of high temperatures. The evidence for this tuber is thus purely literary.[224] Pliny remarked on the mildness of Egyptian radishes and their use as a source of oil. He is one of the few ancient writers who spoke of this vegetable in Egypt.

> In Egypt ... the people are very fond of sowing radish seed if opportunity offers, because they make more profit from it than from corn and have a smaller duty to pay on it, and because no plant there yields a larger supply of oil.[225]

The only other reference to the radish as a staple food is a statement by Herodotus who says it was provided to the builders of the Giza pyramids. The Ancient Egyptian name for radish is uncertain. *Swm* is a general word for herbs or weeds, but it is possible that *swm* referred to radish as well.[226]

Cyperus Grass (**Cyperus esculentus**)

Cyperus grass is distinguished by its pale spikelets, fibrous (not creeping) root system and transversely ridged ovoid tubers. It is easily confused with the wild *Cyperus rotundus* (chapter 1) unless the root system is recovered relatively intact. Cyperus grass grows in moist soils or on sandy seashores. It is cultivated in modern Egypt for its edible tubers called "*Habb el aziz*," which are about the size of a pea. In certain parts of Spain it is made into a popular drink (*horchata de chufa*). Its status as a cultigen in Ancient Egypt is, however, difficult to ascertain because cultivated and wild specimens are so similar. Cyperus grass or its tubers have been recovered from the rectal contents of an individual recovered from Predynastic Nag' ed Der. Tubers have also been recovered from Badari (ca. 4000 BC) and from tombs of the Middle and New Kingdom.

Cultivation of the plant is known to have occurred in recent times in the Rossetta district where it is a summer crop. Täckholm and Drar believe this district also produced cultivated cyperus grass in early times, but no justification for this statement is given.

The ancient name for the plant is thought to be *gaiou* and the tubers *baka*. The tubers contain protein, fat, sugar, and starch and produce an edible oil. They are eaten today as both a novelty snack and for their reported qualities as an aphrodisiac.[227]

VII

EGYPTIAN CATTLE

7.1. Illustration of the last known wild aurochs, Bos primegenous.

Many scholars believe that the domestication of herd animals, cattle in particular, was the most important step in the exploitation of the animal world. The importance of herd animals to humans lies in their ability to obtain nourishment from grasses and other fibrous forage that people cannot directly utilize. Domesticating herd animals opened up a new dimension in cultural lifestyles; the spread of herding throughout the world is evidence of its utility and evolutionary importance.

The Ancient Egyptians classified herd animals into two groups: large cattle and small cattle. "Large cattle" implied *Bos* (bulls, cows, oxen) and small cattle referred to such animals as goats, sheep, and pigs. Of these domestic animals, large cattle (*Bos*) possessed the greatest status. In some extant East African societies, cattle receive similar levels of respect and status. As in Egypt, cattle in these societies are esteemed possessions and are, therefore, equated with wealth. At the root of the Egyptian and East African cattle complexes is a strong personal attachment to the animals themselves. This can be seen in Ancient Egypt and modern East Africa by the affection shown to individual cattle of which many have given names. Cattle do and did serve as food and possess a purely social function. The latter is possible because in modern East Africa as in Ancient Egypt plant cultivation formed the basis for subsistence, allowing cattle raising to fluctuate between valued food resource and a purely cultural entity.

Ruminants (cud-chewing animals) such as cattle, sheep, and goats able to transfer otherwise unusable plants into edible products, take on added significance where grazing lands are unsuitable for maintaining crops. In Egypt, grasses grew in a variety of areas and depending on the availability of water could be tall and lush or sparse, dry, and stunted. Fallow fields also offered forage for ruminants with the added bonus of a direct application of fertilizer. The productivity of grazing lands, however, would have varied from year to year due to the vagaries of Egypt's rainfall, the reluctance to irrigate fields not devoted to cash or food crops and the planting/fallow schedule of given plots. Consequently, a grazing strategy would have to evolve that would acceptably counter the local constraints.

Although a number of grazing and feeding options were available to the Egyptians, they surely did not intentionally choose the most cost-efficient strategy, nor did they actively choose the most proper and efficient balance between herding and cultivating. Over time however, the tendency would clearly be to select a strategy that showed a satisfactory level of success and minimal or acceptable incidence of failure. This balance between success and failure has been referred to as subsistence risk.

In studying land and water relationships, geographers have posed an interesting correlation between planting and herding. On the basis of subsistence risk analysis of modern farmers and herders, when the probability of receiving sufficient water to grow a crop on a particular plot of land reached 0.90 (9 out of ten years), that land was devoted to cultivation and able to support a large number of farmers. Land with a water ratio between 0.50 and 0.30 was characterized by chronic crop failure and considered a high risk area for cultivation, but excellent for pasture. Areas with ratios of 0.10 were seldom if ever cultivated but were useful as pasture land for most years.

Egypt possessed lands with water ratio levels ranging from above 0.90 to those well below 0.10. A mixed system of cultivation, penned animal raising, and range herding would, over time, be an efficient strategy for capturing the most benefits from the natural environment of the Nile Valley. The Nuer living along the Nile in the Sudan provide a modern example of a mixed system in an environment similar in many ways to Ancient Egypt. Observations of the Nuer therefore, may provide some insights into Ancient Egypt's adaptive system.

The Nuer live near the Nile on elevated levees. Land for planting crops is limited due to the quality of land and the availability of water. Given the present climate and Nuer technology, there is no opportunity to expand agriculture land profitability. Herd animals (cattle, sheep, and goats), although they do not provide the basis of Nuer subsistence, are an important insurance factor against crop failure and the most effective means of using the otherwise unproductive grasslands. Raising large herds of cattle, however, does require the Nuer to make seasonal forays, first to small dispersed cattle camps, where fishing is also practiced, and later in the dry season they move to permanent water sources and live in larger settlements. Nuer herds are quite large and overgrazing is a problem. Nuer rationalize their grazing strategy by stating the obvious: if their cattle do not eat all the grass in a given area, someone else will surely move his cattle in to eat it.

The parallels to Ancient Egypt are probably obvious. Egyptian agriculturalists originally lived on the natural levees of the Nile or beyond the reach of floods on the desert border and cultivated the rich inundated lands between the levees and desert. Those areas not receiving enough water to support crops were range lands. As technology increased, more and more land came under cultivation and less land was available for herding. Egyptian herds were large and one must assume that overgrazing was undoubtedly a problem in Ancient Egypt as well. This and the seasonal nature of forage availability necessitated ancient cattle drives to better pasture. Although ancient drives may have crossed hundreds of kilometers and appear to pose hardships on both animals and herdsmen, it has been documented that among non-mechanized agriculturalists, livestock productivity in terms of weight gain, calving rate, and calf survival is better among migratory herds than among sedentary ones. Egyptians further maximized cattle production by also keeping animals in pens or corals, bringing the food to the animals as is done in many modern societies.

The balance between pen raising and herding and cultivation was one, that over the years reached a point of equilibrium as a viable working system. This balance was not necessarily one of maximum efficiency or productivity, but rather, only needed to be successful (i.e., possess a positive risk factor) and culturally compatible. Although the great numbers of cattle recorded as attached to temple and personal estates seems to be an example of an unnecessary over indulgence, large herds do make evolutionary sense under certain conditions.

Modern cattle herders of East Africa and the Sudan likewise emphasize large herds. At one level it could be assumed that the herds are large because of the cultural values attributed to cattle. Cattle are a measure of wealth and prestige and are only slaughtered on certain occasions, butchered in a prescribed manner, and the meat distributed to a number of individuals. Giving beef to others is considered a prestigious act. Cattle are sometimes killed on non-ceremonial occasions, but this is not common practice because the meat in such a hot climate spoils quickly. Large herds, however, do have other advantages over small herds that make them practical in the long run. Primarily, large herds are a means of ensuring the survival of at least some cattle even after a disastrous environmental or disease-invoked tragedy. The Samburo herders of Uganda sum up the large herd philosophy quite well. They fully realize that a certain percentage of the herd dies each year, but in a bad year a man who loses one-third of his stock is better off if he begins with 60 cattle than with six cattle.

For rapid replenishment of a herd, the large herd philosophy works well. When the availability of food is threatened by catastrophe, particularly in groups as advanced as Dynastic Egyptians, that catastrophe will affect all the agricultural products. A large herd would provide immediate food for families as well as leave enough stock to propagate a new herd. A diversified herd incorporating sheep, goat, and cattle would have served as an additional safeguard. Each species thrives under different environmental conditions. Goats are browsers and do not compete with sheep and cattle for food and are more drought tolerant than either. Cattle and sheep are grazers, but sheep are a little more tolerant of drought than cattle. Given an environmental crisis, the three herd animals will have different probabilities for survival depending on the nature of the problem. Because sheep and goat reproduce more rapidly than cattle, their herds can recover relatively quickly. Thus, although the Egyptian herding system would appear to be a pretentious one overemphasizing herd numbers, there is enough evidence to suggest that large herd sizes actually represent adaptive responses to Egypt's environmental uncertainties.

Large Cattle (*Bos* spp.)

The earliest known examples of "culturally controlled" cattle are those from Tell Mureybit, Syria, dated to the end of the tenth millennium BP. The term "cultural control" is used because no biological evidence exists that these animals were domesticated, although Perkins suggests that at Çatal Hüyük, there was some reduction in size (a characteristic of domestication) in a level dated to the early eighth millennium BP. The earliest evidence of controlled cattle with demonstrated metrical and morphological differences comes from Greece at the pre-pottery sites of Argissa-Magula in Thessaly and Nea Nikomedeia in Macedonia. Both sites date to about 8000 BP. At Mehrgarh, Pakistan, domestic cattle were reported to occur in an archaeological context, probably dating to the mid-seventh millennium BP. The earliest undisputed cattle remains from cultural context in Africa comes from Capeletti, Algeria (ca. 6530 +/- 250 BP). It cannot be determined if these finds represent domesticated forms but by 5100 BP securely identified domestic cattle are known from the same site.[228]

A survey of the evidence for domesticated animals in Egypt indicates that the earliest undisputed appearance of domestic cattle and ovicaprids date to about 4800 BC. These remains come from Merimde and the Fayum. Three viable hypotheses have been proposed to explain the origins of Egyptian cattle. The first and, until recently, most widely accepted view was that cattle, like cereal grains, were introduced to Egypt from the Near East and Levant. Early dates for domestic cattle from Turkey (ca. 7750 BP) and Iran (ca. 7500 to 7000 BP) are used to support this view. However, one of the most intriguing questions arising from excavations of the early Holocene occupations in Egypt's Western Desert is the apparent association of cattle with sites dated to ca. 9000 BC.[229]

These finds have given new support to a second hypothesis; that Egyptian domestic cattle arose from the indigenous wild aurochs of North Africa, *Bos primigenius*. A third possibility could be that the concept of domestication diffused from the east, but the domesticated animals were derived from Egypt's wild aurochs. Although there is no conclusive evidence substantiating any of these hypotheses, recent evidence from the Western Desert, albeit of a circumstantial nature, has rekindled the argument that Egyptian cattle were possibly independently and locally domesticated from indigenous stock.[230]

Before proceeding further, it is necessary to settle a problem of nomenclature that has arisen in connection with the development of domestic breeds of cattle in prehistoric North Africa. These problems persist, despite the excellent critical discussions of Muzzolini. When wild cattle became extinct in Europe in the seventeenth century, the name "aurochs" (plural: aurochsen) was applied to the extinct species as well as the extant European bison. The term eventually evolved to mean simply a large wild bovine, which was equated with the only extant representative, the European bison. The term "aurochs," however, technically refers to wild cattle of the genus *Bos*; this usage will be maintained throughout the text.[231]

Some comment is also needed regarding the various species of wild cattle identified from skeletal material recovered in Egypt: *Bos brachyceros, Bos longifrons, Bos ibericus* and *Bos africanus*. It should be pointed out that these identifications are based on limited material and in general on an overly typological approach, which has traditionally underestimated morphological variability, especially sexual dimorphism. Apart from the cattle of Southeast Asia, all cattle are descended from a single wild species, *Bos primigenius*, the extinct wild aurochs and many of the "fossil species" are very likely examples of the inherent variability of this single species. For example, recent osteometric analysis and carbon dates have shown that the formerly recognized species *Bos ibericus* (*africanus*) is most likely the smaller female form of *Bos primigenius*.[232]

The wild aurochs was a ubiquitous species that was very successful in the late Pleistocene and early Holocene, and was widespread over most of the northern hemisphere with the exception of North America. The species declined in numbers as a result of hunting pressure. Aurochsen were browsing and grazing ruminants that inhabited forests, but could also flourish in open scrub. They thrived in temperate regions, but evidence of their existence beyond these borders is not uncommon (e.g., Nubia and India).

The external appearance of the wild aurochs is well-known. The last survivor died in Poland in 1627 and there are several good descriptions available including several illustrations (fig. 7.1). The bulls were large, up to two meters at the shoulder, and possessed very long horns. The bulls were generally black with a white stripe along the back and white curly hair between the horns. The muzzle was white to grey. Southern variants, including the Egyptian varieties, were lighter in color and displayed a light brown or fawn saddle that extended over the flank towards the belly. The calves of both sexes appear to have been red in color until about six months of age. It is conceivable that, rather than turning darker with age, the southerly races retained this lighter coloration throughout their lives. Cattle displaying these wild colorations can still be found in North Africa.[233]

One of the most important characteristics concerning wild aurochsen is that they varied greatly in size, color, and horn shape, both within a single breeding population and across different geographical populations. Unfortunately, few archaeological (or paleontological) finds have been fully described and there are great gaps in our knowledge of the species. Nevertheless, three detailed studies are available. These studies from central Europe, Tuscany, and Rome demonstrated that although there was considerable morphological variability between members of the species, the variability centered around a standard type. Also, because *Bos primigenius* was such a wide-ranging species, a number of geographical races existed forming a cline across Europe. These results, based on skeletal morphology, are further substantiated by studies on Paleolithic rock paintings, which bespeak of regional color variations.[234]

With respect to domestic origins, taking into account the great degree of variability, it seems quite plausible that a referent for any of the early domestic breeds could be found in any population of aurochsen from anywhere within the range of the wild form. There is, consequently, no need to postulate migrations to account for the Egyptian domestic form.

In attempting to determine whether archaeologically recovered aurochsen are domesticates, three principle criteria are used. The first involves constructing age classes of the recovered remains (i.e., how many young, juveniles, and adults were recovered) to see whether the archaeological sample differs significantly from the age profiles of a natural population. The second criterion, sometimes regarded as conclusive, is determining whether significant size differences exist between bones of wild aurochsen and the archaeological specimens. Diminution is thought to occur as a result of breeding in isolation from the natural population. The third and most definitive criterion is the appearance of the animals in areas where they could not have survived without the intervention of humans. An even stronger case can be made if no record exists of the species or its ancestral form in that area.[235]

Several problems do exist, however, in determining whether an animal is a domesticate on the basis of these criteria. For example, morphological changes including diminution in size may not be observable for many generations after human control has been imposed, and there is no exclusive relationship between domestication and diminution. Although Grigson has claimed that the only known occurrence of size-reduction in aurochsen is caused by humans, this does not appear to be the case. Several studies have demonstrated that the Holocene aurochsen in Europe were smaller than the Pleistocene ones. Also, there are many examples of size differences between herds (i.e., interbreeding sub-populations) inhabiting a large area and this is not limited to aurochsen. Changes in natural habitat and long-term genetic isolation are important natural causes of size differences in various mammals and it is now evident that the genetic isolation of controlled cattle was never complete, particularly in the early stages of domestication. Thus, at present, the criterion of size cannot be considered, unconditionally, as evidence for domestication.[236]

The use of age or sex profiles in determining the state (domestic or wild) of an archaeological sample is also open to criticism because it involves at least two non-random variables: human choice and the behavior of the animals themselves while grazing or migrating. In particular cases where the structure of the archaeological population has been found to be very different from a natural one, such as the late glacial reindeer in Europe, other factors can provide equally as plausible or even better explanations than a hypothesis involving human control. Additionally, the very manner in which the structure of a population is determined has been shown to be gravely inaccurate. In fact, a study of American elk (*Cervus canadensis*) killed in the 1983 eruption of Mount Saint Helens was conducted to assess the accuracy of age-profiles as they pertained to archaeologically recovered specimens. In essence, the same criteria used to create profiles from bones recovered from archaeological sites was used in creating profiles of the naturally killed elk. Results indicated that depending on the sample size involved (i.e., how many elk were included in a given test) and how the bones were grouped into different age classes (adults, young, and juveniles versus other combinations), a profile indicative of domestic culling patterns, big game hunting or natural death could be created from the same sample of elk bones. Such studies, therefore, do not necessarily measure ancient herding and culling practices, but rather measure some factor of sample size and how the researcher grouped the bones into different age classes. The bottom line is, because aurochs bones are never abundant in an archaeological site, caution is needed before such studies can be accepted.[237]

The best evidence to date for early domestication in Egypt is the rock art found in the Western Desert and North Africa depicting collared and herded cattle. These scenes leave little doubt that at least some of these animals were domesticated. The question that remains is when pastoralists became established (fig.7.2).[238]

7.2. Tended or domestic cattle of the Western Desert. Saharan Neolithic

Two major arguments have led Gautier to believe that the bovid remains found in the early Holocene (ca. 8000 BP) sites of the Eastern Sahara are indeed those of domesticated cattle. One is ecological: the environment was so severe that it could not support *Bos primigenius*, which requires large amounts of water and forage. The second argument is derived from the osteometric data, which indicate that the cattle bones from the Eastern Sahara are within the size-range of domestic wild cattle. If Gautier is correct, cattle remains from Egypt's Western Desert may be some of the earliest domestic cattle known. The size of the samples, unfortunately, do not permit statistical treatment of the osteometric data or evaluation of the population structure.[239]

Wendorf and his associates believe the most valid argument for early domestication is an ecological one. In the Sahel today only the areas receiving at least 500 mm of seasonal rainfall are considered to be good for cattle; areas receiving 300 to 400 mm are adequate for sheep, and cattle can be raised if water and diet supplements are available; areas with 100 to 200 mm are suitable for sheep and goats; and areas with less than 100 mm can support only goats and camels. Information collected by McHugh supports the Sahel data; herds of cattle are raised in Darfur and Kordofan in areas receiving 400 to 625 mm of rain, but watering facilities such as wells are needed in territories with less than 400 mm of rain. The available ecological data make it extremely improbable that the southern Eastern Sahara could have received more than 400 mm of rain per annum in the early Holocene.[240]

The Eastern Sahara (i.e., Western Desert) was probably too arid to support wild aurochsen except around oases and along the Nile. It, therefore, does not seem likely that abundant wild cattle romed over the desert regions. It is possible that cattle were initially brought under human control elsewhere and then introduced into the desert. The most likely point of origin would be the Nile Valley itself. Gautier has suggested that a special human cattle relationship existed in the Nile Valley as early as ca. 14,500 BP. At Tushka, horncores of large cattle were found directly over two human burials and a horncore was found near the skull of a third burial. These horncores appear to have been grave markers. No connection, however, has been established between the ancient Qadan culture at Tushka and the early Neolithic industries of the Western Desert, and there are no identified domestic cattle in the Nile Valley contemporary with the early Neolithic of the Eastern Sahara.[241]

Why early remains of domestic cattle have not been recovered from the Nile Valley is not really a great mystery. First, it is very unlikely, given the presence of wild forms, that any culturally controlled cattle would be fully isolated genetically, thus skeletal remains would be impossible to separate osteometrically. Second, many early Neolithic sites along the Nile are deeply buried under thick alluvial deposits rendering them nearly unattainable. Third, faunal remains do not preserve well in the moist alluvium near the Nile. For example, *Bos primigenius* ranged from the Delta south to at least Nubia, yet its remains are rare in the Nile Valley. Consequently, the odds of recovering and correctly identifying an early domestic or controlled form is relatively low. Therefore, ecological criteria may be the only means available for identifying the earliest domesticates.

Saharan rock art and Egyptian tomb scenes provide some interesting clues to later developments. The rock art predominantly depicts animals with longhorns of varying morphology, including a lyriform type and a type with horns pointed forward. Short-horned and polled animals are not frequently represented, but polled are more common than short-horned. It is possible that the animals with less developed horns or without horns represent cows, but there is no way to substantiate this contention.[242]

The oldest domestic cattle in Egypt, on the basis of artistic scenes, were long-horn cattle. These were slowly replaced by short-horn cattle, which became the predominant breed during the Second Intermediate Period. The replacement of long-horned by short-horned cattle also seems to have occurred elsewhere in coastal North Africa and adjacent regions of West Africa, but the change is not well-documented. The switch could be the result of the importation of short-horned cattle or could reflect a morphological evolution of long-horned cattle. Zebu cattle were not introduced into Egypt until the New Kingdom.[243]

Summarizing the available data, and allowing for some speculation, cattle probably held special significance for some indigenous cultures of the Nile Valley (e.g., Qadan). As a result of contact with Saharan prehistoric hunters, a wild cattle cult may have spread to the Egyptian deserts. These marginal areas could not support populations of wild cattle; therefore, recovered cattle remains may represent tended animals. These controlled cattle may have been later reintroduced along the Nile, as full domesticates, when the climate deteriorated and forced immigration of desert pastoralists to the Nile Valley and Delta. Other domestic breeds could also have been introduced into Egypt at various times in the prehistoric past.[244]

Egyptian Breeds

On the basis of iconographic evidence, four major physical types of Ancient Egyptian cattle can be identified. The morphological differences are distinct enough that these types may represent different breeds. During the Old Kingdom the most frequently depicted bovid was a long-horned variety called *ng',w*, which is shown as

7.3. Egyptian longhorn (upper), shorthorn (middle) and hornless or fancy (lower) cattle. Tomb of Mereruka, Dynasty VI, Saqqara; New Kingdom, Karnak Temple; Tomb of Nefur, Dynasty V.

being tall, lean, and with everted horns sometimes depicted as lyre-shaped, less frequently crescent-shaped. Further, this bovid appears heavily muscled, possesses a thick bison-like neck, and a large muzzle. Representations of this form closely resemble the wild aurochs (*Bos primigenius*). The *ng',w* was often used in religious sacrifices as well as for its meat. The second type of bovine was a short-horned variety (*wndw*). Evidence of short-horned cattle extends back to Dynasty V, although it does not appear to have been a popular breed until the Hyksos period. Textual evidence suggests that a short-horned bovid was imported into Egypt from Syria, but it cannot be substantiated as to whether there is any relationship between the Syrian cattle and the Egyptian short-horns (fig. 7.3).[245]

Another observation that may offer some insight on the Egyptian breeds is that in central and eastern Europe, long-horn cattle tend to predominate in steppe environments; short-horn cattle appear adapted to cooler, wetter mountainous regions. Moreover, it is common knowledge among Hungarian cattle-breeders that short-horn cattle acquire long horns in a few generations when transplanted to an open steppe environment. Thus, it might be that the short-horned Egyptian cattle are simply the evolutionary product of human control and the accompanying move from desert steppe to the Nile valley and Delta. Interestingly, early domestic cattle tend to have long-horns with short-horn types generally appearing later as a more advanced form of the domestic species. Scenes containing short-horn cattle are represented more frequently in later periods. Whether they were rarer in the earlier periods or this is merely an artistic convention is difficult to surmise.[246]

A third type, a hornless breed (*hred'eb'a*), is also known from at least the Old Kingdom. These cattle seem to have been valued as "fancy" cattle, because they are never depicted engaged as draft animals and the peasants decorated them for amusement (fig. 7.3). This was not a rare breed as Cha'fra'onch was said to have 835 long-horned animals and no less than 220 of the hornless type.[247]

The Zebu (Brahma) was introduced into Egypt during the New Kingdom and constitutes the fourth discernible breed of cattle.

From the painted tomb scenes the colors of the Egyptian cattle ranged from black, brown, brown and white, black and white, white spotted with black and pure white. Overall, they resemble the wild aurochsen depicted in the Lascaux caves of France. Interestingly, the Ancient Egyptian words used to designate different cattle are found in modern use in neighboring areas. The word *neg*, for example, is used in Senegal for ox, *nige* in Guinea, *niga* among the Massi of Senegal, and *nagge* by the Fulbe of northern Nigeria[248]

At least some cattle and perhaps by inference whole herds were inspected and classified as to what their eventual use might be. Herodotus provides one example,

> "One of the priests ... searches to see if there is a single black hair on the whole body, since in that case the beast is unclean. He examines him all over ... after which he takes the tongue out of this mouth, to see if it is clean according to the recognized marks; he also inspects the tail to see if the hairs grow properly. If the animal is pronounced clean in all these various points, the priest marks him by twisting a piece of papyrus round his horns and attaching thereto some sealing-clay, which he then stamps with his own signet ring. After which the beast is led away; and it is forbidden, under the penalty of death to sacrifice an animal which has not been marked in this way."[249]

7.4. Obesity, a common condition of the selected and stall fed bull. New Kingdom, Luxor Temple.

7.5. Shedding a tear over the loss of her milk. Dynasty XI sarcophagus, Queen Kahyat.

If the animal was to be raised for meat, the taste and quality of the beef could be altered by regulating its feeding habits, exercise, and quality of life. The *iw'* bull for instance seems to have been fattened and nurtured for a special purpose, perhaps as a sacrificial offering: they are shown as being exceedingly fat, setting low on their haunches and having pendulous belies. Sacrificial bulls appear in relief on Akhenaten's *Rwd-mnw* Temple at Thebes. There, a scene depicts an enormous bull being pulled in a cart while being force-fed: the bull's hooves are overgrown and turned upward, suggesting a sedentary life. Sacrificial bulls are also shown in the jubilee reliefs of Ramesses II at Luxor Temple (fig. 7.4). Their everted horns are indicative of the *ng',w* breed, but their particular lifestyle has given them a distinctly obese form. Such an inactive lifestyle undoubtedly left them muscularly weak and unstable. Their flavor would certainly differ from that of a range fed *ng',w* or an oxen toughened by hard labor. Only "chosen" bulls and calves were used in sacrifice; cows were not traditionally offered. Their contributions were in procreation and milk production.

The earliest firm evidence for the use of cattle as providers of milk in fact comes from Egypt and Mesopotamia and dates to the fourth millennium BC. Cows being milked and nursing calves are frequently depicted throughout the Dynastic Period, and artists often showed regard for the cows' feelings. In many scenes the cow is shown looking back or shedding tears (fig. 7.5) at the removal of her milk while the calf is denied its meal. Peet and Woolley described a series of sticks recovered from their excavations at Amarna that were thought to be used like a muzzle (?) to prevent calves from drinking their mothers' milk.

Ethnographic evidence from East Africa suggests that milk production of pastured Egyptian cattle was probably quite low when compared to today's standards and breeds. For example, in herds of the Dodoth in Uganda only about 20 per cent of the cows are giving milk at any one time. Among the Karimjong only about 12 per cent of the cows give milk. Because each cow also has to feed her calf, only about one liter of milk is available per lactating cow per day under the best of circumstances. In the dry season as little as one-fifth of a liter might be available.[250] Ancient Egyptian cows probably produced variable amounts of milk depending on their particular feeding history, but average production most likely ranged near or slightly above one liter per day. Herded cows, moving over dry lands would, of course, produce much less.

Cattle Herding

7.6. The assisted birth of a calf. Tomb of Ti, Dynasty V, Saqqara.

Egyptian herdsmen were aware of fundamental breeding practices because certain special bulls were known to be kept for breeding purposes and the herdsmen understood how to assist the cows in calving (fig. 7.6). The bovine life cycle, from birth to mating to death, is displayed in tomb art from all periods and provinces. The tombs of Ti and Mereruka include scenes of calving, grazing, drawing plows, and butchering. The art of roping and throwing a wild (or feral) bull is also depicted in the same tombs. In the latter, several men wrestle an animal to get a rope around its horns and legs and finally bring it to its knees; the actual killing of the beast is shown in a number of tombs.

As discussed, with the exception of chosen individuals, cattle were allowed to graze in open fields whenever possible. By Dynastic times, however, the Nile Valley was heavily cultivated and open range was probably very limited. Tethering cattle by means of ropes fixed to pierced stones or to trees or stumps probably became more common. In fact, tethering stones have been used as a means of identifying ancient animal pens.

It was the job of the herdsmen to see that the food for the cattle was plentiful and properly balanced. One method of adding important proteins and amino acids to the diet was by hand-feeding the cattle fresh green produce and bread dough. In fact, grain feed probably constituted the main diet of the penned and force-fed *iw'* bulls. Judging from the pictures in the tombs, this method must have been in common use in the Old Kingdom. Scenes frequently depict herdsmen patiently feeding their cattle green produce and balls of bread dough (fig. 7.7). This would have been an important supplement in the dry season or any time when green grasses were not available because dried grasses do not provide adequate supples of several important minerals and proteins.

Although grain or bread dough served as a healthy supplement to range-fed cattle, it would not have been economically feasible "as feed" to Egypt's vast herds. Particularly when it would have, ultimately, put cattle in direct competition with humans for the same foodstuffs. Consequently, during the unproductive dry season of the year, cattle were driven to better pasture. There is evidence that the Ancient Egyptian herdsmen sent their cattle to the marshes of the north, because a

7.7. Hand feeding which was practiced for fattening chosen cattle and balancing the diet. Tomb of Ti, Saqqara, Dynasty V.

good part of the delta was still wild and uncleared (relative to Upper Egypt).[251] In these marshy districts the cattle were kept by men who were considered to be of the lowest social class, marshmen. Although such men were highly valued as herdsmen, their personal hygiene is always depicted as being somewhat wanting. Marshmen are usually represented as unshaven and with ruffled hair, suggesting a lack of attention to grooming. Their clothing was also shown to be of a simple type and not the white fine and pressed linen of the upper class.

The herdsmen of the marsh lived off the land with the cattle and, like the cowboy of the American Old West, some probably had no permanent home. Rather, they lived in reed huts that could be built with little effort. Personal possessions were minimal, limited to a few vessels and papyrus mats. On the basis of tomb inscriptions, it can be inferred that some of the herdsmen were not indigenous marsh-dwellers, but had accompanied the cattle to pasture to represent the owner's interests. These herdsmen seem not to have delighted in the romance of marsh life. From textual evidence it seems they longed for the comforts of home, and it was a joyful day when they came "out of the north country and drove their cattle upwards" (fig. 2.11).[252]

Once the herd returned home, scribes inspected the accounts of the herdsmen to determine how many head of each breed and class had returned (fig. 7.8). A written accounting of the herd also had to be presented to the estate owner (e.g., a census: 835 long-horned cattle, 220 hornless cattle, 760 donkeys, 974 sheep, and 2234 goats). Government officials from the office of the "Overseer of Cattle" might also visit the estate to levy taxes on the herds. Such taxes were attached to living cattle as well as products such as hides.

7.8. A cattle census. Tomb of Nebamun, Thebes, Dynasty XVIII.

These periodic inspections possibly served to verify the growth (or loss) of wealth of the estate and ultimately of the state itself.[253]

Large numbers of free-ranging cattle or even smaller herds allowed to graze together required some means of identification. One means suggested by Moustafa, who excavated a Dynasty XXVI (655 to 630 BC) animal cemetery, was to etch or mark the horns of the cattle. Moustafa noted that a remarkably large number of horns of all sizes had been treated in this manner. He suggested that these may have served as markers to distinguish individual cattle or the herd owner, although he could not exclude the possibility of other interpretations.[254] A number of tomb scenes also depict cattle with one horn bent downward, although there is no explanation as to why this might have been done (fig. 7.9). The modern Dinka of the Sudan bend the horns of their cattle by filing or deeply incising one side of a horn. This causes the horn to grow in the direction of the incision. This practice, incidentally, is not done as a means of identification, but rather for religious or aesthetic reasons.[255]

Branding (*ꜣbw*) is an effective means of identification and was probably practiced on large estates of the crown and temples. Branding scenes are known from several Theban tombs (Kenamunt, Netererhotep, and Neferhotep) (fig. 7.10) and the Papyrus Varzy tells of a man apparently involved in cattle stealing who placed his own brand over the brand of the true owner.[256]

Although cattle care was in the hands of herdsmen and farmers, a section of the Kahun gynecological papyrus, which deals with disease of cattle, makes it evident that some physicians also possessed veterinary skills and possibly veterinarians formed a distinct social class. For example, many priests of the goddess Sekhmet were medical physicians (*swnw*) but also "knew cattle," others, although not physicians, also "knew oxen."[257]

Secular and Religious Use

The hunting of (feral or wild) cattle is shown as a favorite sport throughout the Dynastic period. In an Old Kingdom hunting scene in the tomb of Ptahhotep (Dynasty V), hounds are shown attacking antelopes while a lion attacks a bull by seizing it by the nose. The same scene appears in the Middle Kingdom about 1800 BC. At this period bulls are also shown being shot with arrows. Apparently, when brought nearly to a halt they were lassoed and dispatched with an axe, as shown in a scene from Beni Hasan. The most famous scene of wild-bull hunting is that of Ramesses III at Medinet Habu. Here the pharaoh is shown hunting in the reed marshes. These could have been truly wild cattle or as likely they may have been bulls returned to the wild for hunting sport (fig. 7.11).

On the basis of anatomical drawings, draught animals were castrates (i.e., oxen). The *ng',w* appears to be the working animal of choice. Castration has an ancient history in Egypt and is mentioned in the *Book of the Dead*; "... I have come and I have smitten for thee emasculated beasts." It is also mentioned in a New Kingdom command to make preparations for Pharaoh's arrival; "... oxen, five castrated, short-horned cattle of the west."[258]

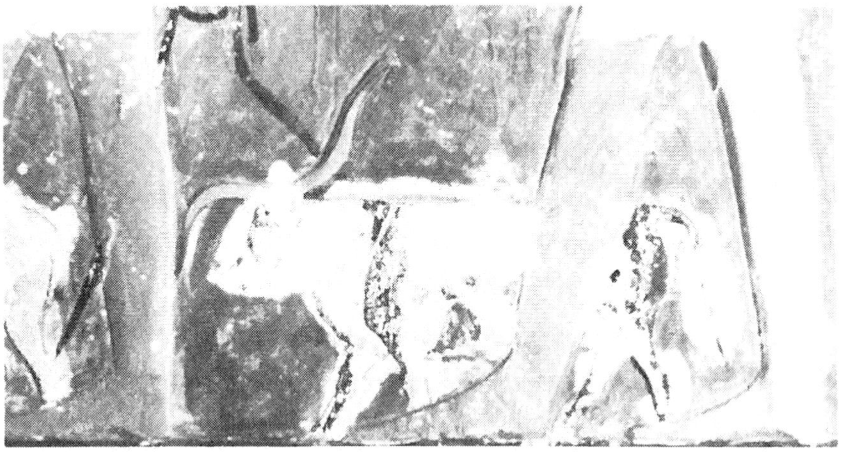

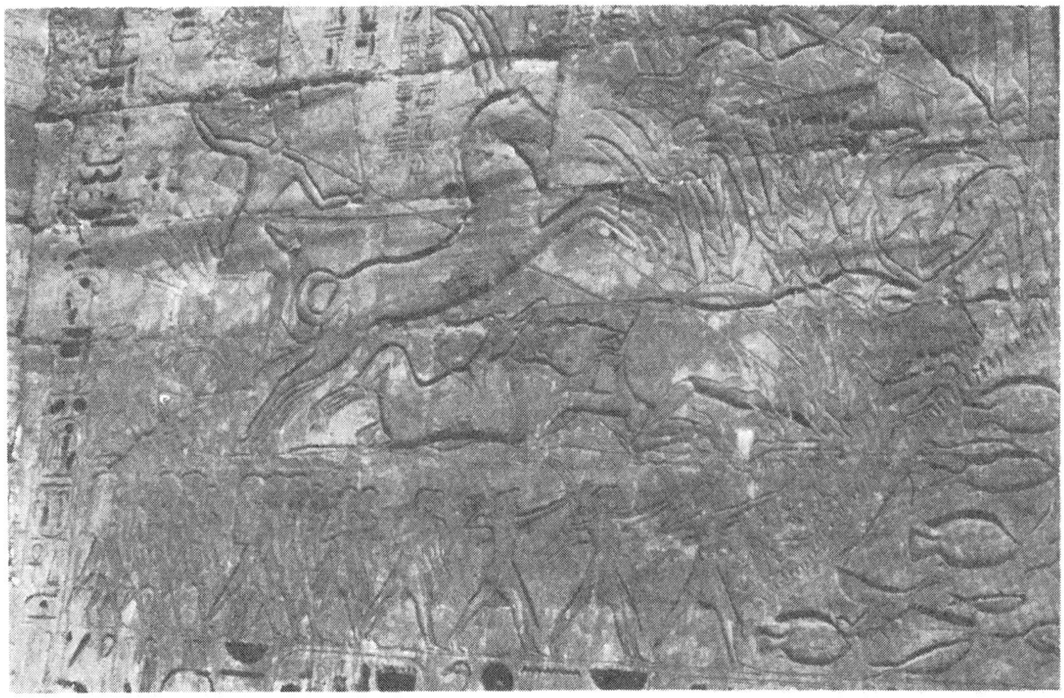

7.9. (top) A purposely deformed horn of an Egyptian cow. Tomb of Mehu, Saqqara, Dynasty VI.
7.10. (centre) Branding cattle in the New Kingdom. Tomb of Nebamun, Thebes, Dynasty XVIII
7.11. (bottom) Ramesses III hunting feral bulls in the marshes. Medinet Habu, Dynasty XX.

Butchering cattle and wild game is a common motif in Egyptian art from all periods and provinces. From the examination of such scenes, Chassinat concluded that the Egyptians had special personnel to select beasts for sacred and secular butchery, to direct the killings in accord with the sacred rites and to examine the flesh for any marks of disease or impurity.[259] Butchers are portrayed as commoners and probably were not supervised by priests or priest-physicians. Cattle were slain by cutting their throats with a knife. They were then bled and skinned. Scenes show priest-physicians smelling blood to make pronouncements on its purity, and a paragraph in the Ebers Papyrus compares *melaena* to cooked blood suggesting that they may have made a dish from it.[260]

After the animal was bled it was skinned, disemboweled, and then dismembered. Select pieces were presented as offerings or exhibited as filets or joints suspended in meat shops. Representations of butchers in association with meat shops are known from the Old Middle and New Kingdoms. Brains too were also eaten. Moustafa noted that cattle skulls recovered from a Dynasty XVI animal cemetery were split along the median (basio-cranial) axis, apparently to permit access to the brains.[261] Numerous medical prescriptions also utilize diverse parts of the cow.[262]

Montet was probably correct in stating that consumption of beef was in general limited to the upper classes of Egyptian society: the large landholders, priests, and royalty. This was probably a function of economics rather than religious restriction. The eating of beef by peasants most likely took place only during special feasts. Normally, the meat most commonly eaten by the peasant class included the smaller, less expensive taxa such as lamb, goat, pig, fowl, and fish. Herodotus offered the first classical evidence of beef avoidance in Egypt when he spoke of the avoidance of the flesh of cows (i.e., females) because they were identified with Isis.[263] Practicality, however, probably outweighed economics or religious restrictions in cattle producing areas. Natural attrition would have made beef more than a sporadic protein source in these areas.

Despite considerable evidence relating to all aspects of cattle raising and butchering, little is known about the preparation of beef for ancient meals. One might expect roasted beef to have been the most common method of preparation, given the many scenes showing Egyptians roasting fowl, but presentations of roasting beef are difficult to find. (One example is in the Tomb of Ukh-hotp, son of Ukh-hotp at Meir.) The cooking method most commonly employed seems to be boiling. Egyptian terminology would indicate, however, that roasted meat was more common than the scenes suggest. It is difficult to know the reason why fowl would be roasted and beef boiled. According to Darby and colleagues the Terabiyin bedouin, whose origins stem from northern Sinai, boil all meats, but roast fowl. Although there is no direct connection to Ancient Egypt, the bedouin believe that boiling kills evil. Roasting, on the other hand, is believed to preserve evil. These explanations do not, however, explain why Terabiyin roast fowl. Personal experience with the Ma'aza bedouin of the Eastern Desert support Darby's experience, but not his contention. On several occasions, ibex was prepared for a meal and each time the meat was boiled. When asked about the method of preparation, it was said that the broth was useful for making rice or for moistening and flavoring the bread that accompanied the meal. No reference was made to "evils."[264]

Cattle Cults

Cattle or more specifically certain chosen individuals were important in religion. The Apis bull, for example, was famous throughout the ancient world and its religious importance probably had its origin in the Predynastic period. The earliest written reference to Apis comes in the reign of Khasekemui (Dynasty II) and is found on the Palermo Stone. Manetho, too, attributed the Apis to a Dynasty II King. Apis was a personification of the god Ptah of Memphis and after death was assimilated into the god Osiris. Only one animal among Egypt's thousands was chosen to be an Apis at any one time and at its death, a search began for its replacement. To be an Apis the animal had to meet certain criteria: it had to have a saddle-marked back – evidently the same pale saddle-patch so common in wild cattle; it also had to have a colored patch on the tongue and forehead. From a variety of scenes it seems that the Apis was a long-horned variety, perhaps of the *ig',w* breed. However, it does not seem that any breed was essential; the special markings were the distinct selective criteria.

In addition to Apis several other bulls were worshipped in similar ways at other localities. The Mnevis bull was associated with the god Re-Atum of Heliopolis and also possessed special markings to demonstrate its authenticity, although the exact nature of the marks remains unclear. The Buchis bull was believed to be a manifestation of the god Mont of Armont (ancient Hermonthis). The Buchis could be recognized as authentic by its long hairs which grew backward, contrary to the nature of other animals and it was reported to change color every hour.[265]

Cattle worship was not limited to bulls. One notable example is Hathor, who took on several personalities in her role as a cow goddess. In the delta she was equated with the sky and in Thebes she was a mortuary goddess. Ironically she was also a goddess of dance, music, and love.[266]

Small Cattle

7.12. Uni-colored and piebald Egyptian sheep sowing grain seeds in the Old Kingdom. Tomb of Ti, Saqqara, Dynasty VI.

Animal domestication is usually associated with the beginning of plant cultivation, but some scholars believe that certain animals such as the dog and more importantly, sheep and goat may have come under human control somewhat earlier than plants. Regardless of the priority of domestication, sheep and goats together with cattle formed the basis of Egypt's domestic animal economy.

The process by which sheep and goats came under human control is not well understood. Sheep and to a lesser extent goats are gregarious animals living in family or larger units. Ancient hunters are known to have hunted wild sheep and goat and undoubtedly followed small herds or family units and learned their behavior. Through hunting it is likely that control over the animals evolved. One possible way in which human control could have been achieved was through maintaining wild herds in favored areas such as near a supply of water or good forage. Given that the native habitat of the animal is in hilly to mountainous regions, the local topography may have aided the hunters in restricting the wandering nature of a given herd. Slowly, over time, a manner of human control was established. Control would have been hastened if adoption and rearing of young was also practiced.

Sheep and goats were probably the first animals domesticated for meat production. The earliest evidence of sheep assumed to have been under human control, if not actually domesticated, comes from Zawi Chemi, Shanindar in northeast Iraq and dates to about 8900 BC. The status of these remains as domesticates, however, has come under recent criticism. The earliest accepted evidence for domestic sheep is in late seventh millennium BC in Iran, and accepted dates for domestic goats or minimally goats under human control predates sheep by more than 1000 years (ca. 8000 BC). These dates too are disputed by some but, by 6000 BC, nearly all scholars agree that domestic sheep and goats had become well established.[267]

The time of introduction of domestic sheep and goats into Africa has long been debated, but Higgs has presented evidence from Neolithic levels of the cave of Haua Fteah in Cyrenaica, Libya. Unfortunately, separating sheep from goat bones is difficult. This was compounded by the fact that most of the bones had been thrown out of the cave by the inhabitants and thereby outside of the excavation area. Higgs, understandably had difficulty distinguishing sheep from goat bone. His problems were further complicated by the presence of a closely related wild form, the Barbary sheep (*Ammotragus*). Nevertheless, he definitely believed that domestic sheep and/or goats were living in Cyrenaica before 4900 BC and possibly as early as 6500 BC. Because both domestic sheep and goats were presumably known in southwestern Asia by this time, and goats presumably this early or earlier at Beidha in the southern end of the Dead Sea drainage, there would seem to be little difficulty in accepting the probability that domestic goats and/or sheep could have been herded by easy stages across Sinai and the north coast of Egypt into the mountains of Cyrenaica. They could also have been moved up the Nile Valley and into the Fayum oasis.[268]

Archaeological remains of sheep and goats are difficult to separate osteologically, particularly if only fragments are available for identification. Artistic representations take on added importance in recreating an image of the early domestic forms. Ancient Egyptian goats, although apparently somewhat larger, appear to be of the same type as those recovered from Jericho and other Near Eastern sites. Sheep as well appear similar to the wild and Neolithic forms of the Near East. Goat and/or sheep bones have been recovered from the Fayum and Merimde, which to date account for the earliest undisputed examples in Egypt. In later Neolithic times, goatskins were used during the early Badarian (i.e., Tasian) and later cultures. Judging from the number of skeletal elements recovered from Neolithic and Predynastic sites, goats and sheep played a significant role in the prehistoric Egyptian economy.[269]

The taxonomy and nomenclature of sheep and goats is very complicated, especially for sheep for which at least forty wild races have been described. There are, however, four basic groups of sheep based on chromosome counts: the Siberian (2n=52), the Euroasiatic (2n=54), the Argali (2n=56); and the Urial (2n=58). The Asiatic mouflon (*Ovis orientalis*), a member of the 54 chromosome group, was probably the ancestor of the early Egyptian domestic forms. The mouflon has a rather small body, long legs, and a relatively short tail. The horns are ringed rather than ridged and are smaller and less twisted than in other groups of wild sheep. The mouflon has a black throat, a well-defined white rump patch, and a white underside. Its coat is dark reddish-brown in color (lighter in southerly forms) and stiff hairs cover a short woolly undercoat that grows only in the winter. The long, bristly outer hairs are known as kemps. In advanced domesticated forms, kemps are absent and the fleece consists entirely of the woolly undercoat. The wool may be white, brown, black, or a mixture of these colors. In wild sheep and in primitive domestic breeds the undercoat is shed each spring and falls in dense mats that can be gathered or plucked from the animal and made into felt or spun. The loss of the ability to shed is an advantageous trait developed through domestication to reduce wool loss, but it requires an added investment in that the sheep must be sheared.[270]

Domestication also brought changes in the color of the hair. Although many wild sheep have white underbellies or rumps, none are entirely white, which is the predominant color of most domestic breeds. Another curious feature present in many domesticated sheep is a long tail. All wild sheep have extremely short tails comprising not more than 13 vertebrae (the number is variously given as 12 to 13 depending on the presence or absence of the vestigial terminal vertebra). Some domestic breeds, however, have more than 35 caudal vertebrae and the tail is long enough to touch the ground. In some breeds, fat is deposited on the tail: the fat-tail sheep of modern Egypt is an example. Its tail is actually of medium length but the tip curls upwards, and two large lumps of fat grow on the sides of the basal portion. The tail can attain a weight of 4 to 5 kilos; the rest of the animal may weigh only 25 kilos. Although one might expect the fat-tail to be a recent breed, they are depicted on the famous Peace Panel of Ur, dated to about 2400 BC. The date of introduction of fat-tail sheep into Egypt is unclear, but Smith believes it was introduced in the Middle Kingdom and is shown in tomb scenes side by side with the earlier form. Despite an intensive search, no examples could be solidly identified as a fat-tail sheep. Rather, it appears Smith might have confused the curved horn breeds depicted in the tombs of Beni Hasan and referred to in the literature as *Ovis platya*, with the fat-tail sheep.[271]

Most of the identifiable features of domestic sheep – an alteration of horn shape, hornlessness in ewes, fattiness and length of the tail, and the woolly white fleece- were already common in western Asia by 3000 BC. Examples can be

7.13. A likeness of the New Kingdom ram displaying its recurved horns. Karnak Temple, Dynasty XIX

7.14. Browsing goats nibbling the ends of a tree, Tomb of Nefur, Saqqara, Dynasty V.

identified in Mesopotamian scenes and they are described in Babylonian texts. Egyptian tomb scenes also display a number of these traits (fig. 7.12).

On the basis of a comparison of scenes, Egypt possessed in succession two different races of sheep that are only once depicted together. Until the Middle Kingdom there was a hairy thin-tailed breed, with twisted horns extending laterally from the head (see fig. 7.12).[272] Woolen textiles are accordingly scarce until the Middle Kingdom. However, the Old Kingdom form already showed an improvement over its wild ancestor in that the kemp was woollier and the hair grew all the year round; hair of the earlier forms would moult only in the spring, discarding hair over the grazing area. The presence of black, piebald, and white animals suggests that the pigment was lost before the development of fleece suitable for use in textiles evolved. The hairy sheep was kept mainly for its meat, milk, and hide, and the flock was used for treading seed into the fields after sowing. The later breed possessed a shorter fatter tail and recurved horns (fig. 7.13). Because the wool of this new race was better suited for spinning and weaving, woolen fabrics become more predominant in later the periods. Interestingly, shears do not appear until the Third Intermediate Period, so wool was evidently plucked or cut with a knife.[273]

In tropical areas today, one can still find breeds that possess some of the early domestic traits depicted on Old Kingdom scenes. Sheep of the Uda of West Africa, for example, have corkscrew horns and some screw-horn sheep still exist in Egypt, although they are not common. The lop ears depicted in the Old Kingdom scenes can also be found on many tropical sheep, and it is thought to be an adaptation for heat loss. Retention of the kemp coat could be a similar adaptation in that domestic breeds in tropical areas would not be managed primarily for their wool thus allowing them to maintain their natural pelage.

Lower Egypt is the chief producer of sheep today, and two distinct breeds can be identified, the Ausimi and Rahmani. These breeds are spreading at the expense of the traditional Fellahi breed of Lower Egypt and the Ibeidi and Saidi breeds of Upper Egypt. Modern Egyptian sheep, as in ancient times, are generally kept in small flocks (2 to 10 individuals) and subsist on wasteland and stubble left after the harvest. They are seldom given supplementary feed as are cattle. Professional herders may look after large flocks consisting of sheep from different owners. Although modern sheep are shorn twice a year (spring and autumn), ancient breeds, like the modern desert Barki breed they resemble, were probably shorn once a year in autumn.[274]

Sheep are grazing ungulates that inhabit hilly regions and the foothills of mountains, but goats are browsers whose natural habitat is on the high, bleak mountain ranges of Europe, Asia, and Ethiopia. Because of their adaptation to a particularly harsh environment, goats are perhaps the most versatile of all ruminants in their feeding habits, a factor that has greatly affected their success as a domestic animal. They also have, relative to sheep and cattle, a wider tolerance of habitat types: they are able to feed and breed on a minimum of food and under extremes of temperature and humidity. The goat could thus provide for many physical needs of the nomadic pastoralist or Neolithic farmer: clothing, meat, milk, tallow, sinew, bones for tools and dung for fuel. Goats also complement a flock of sheep by browsing on thorny scrubland while the sheep graze on grasses (fig. 7.14). Goats may even have been of assistance to the Neolithic farmers in helping to clear land.[275]

Goats are believed to be the dominant food animal at Jarmo and are listed as being abundant in the earliest phase at Tepe Ali Kosh, Deh Luran, Iranian Khuzistan, where their identification as domesticates is based on the high proportions of yearlings. The Neolithic site of Shaheinab in the Sudan, excavated by Arkell and dated to about 3300 BC showed two types of twisted-horn goats. One was small and is referred to in the literature as a dwarf similar in size to the modern Nilotic dwarf goat. Most likely, however, it was just a local variation of the early domesticated breed.[276]

Unlike sheep, domestication resulted in only moderate changes in goats. The horns diminished in size with a slow, albeit arguable, change from scimitar shaped horns to screw horns, (the reasons or actual extent of this change is still debated) and a minor tendency towards hornlessness in females.

In external appearance the Ancient Egyptian goat resembled the sheep in many respects. It was high-legged, short-haired, and had a long face with a straight nose. Scimitar-horned goats appear to have existed in Old Kingdom times but by the Hyksos period the horn appeared twisted, or 'corkscrew' in shape and the profile of the goat's nasal area is straight. The angle between the horns varied a great deal, especially when the horns pointed to the back of the animal. As a rule the females were horned, although a few representations show hornless goats. Among 29 goat skulls recovered from tombs ranging in date from 1000 BC to 100 AD, 14 had thick, well developed horns, 13 had weaker, less developed horns and two were hornless. The more robust skulls tended to have robust screw horns and were thought to represent male goats. Profiles of the goat skulls appeared similar to artistic representations in that male skulls were somewhat concave in the forehead-nasal area while female goats tended to have a straight profile. The modern goat of Egypt with its convex nose, drooping ears and long hair is not a descendant of the ancient forms, but rather is a more recent introduction from the east.[277]

Religious and Secular Use

Although a selective goat-breeding policy was unknown, goats were kept for their meat, skin, and perhaps milk, although less importantly for their hair. Tomb illustrations depict only short-haired varieties that could not have supplied much wool for spinning. This strongly suggests that goats were raised primarily for meat. Otherwise, it is hard to justify the large number of remains recovered from excavations of all periods. Goat and possibly sheep meat was a common dish for the peasant and working class. Goat skin was also used to produce a diverse number of leather objects. Prices of sheep and goat are not as well documented as those of cattle, but Dynasty XIX documents indicate that the price of small cattle (sheep, goats, and pigs) fluctuated between one and three *deben*, presumably copper.[278]

Evidence for some restrictions on sheep consumption is recorded by ancient historians. Herodotus tells us that on occasion rams were sacrificed to Amun at Thebes. Plutarch reported that priests shunned mutton, and added that the inhabitants of Lycopolis (Asyut) were the only people to eat mutton because the wolf, whom they held to be a god, ate it. Plutarch also reported that the Egyptian priests did not wear woolen garments "... priests because they revere the sheep abstain from using wool as well as its flesh..."[279]

The benefits of sheep as providers of wool, butter, cheese, and milk undoubtedly made an impression on the Ancient Egyptians who knowingly kept them until their usefulness as a meat producer outweighed their ability to produce secondary products. The large herds that were reported to have been kept in the New Kingdom probably served, therefore, as a source of wool and dairy products and only after productivity waned were they slaughtered for meat.[280]

Swine

Domestic pigs are all descended from one species, *Sus scrofa*, the wild boar, which is still a relatively common animal throughout Europe, Asia, and North Africa. The wild boar prefers river valleys, marshes, and forested areas. During Egypt's prehistoric period, wild boar could be found in the Delta, Nile Valley, Fayum and Wadi Natrum. In fact, wild boar was so common in the nineteenth century Delta and Fayum that in 1846 a campaign to eradicate the beast from Lower Egypt was undertaken by the government. In that year alone 860 pigs are recorded as being killed. The program was apparently successful as the last sighting of an indigenous boar was one shot in Wadi Natrun in 1894.[281]

The feeding habits of pigs resemble that of dogs much more so than any other artiodactyl (e.g. cattle, sheep) and in many respects pig behavior seems to be intermediate between that of carnivores and artiodactyls. They are very versatile in their feeding habits and flourish by scavenging foods that humans have discarded. Also, like carnivores and unlike all other artiodactyls (except the hippopotamus), pigs seek out and enjoy body contact with other members of their family group – they like to huddle together. Like carnivores pigs have large litters of up to ten young at a time; while other artiodactyls have only one or at most three offspring at a time. Another characteristic that the pig shares with carnivores is the habit of building a nest to birth its young. Once the nest of grasses and twigs is complete, the sow will enter the nest, lie down and give birth on her side. This is again distinct from other artiodactyls, which give birth while standing.[282]

Within minutes or even seconds of birth, wild piglets will try to reach their mother's teat and establish a nipple order. Each piglet will establish itself on a nipple and will always feed from it and defend it against other piglets. This behavior is not always seen in domestic pigs, but explains why it is sometime difficult to introduce piglets from another litter to a foster mother.

Another way in which pigs resemble carnivores rather than artiodactyls is their weak physical development at birth. Most ungulates are born with well-coordinated musculature so that they can stand and even run a few hours after birth, but a litter of piglets has to stay within the protection of the nest for the first few weeks. When they do leave the nest, the sow keeps in contact with the piglets by nose-to-nose contact at frequent intervals and a complicated series of vocalizations. If a piglet is lost, all the others will squeal and try to find it and the mother will become very agitated. When the piglet is finally found, the sow will touch the piglet with her snout. Pigs do not, however, lick their young in the way that carnivores do.[283]

Despite their desire for close bodily contact, wild pigs do not congregate in large herds in the way that cattle and caprines do; the sows and their young stay together as a family group while the boars remain solitary except in the rutting season. The number of sows that a boar will keep together for mating depends on how many he can defend against other males. Usually, at least in present-day groups, wild pigs maintain units of less than ten individuals. However, when domestic pigs were allowed to free-range in European woodlands, a herd of one hundred or more sows with a few boars was not uncommon.[284]

Male pigs can be very aggressive and will fight over food or to defend sows (as will dogs), but like other species of domesticated mammals, *Sus scrofa* is not strongly territorial, which makes them more easily managed by humans. To control the aggressive behavior of males, castration is practiced. With its omnivorous habits it is not difficult to get it accustomed to food available in village settlements. Feeding and sleeping are the two activities that dominate a pig's life. Ruminants will feed for a short time, ruminate, perhaps sleep for a while and then feed again; pigs will feed continuously for many hours and then sleep for many hours. This means that in captivity they do not require food during the night and their sleeping and feeding programs can be easily accommodated to that of humans. In addition, wild pigs have social tendencies that make them suitable for domestication (the social unit being the family).

Since ancient times, there have been two methods of keeping domestic pigs and both methods were practiced in Egypt. The first is to allow large herds of animals to roam at will in the forests under the eye of a swineherd. The second, which is more common today, is the sty.[285]

Archaeological Evidence

The physical stature of the pig, its preferred habitat, and its uncompromising personality make it an unlikely candidate for herding over great distances. It is seems unlikely, therefore, that the pig was domesticated before the establishment of permanent settlements. It is indeed difficult to imagine how a nomadic community or even a semi-sedentary group could cope with pig-drives, given that the animal is notoriously unaccommodating in this respect. The pig was, therefore, more valuable to settled societies. The pig's path of introduction into Egyptian Neolithic villages is still uncertain. Egypt did possess a healthy wild population. However, the co-occurrence of sheep, goat and pigs has convinced many that they were Eastern introductions into Egypt. If so, this probably represents a village-by-village migration. It should be pointed out that the co-occurrence of pig with other introduced species may simply be a factor of the archaeological circumstances. That is, because pigs are beneficial to village farmers and less so to more mobile groups, one would not expect to find domestic pigs until agricultural communities developed. The archaeological record may simply reflect an early balancing of animal resources and not co-introductions of all three forms from a foreign area. Regardless of its origins, the pig filled an open domestic niche in that it complemented cattle, sheep and goats by eating what they did not. As well, through rooting they helped turn the soil and produced conditions conducive to grass growth.[286]

The chief role of the pig was undoubtedly as a source of meat and fat for the kitchen. Pigs are well-suited for this role because they produce two litters a year, are comparatively long-lived, and mature within a year. Their ability to adapt to different environments allows them to freely range and root in the village or be confined to the home or sty. This versatility offers a unique advantage over other domesticates, particularly in densely populated areas.

Changes thought to be the result of the domestication process include decrease in size and the loss of hair and pigmentation. The earliest remains of domestic pig date to the Pre-pottery Neolithic B levels of Jericho (ca. 7000 BC). Skeletal remains of these pigs are marginally smaller than those of the preceding A levels, so it could be argued that domestication or at least human interference with a wild population of pigs was underway. Similar evidence has been found at Jarmo and at the site of Argissa-Magula in Greece, and it is probable that the earliest settled 'farmers' began to manage wild pigs at the same time as they husbanded the first sheep and goats.[287]

During the late Paleolithic and Epipaleolithic in Egypt, the people of Helwan ate pork. Pig bones were also recovered from Epipaleolithic and Neolithic sites in the Fayum. The animals recovered from the Fayum, however, are thought to be of wild stock. The date of the first appearance of domestic swine in Egypt is debatable. It is known, however, that the early settlers at Merimde consumed great quantities of pork, as revealed by thousands of pig bones. Indeed, several archaeologists have concluded that pork consumption was a characteristic of early Delta culture. Although it is difficult to assess morphologically whether these early remains came from hunted or domestic animals, the sheer number of bones recovered and their relative frequency compared to sheep/goat and cattle, ranging from the first to third most abundant animal, strongly suggests that they were kept animals.[288]

Further investigations have revealed that pig bones have been recovered from most Lower Egyptian Predynastic sites, including such settlements as el-Omari, Maadi, and the Archaic and Old Kingdom sites of Minshat Abu Omar, Mendes and Kom el-Hisn. These finds are a good indication that swine were raised and utilized as food in Lower Egypt, from Neolithic times (ca 4000 BC) through the Old Kingdom and beyond.[289]

Parallel information from Upper Egypt is sketchier. That wild pigs were hunted during the Late Paleolithic Sebilian horizon is suggested by the recovery of pig bones in strata correlated to this period. Pig bones have also been identified from early Predynastic sequences at Armont, Toukh, Abydos, Naqada, and Hierakonpolis.[290]

Table 7.1 lists the number of identified skeletal elements per taxon for a series of well-published assemblages from the Delta, Giza, and Hierakonpolis. Interestingly, the relative abundance of pig bones shifts from being the predominant taxon encountered to that of a lesser status as one moves out of the Delta. This perceived shift away from pig as the main source of domestic animal protein probably reflects available habitat – the Delta offering the most hospitable environment for raising pigs – but cultural biases cannot be totally discounted. For example, small figurines of swine have been recovered from Predynastic graves at Abydos, El-Amrah, and from the temple foundation at Hierakonpolis.

Table 7.1. Identifed domestic animal bones from five sites.

Taxon	Site Merimde	Maadi	Kom el-Hisn	Ibrahim Awad	Hierakonpolis
Dog	508	31	12	1	34
Pig	6568	398	397	112	140
Sheep	840	62	0	13	111
Goat	38	32	0	1	136
Sheep/ Goat	5185	1144	311	7	900
Ass	0	20	41	0	5
Cow	3575	311	14	76	851

Unfortunately, pictorial evidence in support of swine and swine raising in the Old Kingdom is lacking. A controversial relief found in the Dynasty VI tomb of Kagemni at Saqqara was described by Firth and Gunn as a "young dog;" Hecker believes it to be a pig. Evidence against the animal being a pig, however, seems more convincing with an examination of the feet, where definite toes and claws are seen rather than sharp hoofs (fig. 7.15). The blunt, tapering face of the young animal, coupled with the distinctive fat abdomen and short curly tail would apparently disqualify it as the pup of the slim saluki, but not rule out the possibility that it is the pup of another variety of canine or hyena.[291]

7.15. Controversial force-feeding scene of a canid or hyena, which has often been misidentified as a pig. Note that the feet display toes, not a cleft hoof. Tomb of Kagemni, Saqqara, Dynasty V.

There is little information on swine during the Middle Kingdom. However, one noble, Menthusweser, who lived during the reign of King Senusret I, held the title "Overseer of Swine". Also, in the Middle Kingdom tomb of Khety at Beni Hasan there is a painting of ambiguous "marsh-animals" that bear a strong resemblance to swine (fig. 7.16). By New Kingdom times, however, references to swine are more frequent and a passage in the *Book of Gates* clearly shows a monkey driving a pig (7.17). A record from the tomb of Reni describes a herd of swine numbering 1500 and some New Kingdom kings offered gifts of swine to temples. Amenhotep III offered 100 adults and 1000 piglets to the temple of Ptah at Memphis and Seti I allowed pigs to be raised inside the temple consecrated to Osiris at Abydos. Paheri, a noble buried at El Kab, had artists portray scenes of swine under the care of a herdsman. Several other tombs have been reported as once having depicted swine, but recent surveys have shown that these scenes have deteriorated to the point that recognition is now impossible. Kees, however, alluded to the recovery of pig bones in trash deposits from Deir el Medina.[292]

The most important discovery relating to hog-farming is the discovery at the Amarna workmen's village of a rather sophisticated pig farm. The animals had been born and raised in sets of specially constructed pens. The pigs were apparently fed grain and most of the animals had been slaughtered in their first or second year of life. The butchering, salting, and packing of meat in pottery jars had been done in special areas coated with white gypsum. The whole complex represents a well-organized operation that so far has no parallel in the main city of Amarna, nor, for that matter, at Deir el Medina, Thebes. The relative care and degree of organization devoted to the farm imply that it was more than a sideline run by some of the villagers for personal use; rather, it appears to have served to supplement income by sales in the main city.[293]

Pork Avoidance in Ancient Egypt

Many reasons have been suggested for the curious attitude towards pork during the Pharaonic Period. The origin of pork avoidance in the Middle East, reflected in the Mosaic and Koranic bans is often attributed to the possible contraction of trichinosis from eating uncooked pork.

Trichinosis is an infestation of a microscopic parasitic worm, *Trichina spiralis*, that may be found coiled in cysts in the muscles of humans, rats, and pigs. When undercooked infected meat is eaten, the cyst is digested and viable parasites mature, reproduce, and deposit larvae in the intestinal mucosa. These are then disseminated by the lymphatic and blood systems to other tissues especially skeletal muscle, where they again encyst. The infected individual experiences diarrhea during the intestinal stage; then during migration, nausea, colic, and fever; followed in the tissue stage by pain, stiffness, swelling, sweating, and insomnia.

Although trichinosis is a concern in most areas of the world, the cause and effect relationship between pork and the parasitic infection is not direct. There are numerous other plants and animals where no taboo of ingestion exists, but whose effects are more directly observable than trichinosis. In fact, the relationship between ingestion of under-cooked pork and trichinosis was not even established until 1846.[294]

From a cultural and economic point of view the development of a taboo on pork in Ancient Egypt seems illogical, but might be explained as an outgrowth of groups descended from pastoralists. Pigs were useless to ancient pastoralists; they could not be easily herded and their bones were too soft for most tools. An intolerance of the species would, therefore, seem appropriate as it would not fit into the mobile lifestyle. If cattle pastoralists did settle in the Nile Valley in early Neolithic times these rules of avoidance would have remained intact. Thus, the same explanations used to support cattle cults in Egypt could also serve to support arguments for pork avoidance.

On the basis of archaeological remains, Herodotus' statements that the Ancient Egyptians refrained from eating pork is unfounded. Although pigs are featured in a few tombs, their bones have never been found in a tomb nor is pork featured in temple offerings. That some restrictions against pork existed, does consequently seem likely. As with fish, restrictions on pork might have been limited to certain classes or to certain periods of the year. Ruffer, one of the early authorities on food and diet in Ancient Egypt, cites as proof of the acceptance of pork examples of slate cosmetic palettes carved in the silhouette of a pig and dated to the Archaic and early Old Kingdom. He argues that had the pig been considered repulsive and an animal to be avoided, no Egyptian woman would wish to use paint from a palette in the shape of such a creature.[295]

Another indication of a permissive attitude towards pigs in the priestly class are the ceramic figures made in their form and found inside the sacred compound of Osiris at Abydos (ca. Dynasty IV). Furthermore, according to some traditions the god Min, a widely accepted deity of fertility, was born of a white sow. There is also the possibility that Min might be linked to a region near Meidum known during the Dynasty IV as the "Domain of the White Sow."[296]

7.16. (top) Animals (pigs) of the marsh. Tomb of Khety, Beni Hasan, Dynasty XI
7.17. A monkey driving a pig through the delta marshes. Tomb of Horemhab, Thebes Dynasty XVIII.

VIII

WORKING AND HOUSEHOLD ANIMALS

8.1. Old Kingdom donkey with shoulder stripe indicative of wild and early domestic forms.

Although oxen were used as draught animals in agriculture and sheep, goats and occasionally pigs were used to seed crops and process grains through trampling, certain animal taxa as a whole were viewed with special affection. Egyptians appear to be very much like modern people with respect to the devotion they felt toward their pets and working animals. There are many examples attesting to the fact that even herd animals had given names and were treated as if they were valued family members. The roots of this attitude probably lay with the Ancient Egyptian belief that humans and animals were created by the gods and that proper treatment of their working partners fell under the concept of *maat*.

It is with the household animals that the distinction between domestic and tame becomes difficult to separate archaeologically. Cats, although they retain to this day much of their innate wild behavior, were indeed Egyptian domesticates. Monkeys and baboons, however, seem to be tame animals accustomed to the company of humans and not genetically altered or dependant in any way on human interactions, at least in the sense of compensating for a genetic disadvantage that would restrict their life in the wild. They were thus not domesticates.

Donkeys and Horses (*Equus asinus*; *Equus caballus*)

Four main species of the genus *Equus* lived in the Old World during the Late Pleistocene and early Holocene: the onagers or half-asses (*E. hemionus*) in Hither Asia (Arabia, Persia and India), the asses in northern and northeast Africa, the zebras in south and east Africa, and the caballine horses in Europe and central Asia. All the species are thought capable of producing hybrids, and all but the zebras have been domesticated.[297]

Donkey (Equus asinus)

Prior to the Roman period there appear to have been three wild races of ass in Africa, one in northwest Africa, one in northeast Africa, and a Somalian race. The northeast African race (the Nubian ass) extended from Nubia to at least southern Upper Egypt, and from the eastern Sudan to the Red Sea. It is also thought to have inhabited parts of the Eastern and Western Deserts of Egypt and cryptic references suggest they were hunted in the New Kingdom[298]

Although in modern times the wild ass (*Equus africanus*) is restricted to North Africa, it is possible that in the late Pleistocene/early Holocene the ass also inhabited Arabia and the drier parts of the Levant. Identification of *Equus asinus* in Asia is complicated, however, by the presence of the onager, *Equus hemionus*. In addition, another now extinct equid, *Equus hydruntinus*, also inhabited western Asia (and southern Europe) until the late prehistoric period; its bones and teeth are found in archaeological contexts. Archaeological remains of the wild African ass in Egypt are not numerous, but have been reported from the Late Paleolithic sites of Kom Ombo in the Nile Valley, Bir Tarfawi and Bir Sahara in the Western Desert, and in early Neolithic sites of the Fayum. Although there is no discernible osteological difference between early domestic asses and their wild counterparts, the Fayum bones are thought to be wild animals. This is based on archaeological interpretations of the sites, which are thought to represent pre-Nelolithic nomadic, rather than settled populations.[299]

The strongest defining evidence for a progenitor of the domestic donkey comes from chromosome studies and observations of hybrids. Although all species of equids will interbreed and produce viable offspring, these offspring are rarely fertile. There is one exception: crosses between the wild ass (*E. africanus*) and the domestic donkey (*E. asinus*). That only the African ass (*E. africanus*) and donkey (*E. asinus*) have the same number of chromosomes and that crosses between these two forms produce fertile offspring provides strong evidence that *E. africanus* is the progenitor of the domestic donkey.[300] It is, therefore, quite probable that Egypt was the original area of ass domestication, although probably not the Nile Valley itself.

In the developing Predynastic, a number of identifiable distinct cultures were evolving in Egypt, the most obvious being the Delta and Upper Egyptian cultures. The peoples of the frontier, however, should not be excluded. These people formed a third culture type based on seasonal or periodic nomadism, relocating their population to take advantage of dispersed available resources.

General studies explaining the rise of nomadism as a way of life have suggested that mobility was the key to success. Yet, at the same time close ties were kept with agricultural communities such as those developing in the Predynastic Nile Valley. The sedentary groups provided needed grains and other commodities to the nomadic peoples in exchange for desert products and other materials traded in distant lands. The domestic ass added to the mobility of these nomadic groups, enabling them to increase their travelling range and load, thereby incorporating a larger sphere of communities within a trading network. That the domestic donkey was first used in desert steppes and then in Egypt is based on several lines of evidence.

First, contrary to the comments of Jacob, who sees the donkey equated with the rise of urbanism in Egypt and elsewhere, the donkey was not present in early urban Mesopotamia. In fact, even by the third millennium BC, cuneform records show that donkey breeding in Mesopotamia was still relatively unsuccessful and stocks were replenished through trading (and raiding) with northern and eastern areas. Second, the horse saw parallel development in Asia and Europe and there it too appears first in the context of nomadic peoples. Again, there is no evidence that it evolved in an urban environment. The donkey like the horse was successful in a nomadic environment because it offered nomads a selective advantage over less mobile groups. Mobility provided the means for survival. The more mobile a group, the better chance that group had in reaching important resources: the donkey enhanced this advantage. Once established in nomadic culture, it was adopted by Egypt as a beast of burden. The donkey is known as a domesticate in Egypt by the mid-Predynastic. Its remains have been recovered from Omari and later sites and it is depicted on several early Dynastic votive palettes. It also appears in Beersheba, Palestine by the mid-Predynastic, but is not known from Mesopotamia until 2900 BC (Jemdet Nasr). The donkey thus joins the cat, *Bos*, and pig as possible indigenous African domesticates.[301]

By the Old Kingdom the donkey was commonly employed as a beast of burden and its duties depicted in numerous tomb scenes (fig. 2.9). During the Old Kingdom it is entirely possible that systematic donkey breeding was undertaken. Large herds of donkeys are suggestive of just such a practice. For example, a Dynasty IV scribe notes a land owner with well over 760 asses. Further evidence of donkey breeding comes from the pictorial record that shows Predynastic and some Old Kingdom donkeys with wild coloring. Most easily identifiable is the dark shoulder stripe of the wild and early domestic form, which decreases in frequency through the Old Kingdom and is lacking in Middle Kingdom and later donkeys (fig. 8.1). By late historic times the end product of donkey breeding is quite well-illustrated by the presence of stronger, larger, and lighter colored animals.

8.2. A large sack being fitted over a donkey, Tomb of Mehu, Saqqara, Dynasty V.

The primary function of the ass was as a beast of burden. Numerous tomb scenes portray donkeys laden with agricultural goods from the fields. Often a saddle-pack composing a basket or leather sack fastened on the back by means of ropes and straps is shown; this enabled the donkey to carry heavy loads (fig. 8.2). A donkey is said to able to carry as much as 200 to 300 kg over short distances and smaller loads over great distances. Prior to the introduction of the camel, trading caravans comprised of donkeys voyaged between Egypt, Arabia, the Levant, and sub-Saharan Africa. During Dynasty VI, Herkhug, the caravan master of King Meren-Re returned from his third journey to Yam with 300 asses ladened with incense, ebony, and grain. Like oxen and sheep they were also employed for threshing, but it seems that donkeys were seldom used for plowing.

It is likely that ordinary Egyptians rode donkey-back, although only foreigners are shown riding (astride) donkeys. Three Old Kingdom reliefs show the tomb owner riding in an elaborate chair suspended over the back of two donkeys and two New Kingdom texts refer to donkeys pulling a chariot.[302]

The Egyptian word for donkey was *cꜣ* (eeyor) a name based on the creature's less than melodious cry. The same word frequently occurs with the connotation "ass-load," a vague measure of quantity for bulky and relatively cheap goods; a term no doubt reflecting the primary function of the donkey as a beast of burden. The purchase price of an average donkey was quite high, about the price of a cow, making it too expensive for most peasants, but it was a good investment. Although they are notoriously stubborn and single minded, donkeys are capable of working for as many as 40 years, are easy to maintain, and are able to survive on relatively little water and poor forage.[303]

For all the donkey offered, it is ironic to find that it was the butt of jokes and insults. When the Egyptians wanted to show their contempt for the Persian ruler Ochus, they called him "the ass", to which he responded by slaughtering and eating the Apis bull. That donkeys were sometimes mistreated is evident from a text from Deir el-Medina relating how a donkey fell ill from being beaten and having to carry too many people. Such treatment was not considered appropriate, however, and many sources record owners caring for their sick donkeys.[304]

Horse (Equus caballus)

There is little evidence, written or archaeological, for the presence of the domesticated horse in Egypt before ca. 1800 BC. Archaeological evidence strongly implies that domestication occurred earlier elsewhere. Three wild races of the species *Equus caballus* have survived until fairly recently. These are Przewalski's horse, a native of Mongolia, of which only a few specimens have survived; the tarpan, which became extinct in the middle of the nineteenth century AD; and the forest wild horse, which survived in Poland until the eighteenth century AD.

The northerly distribution of these wild species suggests that horses were first tamed on the grass steppe-lands of Eurasia. One factor that makes it

8.3. Pairs of horses (above) and hinnies (below) pulling an Egyptian chariot. Tomb of Nebamun, Thebes, Dynasty XVIII

difficult to substantiate the site of early horse domestication is that the skeletons do not show morphological differences from wild horses. The earliest skeletal evidence relating to the domestication of the horse comes from the Ukraine (ca. 4000 BC), where they were being managed not as a beast of burden, but as a food source.[305]

The earliest horse remains in the Near East appear in the fourth millennium BC at Tali Iblis, Norsun-Tepe, and Chogha Mish, located on the periphery of Mesopotamia. The next series of finds come from the Old Elamite levels of Tepe Farukhabad, Iran (ca. 2200 BC), from the Early Bronze Age level of Arad in the northern Negev (ca. 2200-2000 BC), and from Fars, Iran (ca. 2000 BC). The first literary mention of the horse occurs in a text of Third Dynasty Ur (ca. 2100 BC) where the animal, apparently in a caravan, is described as a foreign ass. Even though it was in use in relative proximity to urban areas, its designation as "foreign" seems to support that, like the donkey, the horse originally served non-urban peoples.[306]

All available evidence suggests that the horse was adopted in Egypt sometime after the Hyksos invasion (ca.1730 BC). An Asiatic introduction for the horse is suggested by several words borrowed directly from west Semitic dialects. Terms for horse and especially for chariots came into the Egyptian language in concordance with the expansion of the Egyptian empire northward into Asia. Regrettably, no evidence has been recovered related to horse training. The Egyptians more than likely based their handling practices on the established skills of the Hyksos and other Asiatics. The earliest literary evidence of horses in Egypt comes from texts (ca. 1580 BC) referring to the war of liberation from the Hyksos, and the earliest remains date to the Middle Kingdom fortress at Buhen. Microscopic studies of the animal's teeth suggest, however, that it was controlled with a bit; a practice that postdates the Middle Kingdom. The earliest representations appear at the beginning of the Dynasty XVIII (ca. 1570 BC).[307]

The ancient word for horse was "*htr*" meaning "yoked animal." Ancient Egyptian horses were fairly small compared to today's riding breeds. The adult horse skeleton recovered from Buhen measured only 125 cm high at the shoulders. The Buhen horse, however, may have been somewhat smaller than the average. On the basis of the yoke measurements of surviving chariots, average shoulder height of an Egyptian horse was closer to 135 cm. This compares fairly well to some historic Bedouin horses, but remains smaller than the average Arabian, which stands about 145 cm. Interestingly, on the basis of osteological features, the Buhen horse is thought to be of Arabian stock. Although horse breeding was known in Egypt, it was never a very successful endeavor and most animals were imported, either by trade or as spoils of war, from Syria or elsewhere. The Karnak annals, listing booty captured by Tuthmosis III at Megiddo, specify: 2041 horses, 191 young animals, both male and female, six stallions, and a number of foals.

The ideal horse, based on those produced through systematic breeding was elegant and swift with a long body and slender legs; speed rather than power clearly was the main objective. A light two-wheeled chariot, requiring minimal muscular effort, was almost always pulled by a pair of horses (fig. 8.3). Egyptian chariots originally had four-spoked wheels with a center of gravity above the axles. This type of chariot predominated into Dynasty XVIII when it was replaced by chariots with a six-spoke wheel and a center of gravity (the rider) situated between the horse and axle. Egyptians took great pride in their chariots and horses and are often depicted riding to battle or hunting. Chariot races, however, were never held, although excavations near Malkata on the Theban West bank have uncovered a straight stretch of swept desert (4 km long by 120 m wide) representing what may have been a training course, where such skills as speed and maneuverability were learned and honed.

Horse-back riding does not seem to have been commonly practiced in Egypt and only a few scenes show mounted horsemen. In most cases the scenes represent foreigners, but at least two cases show Egyptians. In both cases, however, the riders were horse groomers. On the basis of textual evidence, riding horseback might have been regarded as undignified. Prince Tefnakhte of Sais (Dynasty XXV) is described fleeing from his conqueror mounted on his horse, having never asked for his chariot. This was thought to be a less than noble retreat.

Although the upper classes may have possessed some horses, most seem to have been state property, royal equids usually being distinguished by plumed head-dresses and individual names. Apart from breaking-in and training, horses were invariably confined to stables, where they received daily rations of grass and forage. The state barracks excavated at Amarna were designed to house up to 200 animals. The chariots here played a role in the Household Brigade, both as a honor guard and as police. A letter relates how "the horse teams of my lord are well: I have their allotted measure mixed before them, and their grooms bring the best grass from the marshes. I assign grass to them daily and give ointment to rub them every month, and their chiefs of the stable trot them every ten days." The leisure lifestyle of these well esteemed animals thus contrasts sharply with that of the valued but exploited donkey.[308]

Mules and Hinnies

A mule is the offspring of a male donkey with a female horse; a hinny is the offspring of a female donkey and a male horse. The hybrids can of course be either male or female and the sexual organs, male and female, are fully developed, although the animals are almost always sterile. In the ancient world as at the present day, the production of mules was easier to manage and more successful than the production of hinnies.

Mules and hinnies have certain consistent identifying characteristics. In general, the head and front end of the hybrids are like the sire; the hindquarters are like the dam. Mules were rare in ancient Egypt, perhaps because horses were much more valuable than donkeys and a hybrid would be worth less than a horse. Additionally, the foals were sterile. A New Kingdom scene depicting two teams of equids (fig. 8.3) might present a unique representation of a pair of hinnies. The upper dark pair of equines represent standard horses, but the lower white pair display a number of subtle hinny features including tail, mane, and a stripe over the shoulder. Mules would not possess the characteristic shoulder stripe nor would the wild Przewalski horse, which would also have possessed a full tail rather than the nearly naked tail depicted in the scene.[309]

Camel (*Camelus dromedarius*)

Camels are even-toed ungulates that fall, physiologically and evolutionarily, somewhere between pigs and true ruminants (e.g., sheep, goats, and cattle). Camels differ from true ruminants in a number of important ways. First, camel dentition bears traces of central incisors in the upper jaw (maxilla and premaxilla) and the third incisor is a well-developed canine-like tusk. In addition, camels possess true canine teeth and the first premolars also appear canine-like and are separated from the cheek teeth by a large gap (i.e., diastema). The second distinctive difference between camels and other ruminants centers on the musculature of the hind limbs. In camels the legs are very long and are attached to the body at the top of the thigh only; in horses and cattle the legs are attached by skin and muscle from the knee upwards. This means that when a camel lies down, it can rest on its knees with its legs tucked under its body in quite a different way than cattle. Third, camel feet do not have functional hooves, rather the toe bones are embedded in a broad cutaneous pad on which the animal walks. Fourth and finally, although camels do ruminate, the stomach has a different construction from that of the true ruminants.[310]

There are two extant Old World camels, the two-humped bactrian camel (*Camelus bactrianus*) and the Arabian or one-humped dromedary camel (*Camelus dromedarius*). The dromedary occurs from North Africa to the Caspian Sea and from Arabia to northwest India. The bactrian camel ranges from the Caspian Sea to Manchuria. The bactrian and dromedary are regarded as different species, but a few authors consider them geographical races of a single species. Proponents of this view cite that osteological differences are restricted mainly to the limb bones, which are shorter in the bactrian camel, and the obvious second hump of the bactrian, which is said to be actually present in vestigial form in the embryonic and adult dromedary. Furthermore, both camels have the same diploid chromosome number (2n=70) and produce viable hybrids; female offspring are fertile, but males often are sterile. In Turkey, female dromedaries and male bactrian camels are intentionally bred to produce a hybrid considered to be more vigorous than either of the parent species.[311]

The Arabian dromedary camel appears to be completely domesticated. There are no living populations of wild one-humped camels, but there is some evidence from the classical literature that they existed in western Asia in the first millennium BC. Wild camels live in the Gobi Desert today, but these camels have two humps and probably represent the wild progenitor of the bactrian camel or are feral forms. The cause of the disappearance of wild camels perhaps lies in the desiccation of their natural habitats or over-predation by humans.[312]

Neither species of camel appears to be much changed by domestication; while under human control, many have been allowed to breed freely and live a life similar to their wild predecessors. Camels, as a group, reproduce and mature slowly. Female camels of northern Arabia are not bred until their sixth year and then only once every two years. The female will give milk for 11 to 15 months and yield one to seven liters per day depending on the season and type of forage. Free-ranging camels are said to be much healthier than those that are constrained, and many domestic camels in the Sahara are allowed to roam free in a semi-wild state for four to five months of each year. Because camels will maintain a home-range, will travel along familiar trails, and will return to wells with which they are familiar, the bedouin can keep track of their herds.

The camel's natural tendency to conserve water is legendary and is what makes it so well-adapted as a beast of burden in the desert. Reducing water loss, rather than storing it, is the key to the camel's success. Camel body temperature is not fixed as in most mammals, but fluctuates (i.e., poikiothermic). In daytime it rises, allowing heat to be stored and reducing the camels need to sweat; at night the body temperature decreases and heat is lost. Camels do not need to drink water during the winter when green pasture is abundant; and even in the most extreme summer conditions, it needs to drink only once every five days. Murray recorded one of his camels going 128 days without water. In contrast, cattle must drink every day, sheep and donkeys must have water every second day, and goats, every third. A female camel (ca. 400 kg) can drink up to 120 liters of water in one draught and a male (ca. 500 kg) as much as 150 liters. In turn, the camel can sustain a 30 per cent loss of body weight through dehydration without ill effect; in comparison, a loss of only 12 per cent is fatal to humans.[313]

Today, Egypt is a camel-consuming and not a camel-producing country. Although ecologically the camel is less well adapted to Delta conditions than elsewhere in Egypt, and mortality rates may reach as high as 25 per cent in some years, they are more numerous in the Delta than anywhere else in the Nile Valley. Four camel breeds can be distinguished in Egypt: the Sudani, Maghrabi, Fellahi, and a cross between the two latter called the Mowalled. The Fellahi and the Mowalled are the two common camels of the Nile Valley.[314]

The Fellahi of the Delta is a large heavy baggage camel, with a well proportioned head, broad face, and wide eyes. The neck is thick and not strongly curved, the hump large and the legs are strong and heavy with thick broad pads. The body is covered with soft hair, commonly white or sand-colored, rarely fawn. The Fellahi is not usually bred in the Delta, but is imported mostly from Upper Egypt. Accustomed to green feed, it lacks stamina and is unfit for desert work. The Mowalled is a heavy camel, fit for farm and desert work. It, however, lacks uniformity in morphology and color.[315]

Origins

Because so little is known about the wild progenitors of the Old World camel and little difference exists between the domestic and wild form, it is very difficult if not impossible to determine from osteological remains when and where camels were first brought under human control. Consequently, archaeological context must be used to ascertain the status of camel remains. The earliest evidence for domestic camels that has so far been documented comes from Iran, where camel dung has been identified from the site of Shari Sholhta and dated to 2600 BC. The excavators believe that the camels at this site were domesticated and that they were more likely to be the bactrian that the Arabian species. For environmental reasons, Mikesell believes Arabia is the center for the domestication of the dromedary. Originally, camels were probably used as pack animals along the southern coast of Arabia; in Egypt and the Levant, the donkey was the main beast of burden. However, once desert trade routes became important avenues for the transport of goods, such as spices, the camel's superiority in stamina and load capabilities made it "the ship of the desert."[316]

The Camel in Ancient Egypt

Because the camel was known in Arabia and Palestine from at least the 1700 BC, and probably much earlier, it is strange to find that evidence for the camel in Egypt is scanty and inconsistent. The scarcity of pictorial representations, given the proximity of Egypt to Arabia, is surprising, but even more so is the virtual absence of literary references. In fact, there was no Egyptian word for camel. Nevertheless, there is hard evidence to demonstrate that the dromedary was present in the Nile Valley from time to time. The most convincing argument comes from the Dynasty I cemetery at Helwan where vertebrae and ribs of a camel were found situated in association with a human grave. The materials are now in the Dokki museum and have been positively identified as camel (fig. 8.4). Indirect evidence includes a drawing of what may be a dromedary on an Amration pot of Predynastic age, which may be the earliest artistic representation of the camel, a camel-shaped receptacle of Dynasty I date found at Abusir el-Melek, and a Dynasty I ceramic head from Abydos, which seems to be of a camel.[317]

8.4. Remains of a camel recorded from Dynasty I Helwan. Agricultural Museum, Dokki.

Indirect evidence for the camel, although sporadic, does exist in later periods. In the Dynasty III (or early Dynasty IV) gypsum mine of Umm es-Sawan (Fayum), Caton-Thompson and Gardner found a cord, a little more than one meter long, made of camel hair. In a Dynasty XIX tomb near Asyut (Dier Fifeh) a ceramic figurine of a camel carrying water jugs was recovered and a similar figurine was found near Benha (Dynasty XIX).[318] It was not until 665 BC that camels reached Egypt in larger numbers. The introduction was associated with the Assyrian and later Persian (525 BC) conquerors. Two hundred years later (331 BC), camels seem to have been relatively common.

On the basis of this evidence, albeit circumstantial, it seems the camel never was an integral part the of the economic structure of pre-Roman Egypt. Because Egypt's main source of heavy transit was the Nile, there was no real need for a large beast of burden. The donkey ably served the needs of most short hauls. In the Ptolemaic period, as the result of the greatly increased commercial relations with the East, the dromedary became more important because it could carry a heavier load and was more water efficient than the donkey. Under Ptolemy Philadelphus (285 to 247 BC) trade routes were established across the Eastern Desert, linking roads with a chain of cisterns for the benefit of camel-merchants. By the beginning of the Roman period, the camel attained its modern position in Egypt.[319]

The Cat (*Felis silvestris*)

Even though the cat has been closely associated with humans for at least 4000 years, it is surprising how little difference there is between the wild and domesticated forms. This is because, although the cat is a fully domesticated animal, its breeding is seldom controlled by humans and consequently, like a wild animal, is subject more to selective pressures imposed by its environment than to artificial selection imposed by humans. This makes it relatively easy to recognize *Felis sylvestris* as the progenitor of the domestic cat, but at the same time the lack of easily definable domestic traits makes it difficult to trace its geographic origins through either morphological or genetic analysis.

In the wild and domestic forms, *Felis sylvestris* must be considered a highly successful carnivore. The wild cat ranges across Africa, Asia, and Europe and, like most mammals with expansive ranges, it has evolved a great many geographical races that are adapted to local conditions of climate and environment. The physical appearance of the wild cat conforms to Allens' law. It is solidly built with thick fur, a rather short face, ears and tail in the northern cold latitudes; in southerly areas like North Africa it is fine-limbed with a long face, long pointed ears, a long tail, and short sleek coat. Examples from the two extremes of this cline are so different that until recent years they were considered separate species: *Felis sylvestris* and the African/Arabian *Felis libyca*. Today, the two forms are considered subspecies of *Felis sylvestris*.[320]

In a study of the population genetics of the domestic cat, Todd examined the three most common variations of the wild color pattern. He suggests that these variations, which arose as mutations in populations of early domestic cats, are related to other traits that are subject to the different selective pressures of domestication. The three variations of the striped wild cat are the blotched tabby, the non-agouti (usually all black), and sex-linked orange (marmalade) tabby, which includes the tortoise and calico. Roughly, one-third of the world's domestic cats are tabbies. The striped domestic tabby, in general, possesses a coat that is commonly seen in the European and the African wild cats. That is, like the wild cat, they have a coat that is blotchy grey with black, tawny-ocherous and lighter-colored spots and stripes.[321]

Todd sampled populations of cats on the basis of these color traits in cities throughout Europe, North Africa, and western Asia and defined their modern distributions. The distributions of the various common pelage colors actually represent a complex set of adaptations that the cat has undergone while shifting from one ecological niche to another. By moving from a wild and predatory lifestyle to a domesticated and subsidized one, the cat has adapted to a new niche, the urban habitat. In this process it experienced a new set of interspecies and intraspecies relations and pelage pattern and color change are examples of the adaptation to the human environment.

The distribution of the three color types is important in that it relates to the time and place of the domestic cat's origin. The basic assumption is that mutant color forms became established because human interference superseded natural selection and created conditions conducive to the survival of cats with coat colors different from that of the wild type. If the centers of origin and relative periods of time can be established for each of the common mutant pelage types, then some inferences can be drawn concerning the earliest phases of the cat's domestication.

Of the three common mutant pelage patterns and colors (the blotched tabby, the non-agouti, and sex-linked orange tabby), the most common type in most parts of the world is the non-agouti. Agouti or tabby coloration (so named because the agouti, a South American rodent, best exemplifies the suit of characteristics) is a basic mammalian condition. The agouti pelage is due primarily to the distribution of melanin in the hair shaft in such a way as to produce bands of reduced pigmentation below the tip of the hair. The result is a salt and pepper or brindle pattern. A simple recessive mutation eliminates the banding, creating hairs that are more or less uniformly pigmented along their entire length. The all-black coat is the most common manifestation of the non-agouti type.

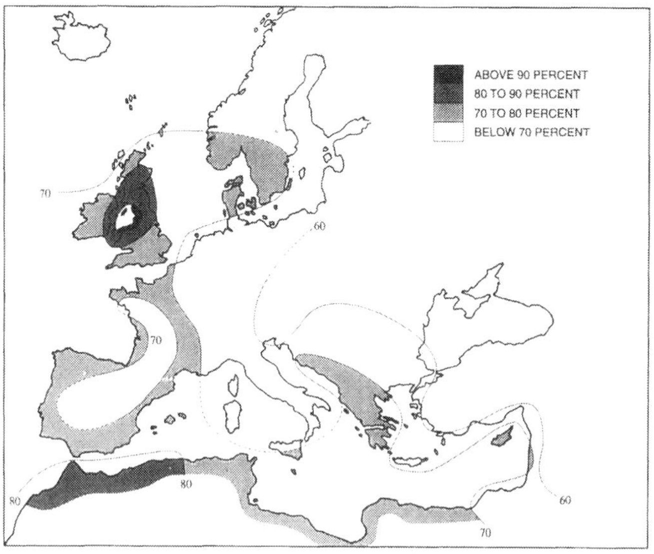

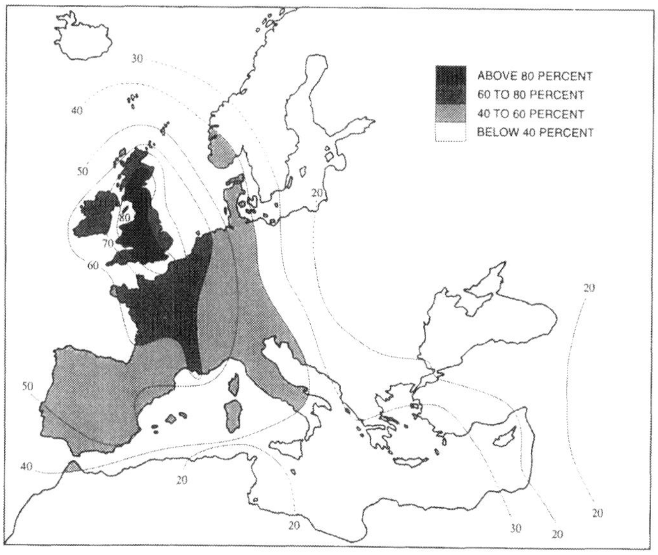

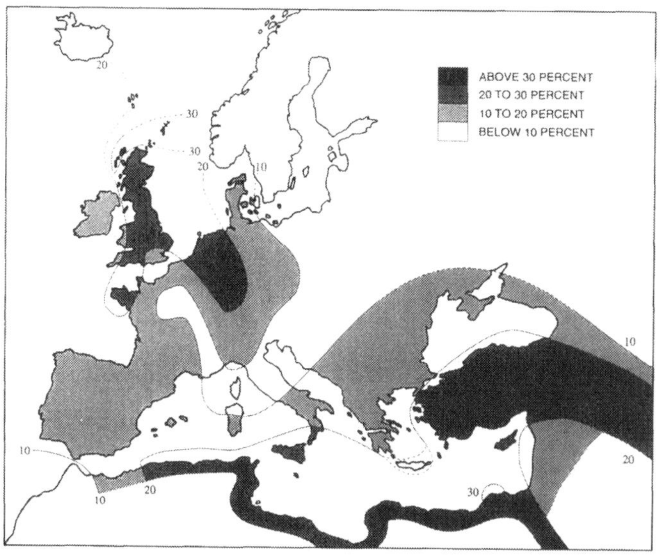

The current distribution of cats
8.5. (top) The non-agouti cat.
8.6. (centre) The blotched tabby.
8.7. (bottom) The orange sex-linked alelle-the-orange tabby.

Most wild mammals are agouti, but most domesticated mammals are non-agouti. Because the non-agouti trait is recessive, these populations represent restricted breeding populations with a high incidence of cats carrying the recessive "domestic" gene.[322]

More than 150 surveys have revealed that the distribution and incidence of occurrence of the non-agouti mutant is closely correlated with urban habitats and thus would likely have evolved in and spread through urban areas. This is supported by the distribution of non-agouti types shown in figure 8.5. The highest areas of incidence occur in Britain and northwest Africa. The high frequencies were created, according to Todd, by the initial seeding of these areas with cats of the non-agouti type. That is, although all pelage types were introduced into a given area there was a higher percentage of non-agouti cats than one would expect from a natural wild population. And, because the cats interbred with other urban cats the incidence of the non-agouti gene increased. Therefore, each time people ventured to establish new urban centers, they took with them an increasingly more concentrated sample of cats adapted to urban environments (i.e., non-agouti cats). The first steps in this process were the Greek, Phoenician, and later Roman colonizations of the Mediterranean region and beyond. For example, domestic cats were quite prevalent in Roman Britain. That it was kept as a domestic pet seems evident because its remains have been found in Roman villages and its footprints are preserved in numerous tiles, across which they must have walked when the tiles were laid out to dry. Cats in such proximity to human activities suggest familiarity and perhaps some level of bonding. Unfortunately, the fur from recovered animals is not preserved so the data on their color is lacking.

Because of its apparent selective advantage in urban areas, the non-agouti is the domestic form that can most easily be traced. However, it probably was not the earliest type of domestic cat. In Egypt, cat skeletons are known from Predynastic cemeteries, indicating that they were already tamed, fed, and kept in what was then almost exclusively an agrarian environment. Even in the New Kingdom, Egypt could not be considered urbanized. Because the archaeological record in Egypt suggests that domestic cats were relatively common throughout agricultural areas as far back as the Predynastic, the non-agouti seems most likely to have evolved from an already domesticated form.

The selective advantage of the second pelage type, the blotched tabby, is uncertain. The type is currently spreading at a rapid rate throughout the world, even to remote areas such as Tasmania. Because it is still spreading at such a fast rate and seems to be displacing the wild color type, it is thought to be a more recent mutation than either the orange tabby or non-agouti. The blotched tabby's highest incidence of occurrence is centered in Britain and France, and it is seems to be spreading to other areas from this focus (fig. 8.6). This leaves the sex-linked orange trait as the best possible avenue of exploration into early genetic change in the domestic cat.[323]

Sex-linked orange is a mutant color responsible for a variety of well-known pelage types (phenotypes), depending on the sex and the genetic make-up of the individual carrying the gene. The most familiar examples are the cats commonly called orange tabby, tortoiseshell, and calico. Tortoiseshell and calico cats are almost always female, because the phenotype depends on heterozygosity. That is, the orange mutation is located on the female, or X chromosome. Because a female has two X chromosomes, she can carry the orange gene on one X chromosome and the non-orange gene on the other X chromosome and simultaneously express both orange and non-orange. Because males have only one X chromosome, the other one being Y, they can only express orange or non-orange, but not both at once. The relevant point is that on the basis of genetic formulae, the frequency of cats expressing the sex-linked-orange allele should be about one in four or 25 per cent of the population. And this level is not exceeded anywhere in the world with one notable exception, the Nile Delta. The Delta, with a figure reaching 36 per cent or greater, has the highest incidence of sex-linked orange cats anywhere in the world (fig. 8.7).

In those areas where the basic level of equilibrium (i.e., 25 per cent) has not been reached, the mutant orange allele is probably a more recent introduction and its incidence will be expected over time to increase. Where the incidence of the allele is higher than 25 per cent, some disturbance to the selection process has occurred. The underlying assumption is that either directly or indirectly, human-induced conditions have selected for this allele, allowing it to reach levels above the expected norm. If Todd's assumption is correct – that the area displaying the highest incidence of an allele is the ancestral area from where the "established" form has or is disseminating – then characteristics of pelage color combined with archaeological and historical data allow for some interesting speculation concerning the origins of the cat.[324]

Origins

On the basis of archaeological evidence, the earliest occurrence for the domestic cat is in the fertile crescent (Southwest Asia-Levant) and Nile Valley where the cultivation of plants first became established. Cat remains have been found in prehistoric Jericho (ca. 7000 BC), India (ca. 4000 BC) and at Badari (ca. 4000 BC) in Egypt. It is difficult, however, to ascertain whether these finds represent wild or domestic forms. Cat skeletons have also been recovered from Predynastic cemeteries; Petrie recovered 150 cats from Giza. Although measurements of the Giza skulls indicated that at least two were wild swamp cats (*Felis chaus*), the others were *Felis sylvestris*.[325]

8.8. (top) An orange tabby on a hunting trip with his master. Tomb of Nebamun, Thebes, Dynasty XVIII.
8.9. (bottom) A sarcophagus of the beloved pet cat, 'Tamyt'. Memphis, Dynasty XVIII

Whether the Predynastic finds represent fully domesticated animals or simply tamed wild cats cannot be ascertained from the skeletal remains. Nevertheless, it seems likely, given the numbers represented in the cemeteries, that cats were quite common in the area, suggesting that they were either domesticates or were tolerated and going through the initial stages of domestication. That Predynastic agrarian communities seem to be a focus of initial domestication should come as no surprise, because the cat is well-noted for its hunting prowess and would not only have been naturally attracted to agricultural areas by an increased rodent population, but would have been beneficial to the early farmer in the control of such pests. This would have created a true symbiotic relationship between cat and agriculturalist. Hunter-gatherer or transient horticulturists would have little need for the cat, and because the cat is territorial, it would not be a willing companion to traveling groups.

The non-agouti, which has a selective advantage in urban areas, would not seem a likely candidate for an early domestic form based in an agrarian environment, but would have likely arisen with the onset of urbanization. The blotched tabby with its focus of highest incidence in northern Europe from which it is still rapidly expanding is most likely a recent form. Based on the fact that the orange allele has reached (or nearly so) a level of equilibrium over much of its current range; that its highest level of incidence is in Egypt; and that it has an even pattern of high incidence around the Eastern Mediterranean and North Africa, it is very likely that the orange tabby allele originated and is spreading from Egypt and represents the first observable genetic change resulting from human involvement and thus possibly the first identifiable domestic cat.

Further evidence for an Egyptian or at least North African origin can be gleaned from skeletal, linguistic, and pictorial data. Although it is difficult to separate the skeletal remains of domestic from wild cats, archaeological provenience and some morphological characteristics make it possible to present some general statements. The anterior and posterior edges of the first molar of the lower jaw, for example, rises more steeply in the African wild cat and domestic cat than in the European wild cat, suggesting that the African cat is the progenitor of the domestic form. Linguistic evidence also implies a North African Berber or a Nubian origin for the word cat (*kadts*) and the subspecies epithet *cattus*. Although artistic evidence for the cat is lacking in the Old Kingdom, during the Middle and New Kingdoms, cats are depicted in a number of circumstances; usually under the chair of their master or in fowling scenes (fig. 8.8). It is important to note that 24 scenes displaying cats were studied for this volume. All cats depicted were tabbies and in those scenes where the original color still existed, the cats were orange tabbies.[326] Inspection of mummified cats with some evidence of pelage remains also show a high incidence of orange tabbies.

The primary role of the cat in Egypt was as a mouser, which, as already noted, was an important function in an agriculturally oriented economy. Outside of this role, cats served as pets and are often portrayed in fowling scenes where they are shown flushing birds. Contrary to some sources, cats were probably not trained to retrieve stunned birds, although some cats do display an innate retrieving behavior. Rather, if present at all during such hunts, the cat's natural stalking instincts or simply its presence were more than likely used to flush fowl for the hunter. The most likely explanation for the presence of cats on such scenes is that they are considered part of the household and are shown in the company of family members.

The cat as a pet was, as in today's society, much loved and at death was at times buried with full ritual as if it were a human (fig. 8.9). Herodotus related that when a cat died the owners were accustomed to shave their eyebrows and to transport their former pet to Bubastis, the city of the cat goddess Bastet for burial. Evidence that cats were buried with the same accord as humans comes from Abydos, where a small Dynasty XII pyramidal tomb contained a cruciform chamber housing 17 cat skeletons. The excavator (Petrie) postulated that a row of rough little pots in small recesses once contained milk, thus representing a rare example of a funerary offering to an animal. More elaborate is an Amarna sarcophagus that had been fashioned for a beloved pet. The offering formula describes the cat as 'Osiris, the Lady Cat', and it is depicted sitting next to an offering table with a feline-headed shwabti, just as if the cat were deceased member of the family.[327]

The Dog

It is generally accepted that the dog was one of the earliest, if not the first, animal domesticated. It could even be said that the dog adopted humans, rather than the reverse. The wolf, (*Canis lupus*) is considered the single ancestor to all modern dogs. This is, however, a debated issue. Since the late 19th century, several other members of the genus *Canis* have been suggested as having played a role in the dog's ancestry. At the head of this list is the golden jackal, *Canis aureus*, believed by Darwin and later by Lorenz to share ancestry with the wolf. In addition, the dingo (*Canis dingo*) and the North American coyote (*C. latrans*) have also been considered possible ancestors. It has even been suggested that the dog and wolf existed separately in the wild, prior to domestication, and that wolves and dogs are related through a common ancestor. This latter position is, however, unsupported paleontologically.[328]

On the basis of several considerations, the case for the wolf as progenitor of the dog is the strongest among the known canids. First, the social behavior and communication systems of wolves and dogs are quite similar. Although wolves exhibit a wide range of behavior, they are, in general more highly social than jackals or coyotes. Second, wolf society is structured in a hierarchical fashion with social relations established and maintained by vocal, facial, and postural communication of dominance and submission. In fact, the patterns of social behavior in wolves and humans are remarkable for their mutual intelligibility. Third, wolves and dogs vocalize in a similar fashion, which differs from that of jackals, and wolves held in captivity are known to bark.[329]

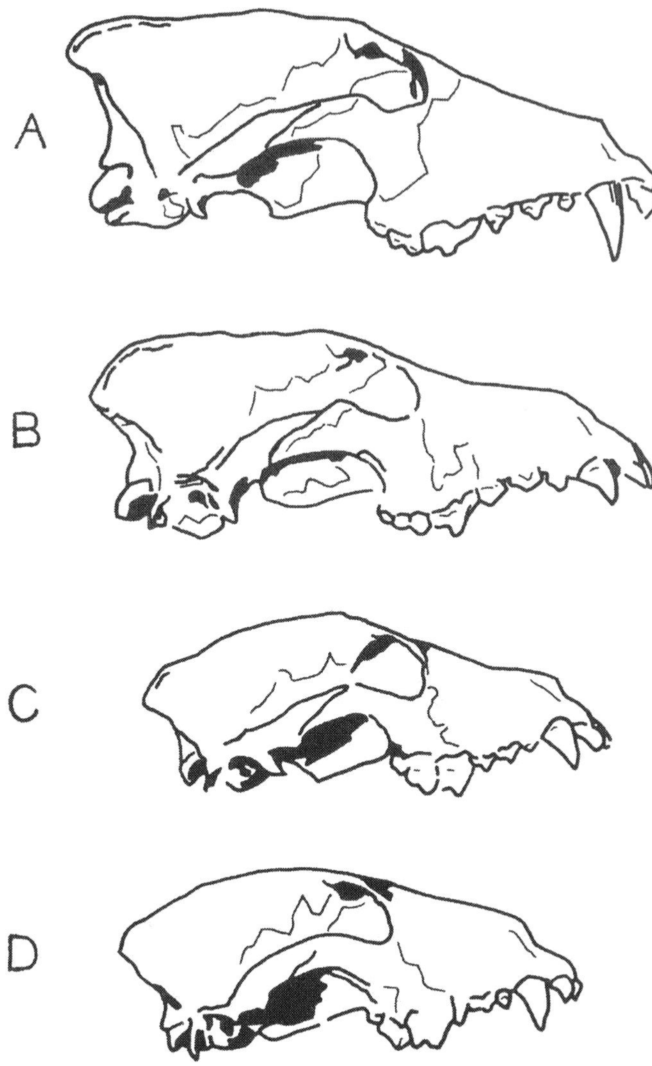

8.10. Four wolf skulls: A. a wild wolf, B. wolf captured as a pup and raised in captivity, C. a wolf born in captivity, D. second generation captive wolf

The argument for a single ancestor for the dog is supported by strong morphological similarities in the cranium and teeth, which in all dogs of all breeds remain fundamentally wolf-like as opposed to jackal-like. Additional criteria have been used to further relegate the jackal, the only serious contender to the wolf for the dog's origin, to a lesser status. Foremost among these criteria is the fact that jackals have a different chromosome count (2n= 74) than dogs, coyotes, and wolves (2n=78) suggesting that they are not as closely related to the dog as the wolf and coyote. In addition, *Canis aureus* is generally smaller than most forms of wolf. Because reduction in size almost always accompanies the initial phases of domestication, the number of early breeds of dogs lárger than the wild jackal make it difficult to consider it a likely progenitor. Additionally, in domestic animals with a body size similar to that of their wild ancestor, the brain is generally proportionally smaller. This phenomenon is consistent between wolf and dog, but does not hold true between jackal and dog; the jackal has a smaller brain than the dog. Another significant difference exists between the skulls of the smaller subspecies of jackals, which tend to have strongly convex profiles, and those of the smallest dogs, which have concave profiles.[330]

Attempts to establish the origin of the dog through skeletal morphology is, however, not without its problems. The genetic similarity between dogs, wolves, and other canids is mirrored in their overall morphology. Although some morphological features, particularly in the skull, can be employed in identification, such criteria are based mostly on the robusticity of muscle attachments, tooth and aperture size, and skull shape. These characteristics are qualitative measures that vary from animal to animal and from area to area. Many examples exist where the remains of dogs and wolves are so similar that it is difficult or nearly impossible to separate them. Overall size has traditionally been used as the main criterion to separate wolf from dog, but there is a considerable overlap in size between the different canids, rendering such criterion somewhat questionable. For example, the length of the base of the skull in the wolf varies from 172 to 236 mm, while jackal skulls measure from about 148 mm to 200 mm.[331]

Although evidence for the wolf as progenitor of the dog, on the basis of morphology, is strongly suggestive, it is not conclusive. For example, one of the strongest criteria for establishing a population as an independent species is reproductive isolation from other forms. Dogs, wolves, and coyotes as well as dogs and jackals are interfertile and produce viable offspring; only isolation of the dog by humans keeps potential cross-breeding at a minimum. Yet, each is considered a distinct species. The chromosome count for the dog, wolf, and the coyote is 78 (the dog actually ranges from 2n=78 to 2n=80). Thus the African Basenji, the European beagle, the Great Dane, the Chihuahua, and wolves represent closely related forms that are theoretically able to cross-breed. In fact, the interfertility between wolves and coyotes has created a controversy within the United States about the possible origin of the endangered red wolf. Studies have suggested that the red wolf may in fact be a coyote-wolf hybrid, rendering the protected status of the red wolf as an "endangered species" questionable. What this degree of interfertility suggests is that there is a considerably closer relationship between canids than would be suggested by the current taxonomic nomenclature. That viable hybrids occur as populations in North America suggests that some wolf populations in Asia, Africa and Europe, likewise might represent hybrid populations with close affinities to the domestic dog.

Perhaps the strongest evidence in support of the wolf as progenitor is the recent biochemical analyses investigating the genetic affinities between canids. These studies analyze DNA, in particular, mitochondrial DNA, which is inherited only from the mother. Once a female reproduces, evidence of her parentage is passed on to future generations, intact, through her DNA. As a result, these molecules can be used to trace the evolution of species over hundreds and in some cases thousands of years. These studies were used in North America to trace the descent of the red wolf, and in the case of the wolf and dog, they demonstrate that at a molecular level, the dog is more similar to the wolf than to any other canid.[332]

If these molecular studies are indeed valid and, as has been generally assumed, the wolf is the ancestor of all dogs, the question that often comes to mind is how the dog can vary so much in size and general appearance? The answer to this question may lie in the current definitions of species, in our vernacular terminology and perceptions of what constitutes a wolf, and in the genetic plasticity of the wolf. The latter directly bears on its adaptability to different environments and ultimately to its overall morphology.

First, the species concept that had been adopted by many biologists actually possesses two philosophical extremes. One side views species as clusters of organisms possessing uniquely shared traits. Opponents, representing the other side, believe species are isolated groups of interbreeding organisms. Adherence to the former definition lends credence to separate species designations for dogs, wolves, coyotes, and the rest, but by strictly adhering to the latter definition, one might lump dogs, wolves, and coyotes under a single species because they do interbreed and produce not only viable offspring but breeding populations of offspring such as the red wolf.

Second, by stating that the dog is a descendant of the wolf, Europeans and North Americans automatically picture the large northern wolf as the ancestral form and exclude other more gracile forms. Wolves are very adaptable and a number of different geographical races encompassing all sizes can (or could) be found throughout the world. The larger northern varieties as well as the smaller southern forms all, most likely, contributed to the genetic pool of the modern dog. There is no reason why different breeds of dog could not have evolved from different geographical races (subspecies) of wolf. Thus, dogs could have differed significantly in size and color very early in their developmental history and, given the adaptability of the wolf, further morphological changes induced by human selection rapidly evolved.

The speed at which morphological change can occur in captive wolves is remarkably rapid. Wolfgramm noted significant differences between the cranium of wild wolves and wolves born and raised in captivity. The skulls of captive wolves were shorter, broader, and had a higher forehead than those of wolves matured in wild surroundings. This trend was even more pronounced in second generation captive-born wolves. Also, the facial musculature and the crests and ridges to which the muscles attach developed considerably less in wolves reared in captivity than in the wild forms, although the degree of divergence largely depended on diet. These changes in cranial conformation (which are not restricted to wolves bred in captivity but apply also to jackals and foxes) were accompanied by changes in the size and position of the teeth: the canines and carnassials grow smaller and the gaps disappear.[333]

Figure 8.10 visually illustrates the changes that occur. Here four skulls are presented: (a) a wild wolf; (b) a wild wolf captured as a pup and raised in captivity; (c) a wolf born in captivity; and (d) a wolf born of parents that were born and raised in captivity. The differences in the skulls are striking. The wild wolf and the cub raised in captivity differ mostly in size and robusticity of the skull, which is probably a reflection of lifestyle and diet. Significant differences in skull shape can be seen, however, in the wolf that was born in captivity: the cranium is more vaulted, the teeth show crowding and the sagittal crest is markedly smaller. The second generation wolf skull appears to look like that of a large dog. Its teeth are not only crowded but, in fact, are overcrowded and turned, the skull is vaulted and the sagittal crest much reduced. These changes, which in effect occurred by the second generation of captivity, illustrate how quickly various breeds of dogs could have developed.[334]

Origins

If the wolf is indeed the ancestor of the dog, the most reasonable scenario for the origins of canid domestication would follow two main premises. First, human hunter-gatherers and wolves existed in overlapping niches and were accustomed to contact with each other; both were social species that hunted for many of the same prey items. Wolves as opportunistic scavengers may have learned to be aware of human hunting activities and to scavenge from human kills and humans may have even learned to do the same with wolves. Second, somewhere, and perhaps more than once, some young wolf pups were found and adopted by humans. Why such an adoption occurred is a matter of speculation. A reasonable suggestion frequently made is that pet keeping is an extension of our nurturing instincts and served as the motivation behind adoption. This position, however, can only be empirically tested after considerably more information is gathered. Although difficult to relegate our canine friends to such a status, another important reason for adoption could have been as a source of food. All domestic animals, with the exception of the cat, entered the cultural environment as a source of food. Horses, cattle, pigs, sheep, goats and dog are all herd (pack) animals, and all are known as food items in extant cultures.[335]

More to the point are the consequences of adoption. Numerous studies have shown that wolf pups taken at an early age and reared by humans are easily tamed and socialized. According to Scott and Fuller the most crucial social bonds of a dog's or wolf's life are formed when the animal is three to eight weeks old. Wolf pups adopted and socialized by humans during this period will form their primary social bonds with members of their "human pack." Although adult animals can be socialized, it is much more difficult with advancing age.[336]

This characteristic of social development among wolves provides an efficient mechanism for the integration of wolves into human society. The remarkable compatibility between humans and wolves in overall social organization and communication systems made wolves especially well suited for domestic life with humans. Of course, some individuals would not possess the necessary temperament to fit into a social setting with dominant humans. Wolves exhibit a wide range or variability in temperament and behavior, and only animals predisposed to a submissive temperament or capable of learning a subordinate role to humans would have been tolerated in human society.[337]

In terms of evolutionary fitness, an adopted wolf's options for contributing offspring to future generations were limited. Individuals whose temperament prohibited their successful integration into human society would likely have been disposed of. If an occasional wolf left the human group as an adult to return to the wild, it could probably survive, but its chances of reproducing successfully would be slim. Wild wolves are not likely to accept unrelated outsiders into their pack, and breeding opportunities are limited by social regulations within the pack. Therefore, for an adopted wolf to contribute to future generations it had to fit into human society and, having been raised by humans, remain there. With that, the domestic relationship that produced dogs from wolves was underway. However, adoption and rearing of tame wolves does not in and of itself define a new species.[338]

As a new species, the dog had certain developed affinities towards a particular niche that allowed it to be evolutionary successful. Wild wolves are carnivorous. In most regions presently inhabited by wolves one or two large ungulate species constitute the principle prey items. For example, deer serve as the main prey animal in many temperate environments and elk, caribou, and moose fill this role in arctic or subarctic regions. However, a variety of smaller animals such as mice, rabbits, and birds are also occasionally consumed. As wolf pups are weaned, their diet shifts to meat regurgitated by one or both parents. Eventually the juveniles are taken to kill locations or rendezvous sites and eat unprocessed meat. As they mature, they begin to accompany adults on hunts and learn the skills necessary for survival.[339]

The early tame wolf grew up quite differently. Humans, the source of their food, are omnivorous and human hunter-gatherers were likely to provide a young wolf with a less than optimal diet. Tame wolves were probably subject to a diverse array of human food refuse, dominated by meat scraps and plant products, much of which may have been undesirable to humans. A wolf with a gourmet's palate probably stood little chance of survival. It is thus reasonable to expect that young wolves brought into captivity experienced nutritional stress during their early months.[340]

The survival skills learned by a maturing domestic wolf would be fundamentally different from those learned by a wild one. For the domestic wolf, there were no experiences available from which to learn the group hunting skills of their wild counterparts. Humans simply could not provide such an environment. Although some captive wolves learned to kill animals like deer, survival skills reinforced through learning experiences by the early tame wolf more likely involved scavenging and solicitation of food from humans. These activities would be supplemented by hunting of small animals (e.g., rabbits, rodents, etc.), whose capture did not require the more refined and usually group-oriented tactics employed in dispatching larger game. In short, their altered (omnivorous) diet continued into adulthood. Only individuals who learned to survive under these circumstances could contribute offspring to future "tame" generations.[341]

Among modern wolves, geographic variations in body size have also been correlated with variation in primary prey size. Schmitz and Lavigne have explicitly related recent changes in body size among canids in Ontario to shifts in modal prey size. This size-prey relationship extends to the domestic wolves and early dogs. Early tame wolves experienced a dietary shift from carnivore to omnivore. This shift, undoubtedly, entailed a dramatic decrease in prey size, probably coupled with an overall decrease of the available bulk of foodstuffs. Smaller tame wolves, with reduced caloric requirements, would have been at a distinct advantage under competition for such resources. Thus, because tame wolves had to also fill a subordinate position with physical survival dependent on the ability to eat scraps, hunt small animals, and solicit food from humans, a new niche was established and no single aspect of structure and physiology is more important than sheer body size in shaping an organism's niche. The dog was the form that filled the new niche.[342]

These human-induced circumstances left their mark on the tame wolf, especially during the early months of normally rapid growth. Tame wolves probably exhibited smaller adult sizes and were shorter in the facial region of the cranium with their large teeth consequently crowded into shorter jaws. As Clutton-Brock and Bökönyi have noted, the large teeth eventually became reduced in size as dog evolution proceeded during the Holocene. Although size reductions and changes in head shape could be based on purely developmental grounds, these morphological traits (i.e., head shape, tooth size, body size) are clearly inherited in modern dogs. Thus, although individually altered development might result in reduced adult body size, there are sound reasons for expecting smaller body size to have been a target of selection under conditions of abrupt and dramatic dietary change.[343]

The majority of the remains belonging to the earliest domestic dogs have been retrieved from archaeological sites in western Asia, although examples have also been found in North and South America, northwest Europe, Russia, and Japan, but nowhere are they common prior to the establishment of pastoral or farming activities.

The specimen most frequently cited as the earliest domestic dog is a partial mandible from Palegawra Cave, Iraq, reported by Turnbull and Reed. The specimen is associated with deposits that date to about 12,000 BP. Turnbull and Reed's (rather subjective) identification is based primarily on the relatively close spacing of the teeth and its overall small size compared to modern wolves of the region. The status of an early dog from Belt Cave in Iran, with a C-14 age of 11,480 +/-550 BP must await the result of a study by specialists in canid osteology.[344]

Elsewhere in the Near East, Davis and Valla have reported canid remains from Natufian (ca. 11,000 to 12,000 BC) contexts in Israel. The lengths of the two lower first molars were compared to corresponding lengths from a variety of recent wolves. The Natufian specimens are small compared to recent wolves and based on this, they were identified as domestic dogs. However, the Natufian specimens do fall close to the lower limits of wolf and one specimen (Ein Mallaha) clearly falls within the range of the smallest wolf (Arabian Peninsular Wolves). Although Davis and Valla's analysis is strengthened by consideration of the Pleistocene-Holocene trends in size reduction among wild *Canis* in the region, the identification remains subject to uncertainty. Remains of Natufian dogs (ca. 10,000 BP) were also identified from Mount Carmel, but a re-examination of this material has convinced many specialists that the skull in question cannot be distinguished from that of the small Arabian wolf. If the Natufian dogs are discounted, the strongest evidence for dogs in the Near East would seem to be from seventh millennium BC Jericho. Many of the Jericho dogs were small, about the size of a fox terrier, and were reported in the company of dog remains almost the size of wolves. Domestic goats are also known at this time, which is important evidence given that there is some debate as to whether the domestic dog was even a useful animal outside of its dietary potential until herd animals and sedentism became a dominant cultural force.[345]

From the onset of the Neolithic, dog remains become more prominent. Examples from Europe include a fragmented cranium of a dog (?) from Starr Carr, England, dated to about 9,500 BP. Dog remains have also been recovered from Vlasac, Romania (ca. 5,400 to 4,600 BC), Senchenberg (9,000 to 10,000 BP) and Bonn-Øberkassel, Germany, and Dobritz-Kniegrotte, Czechoslovakia. In North America, Danger Cave, Utah, has produced the oldest evidence for the dog (ca. 9,000 to 10,000 BP).[346]

The Dog in Ancient Egypt

In Egypt the first valid evidence of the dog comes from Merimde Beni Salame (ca. 4,800 BC). There has been no claim for the presence of the dog in the Neolithic Fayum or Badari. Pictorially, the earliest datable representations of dog comes from several ceramic bowls dated to the Amration period. Dogs probably entered Egypt via the same eastern path as the early domestic ungulates and their earliest appearance is concordant with that of herding animals. It is also possible, although the early dates seems to indicate it not likely, that dogs were introduced into North Africa from Europe across the Iberian Peninsula.[347]

Although reliable dates cannot be substantiated, perhaps the oldest evidence for the dog in Egypt is the rock art found in the Western and Eastern Deserts, where paintings of cattle, giraffes, antelope, and human figures accompanied by dogs are found (fig. 8.11). Winkler classified the rock art of the Eastern and Western Desert into a series of basic styles. The earliest group, the western hunters, depicted dogs that look much like the dogs found today among Berber peoples; in the drawings they have long bodies, long legs, pricked ears, and tails carried high over the back. The elevation of the tail appears to be one of the first effects of domestication; already in wolves and

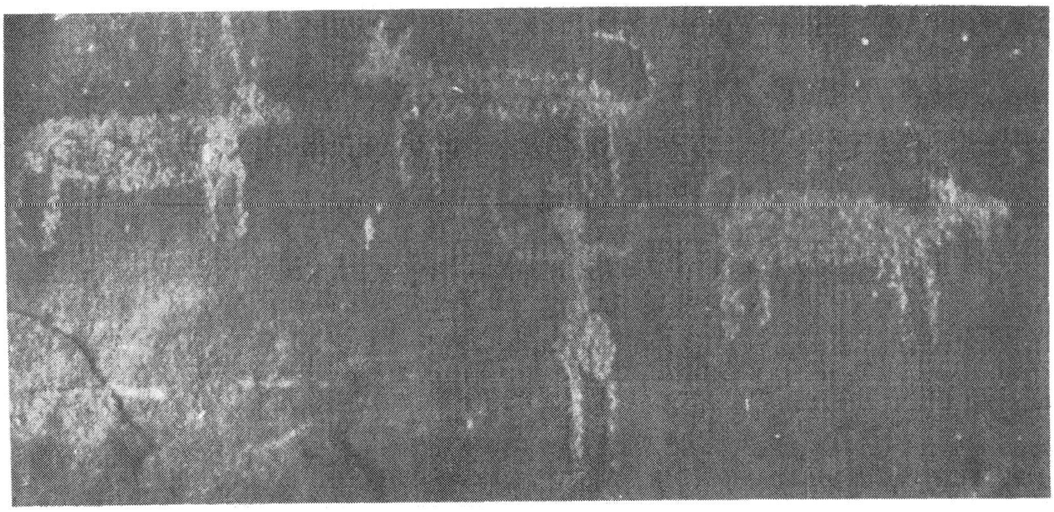

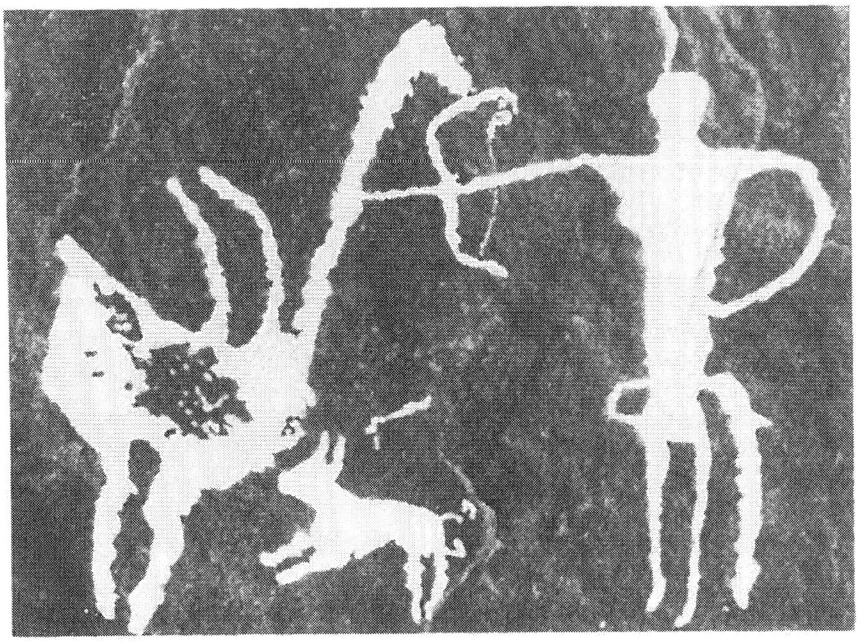

8.11. (top) A petroglyph from the Eastern Desert depicting an early domestic dog. Wadi Hammamat.
8.12. (centre) A short stocky dog thought to represent a distinct form or breed used in Predynastic desert hunts. Eastern Desert.
8.13. (bottom) An ibex hunting scene from the painted tomb of Hierakonpolis. Late Gerzean.

jackals born wild but reared in captivity the raising of the tails is observed as an expression of excitement and expectation.[348]

The rock drawings of the early hunters are followed by scenes that differ in style and represent primarily cattle and pastoral activities. These scenes grouped as a unit seem to suggest two types of dog: a rather large form similar to the dog represented with the early hunters, and a prick-eared greyhound type. Associated with a third style of pictures, which often depict boats, is a third breed of dog. This variety is smaller and stockier in build than either the hunter or pastoralist type dogs and possess a short neck, short legs, long, pricked ears, and a straight tail (fig. 8.12). It is difficult to verify whether the greyhound-type dog that occasionally appear in the drawings represent a different type of greyhound or a change in artistic convention.[349]

Skeletal Evidence. Based on a collection of skulls of mummified dogs from Abydos, Thebes, and Asyut, Haluck derived three major types that compare closely with those identified from rock art: a large and small (early hunter's) dog; a medium, small and dwarfed Pomeranian-like dog; and a small and large greyhound-type dog. Hilzheimer noted, however, that the majority of Egyptian dogs were the large and small dog resembling those depicted in the early hunter rock art scenes.[350]

That two independent sources of evidence (pictorial and skeletal) support the presence of separate canid forms implies that by Dynastic times at least two different breeds, perhaps maintained for different purposes, had become established. Although it is possible that these forms represent two end points along a long continuum of canid shapes and sizes, the frequency of representation in skeletal and artistic samples lends stronger support to the development of rudimentary breeds.

Ancient Egyptian Breeds

The Pariah. Examples of the pariah dog can be seen almost everywhere in modern Egypt. Two different hypotheses have been advanced on the origin of the pariah: that they represent a transitional state in evolution between wild and domestic dogs or that they are descendants of domesticated dogs that have turned feral. Although the latter hypothesis is favored, left to fend for themselves, wild or feral, dogs with their indiscriminate breeding revert to a pariah type identified by erect ears, yellow coloring, and bushy tail. They are about the size of a small sheep dog or collie (ca. 55 cm at the shoulder), but of a stockier build. In essence, the pariah is the ultimate mutt, whose genetic background is the product of continuous indiscriminate breeding between any number of domestic or wild forms. This type is probably similar to the dogs shown in desert rock art and the early Dynastic tomb scenes. The painted tomb from Hierakonpolis shows several dogs of a sturdy build, working an ibex – the pariah is the best candidate (fig. 8.13).[351]

Greyhounds: the Tesem and Saluki. The greyhounds are generally characterized by a long narrow muzzle, nearly straight facial profile, slender body, long neck and limbs, and the habit of hunting by sight rather than by smell.

The earliest record of greyhound-type dogs in Egypt is found on an Amration bowl and, on the basis of skeletal evidence, is also known from the Ubaid period in Mesopotamia. The tesem, which possesses a curved tail, is the earliest breed of greyhound from Egypt. Tesem-like greyhounds are depicted in the rock drawings of the early pastoral peoples in the Eastern and Western Deserts and prick-eared greyhounds are shown in rock art of the Atlas countries. The range of the tesem thus must have extended across North Africa.[352]

During the Dynastic Period, tesems were repeatedly imported into Egypt from Nubia and the Land of Punt (near Somalia), which may have been an early breeding center. Whether the original parent stock from which the Egyptian breed evolved was indigenous to East Africa or introduced from western Asia is still uncertain, although the recovery of skeletal remains of a tesem-like dog from the Ubaid period in Mesopotamia tends to favor the latter alternative. Independent evolution of the Egyptian and Mesopotamian breeds is unlikely because the steppe and desert country between the Nile Valley and Mesopotamia forms no barrier to the greyhound, which is particularly well-adapted to such an environment.[353]

Comparing representations from the Late Predynastic Period to the Dynastic shows that a change in the characteristics of the greyhound-type dog occurs. The thick body and tail of the

8.14. (top) An Old Kingdom Tesem. Tomb of Ti, Saqqara, Dynasty VI.
8.15. (bottom) A Saluki, named "The brave one". Tomb of User, Thebes, Dynasty XVIII.

Predynastic tesem is replaced by a smooth curved tail, erect ears and a more gracile body, and in the later dynasties, the long pricked ears give way to drooping ears similar to those of modern greyhounds (fig. 8.14).

Although the tesem was widespread over many parts of North Africa, Przedziecki believed that in ancient times the saluki (fig. 8.15) was restricted to Egypt, and that it spread across North African countries with the Arab invasion. Interestingly, the saluki is better adapted to both the desert and desert hunting that the tesem. It is, therefore, quite likely that the range of the saluki extended beyond Egypt's borders during the Dynastic period.[354]

Mastiffs. Evidence for the large and massive mastiff-type dog in Egypt during the Prehistoric Period is suggestive at best. At Hierakonpolis a serpentine vase was recovered with handles shaped in the form of an animal head. The handles have been identified as bulls by Quibell, but Hilzheimer believed they represented mastiffs.[355]

It remains uncertain whether mastiff-type dogs existed in Egypt at any time prior to the Middle Kingdom. It may be that the predynastic depictions represent copies of Mesopotamian motifs. However, Hilzheimer was convinced that Egypt was the most southerly point reached by this mastiff-type dog in prehistoric times. He believes that they probably were introduced into Egypt by nomadic tribes, but did not survive as a breed because of the lack of sufficient numbers to establish a breeding population. It is likely that these early mastiffs, if they existed at all, resembled the huge Babylonian dog, from which they were probably descended.[356]

A example of a mastiff-type dog is known from the Middle Kingdom. There is a colored painting from the tomb of Redmea at Thebes, which illustrates tribute from various parts of Asia. Eight dogs form a part of the tribute, and among them is a mastiff. Also, among 38 skulls of mummified dogs from Abydos, Thebes, and Asyut, one cranium resembles a mastiff skull. From the limited pictorial and skeletal evidence, it appears that mastiff-type dogs may have existed in Egypt as an exotic pet, but was present only in limited numbers and probably never reached the numbers needed to establish it as a true breeding population.[357]

Hounds. There is some evidence that hounds made an appearance in Egypt near the end of the Predynastic period. It is, of course, difficult to separate greyhound representations from the bulkier, thicker hound as they possess similar identifying features and only vary in body proportions. Perhaps the best evidence is the condition of brachymely. This is a common mutation whereby the legs of the dog are quite short (fig. 8.16). Skeletal evidence also supplies supportive data for the presence of hounds: Hilzheimer reported two skulls from Asyut that possessed the short, broad skull dimensions of a hound.[358]

The Egyptian Attitude Towards Dogs

Most of the dogs living in Egypt at any one time were probably pariahs living on the fringes of society. Such dogs were very likely despised by the ancient villagers, an attitude that persists to this day. Conversely, numerous tomb scenes show that pets and hunting dogs were obviously much loved. A New Kingdom scribal instruction states: "the dog obeys the word and walks behind its master." The pet dog also stood as a symbol of the faithful retainer. A Middle Kingdom official describes himself as "a dog who sleeps in the tent, a hound of the bed, whom his mistress loves." Hunting and pet dogs are often depicted wearing collars, some adorned with metal studs and animal motif decorations.[359]

It is not surprising, given the special affection pets and hunting dogs received, that they had individual names of which nearly 80 have been recorded. The names refer to color (Blacky, Ebony), character (Good Herdsman, Reliable or Brave One) and to qualities such as speed (North Wind, Antelope). Some names were even numbers such as Fifth or Sixth. On some stele foreign names of dogs also appear; many are thought to be Libyan and some perhaps Nubian in origin.

Aside from their role as pets, dogs also served as watch and police dogs. A Middle Kingdom stele belonging to a member of the desert police, testifies that he patrolled the Western Desert in search of fugitives. He was subsequently promoted for his loyal service, in which he was assisted by five dogs. Each member of the pack had a name and it was inscribed next to his.

As a testimony of their love, dogs were often buried with human-like care. Dogs were provided with individual coffins bearing their own inscriptions. One Old Kingdom stele mentions a royal guard dog: Abutiu (with pointed ears [?]), which kept watch over his master. The dog was ordered by Pharaoh to be buried, a sarcophagus was made for him and he was wrapped in fine cloth dusted with incense and scented oil. Pharaoh also had a tomb constructed for his pet by the crews of tomb builders. Such special devotion may have been an exception, although erecting a stele over an interred dog was not atypical, and Herodotus mentions the habit of burying dogs in tombs.[360]

Evidence for eating dog flesh is confined to one single incident, which was a case of religious vengeance. Plutarch stated that "in my day the people of Oxyrhynchus caught a dog and sacrificed it and ate it up as if it had been sacrificial meat, because the people of Cynopolis (city of the dog) were eating the fish know as the Oxyrhynchus (*Mormyrus* sp.)." As a result of this they became involved in a war and "inflicted much harm upon each other" and it took the Roman army to quell the disturbance.[361]

Deification

Three important deities took canid form: *Wp-w;wt*, Khentiamentu (*Hnty-'imntyw*), and Anubis (*Inepw*).

Wp-w;wt "the opener of the way" was worshipped at Asyut. Its role was apparently to guide kings and divine boats. Though closely connected with Khentiamentu and Anubis, it never became a god of the dead or of cemeteries. Under the Middle Kingdom it started to play a role at Abydos in the Osiris festival, where it represented the young Kinshi of Horus as heir to the older generation.

Khentiamentu "the first in the west " (the land of the dead) was the local god of Abydos, the cemetery of the Archaic period (Dynasty I & II) kings. During Dynasty V, Osiris absorbed and entirely superseded him as Lord of the Dead.

Anubis, the most famous of the canine gods, was said in later periods to be the son of Isis and Osiris, although Plutarch asserted that Osiris begat him from his other sister, Nephthys, whom he mistook for Isis. More generally he was considered the offspring of *hesat*, a sky-cow, which may account for his being called: "Lord of the Milch Cows" besides his other titles that designated him as the embalmer of Osiris, the patron of embalmers.

In addition, he was one of the judges of the dead, and he verified the scales on which souls were weighed. Anubis was, therefore, one of the most important gods of the Egyptian Pantheon. Of his many sanctuaries the most famous was in the city the Greeks called Cynopolis. He was represented either as a human with a jackal head or as a black jackal sitting on all fours. Black was a symbolic color of the dead and the embalming resin. The embalming priests identified themselves with Anubis during the embalming rituals by wearing a jackal-head mask, of which several examples are known.

Anubis was further connected with the creation god Khnum in the well-known scene of the divine birth of Queen Hatshepsut at Deir el Bahari; and is interchangeable with *Wp-w;wt*.[362]

Monkeys and Baboons

Although a number of scenes depict monkeys or the larger stockier and more aggressive baboon, there is no conclusive evidence that these animals were domesticated in the sense that they underwent specific genetic changes as a result of human control. Monkeys are usually seen as pets providing entertainment to their owners. That they were imported is obvious from numerous scenes of ships with monkeys on the masts and cavorting on deck. Baboons because they can be aggressive and are shown assisting the police and at the other end of spectrum robbing figs and other fruits from orchards and markets. Animals depicted in trees were not likely trained fruit-pickers, as some have proposed, but rather robbers and competitors for the sweet produce. Baboons, as a personification of Thoth, probably took advantage of religious tolerance and robbed many orchards. Also, as a personification of Thoth, menageries of Pharaoh and other powerful nobles probably held baboons and numbers of different types of monkeys on their estates, and many scenes could be reminiscent of this luxury.

8.16. Two examples of dogs displaying brachymely: Beni Hasan, Dynasty XII, British Museum, New Kingdom (?).

IX

THE BIRDS AND BEES

Domestic Fowl[363]

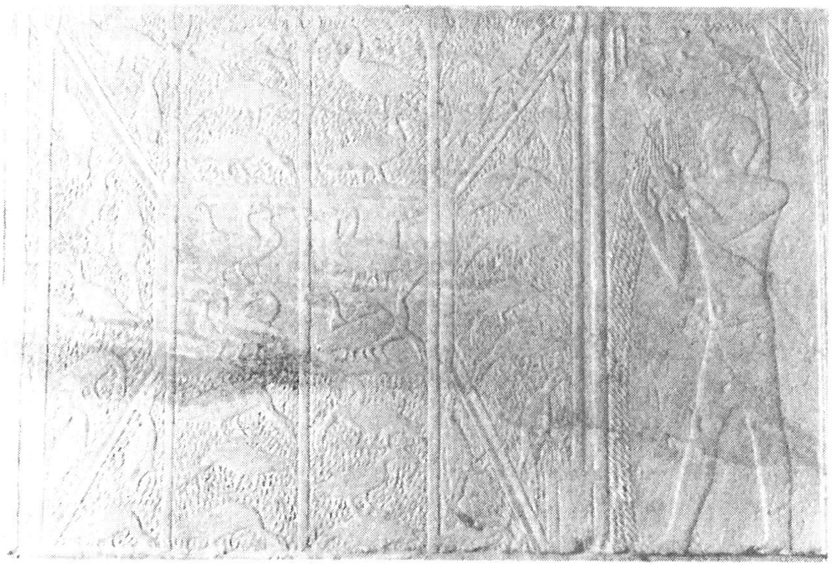

9.1. A poultry yard from the Tomb of Kagemni. Saqqara, Dynasty V.

The Nile Valley and Delta offer an excellent haven for birds. Migratory and non-migratory birds served as important sources of food. Additionally, during the Predynastic and Dynastic Periods the goose, hawk, ibis, and vulture served as political and religious icons. Unfortunately, very little is known about the domestication of birds. Being capable of flight, and on the whole extremely cautious, opportunities for prolonged contact between birds and humans were limited prior to the onset of cultivation. Because the important early domestic bird species were seed eaters (pigeons and fowl) or grazers (geese and ducks), crop-robbing may have been the initial focal point for increased interactions. Also, as in mammals, those species that were first domesticated, such as goose and fowl, possess a rudimentarily social order.[364]

Egyptian palaces, villas, and even modest peasant dwellings contained poultry yards and aviaries. Poultry yards, commonly depicted in Old Kingdom reliefs, show some of the earliest attempts to tame and raise birds (fig. 9.1). It is likely that for many species, captivity and domestication was not completely successful and the bird-pens were supplied with new specimens during the yearly migrations. Poultry cages are illustrated as large structures filled with cranes, ducks, geese, and pigeons. Sometimes species are isolated from one another; in some cases the different species are allowed to freely roam within the enclosed area. Bird behavior, (fighting, pecking, and preening) is often depicted with humor. Penned birds were fed by scattering grain inside the enclosure, but some cranes and geese were hand or force-fed, possibly to fatten them or to enlarge their livers for the production of *foie gras*, which has been documented in the Roman period (fig. 9.2). The few surviving prices for birds indicate that their value was lower than that of a pair of papyrus sandals or a simple basket, and barely higher than a small loaf of flat round bread.[365]

Of the more than 70 species of birds recognized in Egyptian art and the 24 birds identified as hieroglyphs, only the greylag and the white-fronted goose seem fully domesticated. However, other species of geese as well ducks, cranes, pigeons, ibis and possibly chickens were kept and possibly bred with some success. The fact that the "goose" and "pigeon" were used as given names suggest that Egyptians were quite familiar with these birds.[366]

Birds known to be held in captivity, but not domesticated, include the pelican, cormorant,

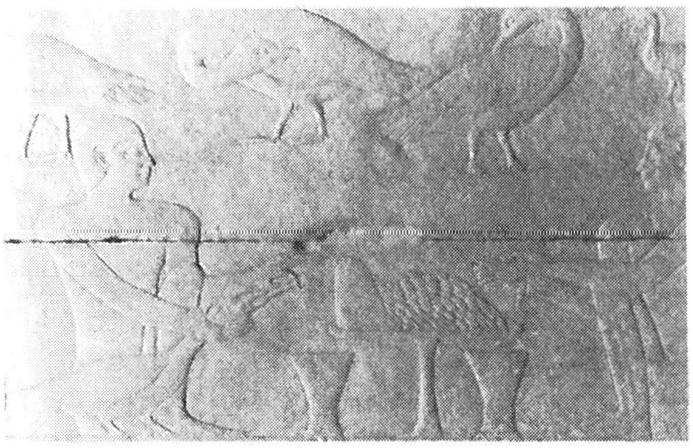

9.2. (top) Force-feeding a goose. Tomb of Kagemni, Dynasty V.
9.3. (top centre) White-fronted geese pictured in the famous scene from Meydum. Tomb of Atet, Meydum, Dynasty IV.
9.4. (bottom centre) The only known represen-ation of a greylag goose from Egypt. El-Amarna, Dynasty XVIII
9.5. (bottom) Nebamun's pet Egyptian goose. Thebes, Dynasty XVIII.

hawk, falcon, and ibis. In late periods the ibis was actually bred in captivity on a massive scale to meet the demands of a flourishing pilgrim industry. When these religious beliefs fell out of favor and as the habitat of the ibis was reduced through agriculture and industrialization, the species became locally extinct.

***Geese* (Anatidae: *Anser* spp., *Aloposhcen* sp., *Branta* sp.)**

There is little doubt that geese were kept by the Ancient Egyptians from at least the Old Kingdom. Although geese are frequently portrayed, they were usually treated by artists in only a summary fashion: they were carved or painted with just enough detail to establish that they were geese. Thus, although the white-fronted, grey-lag, Egyptian, bean, and red-breasted, goose have been identified in Egyptian art, only the white-fronted goose appears with any degree of regularity.

The wild white-fronted goose (*Anser albifrons*) summers and breeds in parts of northern Europe and Asia (fig. 9.3). It winters in southern Europe, Asia, the Middle East, and North Africa, and is a common winter visitor in the Nile Delta. In captivity the white-fronted goose has shown itself to be a sociable and peaceful bird, and because of this would have been an excellent goose to domesticate. Remains of white-fronted geese have been found in the Queen's burial chamber in the Dynasty XII pyramid of Amenemhat III at Dashuur and in five New Kingdom tombs at Thebes.

The greylag goose (*Anser anser*) is the wild ancestor of our own domestic farmyard goose. Although only one badly damaged representation exists, skeletal evidence seems to suggest that this goose was fairly well known in Ancient Egypt. Remains of greylag geese were also identified from the queen's burial chamber in the Dynasty XII pyramid of Amenemhat III (Dashuur) and from New Kingdom tombs in the the Valley of the Queens, where they had been placed as food offerings.[367]

The greylag is a very social bird and does well in captivity (fig. 9.4). Once tame, they soon adapt to a domestic environment and will breed without much difficulty. Interestingly, in modern Egypt, the wild greylag is only an occasional visitor. This may explain why only one representation can be positively identified.[368]

9.6. (left) A bean goose from Meydum. Tomb of Atet, Meydum, Dynasty IV.
9.7. (right) The redbreasted goose. Tomb of Atet, Meydum, Dynasty IV.

The Egyptian or Nile goose (*Alopochen aegyptiaca*) has a nasty and belligerent temperament (fig. 9.5). It is a breeding resident of the Upper Nile Valley and winters in Egypt. Egyptian geese often spend much of the daylight hours sunning themselves on mud flats and sandbanks. In the evening, these birds invade grain fields where they can cause severe damage to crops. The habits of this goose were noted in a passage from the lesson of a scribal student;

> "worse than the Nile goose of the riverbank, busy with mischief. It spends the summer ravaging dates, the winter destroying the seed grain; its free time of the year in pursuit of peasants. One cannot catch it by snaring. One does not offer it in the temple, sharp eyed bird that does not work."[369]

In poultry yards and other related scenes of the Old Kingdom the presence of Egyptian geese can sometimes be inferred by the associated hieroglyphics rather than the morphological characteristics or coloring of the depicted birds. Apparently by the Old Kingdom, the Egyptian goose was already being kept along with other poultry and was apparently tamed for the table. It is not until Dynasty XVIII, however, that the Egyptian goose can regularly be identified from pictorial or archaeological material. In the foundation deposits of the mortuary temple of Thutmosis III at Thebes (Dynasty XVIII), remains of five Egyptian geese were recovered. The birds had been ritually sacrificed, probably as a foundation deposit offering. The Egyptian goose may also have been frequently represented under the chair of the tomb owner, but because it was held sacred to Amun of Thebes, many depictions of this goose may have been defaced by Akhenaten, who wished to obliterate all images and references to Amun.

Although the bean goose (*Anser fabalis*) and red-breasted goose (*Branta ruficollis*) are represented in Egyptian art, they are, at least in modern times, rare visitors to Egypt (figs. 9.6 and 9.7). The remains of two bean geese were recovered from Tutankamun's funerary meal, but little archaeological evidence is available on the red-breasted goose. Modern researchers have only reported it twice in Egypt, once in 1874 and once in 1882. The red-breasted goose, as with other Nile waterfowl has experienced a significant decline in numbers and range within the last two hundred years. This is predominantly due to over exploitation by humans and the loss of habitat. These same factors, in varying degrees, may also apply to the greylag and bean goose, as well as other species of waterfowl, many of which were more common in ancient times.[370]

Of the geese identified from archaeological or pictorial sources, the greylag and the white-fronted goose are the most common. It is difficult to determine when these birds ceased to be captive wild forms and began to be true domesticates. By New Kingdom times, however, the greylag and white-fronted goose were fully domesticated. Grey-lag, white-fronted, and Egyptian geese were used for food as well as religious sacrifices. There is evidence that the Egyptian goose was less preferred as a food than as a pet. Although its quarrelsome nature rendered it a troublesome and unproductive domesticate, it was this very quality that many found endearing in a household pet.[371]

Geese were also dedicated to Egyptian gods and left to flock in various temple pools. Thutmosis

III is said to have created a flock of greylag geese to fulfill the needed offerings to the gods. Seti I is said to have had a farm for Osiris at Abydos where the number of birds was like grains of sand. Temple flocks are also mentioned in the *Book of the Dead* (Papyrus of Nu) where the deceased, questioned by various assessor gods, was required to swear "... I have not snared the geese in the pens of the gods ...". That enormous numbers of birds were raised in Egypt is substantiated by textual reference to King Usermare's gift to Amon of 8140 live geese and 20 fat geese from his flocks, and if we can suppose some truth exists behind what must be an exaggerated figure more than 253,000 geese were listed as gifts to Phenhetep's mortuary cult. Roasted goose was a common dish throughout the Dynastic Period, and dressed geese were frequently included in funerary offerings to the deceased; examples of preserved remains are known. For example, a specially prepared goose wrapped with strips of fine linen was found among the meat and food offerings to King Amenhotep II (Dynasty XVIII, ca.1425 BC).[372]

Reverence of the goose dates to the beginning of Egyptian cosmological thought. It was imagined that the great cackler or cosmic goose fathered the primordial egg from which the sun was born. It is interesting to contrast the status of the goose, which was eaten, with that of the ibis, also a sacred bird, which was prohibited as food. This inconsistency perplexed the early Greek visitors to Egypt – in particular Herodotus, who was amazed that the goose, which was sacred to the Nile god, was also a major component in the diet of Egyptian priests. Apparently the Egyptians were as practical with their culinary habits as they were in other aspects of life.[373]

Ducks (Anatidae:*Anas* spp., *Tadorna* spp.)

Although bones of duck are regular components of archaeological sites throughout all periods, they are never very abundant. Whether this is due to preservational bias or relates more to their general rarity compared to mammals is difficult to determine. There is no definitive evidence to suggest that ducks were domesticated. They were almost certainly captured and held in captivity, but breeding and raising ducklings to maturity is not recorded. The large quantities of ducks that seasonally passed through Egypt as well as those that stayed year-round lead one to conclude that the number of wild ducks was so large that augmenting this supply through domestication was unnecessary.[374]

Doves and Pigeons (Columbidae)

Although the evidence is sketchy, pigeons and doves seem to have been a favorite food throughout most of Egyptian history. These birds are depicted in tombs of all periods either as offerings to the deceased or as one of the main species occupying the poultry yards. In addition to the pictorial evidence, Emery found remains of a pigeon stew with the funerary meal in a Dynasty II tomb at Saqqara. Nearly 2000 years later, King Ramesses III (Dynasty. XX, ca. 1182-1151 BC) offered 57,810 pigeons to the god Amon at Thebes. It is likely that pigeons and doves were part of the diet from Archaic through New Kingdom times.[375]

The most common method of raising doves/pigeons in dynastic times was in pens, but in the Greco-Roman period cotes were used, which differ little from the pigeon towers that dominate present day Egyptian villages. Official indication of a prosperous pigeon economy is the pigeon house tax levied by Augustus. A by-product of this industry was the dung deposited in the pigeon towers, which was considered highly valuable and a proportion of which was sometimes returned to the lessor as rent. Today, pigeon dung is still a prized fertilizer in Egypt, especially for vegetables and fruits.[376]

Cranes (Gruidae)

That cranes and related species were kept for food is suggested by the large numbers depicted in poultry yards and some being force-fed. Because these birds were tamed, but never domesticated, the flock was likely replenished during the seasonal migration.

Additional evidence for the capture and taming of cranes comes from a text relaying how Ramesses III offered a selection of cranes to the god Amon at Thebes. Other texts also mention cranes, but it is not certain whether the ancient terms used refer specifically to cranes or include other related species such as herons and egrets.[377]

Bustard (Otis tetrax, Chlamydotis undulata)

Two species of bustard are indigenous to Egypt; because the Haubara bustard attains great size, it would have probably aroused considerable attention in antiquity. There is, however, no evidence to substantiate Wilkinsons' suggestion that it was prized for the table during the Dynastic Period. The bustard was not a domestic species and in the Ptolemaic Period was apparently imported from Libya.[378]

Chicken (Gallus gallus)

9.8. An ostracon of a jungle fowl (chicken) recovered from Tutankhamun's tomb, Dynasty XVIII.

The earliest remains of the chicken in Egypt are the eggs and bones dated to Dynasty XVII and now housed in the the Egyptian Agricultural Museum at Dokki. The earliest pictorial evidence is on a limestone fragment recovered by Carter and thought to date to Dynasty XIX (ca. 1350 BC). It bears the distinct profile of the red jungle fowl (fig. 9.8).[379]

Evidence suggesting early knowledge of the chicken comes from the eighth campaign into Asia of King Thutmosis III (Dynasty XVIII) who received, as tribute, several birds that appeared so unusual that he ordered the event to be recorded "... four wild fowl of the country which [???] every day". During the Late Period, chickens appear to have been better known. In the fourth century BC in the tomb of Petosiris at Tuna el Gebel, two paintings of fowl easily identified as chicken appear among the main offerings presented to the deceased and further excavations at this site revealed other representations of the same bird.[380]

During excavations at Memphis, Petrie discovered oil lamps decorated with camels and the heads of roosters, but because of stratigraphic problems these objects could only generally be dated to sometime prior to 70 AD. It is most likely, however, that they date to the Ptolemaic or Early Roman Period.[381]

On the basis of this scanty archaeological evidence, one cannot ascertain when chickens were first introduced into Egypt. Moreau, one of the major authorities on Egyptian birds, believed that chickens were unknown before the Ptolemaic Period. Concerning its arrival in Ancient Egypt, Carter and others, on the basis of etymological studies of ancient Sumerian words, believed chickens were imported from western Asia, where they think chickens existed as early as 2500 BC, nearly 1000 years before they were introduced into Egypt! But finding a rooster in a Dynasty XVIII painting of Createn origin suggests a possible diffusion into Egypt from the north, and further complicates the problem of introduction.[382]

In the cultures of ancient Southeast Asia (where the chicken was first domesticated) and later in the eastern Mediterranean regions, the chicken was a sacrificial animal. It was held to have affinity with the gods because the cock signaled the coming of the morning sun; its entrails were, therefore, commonly inspected by priests for a wide variety of signs. Plutarch wrote that the Egyptians of his day sacrificed chickens to the god Anubis.[383]

Quail (Coturnix coturnix)

There is a wealth of information relative to quail-like birds in Ancient Egypt (fig. 9.9). It is difficult, however, to identify the exact varieties described. Emery described quail among the foods he found preserved in a Dynasty II tomb at Saqqara. This discovery coupled with the linguistic and phonetic evidence suggests that quail was a relished food during the early years of the Old Kingdom. During the Middle Kingdom, the archaeological record lacks evidence relative to quail consumption, but under the New Kingdom, this bird again occurs in a dietary context. The first historical record that quail served as a substantial dietary element in Ancient Egypt was made by Herodotus, who stated that dried and salted quail was a dietary favorite of the Egyptians.[384]

Quail was, however, not a domestic species and fresh quail must have been only a seasonal food item. Twice yearly, quail pass through Egypt; northward in March-April and the southward in September-November. During their long overseas flight, the quail returning to Egypt have few places

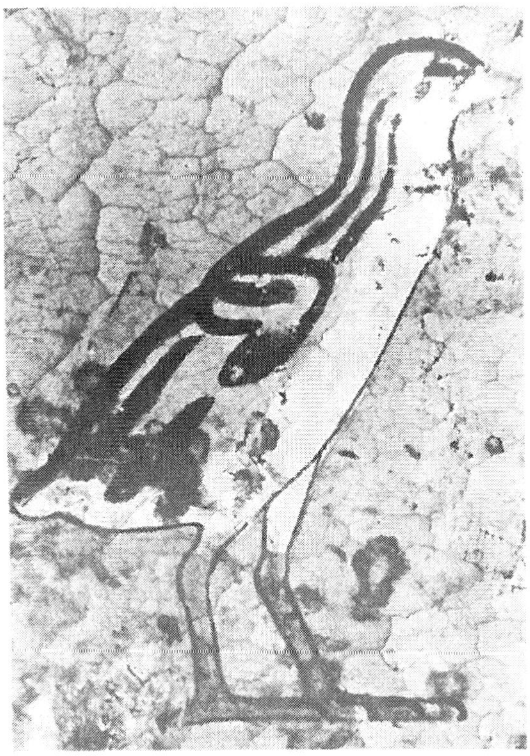

9.9. A common quail chick. Tomb of Atet, Meydum, Dynasty IV.

to land except for an occasional island. When they reach the shoreline of North Africa, they are exhausted and can easily be captured from the coastal regions of the Sinai in the east to Algeria and Morocco in the west.[385]

The Honey Bee

> "One day, the god Re wept, and the tears that dropped from his eyes turned into bees." [386]

It is ironic that the last entry in this volume should be the honey-bee. As stated at the onset of this treatise, domestication was one of the important catalysts in the development of complex societies such as that which evolved in Egypt. Yet the honey-bee possessed a complex social organization (as did ants) thirty million years before modern humans had even evolved. Bee colonies, like human societies, possess distinct divisions of labor, create artificial (domestic) environments, wage war on neighbors, and communicate with each other in complicated ways.[387]

Wild honey collecting, or more technically, "robbing" by humans was certainly carried out long before the onset of the Neolithic. Although wild bee colonies existed throughout Egypt, the Delta with its varied wild flora and later its large tracts of cultivated land would most likely have been the greatest producer of wild and later domestic honey. In fact, one of the earliest designations of Egyptian Kings was their *bity* name, meaning "the one of the bee," referring to the king's role as ruler of the Delta. The symbol does not seem to indicated rulership, but rather is a topographical symbol for Lower Egypt, perhaps suggestive of the bee's importance or abundance in that area. As befitting a king, the bee represented in the royal titulary with its large and extended abdomen appears to be a "queen-bee."[388]

The Egyptian queen-bee beside its larger and more extended abdomen has a slightly different coloring than the worker-bee. Its body segments are generally reddish brown with variations ranging between brown and red. The Egyptian worker-bee is smaller in size than the queen and has a more slender and pointed abdomen. The first three segments of the worker are light yellow to red, with a black border. The abdomen is colored with grey-white hairs.

The Egyptian bee has a much less accommodating temperament than either the European or North American honey bee. It is more easily excited and therefore more likely to attack and sting what it perceives to be a threat. It is very susceptible to cold and produces an enormous number of queens, sometimes more than 100 per hive. Probably as a consequence of so many queens, the Egyptian bee tends to swarm more frequently than other honey bees.

Although the personality traits of the Egyptian bee make it less than desirable for modern beekeepers, in Ancient Egypt these same characteristics would have been highly advantageous. Numerous queens and frequent swarming meant a ready supply of colonies to occupy human-tended hives and large numbers of hives meant a higher incidence of crop pollination, leading to higher yields and to more honey.

A simple but convincing experiment showing the benefits bees provide the farmer was conducted using insect-proof cages set up around four apple trees; in two cages a hive of bees was introduced. At the end of the flowering period the number of set fruit was counted. Trees with bees out-produced those without by a staggering figure ranging from 390 per cent more fruit for one apple species to an 1800 per cent increase in fruit for the second apple species.

The origin of beekeeping is still a mystery, but Egypt is one of the earliest cultures known to keep bees and may have pioneered ancient apiculture. Although many forward the idea that bees were originally kept in Egypt and elsewhere in hollow logs, no proof can be found for this common statement. In all probability, given the earliest records and knowledge of Ancient Egyptians, the first colony to be tamed was probably a swarm that established itself in an ceramic vessel near a human dwelling. Left unmolested for some time, human landlords with experience in wild honey collecting knew that, in due course, the hive would be productive.

Turn of the century Egyptian and present central African beekeeping probably resembles the early Ancient Egyptian methods. Central African beekeeping is referred to as "pastoral" because the beekeepers provide the hives but nature provides bees to occupy them. Nests are rolled pieces of bark plugged at one end with an attractant placed on the entrance of the nest. Eventually a bee swarm occupies the hive and when adequate time has elapsed the bees are killed and the honey taken. Rather than kill the bees the Egyptians soon learned that the bees could be removed by smoke or other means thereby allowing for removal of honey without inducing harm to the hive. As beekeeping develped, the Egptians may have practiced "migratory" beekeeping. Because the flowering season in Upper Egypt arrives a little earlier than in Lower Egypt, beekeepers could move their bees by raft down the Nile pollenating the various crops. Upon arriving at Memphis, the hives could be tapped for their honey. Migratory beekeeping is still practiced over much of the middle and western agricultural areas of the United States. The bees apparantly have no difficulty in locating their mobile home.

In Ancient Egypt honey was an expensive commodity that only the wealthy could afford. Based on the depictions of bees and honey-combs, the honey bee (*Apis* spp.) appears the likely source of Egyptian honey, although several other types of bees do produce honey as well (e.g., bumble bees and some stingless bees). As early as Dynasty V, apiculture as a profession was illustrated. A bas-relief in the Chamber of Seasons of Niuserre's solar temple at Abu Gurob clearly shows a man kneeling in front of a pile of cylindrical vessels and holding one to his mouth, exhaling or breathing (*nft*) into it (fig. 9.10). This has been interpreted as "blowing" smoke into the hive, or as possibly imitating the call of a "queen" as do beekeepers in Egypt today. That both calling and smoking techniques were used to extract bees seems probable given existing scenes and texts. In the Leyden Papyrus, for example, is a phrase that " ... they (the bees) are called with a flute."[389]

To the the right of the keeper exhaling into the cylinder in figure 9.10 is another worker shown pouring the liquid contents into a second large, wide-mouthed vessel; another group pours something from a low, rounded vessel into high

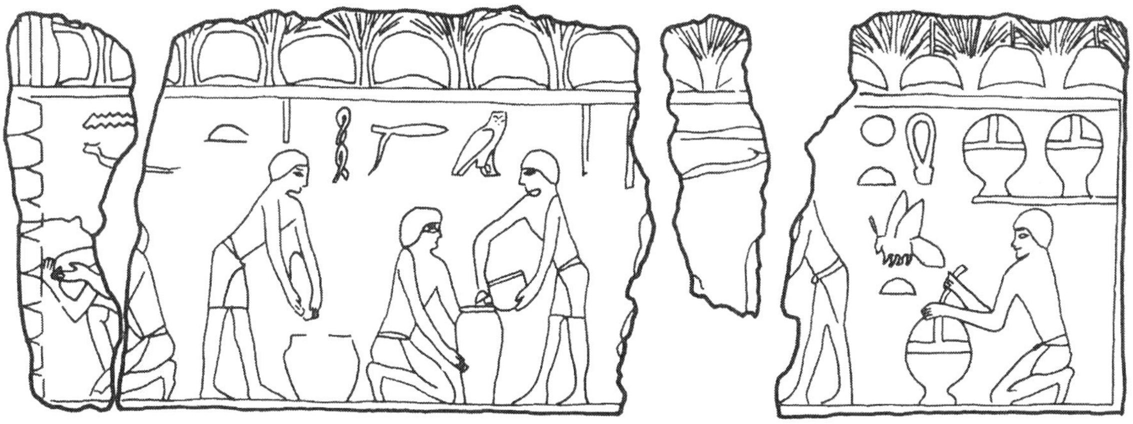

9.10. Breathing or blowing smoke into a hive. Niuserre's Temple, Abu-Gurob, Dynasty V.

narrow jars. On the extreme right a spherical pot is shown being sealed; two already sealed pots are shown being stored and a bee is very obviously displayed, giving meaning to the whole scene.

Only four representations of apiculture are known. Except for the example from Abu Gurob, all are from Thebes: the Dynasty XVIII tomb of Rekhmara (fig. 9.11; above), the tomb of Pebes (Dynasty XXV) (fig. 9.11; below) and a Dynasty XVIII tomb where the scene is barely visible. Honey itself is shown in scenes in at least eight tombs.[390]

In Rekhmara's tomb, the tomb owner is shown presiding over a function called "reception of grain, honey and all precious things ..." He receives a number of local officials offering dues (taxes or revenue?). The list of offerings presented by the officials is damaged, but 31 presentations are preserved and 10 mention honey. Elsewhere in the scene, Rekhmara oversees the workmen removing bees with lamp smoke, filling jars with honey and sealing them (fig. 9.11; above) The two remaining illustrations are both badly preserved but show an arrangement of structures used to house bees. The scene is similar to the traditional methods still used in Egypt today- clay pipes are piled up in rows and stoppered with mud (fig. 9.11; below). In ancient times due to the limited amount of bark, papyrus rolls might have been used, but most likely ceramic pipe was employed. The conical shape of jars in the extant scenes seem to indicate a vessel opened at one end, but a stopper or plug was probably removed from the back-end to allow the bees to escape when honey was extracted; again a practice employed today. Smoke applied directly into the nest with no "back door" would have resulted in asphyxiation of the bees and very probably a concerted attack on the bee handler.[391]

Kuény, reviewing present day apiculture practices in Egypt, finds several other similarities between modern and ancient beekeeping. Some areas in Egypt were well-suited to beekeeping and honey production, other areas were not suitable because of a lack of proper flowering vegetation or climatic conditions. Egyptian honey-bees are greatly influenced by temperature. When temperatures approach 37°C bees remain in the hive and do not collect pollen. When temperatures dip below 10°C they are unable to fly, and cannot move at all at temperatures less than 7°C. Kuény notes that present day honey producers prepare three grades: virgin honey, which is the first honey expressed from the combs, and is usually kept for personal consumption of the producer; second grade, obtained by pressing the combs with six to 12 per cent water, destined for the market; and third grade, obtained by further crushing the residue. Kuény suggests that the three types of jars in both Niuserre's and Rekhmere's illustrations might represent the production of different grades of ancient honey: *stf* (light colored), *dsrt* (red), *pw-g'*, *mh-tt* and honey for cakes.[392]

Kuény believes that originally honey was restricted to religious use because no secular documents or private tombs mention it. But, the biography of Sabni mentions that he took honey, among other things, with him to the land of the "negros" as gifts. In Dynasty XVIII honey is listed as a funerary offering and was among the tribute brought from the campaigns in Palestine and Syria. Ramesses III included it in almost every one of his offerings. Under Dynasty XXI the great chief Namlot is recorded as having made a payment for honey. Documented examples of honey consumption by the common class are rare, but they do exist. In Dynasty XVIII, Ineni who was in great favor with Thutmosis II, boasted of having been supplied with honey from the royal table and in Dynasty XIX, honey is mentioned as part of the daily rations of the kings' messenger and standard bearer. It was not, however, distributed down the ranks.[393]

The presence of royal or state controlled hives is suggested in the Middle Kingdom by the titles of a man named Intet, "Nomarch, Royal Acquaintance, and Overseer of Beekeepers," and another Middle Kingdom title "Overseer of Beekeepers of the Entire Land." By the Ptolemaic period both royal and private bee farms are known to have existed.[394]

Honey was especially agreeable to the god Min, and the Harris Papyrus mentions large quantities were needed for temple rituals. Montet could identify the titles of two high officials involved in the provisioning of honey in Min's rituals: the *;fty*, who probably kept bees and the *bity*, who was more concerned with the gathering of honey, and possibly took part in desert expeditions to collect wild honey. One of the high officials of Ramesses IV, Ouser-mare-nakhty bore the titles, among others, of "Purveyor of Honey to Min, who is in the Laboratory at Coptos" (a center of the Min

9.11. Apiculture as depicted in Dynasty XVIII and XXV, Tomb of Reckmara, Dynasty XVIII, and Tomb of Pebes, Dynasty XXV, Thebes.

cult) and "Messenger to the Mysterious District." Montet concluded that the Coptos laboratory was the place where sacred preparations were made, such as the "divine matter" prepared by the *sm;ty* priest of Min as an ointment to be applied to the divine member of the statue of Min. Special gatherers were appointed and armed guards accompanied them to their work; "I made for thee archers and collectors of honey ... I established for them tax officials to collect their annual impost for thy august storehouse."[395]

Apart from the finds described by Maspero there have been, according to Kuény, many specimens of honey discovered in tombs from the Middle Kingdom onwards. Two small jars from Tutankhamon's tomb labelled "honey of good quality," were examined by Lucas but their contents could not be identified, although, when one jar was treated with hot water a slight caramel smell was detected. Another material from the same tomb was black and resinous-looking, and covered with the remains of beetles and innumerable crystals of some sugar, suggesting that the material had been either honey or a fruit juice.[396]

Zander described a honeycomb found at Deir el-Medineh in a tomb dating to Dynasty XIX (ca. 1350 B.C.). The typical hexagonal design indicated its source as an *Apis* bee, and the small size of the cells (when compared to present-day honey-combs) suggest the species *Apis mellifica unicolor fasciata*. When the hardened honey was analyzed, a predominance of pollen of *Mimusops schimperi* and *Balanites aegyptiaca* with scant examples of Graminae, Caryophyllaceae, *Trifolium, Melilotus, Vicia*, Cruciferae, Rosaceae, Thymelaceae, and Polygonaceae was identified.[397]

Apart from its use in the pure state, honey was incorporated in cakes and pastries, and was used to prime beer and wine. In the field of Ancient Egyptian medicine about 60 prescriptions included honey.[398]

One by-product of apiculture was beeswax. It was used by the Ancient Egyptian not only to seal the nose, eyes, and mouth of mummies but also to model the funerary mask. The realism of objects made with beeswax was also appreciated by the magicians of Ancient Egypt. Breasted refers to a lawsuit in which certain individuals were prosecuted for plotting to bring harm to Ramesses III by practising on a wax image.[399]

References

1 Redman 1978, p. 89; Childe 1925, 1936; de Candolle 1884; Harlan 1975, p. 3.
2 Bökönyi 1989, p. 22.
3 Ducos 1978, p. 54; Harlan 1975, p. 4.
4 This definition is based on a personal communication with D.K. Grayson and that published by Ducos 1978.
5 Harlan 1975, p. 107.
6 Morey 1990, p. 9.; Chaplin 1969, p. 231.
7 Harlan and de Wet 1965; Hawkes 1969; Harlan 1975, p. 79.
8 Adapted from Zuener 1963, pp. 57-58.
9 Zohary 1969, pp. 59-64; Zohary 1989, pp. 31-34; De Wet and Harlan 1975, pp. 102-105; Harlan 1975, p. 176.
10 Lee 1968; Redman 1978, p. 90.
11 Sponsel 1989; Vickers 1989; Rosman and Rubel 1989; Cook 1909; Cooke 1931; Morley 1920; Ricketson and Ricketson 1937; Meggers 1954; Cowgill 1962; Sabloff and Willey 1967; Willey and Skimkin 1971; Sheets 1982; Flannery 1982; Marcus 1982; Miller 1992.
12 Diamond 1989.
13 Lovell 1993; Armelegos et al. 1984; Harlan 1967, 1975, pp. 12-13.
14 Jarman and Wilkinson 1972, p. 83; Bökönyi 1969, pp. 221-222.
15 Wendorf et al. 1992, pp. 721-724; Harlan et al. 1976, pp. 3-6.
16 Wendorf et al. 1992, pp. 721-724; Hillman 1989; Hillman et al. 1989, pp. 180-181; Wetterstrom 1993, pp 175-176.
17 Stemler and Falk 1980; Wendorf and Schild 1980, p. 266; Wendorf et al. 1984, p. 5.
18 Hassan 1986; Banks 1984 cited in Clutton-Brock 1989; Brewer 1991a, 1992; Clark 1980, p. 577.
19 Hassan 1984, p. 61, 1988; Arkell 1975 ; Arkell and Ucko 1965; Gabrial 1987; Holmes 1989; McDonald 1982; Wendorf et al. 1984; Brewer 1991a.
20 Brewer 1991a, 1991b, 1992; Hassan 1988; Harlan 1975, p. 58.
21 Petrie 1920.
22 Hassan 1980, p. 439.
23 Part of a Nile hymn. Helck 1972.
24 Holy Bible, Genesis 42 (May and Metzger 1977).
25 Wenke and Brewer 1993; Daumas 1965, pp.218-219. Darby et al. 1977, p. 52.
26 Butzer 1960; 1976.
27 Papyrus Harris 57, 8-9, 67,6.
28 L'Égypte, p. 160 in Darby et al. 1977, p. 52; Egypt's present population now exceeds 40 million and a large percentage of its food must be imported.
29 Sethe 1932 autobiography of Karhkuf, Urkunden I, 122.
30 Kemp 1991, pp. 307-308; Gardiner 1948; see also Kemp 1991, pp. 310-11.
31 Millet 1990.
32 Dunham 1938.
33 Breasted 1988, I, 188-189.
34 Newberry 1893, pl. 8; James 1984, p. 113.
35 Redford 1990.
36 Černý 1954.
37 The earliest reference for the *deben* is in the Second Intermediate Period. It has been estimated that at its inception the *deben* was worth 12 *shaty*. Reasons behind the change in monetary units is unknown, but evidence suggests that an increase in the quantity of precious metal during the New Kingdom might account for the shift. Other monetary units and names for the deben and shat were recognized (e.g., *senw*, *snc*, *shat*) but for the sake of simplicity only the *deben* and *kite* will be presented here (see Daumas 1965; Janssen 1975; Montet 1985; Černý 1954).
38 Gardiner 1932, pp. 5, 8f, 43f.
39 Baer 1962.
40 Černý 1954; Brewer and Friedman 1989; Baer 1962; Darby et al.1977.
41 Diodorus I, 36,1-8. Sethe 1906, pp. 742-743.
42 Gardiner 1948; Menu 1970, 1982.
43 Berger 1934, p. 54; Davies 1923, p. 11; James 1985, pp. 32-33; Baer 1962.
44 James 1984, pp. 100-120; see also Hayes 1955, p. 47.
45 also see James 1984, pp. 100-120.
46 Taylor and Griffith 1894, pl. 3 and 4; Herodotus II, 14; Ephron et al. 1939 pl. various; Bedigian and Harlan 1983.
47 cf. James 1984, pp. 107-112; Erman 1971, pp 427.
48 Diodorus I,14; Gastier 1961, p. 31; Herodotus II, 79; Montet 1925, p. 201, pl. 16; Mekhitarian 1954, p. 73; Bohrer 1972.
49 There was an honorary tile of "Superintendent of the Herds of Kings or gods, but this was a high and distinguished post, not apparently related to actual supervision of livestock.
50 Newberry n.d., I, pl. 18.
51 Erman 1971, p. 440.
52 Helck 1975, pp. 15-16, 85f.
53 James 1984, p. 102; Budge 1967, pp. 194-200.
54 DJB, personal interpretation.
55 DeBuck and Gardiner 1938 (Coffin Texts) II, 1938, p. 368.
56 Budge 1967, p. 362.
57 Zohary 1971; Feldman 1976 pp. 120-122; Berrie 1977, pp. 1-3; Bender 1975, pp. 56-57 and references cited there.
58 After Harlan and Zohary 1966; Zohary et al. 1969; also see McCorriston and Hole 1991; Wright 1971; Struever 1971; Reed 1977 and references cited there.
59 Hassan 1986; Brewer 1989; Wendorf et al. 1984; Harlan 1977; A shift in climate could also account for a disjunct population of freshwater clams now found in Abyssinia and S.W. Asia; see Brewer 1993, in press.
60 Over time, silica from grass stocks builds up on the cutting surface and these deposits are distinctly visible; Harlan 1977.
61 Wendorf et al. 1979, pp. 1341-1342; Wendorf et al. 1992; Hillman 1989; Hillman et al. 1989; Wetterstrom 1993.
62 Wendorf et al. 1970, p. 1168; Täckholm and Täckholm 1941, pp. 239, 284; Hassan 1985, 1988, p. 151.
63 Arkell and Ucko 1965, p. 147; Trigger 1968, pp. 68-69; Junker 1929, pp. 218-219; Eiwanger 1980, p. 69; 1982, pp. 68-81; 1984, pp. 12, 14, 59; Hassan 1985, 1988, p. 151.
64 Debono 1948; Lauer et al. 1951; Dixon 1969; Helbaek 1953, 1955.
65 Peterson 1965 pp. 9-10; Percival 1927 cited in Täckholm and Täckholm 1941; Helbaek 1955; Schulz in Täckholm and Täckholm 1941; Schiemann in Täckholm and Täckholm 1941.
66 Zohary 1971; Orlov 1931; Harlan 1976, p. 93. Zohary and Hopf 1988, p. 56.
67 Zohary and Hopf 1988, pp. 58-61.
68 Jackson 1934 in Caton-Thompson and Gardner 1934, p.46 "Grain;" Helbaek 1959. The wooden and ivory carvings of cereal spikes found in the tomb of Djer at Abydos by Petrie, who described them as bearded barley, actually represent emmer wheat.
69 Dixon 1969; model now in the Museum at Florence (Loret 1892); Carter 1933; Quibell 1908; Dixon 1969.
70 see other volumes in this series.
71 Černý 1934; Dixon 1969 p. 137; Gardiner 1941; Täckholm and Täckholm 1941; Berrie 1977.
72 Dixon 1969, p. 138; Emery 1958; Gardiner 1947 and references cited there; Percival 1921.
73 Caminos 1964.
74 Griffith 1909.
75 Gardiner 1941; see also Dixon 1969, p.138.
76 Hamada 1938; Täckholm and Täckholm 1941; Lauer et al. 1951; Helbaek 1953.
77 Griffith 1898; Nims 1958; Dixon 1969, p. 139.
78 Gardiner 1947; Nims 1958; Hartman and Oppeneheim 1950.
79 Brunton and Caton-Thompson 1928; The yeast was named after the supplier of the material H. E. Winlock; Grüs 1928, 1929.
80 Lucas 1989; Brewer pers. observation. The flavor is not bad although the general consistency is not appealing to most Western tastes. Diarrhea has usually followed various taste tests.
81 Kemp 1991, pp. 124-125.
82 Brewer Pers. observation and pers. communcation with J. Geller, Hierakonpolis staff member.
83 For bread making see Erman 1971; Kees 1977; Montet 1985; Wilkinson 1878; Lucas 1989. Bedouin bread making was observed by Brewer.
84 Brunken et al. 1977; Unger 1859 in Dixon 1969 (Unger cited as SAWW, Math.-naturw. 1859, p.100, could not be independently verified); Täckholm and Täckholm 1941; Germer 1985, p. 221; Anderson and Martin 1949, pp. 268-269.
85 de Wet and Harlan 1971, p. 133; Karper and Quinby 1947, p. 357; Netolitzky 1914 in Dixon 1969.
86 in Dixon 1969; Daressy 1922; Täckholm and Täckholm 1941.
87 Zohary and Hopf 1988, p. 113.
88 Hall 1986, p.9; Stemler 1980; Caton-Thompson and Gardner 1934; Brunton and Caton Thompson 1928, p. 63; Durant 1976, p. 190.
89 Pliny in Warden, full citation not given; Warden 1864, p. 146-150.
90 Gill and Yermanos 1967; Zohary and Hopf 1988, p. 114-115.
91 Legget 1945, pp.1-5; Hodges 1964, p. 126; Durant 1976, p. 190; Bedigian and Harlan 1986, p. 139.
92 Warden 1864; Kilany 1939.
93 Legget 1945, p. 4.

94 Legget 1945, p.5; Kilany 1939; Warden 1864, pp. 147-148; Lucas 1989, p. 143.
95 Hall 1986, pp. 12-13; Hodges 1964, p. 128; Brewer pers. observation.
96 cf. Hall 1986, pp. 14-15, fig. 5; Hodges 1964, p. 133.
97 Hall 1986, p. 15-16.
98 Täckholm and Drar 1950, p. 129.
99 Pliny xii, 21-26; xxiv, 51; Lucas 1989, p. 139; Täckholm and Drar 1950; Brewer pers. observation of papyrus made for tourist industry.
100 Täckholm and Drar 1950, p. 129.
101 Muthuri and Kinyamario 1989, p. 28; el-Hadidi 1971.
102 Minutoli 1827, cited in Täckholm and Drar 1950, p. 134. e.g., Thiselton-Dyer 1875.
103 Täckholm and Drar 1950.
104 Täckholm and Drar 1950, p.100.
105 Darby et al. 1977, p. 778; Plutarch I, 2,4; Elder and Rathman 1962.
106 Binger 1952; Darby et al. 1977; Bouche-Leclercq 1963: III, p. 253.
107 Zohary and Hopf 1988; Hepper 1990; Davies 1936, pl. ix(c); Schweinfurth in Lucas 1989, p. 335; Simmonds 1976, p. 219; Hartman 1948, p. 344. The rarity of olives in Egypt was attributed to a statement by Borchardt in Goor 1966, p. 231, but the citation was incomplete and thus unable to verify.
108 Theophrastus 4, 29; Strabo XVII, 1, 35; Grenfell and Hunt 1906 (Hibeh Papyri), pp. 192-193; Edgar 1931, (Zenon Papyri) I, 2.
109 Mehra 1967, p.12; Hepper 1990; Bedigian and Harlan 1986; Petrie and Quibell 1896, p. 54; for a review see Bedigian 1985; Nayer 1976.
110 Hepper 1990, p. 28; Manniche 1989, p 147; Singh et al. 1960; Rheenen 1968a; Dioschorides II, 121, also reports that the Egyptians made sesame oil for consumption; Lucas 1989; Tebtunis Papyri 3 (pt 2) no. 844 (trans. D. Redford); Hunt and Edgar 1932 I, p. 277, 287, II pp. 11-35; Bedigian and Harlan 1986.
111 Burkill 1953; De Candolle 1884; Loret 1892, p. 57; Bedigan and Harlan 1986.
112 Rheenen 1968b, p. 204.
113 Gunter 1959, 1, 38; Manniche 1989, p. 142; Herodotus II, 94; Diodorus I, 34; Strabo XVII, 2, 5; Brunton and Caton-Thompson 1928, p. 38; Singh 1976; Knowles 1967; Weibel 1948.
114 Pliny xxi, 107; Manniche 1989, p. 84; Bauman 1960, p. 95.
115 Manniche 1989, pp. 83-84; Hepper 1990, p. 32; Lucas 1989, p. 336; Knowles 1955, 1967, 1976; Classen 1949.
116 Pliny XIII,11,8; see also Darby et al. 1977; Lucas 1989, p. 329.
117 Lucas 1989; Täckholm 1961: III, p. 23; Lauer et al. 1951; Darby et al. 1977.
118 Pliny XV, 7, 30.
119 Zohary and Hopf 1988, p. 128; Zohary and Spiegel-Roy 1975, p.319.
120 Zohary and Hopf 1988, p. 146; Nixon 1951, p. 272.
121 Zohary and Hopf 1988, p.146.
122 Oudejans 1969; Nixon 1951, p. 275.
123 Zohary and Spiegel-Roy 1975;; Caton-Thompson and Gardner 1932, p. 84; Täckholm and Drar 1950, p.209; Darby et al. 1977; el-Hadidi 1980, p. 348.
124 Zohary and Spiegel-Roy 1975, p. 323.
125 Campbell-Thompson 1949; Breasted 1988, I, 785.
126 Manniche 1989, p. 134.
127 Ebbell 1937, various; Zeven 1967, p.8, pl. 2; Kamal 1967, p. 130; Cunningham and Wehmeyer 1988; Nixon 1951, p. 277. Medically, dates were consumed to purge the body of ills or to regulate urine flow. In vaginal pessaries, with other ingredients, they enhanced fertility. They were also used in various fumigations, or ointments for various troubles.
128 Petrie et al. 1903, II, pl 1; also see Legge 1900; Darby et al.1977.
129 Täckholm and Drar 1950, pp. 227-236; Nixon 1951, p. 277.
130 Engelbach 1946, p. 260; van de Walle and Vergote 1943; Wallert 1962, p. 76; Darby et al. 1977, p. 729; Nixon 1951; Goor, 1967.
131 see Brugsch 1878; Klebs 1934; Täckholm and Drar 1950, p. 274.
132 Newberry 1900, p. 31; Täckholm and Drar 1950, p. 276-277.
133 Manniche 1989, p. 109; Theophrastus II, 6, 10; Dioscorides I, 149. The astringent pulp of the fruit was likely used medicinally, but no texts record their use. Classic authors note, however, that the fruit was used to make bread and as a remedy for stomach ailments and fevers.
134 see Farinà 1929, pl. 172; Zulficar 1937; Davies 1927, p. 26: pl 16; Keimer 1939; Wallert 1962, p. 86-87.
135 Manniche 1989, p. 119; Täckholm and Drar 1950, p. 297; Boussac 1896 and Darby et al. 1977 state the argon palm is depicted in the tomb of Ana, Thebes, but this could not be verified.
136 Darby et al. 1977, p. 722.
137 Zohary and Spiegel-Roy 1975, p. 145.
138 Zohary and Hopf 1988 p. 142; Zohary and Spiegel-Roy 1975, p. 145.
139 Galil and Neeman 1977; Zohary and Hopf 1988, pp. 142-143; Zohary and Spiegel-Roy 1975, p. 145.
140 Zohary 1973, II, p. 631; Zohary and Hopf 1988, p. 143; Storey 1976, p. 205; Goor 1965, p. 130.
141 Hopf 1983; Keimer 1929a; Bruyère 1937; Darby et al. 1977; Storey 1976, p.205.
142 Plutarch V:378,68; Pliny XV, 19,70; Zohary and Hopf 1988:143; Herodotus II:40. In modern Egypt the medicinal use of figs as a laxative is well-known. This observation did not escape the attention of the ancient Egyptians. They mixed figs with milk and steeped the concoction overnight in sweet beer. The desired effect apparently came quite soon after consumption.
143 Zohary and Hopf 1988, p. 145; Hepper 1990, p. 58; Galil 1968, p.79.
144 Hayes 1964, p. 119.
145 Darby et al. 1977, p. 745; see also Galil et al. 1976; Petrie 1901, p. 36, 48; Mond et al. 1937, p. 7, 138.
146 Diodorus I:34, 9; Hepper 1990, p. 58; Harlan 1986.
147 Galil et al. 1976; Theophrastus I, 4, 21.
148 Zohary and Hopf 1988, p. 145; Zohary and Spiegel-Roy 1975, p. 322; Hepper 1990, p. 58; Galil 1968.
149 Galil et al. 1976; Zohary and Hopf 1988, p. 146; Galil 1968; Harlan 1986. Medicinally, sycamore figs were prescribed against numerous ailments. They was used to combat the mysterious "blood-eater" (scurvy?). As part of a drink they could distinguish fertile from sterile women. They also served in a number of medical potions designed to aid stomach and intestinal disorders. Crushed leaves were used in a mixture to cure constipation, and, leaves were applied to hippo bites. The sap of the tree was used to darken scars. Ebbell 1937, lxxxviii; Wreszinski 1909, p. 193; 1912; Manniche 1987, pp. 103-104; Darby et al. 1977, pp. 746-748; Kamal 1967, pp. 460-461.
150 Zohary and Spiegel-Roy 1975, p. 321-322; Zohary and Hopf 1988, p. 136-137; Manniche 1989, p. 156; Hepper 1990, pp. 67-68; Winkler 1948, p. 47.
151 Zohary and Spiegel-Roy 1975, pp. 321-322; Zohary and Hopf 1988, p. 141; also see Lauer et al. 1951; the citation as to the earliest remains of grapes in Egypt (Helbaek 1966) could not be verified, see Darby et al. 1977, p. 713; Olmo 1976, p. 295; Winkler 1948, p. 50; Stager 1985; Breasted 1988, I, 173; Posener 1962, p. 300; Lesko 1977, p. 11.
152 Einset and Pratt 1975; Olmo 1976; Lutz 1922, p. 51; Zohary and Hopf 1988, p. 139.
153 Athenaeus 7, 33, D-E; Lutz 1922, p. 7.
154 Budge 1960, pp. 211-212; Erman 1971, pp. 196-197; Kees 1977, pp. 81-82
155 Lucas 1989, p.19; Lesko 1977; A. Phillips pers. comm. on Portuguese wine making.
156 Darby et al. 1977; Piankoff 1968, utt. 153,155; Winkler 1948.
157 Herodotus (Rawlinson 1885), I, 87; Lutz 1922, p. 56.
158 Lutz 1922, pp. 56-7; Montet 1985, p. 88; Montet's statement could not be verifed in Strabo 17:1,35; Lucas 1989, p.20.
159 Harer 1985, p. 54; Athenaeus I, 34b.
160 Athenaeus 10, 438,b; Darby et al. 1977; Herodotus II:173; Tylor and Griffith 1895, pl. 7.
161 Loret 1892; Breasted 1988:IV:301.
162 Zohary and Hopf 1988, p. 140.
163 Watkins 1976, 1981; Browicz 1972; Zohary and Hopf 1988, p. 152.
164 Zohary and Hopf 1988, pp. 151-152; Watkins 1976, pp. 247-248.
165 Manniche 1989, pp. 85-86; Coit 1951, p. 82, 92.
166 Loret 1892, pp. 87-89; Newberry 1890, p. 47, 48, 50; Lucas 1989, p. 443; Breasted 1988:I:372,667; II:436, 490, 755; IV:391; Coit 1951, p. 90.
167 One recipe calls for carob, milk, honey, cyperus grass, wine strained and drunk for four days --Manniche 1989, p. 86; Theophrastus IV, 2,4; Darby et al. 1977; Lucas 1989, p. 443.
168 M. Zohary 1973; Täckholm 1974, p. 345; van Zeist 1983; Wetterstrom 1984; Emery and Saad 1938, p. 52; Lauer et al. 1951; Petrie 1920, p. 44; 1890; pp. 46-50; Schweinfurth 1885; 1886; Hepper 1990, p. 68; Ebbell 1937: XLIII: 210, XXXIII:159, XLIX:272; Lucas 1989, p. 446; Abulafatih 1987, p. 356; Baumann 1960, p. 101.
169 There is some uncertainty as to what species of Persea is represented archaeologically, but the concensus seems to favor *M. laurifolius* --Darby et al. 1977, p. 736; Petrie 1889; Lauer et al. 1951; Schweinfurth 1885; Zander in Hepper 1990.
170 Alpin 1980; Manniche 1989; Hepper 1990; N. de G. Davies 1927.
171 Darby et al. 1977, p. 740; Plutarch V, 359, 20; 378, 68.

172 Boussac 1896; Schweinfurth 1886; Keimer 1924; Zohary and Hopf 1988, p. 151; Zohary and Spiegel-Roy 1975, p. 324; Goor 1967, pp. 215-216; Erman in Goor 1967, p. 216 was not fully cited and could not be verified.
173 Hepper 1990; Manniche 1989; Darby et al. 1977, p. 741; Zohary and Spiegel-Roy 1975, p. 324; Zohary and Hopf 1988, p. 151; Smith 1976, p. 320.
174 Zohary and Hopf 1988, p. 167.
175 see Jeffrey 1980; Whitaker and Bemis 1976, p. 65, 67.
176 The Indian and east Asian cultigens show their closest affinity to a more tropical wild melon race.
177 Schweinfurth 1885; Keimer 1924, pp.14-17; Holy Bible, Numbers 11,5 (May and Metzger 1977); Hunt and Edgar 1932, I, 18.
178 Jeffrey 1980; cf. Manniche 1989, p. 96; Whitaker and Bemis 1976, p. 67.
179 Zohary 1983; Zohary and Hopf 1988, p. 176.
180 Osborn 1968, p. 171; Brewer pers. observ.
181 Zohary and Hopf 1988, p. 168; Loret 1892, p. 73; Keimer 1924, pp. 17-18; Hepper 1990, p. 56; Manniche 1989, p. 92.
182 Täckholm and Drar 1954, pp. 58-59.
183 McCollum 1976; Zohary and Hopf 1988, p. 169.
184 McCollum 1976, p. 187; Keimer 1924; Täckholm and Drar 1954, p. 86, 104; Campbell Thompson 1949; Hopf 1983; Leaves recovered from Dra' Abu el-Naga and originally identified as *A. abpeloprasum* (Schweinfurth 1886) were determined by Täckholm and Drar (1954, p 104) to be *A. sativum*.
185 Täckholm and Drar 1954, p. 84; Wreszinksi 1912, p. 237; Ebbell 1937, lxiv, 432, 501. In medicine, leeks were prescribed for wounds and diseases of the limbs, to darken burn scars; and as applications to human bites.
186 McCollum 1976, p. 188; Zohary and Hopf 1988, p. 169; Stearn 1978.
187 Schweinfurth 1886, p. 49; Hepper 1990, p. 55; Darby et al. 1977, p. 657; Dioscorides II, 181; Sickenberger 1901, p. 295; Loret 1904; Brewer pers. observation.
188 Täckholm and Drar 1954, p. 102-103; Zohary and Hopf 1988, p. 169; see also Petrie 1920, pl. 46.
189 Loret 1892; Lefebvre 1956, p. 102, fn. 10; Ebbell 1937, lxx, 519; Griffith 1898, p. 28; Darby et al. 1977, pp. 656-660. Regardless of its origins, one cannot fail to be impressed with the lasting belief in its therapeutic value. Pliny (XX, XXIII, 50-57) cited several examples of its medicinal applications: its smell reportedly kept away serpents and scorpions, mixed with honey, it was an ointment for dog and serpent bites and bruises were treated with garlic roasted in oil. When cooked with honey and vinegar it was used to expel tapeworms and other parasites of the intestines. When mixed with goose grease, it was used for ear drops.
190 Stearn 1978; Hanelt 1985.
191 Green 1973, pp. 165-166; Lefebvre 1956; Ebbell 1937, various; Faulkner I962; Tackholm and Drar 1954, pp. 102-103; Although providing no detail Ruffer (1919, p.76) states that onions were found with mummies as early as Dynasty XIII; this statement is contradicted by Elliot Smith and Dawson (1924, p. 165), who date the use of onions in embalming to Dynasty XVIII; see also Keimer 1933, p. 52-60. The Ebers Papyrus contains many medical recipes that use onions. Onion juice is a known antibiotic, diuretic, and expectorant. In Ancient Egypt onions or extracts were taken orally, used in vaginal douches, and applied in ointments and dressings. Onion was also used as a means of assessing female fertility. Introduced *per vaginam*, its smell could be perceived the next day in the mouth of a fertile, but not in that of sterile, women. This curious test was apparently based on a presumed connection between the digestive and genital tract. Manniche 1989, p. 69; Ebbell 1937, xxxvii, 192b; xcvi, 828; lxxix, 634; Wreszinksi 1912, p. 237; 1909, p.54; Griffith 1898, p. 28.
192 Zohary and Hopf 1988, p. 83; Doughty and Orraca-Tetteh 1966, p. 10.
193 Zohary and Hopf 1973, p. 83; van Zeist 1980; Zohary 1989; see also Ladizinsky 1987.
194 Ladizinsky et al. 1984; Zohary and Hopf 1973, p. 83-84; Zohary 1972, 1976.
195 Ladizinsky et al. 1984.
196 Barulina 1930; Zohary 1972.
197 van Zeist 1970; Hillman 1975; Zohary and Hopf 1973.
198 Darby et al. 1977, p. 687; Zohary and Hopf 1988, p. 85, 91; Brunton 1948; Lauer et al. 1951; Zohary 1972, p. 329; Schweinfurth 1885; Täckholm 1961, p. 19; Breasted IV, 1988, 582; Plutarch V 377, 65; Petrie 1889 p. 53.
199 Zohary and Hopf 1973; Davies 1976, p 172;.
200 Zohary and Hopf 1988, p. 92; Davies 1976, pp. 172-173..
201 Davis 1970, 1976, pp. 172-173; Waines 1975; see also Ben Ze'ev and Zohary 1973.
202 Zohary and Hopf 1988, p. 98; Wetterstrom 1981, p. 21; Newberry in Petrie 1889, pp. 49, 53; Newberry in Petrie 1890, pp. 46-50; Zohary and Hopf 1973; Davis 1976, p. 173.
203 Medically they were prescribed to be taken internally with other ingredients for a condition that may have been angina pectoris, and for paresis. It was used externally to "cool" the members and to induce maturation in inflamed glands. Peas were mixed with other ingredients to soften the knees and to cool the members. When mixed with leeks, it was used to darken burns, and peas mixed with beer was used to cure stomach aches. To stop a woman from bleeding, peas mixed with acacia leaves, moringa oil, honey, and another unidentified oil and plant were administered vaginally. Dawson 1935; Lefebvre 1956, p. 130; Ebbell 1937, xxxvii, lxxvii, lxxxv; Ebers Papyrus also cited in Manniche 1989, p. 137.
204 Bond 1976.
205 Lawes 1980; Some broad beans, particularly those from India and Afghanistan (e.g., *V. f. paucifuga*), are able to self-propagate.
206 Muratova 1931; Hanelt 1972; Zohary and Hopf 1988. Some small seed forms grown mainly in India and Afghanistan also show reduced numbers of leaflets and have very small flowers. These are frequently regarded as a distinct intraspecific taxon (*V. f. paucifuga*); Bond 1976, pp. 179-180; Zohary and Hopf 1973.
207 Zohary 1977, pp. 39-40; Schäfer 1973; Ladizinsky 1975; Cubero 1973.
208 Kislev 1985; Manniche 1989, p. 154.
209 Schweinfurth in Keimer 1929a; Newberry in Petrie 1890, pp. 46-50; Petrie 1891.
210 Schweinfurth in Keimer 1929a.
211 Newberry in Petrie 1889, p. 49, 53; Hepper 1990, p. 55; Darby et al., 1977, p. 685.
212 Keimer 1929b, p. 88; Hunt and Edgar 1932, I,92; Ramanujam 1976, p. 157.
213 Zohary and Hopf 1988; Gladstones 1970; 1974; Maesen 1972.
214 Wilkinson 1878, II, p. 143; Maspero 1901, p. 65; Täckholm 1961, p. 20; Gladstones 1974. Schweinfurth (1886, p. 256) noted husks at Dra' Abu el Naga, but these were later determined to be modern. Newberry in Petrie 1890, p. 47.
215 Darby et al. 1977, pp. 683-684; Diodorus I, 89,4; Pliny XVII, XXX, 118-119; Wilkinson 1854, I, 323; Breasted 1988, IV, 301, 350; Ebbell 1937, xlix, lxxi, lxxx, lxxxvi, Wrezinski 1909 p. 78. Medically, beans were used in mouth rinses, dressings, applications to soften stiff limbs, and fumigations. Bean meal paste mixed with honey was applied to a prolapsed rectum. When mixed with oil, bean meal paste was applied to the penis to regulate urine.
216 Wetterstrom 1981, p. 21; Brunton and Caton-Thompson 1928, p. 63; Moens and Wetterstrom 1988.
217 Keimer 1924, p. 290; Darby et al.1977, pp. 675-676.
218 Zohary 1983; Zohary and Hopf 1988, p. 170.
219 Darby et al. 1977, p. 678; Lurker 1980, pp. 76, 80-81; Ryder and Whitaker 1976, p. 39.
220 Harlan 1986, pp. 8-9; Gauthier 1931, p. 166. Lettuce representations have often been identified as artichoke or pine cone.
221 Loret 1892, p. 69; Keimer 1924, p. 126; von Deines and Grapow 1959, p. 21. Internally, its use seems to have been restricted to the treatment of *ååå*. Its seeds, hair, and oil were utilized in ointments to soften the limbs and to relieve headache. In view of the claimed influence of lettuce on sexual functions, it is not surprising to find that the Ebers papyrus, recommends it as a cure for impotence. Ebbell 1937 xlvi,; xxvi, lxxi, xliii, lxxxiii.
222 Hepper 1990, p. 14; Manniche 1989, pp. 76-77.
223 Apicus, 10,1,6 in Darby et al. 1977, p. 670; Lefebvre 1956, p. 149, 214; Ghalioungui 1962; Smith 1976, pp. 322-323. Medicinally, celery was used to treat a variety of diseases. It was prescribed for the mysterious *ååå*. It was also given to retain urine, which is interesting because fresh celery juice is a diuretic. It was applied externally to wounds and stiff joints. Together with sweet beer and another unidentified plant, it was used to treat and fix the teeth. A remedy to cool the uterus included celery, and mixed with oil (or fat) and sweet beer, it was taken as a contraceptive. Ebbell 1937, l, lxviii, lxxx; Darby et al. 1977, p. 670; Dioscorides (III, 64) gave its Egyptian name as *mith*. Dawson (1933) proposed that *mith* referred to mandrake, but Faulkner (1962, p. 103) was skeptical of this interpretation.
224 Banga 1976, p. 60; Petrie 1890; 1891; Darby et al. 1977, p. 664.
225 Pliny xix, xxvi, 84; xxxvi, 80.
226 Herodotus II, 125; von Deines and Grapow 1959, p. 140, 440; In some translations the word purge is used instead of radish.

227 Tubers of *C. rotundus* are small aromatic black tubers about the size of a small grape; Täckholm and Drar 1950, p.62, 65-67; Darby et al. 1977, p. 649; Manniche 1989, p. 98; Brunton and Caton-Thompson 1928, p. 63; Brunton and Morant 1937.

228 Zeuner 1963, pp. 240-241; Bökönyi 1974, p. 95; Ducos and Helmer 1980, p. 525; Perkins 1969; Boessneck 1962; Higgs 1962; Meadow 1981; Haaland 1977; Gulliver 1955; Porter 1965; Netting 1986; International Lifestock Research Center 1978; Spencer 1965.

229 Epstein 1971; Boston 1963; Perkins 1969; Hole et al. 1965; Wendorf et al. 1984.

230 Mori 1965; Carter and Clark 1976.

231 Muzzolini 1980a, 1980b, 1981, 1982; Zeuner 1963; see also Herre 1969; Herre and Rohrs 1973; Bökönyi 1974; Banks 1984 in Clutton-Brock 1987, p. 201.

232 Gautier 1984; Clutton-Brock 1987, p. 64.

233 Zeuner 1963; There have been several attempts to back-breed to the exinct aurochs, but the products were lost in the Second World War.

234 La Baume 1947; Portis 1907; especially see Clutton-Brock 1987.

235 Chaplin 1969; Ducos 1969; Perkins 1964; Higgs and Jarman 1972; Legge 1977; Ducos and Helmer 1980; Hecker 1982a; Zeuner 1963; Grigson 1969; Bökönyi 1969, 1974.

236 Grigson 1969, p. 287; Lasota-Moskalewska 1977, 1980, p.121 and references cited there; Jarman 1969; Kurten 1968; Bökönyi 1974.

237 Sturdy 1975; Bokelmann 1979; Lyman 1987.

238 Winkler 1938.

239 Gautier 1984.

240 Wendorf et al. 1984, p. 421; Heussel 1981, p. 142; McHugh 1971, p. 245

241 Gautier 1984, p. 71; Wendorf 1968, p. 875; Perkins 1965; Hall 1962; Geus 1981.

242 Muzzonlini 1980a.

243 Pia 1942; Gautier 1984, p. 69; Epstein 1971.

244 see Wendorf et al. 1984; Hassan et al. 1980; Brewer 1991a, 1992; Gautier 1984.

245 Smith 1969

246 Bökönyi 1974; Bökönyi, pers. communication in Gautier 1984, p. 69.

247 Erman 1971, p. 437.

248 Gautier 1984, p. 69; Ruffer 1919; Darby et al. 1977; Zeuner 1963; Smith 1969; Redford 1988, p. 10, pl. 31; Winkler 1938.

249 Herodotus II, 38. 22b. Darby et al. 1977, p. 93-98.

250 Tannahil 1973, p. 41; Darby et al. 1977: Peet and Woolley 1923, p. 75; Deshler 1965.

251 Erman 1971; Peet and Woolley 1923, pp. 49, 60,68, 74, 81, 91; von Ricke 1967, p. 38; Pendlebury 1951, III, p. 133; Williams 1993; Vandier 1952, p. 26; Selim 1935 IV, p 38.

252 Erman 1971.

253 Kees 1977; Winklock 1955.

254 Moustafa 1964.

255 The Dinka do not, however, disfigure the horn for identification purposes (Darby et al. 1977).

256 Darby et al. 1977, p. 109; Gardiner 1948, pp. 59-60; Wb I, 6, 18..

257 Griffith 1898; Ghalioungui and Dawakhly 1965, p. 13, fg. 26; Darby et al. 1977, p. 114.

258 Budge 1949, p. 591; Caminos 1954; Smith 1969.

259 Chassinat 1905.

260 Ebbell 1937, xxxiv,198; Darby et al. 1977.

261 Montet 1910; Moustafa 1964.

262 Ox-liver, blood, horn, spleen, grease, and raw flesh are employed in various formulas. One of the most frequently encountered substances in the Egyptian medical papyri is ox grease. In certain instances it was ingested in other cases it was applied externally. The organs and blood of cattle were also important and sometimes more than one was incorporated into the same formula.

263 Montet 1985, p. 89; Herodotus II, 41.

264 Darby et al. 1977; Brewer pers. observ.

265 Wilkinson 1878, III, p. 307-308; Aelian II, 11, VII-38; Darby et al. 1977.

266 Lurker 1980, p. 58-59.

267 Uerpmann 1979, 1987; Clutton-Brock 1987, p. 56; Zuener1963, pp. 63-64; Bökönyi 1974; p 156; Crabtree 1993, pp.218-224.

268 Higgs 1967; Reed 1969.

269 Brunton and Morant 1937; Brunton and Caton-Thompson 1928; Bökönyi 1974, pp. 192-193; Reed 1959; Epstein 1971, p. 224.

270 Clutton-Brock 1987, p. 53.

271 Zeuner 1963; Smith 1969, p. 308; Also, compare Darby et al. 1977, p. 213 and Smith 1969, p. 308; Bökönyi 1974, pp. 159-160.

272 The shape of the horns is one of the main criteria used to identify sheep breeds.

273 Clutton-Brock 1987; Zeuner 1963; Janssen and Janssen 1985.

274 Ryder 1984, p. 70; Mason 1967.

275 Clutton-Brock 1987; Zuener 1963, pp. 145-146; Bökönyi 1974, p. 190.

276 Stampfli 1966; Hole et al. 1965; Zeuner 1963; Reed 1959, p. 1632; 1960, p. 132; Bate in Arkell 1953, pp. 53-67

277 Zeuner 1963, p. 140, 1; Pia 1942; Epstein 1971, p. 267-271.

278 Janssen 1975, p. 166.

279 Herodotus II, 327; Plutarch V, 352, 4; 352, 5. The god Khnum resembles the Old Kingdom breed while the Ram head of Amun Re appears to be modeled after the Middle Kingdom breed.

280 Ruffer 1919, p. 19.

281 Clutton Brock 1987; Osborn and Helmy 1980, p. 476; Strekalovsky 1949; Epstein 1971; p. 356.

282 Clutton-Brock 1987.

283 Frädrich 1974; Clutton-Brock 1987.

284 Clutton-Brock 1987.

285 Clutton-Brock 1987.

286 Zeuner 1963.

287 Reed 1969; Clutton-Brock 1979; Bökönyi 1974, p. 204-205.

288 Hayes 1964, p. 71; Wenke et al. 1983; Caton-Thompson and Gardiner 1934; Junker 1929, p. 218; von den Driesch and Boessneck 1985; Darby et al. 1977.

289 Debono 1948, p. 567; Menghin and Amer 1932, p. 52; Brewer and Wenke 1992; Wenke et al. 1988; Bökönyi n.d.

290 Sanford 1934, p. 86; Gaillard 1934, pp. 66-72; Brunton and Caton-Thompson 1928, p. 77; Mond et al. 1937, p. 258; Ruffer 1919, p. 2; Hassan 1981; McArdle 1982.

291 Firth and Gunn 1926, p. 114; Hecker 1982b; Epstein 1971, p. 341; Randall-McIver and Mace 1902; Quibell and Green 1900.

292 Newberry 1928, p. 211; Sethe 1906, 4, 75, 1; Kees 1977, p. 92; Darby et al. 1977. The Tomb of Inena, Neb-Amon and Amenemhat depict swine.

293 Kemp 1991, p. 256.

294 Leidy 1846; Darby et al. 1977.

295 Janssen and Janssen 1989; Brewer and Friedman 1989; Ruffer 1919; Darby et al. 1977.

296 Petrie et al. 1903, p. 25; Newberry 1928, p. 214; Jacquet-Gordon 1962, p. 466. Ebbell 1937, xcv, 814; Darby et al. 1977. Medical treatments using pig are not numerous. Humour of pigs eye was injected into the ear to cure blindness. Pig's tooth was crushed and added to other ingredients and used as an liniment to expel exudation and pig's brains (or viscera) mixed with other ingredients was a cure for "eating" (cancer ?).

297 cf. Drower 1969; Epstein 1971, p. 377; Zuener 1963.

298 Zeuner 1963; Osborn and Helmy 1980; Talbot 1960; Epstein 1971, p. 377.

299 Clutton-Brock 1987; Gautier 1980; Churcher 1972; Caton-Thompson and Gardner 1934; Mengin and Amer in Hoffman 1980, p. 205.

300 Clutton-Brock 1987, p. 95; Zarins 1976, pp. 521-522.

301 Jacob 1970, p. 18. compare to Zeuner 1963, p.375; Clutton-Brock 1977; Stager 1992, p. 40.

302 Epstein 1971, p. 393; Zeuner 1963; in Janssen and Janssen 1989, no citation given; Hassan 1988, p. 158; Breasted 1988, I, 336.

303 in Janssen and Janssen 1989, no citation given.

304 Janssen and Janssen 1989, no citation given. Plutarch V, 363, 31; Janssen and Janssen 1989.

305 Bibikova 1967, 1969, 1970; Nobis 1971.

306 Redding 1981, pp. 243-244; Davis 1987; Zeder 1986; Littauer and Crouwel 1979, p. 43.

307 Emery 1960; Clutton-Brock 1974; Anthony and Brown 1989, pp. 112-113; Hoch 1991; Clark 1941; Paton 1925; Drower 1969.

308 Janssen and Janssen 1989, pp. 36-43, no citation given; Nibbi 1979; Chard 1937; Wiesner 1939; Reinhardt 1912.

309 Clutton-Brock 1987, pp. 95-96.

310 Clutton-Brock 1987.

311 Lobardini in Zeuner 1963; Curasson 1947.

312 Clutton-Brock 1987; Zeuner 1963; Epstein 1971.

313 Hobbs 1989, p. 36; Murray 1967, p. 27; Schmidtz-Nielson 1964, p. 67; Cloudsley-Thompson 1977, p. 103; Sweet 1965.

314 Flower 1932; Wahby 1938.

315 Müller 1903; Epstein 1971.

316 Compagnoni and Tosi 1978; Mikesell 1955.

317 Saad 1951, p. 38; Brewer 1992, pers. observ.; Childe 1952, p. 51; Scharff 1957, p. 201, pl. 24.

318 Caton-Thompson and Gardner 1934, p. 88, 119, 123; Petrie 1907; Lefébure 1906.

319 Strabo 17, 4-45.

320 Clutton-Brock 1987.

321 Clutton-Brock 1987; Todd 1977.

322 Todd 1977.

323 Todd 1977; Howard 1951, p. 151. The blotched tabby is now found in Egypt and its population is increasing (Brewer, personal obervation.)

324 Todd 1977, p. 104. The term "established" is emphasized because the area of origin of the first cat of a given color is not what is inferred, but rather, the area where the *population* first became established.

325 Zeuner 1958; Prashad 1936; Brunton and Morant 1937; Morrison-Scott 1952.

326 Zeuner 1963; Keller in Zeuner 1963, p. 390; Malek 1993.

327 in Janssen and Janssen 1987, no citations given; Malek 1993. Medical prescriptions employing the cat include a recipe: for not letting mice come at things: the fat of a tom, put on everything;" to improve the hair, fat from six animals one of which was the cat, would be applied." Ebbell 1937; LXVI.

328 Darby et al. 1977; Clutton-Brock 1987; Epstein 1971; Siber 1899; Darwin 1868; Newsome et al. 1980; Skaggs 1946; Dahr 1942; Lorenz 1954; Fox 1978, p. 248. For critical review of recent finds see Morey 1990 and Olsen 1985.

329 Scott 1950, p. 1019, 1968, p. 257; cf. Mech 1970; Peterson 1977; Fox 1971, 1975; Beuler 1973; Clutton-Brock 1977, 1981, p. 34; Schenkel 1967; Morey 1990, p. 17; Zimen 1975; Clutton-Brock 1984, p. 206; Epstein 1971.

330 Morey 1990; Matthey 1954; Borgaonkar et al. 1968; Herre 1955; Schäme 1922; Epstein 1971.

331 Werth 1944; Iljin 1941; Williams 1966, p. 252; Wilson 1975, p. 9; Mayr 1982, p. 270-275; Clutton-Brock 1984, p. 203; Hilzheimer 1932.

332 see Simonsen 1976; Wayne and O'Brien 1987 for examples; see also DeBlieu 1992, Wayne 1992, Ferrell et al. 1980; Lawrence and Bossert 1967; Lehman et al. 1991; Wayne and Jenks 1991; Nowak 1992; Phillips and Henry 1992; Dowling et al. 1992a,b; Parker 1989; Nowak et al. 1992.

333 Wolfgram 1894.

334 Strebel 1905; Zeuner 1963.

335 cf. Serpell 1989; Zeuner 1963, p. 39; Reed 1969; 1984, p. 5; Clutton-Brock 1984, p. 204. For further discussion see Morey 1990.

336 Fentress 1967; Pulliainen 1967; Scott and Fuller 1965; also see Woolpy and Ginsburg 1967.

337 Murie 1944, p. 25; Sullivan 1978; MacDonald 1987; Morey 1990; Clutton-Brock 1981; also see Belyaey and Trut 1975.

338 cf. Mech 1970, p. 51-56; Peterson 1977, pp. 80-85; Jenks and Ginsburg 1987; Schotté and Ginsburg 1987.

339 Mech 1970; Pulliainen 1975.

340 Morey 1990.

341 Mech 1970, p. 138; Morey 1990.

342 Rosenweig 1966, p. 603; Gittlemen 1985; Kolenosky and Standfield 1975; Schmitz and Lavigne 1987; Peters 1983; Calder 1984; Werner and Gilliam 1984; LaBarbara 1986; also see Morey 1990. Morphological differences could simply be allometric consequences of size reduction. (see Lumer 1940); Epstein 1971; Wayne 1986a.

343 Epstein 1971, pp. 83-86; Stockhaus 1965; Clutton-Brock 1970, p. 305; 1981; 1984; Zeuner 1963; Lawrence 1967; Bökönyi 1975; Olsen 1985; Degerbøl 1961, p. 41; see also Stockard 1941.

344 Clutton-Brock 1984; Turnbull and Reed 1974. Olsen (1985, pp. 72-73) has cautioned that the Belt Cave specimen could have come from an atypical wolf.

345 Davis and Valla 1978, p. 10, Table 1; Bate 1937; Zeuner 1958; 1963.

346 Degerbøl 1961; Bökönyi 1975; Mertens 1936; Nobis 1979, 1986; Musil 1974, p. 47; 1984; Bökönyi 1975, p. 167; Grayson 1988, p. 23; see also Clutton-Brock 1979, 1987, pp. 42-43. The North American canid remains from Jaguar Cave, Idaho, long regarded as the oldest domestic dog remains in the world (ca. 10,000 BP) have been determined under re-analysis to be no more than 2000 to 3000 years old (compare Lawrence 1967, p. 44; 1968, to Gowlett et al. 1987, pp. 145-146). For a review of early canid finds see Clutton-Brock 1975; Morey 1990; Benecke 1987; and Olsen 1985.

347 Junker 1929; von den Driesch and Boessneck 1985; Caton-Thompson and Gardner 1928; Brewer 1989; Brunton and Caton-Thompson 1928; Reed 1960; Hilzheimer 1932; Massoulard 1949; Kantor 1953.

348 Winkler 1938; Epstein 1971.

349 Schweinfurth 1912.

350 Hauck 1941; Hilzheimer 1908.

351 Epstein 1971.

352 Tobler 1950, pl. 37b; Frankfort 1939, pl. IVa; Hilzheimer 1932; Winkler 1938.

353 Clark 1954; Epstein 1971.

354 Przedziecki 1954.

355 Quibell and Green 1900; Hilzheimer 1926.

356 Hilzheimer 1932.

357 The identification of a mastiff in the Tomb of Redmea could not be verified. Gwatkin 1933, 1934; Hilzheimer 1908; Epstein 1971.

358 Hilzheimer 1908.

359 in Janssen and Janssen 1989, no citation given.

360 in Janssen and Janssen 1989, no citation given.

361 Plutarch V, 380, 72.

362 see Darby et al. 1977; Budge 1960 and 1967 various, 1969, pp. 261-266; 196; Lurker 1980; Helck and Otto 1956, p. 388; Plutarch V, 366b.

The Ancient Egyptians did, however, prescribe parts of the dog for medical treatments. Hound legs, dung, and blood were used in external applications for pain in the limbs. One prescription " prepared for the mother of his majesty the King of Upper and Lower Egypt" included, among other ingredients, the leg of a hound and the hoof of an ass. To remove hair, one prescription call for the genital blood of a bitch and to prevent whitening of hair the genitals of a bitch. For rabies, the liver of the mad dog eaten and roasted was suppose to protect the bitten from the fear of water. The prescription for a dog bite calls for the tooth of the dog that did the biting be put into a bag and tied to the arm of the victim. Ebbell 1937: lxxiv, 578, 580; lxxv, 784; lxv, 460; Wreszinski 1912, pp. 41, 49.

363 Because birds are treated at length by another volume in this series, only a cursory survey focusing on known domesticates is presented. Readers are referred to Houlihan 1986 for further details.

364 Zeuner 1963, p. 441; Darby et al. 1977, p. 265.

365 Moreau 1966; Meinertzhagen 1930:I, p. 68; Darby et al. 1977, p. 273; Mackworth-Praed and Grant 1952.

366 Gardiner 1950; Houlihan 1986; Janssen and Janssen 1989.

367 Boessneck and von den Driesch 1982, pp. 121, 124-125; Lortet and Gaillard 1908, p. 147-148; Houlihan 1986, p. 56; Darby et al. 1977, p. 283.

368 Houlihan 1986.

369 Houlihan 1986; Caminos 1954, p. 381-382.

370 Houlihan 1986, p. 56.

371 Boessneck 1960; Houlihan 1986; Darby et al. 1977, p. 283.

372 Breasted 1988, II, 559; IV, 235; Budge 1960, p. 575; Houlihan 1986; Darby et al.1977; Davies 1900, p. 11.

373 Ames 1965, p. 27, 35, 52; Herodotus II, 37, 72.

374 Houlihan 1986.

375 Abu-Baker and Badawy 1953, pp. 54-55; Davies 1900, p.11; Emery 1962, pp. 6-7; Breasted 1988, IV, 242.

376 Lichtheim 1957, p. 110; Lindsay 1966, p. 233.

377 Breasted 1988, IV, 242.

378 Houlihan 1986; Wilkinson 1878, II, p. 103.

379 Carter and Mace 1923; Houlihan 1986.

380 Gabra et al. 1941; Darby et al. 1977.

381 Petrie et al. 1910, p. 45.

382 Moreau 1927, p. 6; Carter 1923.

383 Simoons 1961, p. 65-78.; Plutarch, V, 375, 61D-E.

384 Emery 1962, p. 6-7; Herodotus II, 77.

385 Numerous medical prescriptions in Ancient Egypt included parts of birds. For example, "gall-of-a *wj;t*-bird" or heart of a *ms* bird were components of medical cures. Even more frequently preparations included goose fat or goose grease. These ingredients usually were included in emollients serving as bases for various external salves, but in some instances they were ingested: "To treat the belly and to treat the anus: milk, goose fat, powder of manna, colocynth, and raisins are strained and taken in one day;" "To cause the stomach to receive bread: sweet beer, *shpt*, *dsrt*-beer, powder of dates, powder of wheat, fruit of juniper, frankincense, *smt*, raisin, figs and goose-grease are boiled, strained and taken for four days;" "To expel illness of the tongue: brain, milk and grease of the goose are rinsed in the mouth." Ebbell xxii, 81; xxx, 132; xxxiii, 146; li, 285.

386 Derchain 1965, p. 137.

387 Zeuner 1963; Clark 1942.

388 Darby et al. 1977; Fraser 1951, p. 36.

389 Fraser 1951; Kuény 1950; Spiegelberg in Kuény 1950; Petter 1946, p. 1.

390 Darby et al. 1977; Kuény 1950; Lucas 1989; Säve-Söderberg 1957, p. 9. pl. ix, b. Scenes depicting honey include: Menna, Suemnut, Kanamun, Thanuro, Amenuser, Antef, Amenemonet, Neferhotep.

391 Breasted 1988, I, 366, II, 717; Säve-Söderbergh 1957.

392 Kuény 1950; Hayes 1951; Breasted 1988, IV, 300-350.

393 Breasted 1988, II, 117, 518, 562, 571; III, 208; IV, 300, 350.

394 Martin 1971, p. 234; Lange and Schäfer 1901-25: I-IV, 20181.

395 Montet 1950; Breasted 1988, IV, 206, 324; Darby et al. 1977, p. 431.

396 Kuény 1950, Lucas 1989, p. 26.

397 Zander 1941, pp. 180, 216-218.

398 Lefebvre 1956, p. 196.

399 Lucas 1989, pp. 132, 301, 352-353. Pliny xxv, 2; xxi, 49; Breasted 1988, IV, 454; Darby et al. 1977; Elliot Smith and Dawson 1924; pp 113, 117, 124.

Bibliography

Abulafatih 1987 H. Abulafatih. "Medicinal Plants in Southwestern Saudi Arabia," *Economic Botany* 41 (1987), pp. 354-360.

Aelian *On the Characteristics of Animals* I, A. Scholfield (trans.), Cambridge, U.S.A., 1958.

Abu-Baker and Badaway 1953. A. Abu-Baker and A. Badaway. *Excavations at Giza* 1949-50. Cairo, 1953.

Alpin 1980 Prospero Alpin. *Plantes d' Egypte*. R. de Fenoyl (trans.). L' Institut Français d'Archéologie Orientale du Caire, 1980.

Ames 1965 D. Ames. *Egyptian Mythology*. New York, 1965.

Anderson and Martin 1949 E. Anderson and J. Martin. "World Production and Consumption of Millet and Sorghum," *Economic Botany* 3 (1949), pp. 265-288.

Anthony and Brown 1989 D. Anthony and D. Brown. "Looking a Gift Horse in the Mouth: Identification of the Earliest Bitted Equids and the Microscopic Analysis of Wear," *Animal Domestication and its Cultural Content*, P. Crabtree, D. Campana, K. Ryan (eds), pp. 111-115, Philadelphia, 1989.

Arkell 1953 A. J. Arkell. *Shaheinab*. London. (1953)

Arkell 1975 A.J. Arkell. *The Prehistory of the Nile Valley*, Handbuch der Orientalisk 1, Leiden, 1975.

Arkell and Ucko 1965 A. Arkell and P. Ucko. "Review of Predynastic Development in the Nile Valley," *Current Anthropology* 6 (1965), pp. 145-166.

Armelagos *et al.* 1984 G. Armelagos, D. van Gerven, D. Martin and R. Huss-Ashmore. Effects of Nutritional Change on the Skeletal Biology of Northeast African (Sudanese Nubian) Populations, *From Hunters to Farmers*, J. Clark and S. Brandt (eds), pp. 132-146, Berkeley, 1984.

Athenaeus *The Deipnosophists* VII. C. Gulick (trans.). New York, 1941.

Avicenna *A Treatise on the Canon of Medicine of Avicenna Incorporating a Translation of the First Book*. O. Gruner (trans.), London, 1930.

Baer 1962 K. Baer. "The Low Price of Land in Ancient Egypt," *Journal of the American Research Center in Egypt*, 1 (1962), pp. 25-42.

Banga 1976 O. Banga. "Radish," *Evolution of Crop Plants*, N. Simmonds (ed), pp. 60-61, New York, 1976.

Banks 1984 K. M. Banks. *Climates, Culture and Cattle: The Holocene Archaeology of the Eastern Sahara*, Dallas, 1984. (cited in J. Clutton Brock 1989).

Barulina 1930 H. Barulina. "Lentils of the U.S.S.R. and Other Countries," *Bulletin of Applied Botany, Genetics, and Plant Breeding* (Leningrad) suppl. 40 (1930), pp. 1-319.

Bate 1937 D. Bate. "The Fossil Fauna of the Wady El-Mughara Caves," *The Stone Age of Mount Carmel* I, D. Garrod and D. Bate (eds), pp. 139-240, Oxford, 1937.

Baumann 1960 B. Baumann. "The Botanical Aspect of Ancient Egypt Embalming and Burial," *Economic Botany* 14 (1960), pp. 84-103.

La Baume 1947 W. La Baume. "Diluviale Schädel vom Ur (*Bos primigenius* Bojanus) aus Toscana," *Encylopedia Geologica Helvetiae*, Basel 40, 2, (1947), pp. 299-308.

Bedigian 1985 D. Bedigian. "Is *se-gis-i* Sesame or Flax?" *Bulletin on Sumerian Agriculture* 2 (1985), pp. 159-178.

Bedigian and Harlan 1983 D. Bedigian and J. Harlan. "Nuba Agriculture and Ethnobotany with Particular Reference to Sesame and Sorghum." *Economic Botany* 37 (1983), pp. 384-395.

Bedigian and Harlan 1986 D. Bedigian and J. Harlan. "Evidence for Cultivation of Sesame in the Ancient World", *Economic Botany* 40 (1986), pp. 137-154.

Belyaey and Trut 1975 D. Belyaey and L. Trut. "Some Genetic and Endocrine Effects of Selection for Domestication in Silver Foxes," *The Wild Canids*, M. Fox (ed), pp. 416-426, New York, 1975.

Ben Ze'ev and Zohary 1973 N. Ben Ze'ev and D. Zohary. "Species Relationships in the Genus *Pisum* L.," *Israel Journal of Botany* 22 (1973), pp. 73-91.

Bender 1975 B. Bender. *Farming in Prehistory: From Hunter-Gatherer to Food-Producer*. London, 1975.

Benecke 1987 N. Benecke. "Studies on Early Dog Remains from Northern Europe," *Journal of Archaeological Science* 14 (1987), pp. 31-49.

Berger 1934 S. Berger. "A Note on Some Scenes of Land Measurement," *Journal of Egyptian Archaeology* 20, (1934), pp.54-56.

Berrie 1977 A. Berrie. *An Introduction to the Botany of the Major Crop Plants*. London, 1977.

Beuler 1973 L. Beuler. *Wild Dogs of the World*. New York, 1973.

Bibikova 1967 V. Bibikova. "Kizucheniiu Drevneishikh Domashnikh Loshadei Vostochnoi Evropi", *Biulleten Moskovskogo Obschestva Ispytatelei Prirodi, Otdel Biologicheskii* 72, 3 (1967), pp. 106-117.

Bibikova 1969 V. Bibikova. "Do Istorii Domesticatsii konya na Pivdennomu Skhodi Evropi", *Arkeologiia* (Kiev) 22 (1969), pp. 55-67.

Bibikova 1970 V. Bibikova. "Kizucheniiu Drevneishikh Domashnikh Loshadei Vostochnoi Evropy", Soobshchenie 2. *Biulleten Moskovskogo Obschestva Ispytatelei Prirodi, Otdel Biologicheskii* 75, 5 (1970), pp. 118-126.

Binger 1952 J. Binger. *The Revenue of Laws of Ptolemy Philadelphus Edited from a Greek Papyrus in the Bodleian Library* I-II. Oxford, 1952.

Boessneck 1960 J. Boessneck. Zur Gänsehaltung im alten Ägypten, *Festschrift der Wiener Tierarztlichen Monatsschrift Herrn Professor Dr. Josef Schreiber* 70, pp. 192-206. Vienna, 1960.

Boessneck 1962 J. Boessneck. "Die Tierreste aus der Argissa-Magula vom Präkeramischen Neolithikum bis zur mittleren Bronzezeit," *Die Deutschen Ausgrabungen auf der Argissa-Magula in Thessalien*. I, V. Miloucic, J. Boessneck and M. Hopf (eds) (1962), pp. 27-99.

Boessneck and von den Driesch 1982 J. Boessneck and A. von den Driesch. *Studien an Subfossilen Tierknochen aus Ägypten, Muncher Ägyptologische Studien* 40, Munich, 1982.

Bohrer 1972 V. Bohrer. "On the Relation of Harvest Methods to Early Agriculture in the Near East," *Economic Botany* 26 (1972), pp. 145-155.

Bokelmann 1979 K. Bokelmann. "Rentierjäger am Gletscherrand in Schlezwig-Hodstein?" *Offa* 36 (1979), pp. 12-22.

Bökönyi n.d S. Bökönyi. *The Animal Remains of Maadi, Egypt: A Preliminary Report*. Ms in possesion of author.

Bökönyi 1969 S. Bökönyi. "Archaeological Problems and Methods of Recognizing Domestication," *The Domestication and Exploitation of Plants and Animals*, P. Ucko and G. Dimbleby (eds), pp. 219-230. Chicago, 1969.

Bökönyi 1974 S. Bökönyi. *History of Domestic Animals in Central and Eastern Europe*. Budapest, 1974.

Bökönyi 1975 S. Bökönyi. "Vlasac: an Early Site of Dog Domestication," *Archaeozoological Studies*, A. Clason (ed), pp. 167-178. New York, 1975.

Bökönyi 1989 S. Bokonyi. "Definitions of Animal Domestication," *The Walking Larder: Patterns of Domestication, Pastoralism and Predation*, J. Clutton-Brock (ed), pp. 22-27. London, 1989.

Bond 1976 D. Bond. "Field bean," *Evolution of Crop Plants*, N. Simmonds (ed), pp. 179-182. London, 1976.

Borgaonkar et al. 1968 D. Borgaonkar, O. Elliot, M. Wong, and J. Scott. "Chromosome Study of Four Breeds of Dogs," *The Journal of Heredity* 59, 2 (1968), pp. 157-190.

Boston 1963 E. Boston. "Cattle Breeds in Europe and Africa," *Man and Cattle*. Royal Anthropological Institute, Occasional Paper No. 18, 1963.

Bouché-LeClercq 1963 A. Bouché-LeClercq. *Histoire des Lagides* III. Bruxelles, 1963.

Boussac 1896 H. Boussac. *Le Tombeau d'Anna*. Mémoires de la Mission Archéologique Française au Caire, 1889.

Breasted 1988 J. Breasted. *Ancient Records of Egypt* I-V. London, 1988.

Brewer 1989 D. Brewer. *Fishermen, Hunters and Herders*. British Archaeological Reports, International Series 478, 1989.

Brewer 1991a D. Brewer. "Temperatures in Predynastic Egypt Inferred from the Remains of the Nile Perch," *World Archaeology* 22 (1991), pp. 288-303.

Brewer 1991b D. Brewer. "Fishing in Prehistoric Egypt: Inferences from Faunal Remains," *Beamers, Bobwhites, and Blue-Points: Tributes to the Career of Paul W. Parmalee*. J. Purdue, W. Klippel and B. Styles (eds), Illinois State Museum Scientific Papers 23, pp. 333-340, Springfield, 1991.

Brewer 1992 D. Brewer. "Incremental Growth Structures in Nile Fish and Shellfish from Archaeological Sites as Indicators of Holocene Environmental Change in Egypt," *The Holocene* 2 (1992), pp. 21-36.

Brewer 1993 D. Brewer. Freshwater Mollusks from Kom Ombo, Egypt and their Archaeological Implications," *The Archaeology and Geology of Kom Ombo*. J. Phillips (ed.) Smithsonian Research Reports (in press).

Brewer and Friedman 1989 D. Brewer and R. Friedman. *Fish and Fishing in Ancient Egypt*. Warminster, 1989.

Brewer and Wenke 1992 D. Brewer and R. Wenke. "Transitional Late Predynastic-Early Dynastic Occupations at Mendes: A Preliminary Report," *The Nile Delta in Transition 4th-3rd millenuium BC*, E. van den Brink (ed.), pp. 191-197. Tel Aviv, 1992.

Browicz 1972 K. Browicz. *Malus*, *Flora of Turkey* IV, P.H. Davies (ed), pp. 157-159. Edinburgh, 1972.

Brugsch 1878 N. Brugsch. *Reise nach der Grossen Oase el Khargeh in der Libyschen Wuste*. Leipzig, 1878.

Brunken et al. 1977 J. Brunken, J. de Wett and J. Harlan. "The Morphology and Domestication of Pearl Millet," *Economic Botany* 31 (1977), pp. 163-174.

Brunton 1948. G Brunton. *Matmar*. London, 1948.

Brunton and Caton-Thompson 1928 G. Brunton and G. Caton-Thompson. *The Badarian Civilization*. London, 1928.

Brunton and Morant 1937 G. Brunton and G. Morant. *Mostagedda and the Tasian Culture*. London, 1937.

Bruyère 1937 B. Bruyère. *Deir el Médineh II: La Nécropole de l'Est*. Fouilles de l'Insitut Français d' Archéologie Orientale Années (1934-5), Caire, 1937.

Budge 1949 E. Budge. *The Book of the Dead*. New York, 1949.

Budge 1960. E. Budge *The Book of the Dead*. New York, 1960.

Budge 1967 E. Budge. *The Egyptian Book of the Dead*. New York, 1967.

Budge 1969 E. Budge. *The Gods of the Egyptians* II. New York, 1969.

Burkill 1953 I. Burkill. "Habits of Man and the Origin of the Cultivated Plants of the World," *Proceedings of the Linaean Society London* 164, 1953.

Butzer 1960 K. Butzer. "Archaeology and Geology in Ancient Egypt," *Science*, 132, (1960), pp. 1617-1624.

Butzer 1976 K. Butzer. *Early Hydraulic Civilizations in Egypt*. Chicago, 1976.

Calder 1984 W. Calder. *Size, Function and Life History*. Cambridge, U.S.A., 1984.

Campbell-Thompson 1949. R. Campbell-Thompson. *A Dictionary of Assyrian Botany*. London, 1949.

Caminos 1954. R. Caminos. *Late-Egyptian Miscellanies*. London, 1954.

Caminos 1964. R. Caminos. "The Nitocirs Adoption Stele," *Journal of Egyptian Archaeology* 50 (1964), pp. 75-76.

de Candolle 1884. A. de Candolle. *Origin of Cultivated Plants*. London, 1884.

Carter 1923. H. Carter. An Ostrecon Depicting a Red Jungle Fowl. The Earliest Known Drawings of the Domestic Cock. *Journal of Egyptian Archaeology* 9 (1923), pp. 1-4.

Carter 1933. H. Carter. *The Tomb of Tut-Ankh-Amen* III. London, 1933.

Carter and Clark 1976. P. Carter and J. Clark. "Adrar Bous and African Cattle," *Proceedings of the Seventh Panafrican Congress of Prehistory and Quaternary Studies*, pp. 487-493. Addis Ababa, 1976.

Carter and Mace 1923. H. Carter and A. Mace. *The Tomb of Tut-Ankh-Amen* I. London, 1923.

Caton-Thompson and Gardner 1932. G. Caton-Thompson and E. Gardner. *Kharga Oasis in Prehistory*. London, 1932.

Caton-Thompson and Gardner 1934. G. Caton-Thompson and E. Gardner. *The Desert Fayum*. London, 1934.

Černý 1934. J. Černý. Fluctuations in Grain Prices during the Twentieth Egyptian Dynasty, *Archiv Orientalini* 6, (1934), p. 175.

Černý 1954. J. Černý. "Prices and Wages in Egypt in the Ramesside Period," *Journal of World History* 1 (1954), pp. 903-922.

Chaplin 1969 R. Chaplin. "The Use of Non-Morphological Criteria in the Study of Animal Domestication from Bones Found on Archaeological Sites," *The Domestication of Plants and Animals*, P. Ucko and G. Dimbleby (eds), pp. 231-245, London, 1969.

Chard 1937 T. Chard. "An Early Horse Skeleton," *Journal of Heredity* 28, 9. Washington, 1937.

Chassinat 1905 E. Chassinat. "Note sur le Titre...," *Bulletin de l'Institut Français d' Archéologie Orientale* IV (1905), p. 223.

Childe 1925 V. Childe. *The Dawn of European Civilization*. New York, 1925.

Childe 1936 V. Childe. *Man Makes Himself*. London, 1936.

Childe 1952 V. Childe. *New Light on the Most Ancient East*. London, 1952.

Churcher 1972 C. Churcher. *Late Pleistocene Vertebrates from Archaeological Sites in the Plain of Kom Ombo, Upper Egypt*. Life Science Contributions, Royal Ontario Museum 82. 1992.

Clark 1954. D. Clark. *The Prehistoric Cultures of the Horn of Africa*. Cambridge, 1954.

Clark 1942 G. Clark. "Bees in Antiquity," *Antiquity* 16 (1942), pp. 208-215.

Clark 1941. J. Clark. "Horses and Battle-Axes," *Antiquity* 15 (1941), pp. 50-70.

Clark 1980. J. Clark. "Human Populations and Cultural Adaptations in the Sahara and Nile During Prehistoric Times," *The Sahara and the Nile*, M. Williams and H. Faure (eds.), pp. 527-582. Rotterdam, 1980.

Classen 1949. C. Classen. "Safflower," *Economic Botany* 3 (1949), pp. 143-149.

Cloudsley-Thompson 1977 J. Cloudsley-Thompson. *Man and the Biology of Arid Zones*. Baltimore, 1977.

Clutton-Brock 1970 J. Clutton-Brock. "The Origins of the Dog," *Science in Archaeology*, D. Brothwell and E Higgs (eds). New York, 1970.

Clutton-Brock 1974 J. Clutton-Brock. "The Buhen Horse," *Journal of Archaeological Science* 1 (1974), pp. 89-100.

Clutton-Brock 1977 J. Clutton-Brock. "Man-made Dogs," *Science* 197 (1977), pp. 1340-1342.

Clutton-Brock 1979 J. Clutton-Brock. *The Mammalian Remains from the Jericho Tell*. Proceedings of the Prehistoric Society 45, pp. 135-158. 1979.

Clutton-Brock 1981 J. Clutton-Brock. *Domesticated Animals from Early Times*. Austin, 1981.

Clutton-Brock 1984 J. Clutton-Brock. "Dog," *Evolution of Domestic Animals*, I. Mason (ed), pp. 198-211. London, 1984.

Clutton-Brock 1987 J. Clutton-Brock. *A Natural History of Domesticated Mammals*. Austin, 1987.

Clutton-Brock 1989 J. Clutton-Brock. *The Walking Larder: Patterns of Domestication, Pastoralism and Predation*. London, 1989.

Coit 1951. J. Coit. "Carob or St. John's Bread," *Economic Botany* 5 (1951), pp. 82-96.

Compagnoni and Tosi 1978 B. Compagnoni and M. Tosi. "The Camel: Its Distribution and State of Domestication in the Middle East During the Third Millennium BC in Light of Finds from Shahr-I Sokhta," *Approaches to Faunal Analysis in the Middle East*, R. Meadow and M. Zeder (eds), Peabody Museum Bulletin 2, pp. 91-103, 1978.

Cook 1909 O. Cook. *Vegetation Affected by Agriculture in Central America.* U.S. Department of Agriculture, Bureau of Plant Industry, Bulletin 145, Washington D.C., 1909.

Cooke 1931. C. W. Cooke. "Why the Mayan Cities of the Peten District, Guatemala were Abandoned," *Washington Academy of Sciences* 21 (13), (1931), pp. 283-287.

Cowgill 1962 U. Cowgill. An Agricultural Study of the Southern Maya Lowlands. *American Anthropologist* 64 (1962), pp. 273-286.

Crabtree 1993 P. Crabtree. Early Animal Domestication in the Middle East and Europe, *Archaeological Method and Theory* V, M. Schiffer (ed), pp. 201-246, 1993.

Cubero 1973 J. Cubero. "Evolutionary Trends in *Vica faba* L.," *Theoretical and Applied Genetics* 43 (1973), pp. 59-65.

Cunningham and Wehmeyer 1988 A. Cunningham and A. Wehmeyer. "Nutritional Value of Palm Wine from *Hypaene coriacea* and *Phoenix reclinata*," *Economic Botany* 42 (1988), pp. 301-306.

Curasson 1947. G. Curasson. *Le Chameau et ses Maladies.* Paris.

Dahr 1942 E. Dahr. Über die Variation der Hirnschale bei Wilden und Zahmen Caniden. *Arckiv für Zoologi* 32a (1942) pp. 1-56.

Darby et al. 1977 W. Darby, P. Ghalioungui and L. Grivetti. *Food: the Gift of Osiris* I-II, London, 1977.

Daressy 1922. G. Daressy. "Le Riz dans l'Egypte Antique," *Bulletin de l'Institut d'Egypte* 4 (1922), p. 37.

Darwin 1868 C. Darwin. *The Variation of Plants and Animals under Domestication* I, New York, 1868.

Daumas 1965 F. Daumas. *La Civilisation de l'Egypte Pharonique.* Paris, 1965.

Davies 1976 D. Davies. "Peas," *Evolution of Crop Plants*, N. Simmonds (ed.), pp. 172-174. London, 1976.

Davies 1900 N. de G. Davies. *The Mastaba of Phahhetep and Akethetep at Saqqara* I. London, 1900.

Davies 1923 N. de G. Davies. *The Tombs of Two Officials of Thutmosis* IV. London, 1923.

Davies 1927 N. de G. Davies. *Two Ramesside Tombs at Thebes.* New York, 1927.

Davies 1930 N. de G. Davies. *The Tombs of Kenamun at Thebes* I. New York, 1930.

Davies 1936 N. de G. Davies. *Ancient Egyptian Paintings* I-II, Chicago, 1936.

Davies and Gardiner 1923 N. de G. Davies and A. Gardiner. *The Tombs of Two Officials of Thutmosis IV, Nos. 75, 90.* London, 1923.

Davis 1970. P. Davis. "Pisum L.," *Flora of Turkey* III, P. Davis (ed.), pp. 370-373. Edinburgh, 1970.

Davis 1976 P. Davis. "Peas," *Evolution of Crop Plants*, N. Simmonds (ed), pp 172-174. London, 1976.

Davis 1987 S. Davis. *The Archaeology of Animals.* New Haven, 1987.

Davis and Valla 1978. J. Davis and F. Valla. "Evidence for Domestication of the Dog 12,000 Years Ago in the Natufian of Israel," *Nature* 276 (1978), pp. 608-610.

Dawson 1933 W. Dawson. "Studies in the Egyptian Medical Texts II," *Journal of Egyptian Archaeology* 19 (1933), pp. 133-137.

Dawson 1935 W. Dawson. "Studies in the Egyptian Medical Texts V," *Journal of Egyptian Archaeology* 21 (1935), pp. 37-40.

DeBlieu 1992 J. DeBlieu. "Could the Red Wolf be a Mutt?" *New York Times Magazine*, 14 June (1992), pp. 30-46.

Debono 1948 F. Debono. "El Omari (près d'Helouan), Exposée Sommaire sur les Campagnes des Fouilles 1943-1944 et 1948. *Annales du Service des Antiquités de l'Egypte* 48 (1948), pp. 561-569.

De Buck and Gardiner 1938 A. De Buck and A. Gardiner (eds), *The Egyptian Coffin Texts*, Vol II. Chicago, 1938

Degerbøl 1961 M. Degerbøl. "On a find of a Preboreal Domestic Dog (*Canis familiaris* L.) from Starr Carr, Yorkshire, with Remarks on Other Mesolithic Dogs." *Proceedings of the Prehistoric Society* 27 (1961), pp. 35-55.

von Deines and Grapow 1959 H. von Deines and H. Grapow. Wörterbuch der Ägyptischen Drogennamen, *Grundriss der Medizen der Alten Aegypter* 6, Berlin, 1959.

Derchain 1965 P. Derchain. Le Papyrus Salt 825, II, 5-7, p. 137. Bruxelles: Académie Royale de Belgique. *Mémoires Classés des Lettres* 58.

Deshler 1965 W. Deshler. "Native Cattle Keeping in East Africa," *Man, Culture and Animals*, A. Leeds and A. Vayda (eds), Washington, 1965.

Diamond 1989. J. Diamond. "Everything Else You Always Wanted to know about Sex ... But that We Were Afraid You'd Never Ask." *Anthropology* 89/90, pp. 66-77.

Diodorus *Diodorus of Sicily* I. C. Oldfather (trans.), Cambridge, 1989.

Diodorus Siculus *The Antiquities of Egypt: A Translation of Book I.* E. Murry (trans.), London, 1990.

Dioscorides. R. T. Gunter 1959. *The Greek Herbal of Dioscorides*, R. Gunter (trans.), New York, 1959.

Dixon 1969 D. Dixon. "A Note on Cereals in Ancient Egypt," *The Domestication and Exploitation of Plants and Animals.* P. Ucko and G. Dimbleby (eds), pp 131-142. Chicago, 1969.

Doughty and Orraca-Tetteh 1966. J. Doughty and R. Orrace-Tetteh. "The Contribution of Legumes to African Diets," *Grain Legumes in Africa*, W. Stanton (ed), Rome, 1966.

Dowling et al. 1992a T. Dowling, B. DeMarais, W. Minckley, and M. Douglas. "Use of Genetic Characters in Conservation Biology," *Conservation Biology* 6 (1992), pp. 7-8.

Dowling et al. 1992b T. Dowling, W. Minckley, M. Douglas, P. Marsh, and B. Demarais. "Response to Wayne, Nowak and Phillips and Henry: Use of Molecular Characters," *Conservation Biology* 6 (1992), pp. 600-603.

von den Driesch and Boessneck 1985 A. von den Driesch and J. Boessneck. *Die Tierknochenfunde aus der Neolithischen Siedlung von Merimde-Benisalâma am westlichen Nildelta.* Deutsches Archäologisches Institut, Abteilung. Kairo, 1985.

Drower 1969 M. Drower. "The Domestication of the Horse," *The Domestication and Exploitation of Plants and Animals*, P. Ucko and G. Dimbleby (eds), pp. 471-479. Chicago, 1969.

Ducos 1969 P. Ducos. "Methodology and Results of the Study of the Earliest Domesticated Animals in the Near East (Palestine)," *Domestication and Exploitation of Plants and Animals*, P. Ucko and G. Dimbleby (eds), pp. 265-275. London, 1969.

Ducos 1978 P. Ducos. "Domestication Defined and Methodological Approaches to its Recognition in Faunal Assemblages," *Approaches to Faunal Analysis in the Middle East*, R. Meadow and M. Zeder (eds.), Harvard Peabody Museum Bulletin 2, (1978), pp. 53-56.

Ducos and Helmer 1980 P. Ducos and D. Helmer. "Le Point Actuel sur l'Apparition de la Domestication dans le Levant." *Préhistoire du Levant*, J. Cauvin and P. Sanlaville (eds), pp. 523-528, Paris, 1980

Dunham 1938 D. Dunham. "The Biographical Inscription of Nekhebu in Boston and Cairo," *Journal of Egyptian Archaeology* 24 (1938), pp. 1-8.

Durant 1976 A. Durant. "Flax and Linseed," *Evolution of Crop Plants*, N. Simmonds (ed), pp. 190-193. London, 1976.

Ebbell 1937 B. Ebbell. *The Papyrus Ebers.* Oxford, 1937.

Edgar 1931 C. Edgar. *Zenon Papyri in the University of Michigan Collection.* Ann Arbor. 1931.

Einset and Pratt 1975. J. Einset and C. Pratt. "Grape Vine," *Advances in Fruit Breeding*, J. Janick and J. Moore (eds), West Lafayette, 1975, pp. 130-153.

Eiwanger 1980. J. Eiwanger. "Dritte Vorberiche über die Wiederaufnahme der Grabungen in den Neolithischen Siedlung Merimde-Benisalâme, *Mitteillungen des Deutschen Archäologischen Institut, Abteilung*, Kairo 36, pp. 61-70 (1980).

Eiwanger 1982. J. Eiwanger. "Die Neolithische Siedlung von Merimde-Benisalâme: Vierter Bericht," *Mitteilungen des DeutschenArchäolologischen Institut, Abteilung*, Kairo 38 (1982), pp. 67-82.

Eiwanger 1984. J. Eiwanger. *Merimde-Benisalâme I: Die Funde der Urschicht*. Archäolologische Veroffentlichungen 47, DeutschesArchäolologisches Institut Abteilung, Kairo, 1984.

Elder and Rathman 1962 A. Elder and D. Rathman. "Seed Oils in Human Nutrition," *Economic Botany* 16 (1962), pp. 196-205.

Elliot Smith and Dawson 1924 G. Elliot Smith and W. Dawson. *Egyptian Mummies*. London, 1924.

Emery 1958 W. Emery. *Great Tombs of the First Dynasty* III. London, 1958.

Emery 1960 W. Emery. "A Preliminary Report on the Excavations of the Egypt Exploration Society at Buhen, 1958-9," *Kush* 8 (1960), p. 7.

Emery 1962 W. Emery. *A Funerary Repast in an Egyptian Tomb of the Archaic Period*. Leiden, 1962.

Emery and Saad 1938 W. Emery, and Z. Saad. *The Tomb of Hemaka*. Cairo, 1938.

Engelbach 1946 R. Engelbach. *Introduction to Egyptian Archaeology with Special Reference to the Egyptian Museum, Cairo*. Service des Antiquités de l'Egypte, Cairo, 1946.

Ephron *et al*. 1939.L. Epron, F. Daumas, G. Goyon and P. Monet. *Le Tombeau de Ti* I-II. Le Caire Imprimerie de L'Institut Français D'Archéologie Oriéntale.

Epstein 1971 H. Epstein. *The Origin of Domestic Animals in Africa*, I-II. New York, 1971.

Erman 1971 A. Erman. *Life in Ancient Egypt*. New York, 1971.

Farinà 1929 G. Farinà. *La Pitture Egiziana*. Milana, 1929.

Faulkner 1962 R. Faulkner. *A Concise Dictionary of Middle Egyptian*. Oxford, 1962.

Feldman 1976 M. Feldman. "Wheats," *Evolution of Crop Plants*, N. Simmonds (ed), pp 120-128. London, 1976.

Fentress 1967. J. Fentress. "Observations on the Behavioral Development of a Hand Reared Male Timber Wolf," *American Zoologist* 7 (1967), pp. 339-351.

Ferrell et al. 1980 R. Ferrel, D. Morizot, J. Horn, and C. Carley. "Biochemical Markers in a Species Endangered by Introgression: The Red Wolf," *Biochemical Genetics* 18 (1980), pp. 39-47.

Firth and Gunn 1926 C. Firth and B. Gunn. *Teti Pyramid Cemeteries Excavations at Saqqara* I. Cairo, 1926.

Flannery 1982 K. Flannery (ed.). *Maya Subsistence*. New York, 1982.

Flower 1932 W. Flower. "Notes on the Recent Mammals of Egypt with a List of the Species Recorded from that Kingdom," *Proceedings of the Zoological Society of London*, pp. 369-450. 1932.

Fox 1971 M. Fox. *Behavior of Wolves, Dogs and Related Canids*. New York, 1971.

Fox 1975 M. Fox. "Evolution of Social Behavior in Canids," *The Wild Canids*, M. Fox (ed.). pp. 429-460. New York, 1975.

Fox 1978 M. Fox. *The Dog: Its Domestication and Behavior*. New York, 1978.

Frädrich 1974 H. Frädrich. "A Comparison of Behavior in the Suidae," *The Behavior of Ungulates and its Relation to Management*, V. Geist and F. Walther (eds), IUCN Publications New Series 24, (1974), pp. 133-144.

Frankfurt 1929 H. Frankfurt. *Mural Paintings of El-Amarneh*. London, 1929.

Frankfort 1939 H. Frankfort. *Cylinder Seals*. London, 1939.

Fraser 1951 *Bees in Antiquity*. London, 1951.

Gabra et al. 1941 S. Gabra, E. Drioton, P. Perdrizet and W. Waddell. *Rapport sur les Fouilles d'Hermoupolis Ouest (Touna el Gebel)*. Université Fouad I, L'Institut Français d'Archéologie Orientale, Cairo, 1941.

Gabrial 1987 B. Gabrial. "The Palaeoecological Evidence from Neolithic Fireplaces in the Sahara," *The African Archaeological Review* 5 (1987), pp. 93-105.

Gaillard 1934 Cl. Gaillard. *Contribution à l'Etude de la Faune Préhistorique de l'Egypte*. Extrait des Archives du Museum d'Histoire Naturelle de Lyon 14. 1934.

Galil 1968 J. Galil. An Ancient Technique for Ripening Sycamore Fruit in East Mediterranean Countries. *Economic Botany* 22 (1968), pp. 178-190.

Galil et al. 1976 J. Galil, M. Stein and A. Horowitz. "On the Origin of the Sycamore Fig (*Fiscus sycomorus* L.) in the Middle East," *Gardens' Bulletin* 29 (1976), pp. 191-205.

Galil and Neeman 1977 J. Galil and G. Neeman. "Pollen Transfer and Pollination in the Common Fig (*Fiscus carica* L)," New Phytolologist 79 (1977), pp. 163-71.

Gardiner 1932 A. Gardiner. *Late Egyptian Stories*. Bruxelles, 1932.

Gardiner 1941 A. Gardiner. "Ramesside Texts Relating to the Taxation and Transport of Corn," *Journal of Egyptian Archaeology* 27 (1941), p. 24.

Gardiner 1947 A. Gardiner. *Ancient Egyptian Onomastica* II. Oxford, 1947.

Gardiner 1948 A. Gardiner. *The Wilbour Papyrus*. Oxford, 1932.

Gardiner 1948 A. Gardiner. *Ramesside Administrative Documents*, London, 1948.

Gardiner 1950 A. Gardiner. *Egyptian Grammar*. London, 1950.

Gastier 1961 T. Gastier. *Thespis*. New York, 1961.

Gauthier 1931 H. Gauthier. *Les Fêtes du dieu Min*. Institut Français d'Archéologie Orientale. Cairo, 1931.

Gautier 1980 A. Gautier. "Contributions to the Archaeozoology of Egypt," *Prehistory of the Eastern Sahara*, F. Wendorf and R. Schild (eds), pp. 317-342. New York, 1980.

Gautier 1984 A. Gautier. "Archaeozoology of the Bir Kiseiba Region, Eastern Sahara," *Cattle Keepers of the Eastern Sahara*, F. Wendorf, R. Schild and A. Close (eds). Dallas, 1984, pp. 49-72.

Germer 1985 R. von Germer. *Flora des Pharaonischen Ägypten*. Cairo, 1985.

Geus 1981 F. Geus. Fouille à el Kadada-IVe Campaigne (17 Janvier-15-Février, 1980). *Rapport Annuel d'Activité 1979-1980*, Director Géneral des Antiquités et des Musées Nationaux du Soudan, Section Française de Recherche Archéologique (1981), pp. 5-18.

Ghalioungui 1962 P. Ghalioungui. "Some Body Swellings Illustrated in Two Tombs of the Ancient Empire and Their Possible Relation to âââ," *Zeitschrift für Aegyptische Sprache und Alterumskunde* 87, II (1962), pp. 108-114.

Ghalioungui and Dawakhly 1965 P. Ghalioungui and Z. Dawakhly. *Health and Healing in Ancient Egypt*. Cairo, 1965.

Gill and Yermanos 1967 K. Gill and D. Yermanos. "Cytogenetic Studies on the Genus *Linum* I. Hybrids Among the Taxa with 15 as the Haploid Chromosome Number," *Crop Science* 7 (1967), pp. 627-231.

Gittlemen 1985 J. Gittlemen. "Carnivore Body Size: Ecological and Taxonomic Correlates," *Oecologia* 67 (1985), pp. 540-554.

Gladstones 1970 J. Gladstones. "Lupins as Crop Plants," *Field Crop Abstracts* 23, 2 (1970), pp. 123-148.

Gladstones 1974 J. Gladstones. "Lupins of the Mediterranean Region and Africa," *Western Australian Department of Agriculture, Technical Bulletin* 26 (1974), pp. 1-48.

Goor 1965 A. Goor. "The History of Figs in the Holy Land," *Economic Botany* 19 (1965), pp. 124-135.

Goor 1966 A. Goor. "The Place of the Olive in the Holy Land and its History Throughout the Ages," *Economic Botany* 20 (1966), pp. 223-243.

Goor 1967a A. Goor. "The History of the Date in the Holy Land," *Economic Botany* 21 (1967), pp. 320-340.

Goor 1967b A. Goor. "The History of the Pomegranate in the Holy Land," *Economic Botany* 21 (1967), pp. 215-230.

Gowlett et al. 1987 J. Gowlett, R. Hedges, I. Law and C. Perry. "Radiocarbon Dates from the Oxford AMS System: Archaeometry Datelist 5," *Archaeometry* 29 (1987), pp. 125-155.

Grayson 1988 D. Grayson. *Danger Cave, Last Supper Cave and Hanging Rock Shelter: The Faunas*. Anthropological Papers of the American Museum of Natural History 66 (1). New York, 1988.

Green 1973 J. Green. "Note on the Use of Flies for Onion Pollination Under Arid Conditions," *Samaru Research Bulletin* 193 (1973), pp. 165-167.

Grenfel and Hunt 1906 B. Grenfell and A. Hunt. *Hibeh Papyri*. London, 1906.

Griffith 1898 F. Griffith. *Hieratic Papryi from Kahun and Gurob*. London, 1898.

Griffith 1909 F. Griffith. Catalogue of the Demotic Papyri in the John Rylands Library, Manchester, III (1909). Manchester.

Grigson 1969 C. Grigson. "The Uses and Limitations of Differences in Absolute Size in the Distinction Between the Bones of Aurochs (*Bos primigenius*) and Domestic Cattle (*Bos taurus*)," *Domestication and Exploitation of Plants and Animals*, P. Ucko and G. Dimbleby (eds), pp. 277-294. London, 1969.

Grüs 1928 J. Grüs. *Tageszeitung für Brauerei* 26, (1928) pp. 1123-1124.

Grüs 1929 J. Grüs. *Tageszeitung für Brauerei* 27, (1929) pp.681-683.

Gunter 1959 R. Gunter. *The Greek Herbal of Dioscorides*. New York, 1959.

Gulliver 1955 P. Gulliver. *The Family Herds*. London, 1955.

Gwatkin 1933 R. Gwatkin. "Dogs and Human Migrations," *The Journal of South African Veterinary Medical Association* 4, 3-4 (1933).

Gwatkin 1934 R. Gwatkin. "Dogs and Human Migrations," *The Journal of South African Veterinary Medical Association* 5, 1, (1934).

Haaland 1977 G. Haaland. "Pastoral Systems of Production: the Socio-cultural Context and Some Economic and Ecological Implications," *Land Use and Development*, P. O'Keefe and B. Wisner (eds), pp. 179-193. London, 1977.

el-Hadidi 1971 N. el-Hadidi. "Distribution of *Cyperus papyrus* L. and *Nymphae lotus* L. in inland waters of Egypt," *Mitteilungen der Botanischen Staatssammlung Muenchen* 10 (1971), pp. 470-475.

el-Hadidi 1980 N. el-Hadidi. "Vegetation of the Nubian Desert (Nabta Region)," *Prehistory of the Eastern Sahara*, F. Wendorf and R. Schild (eds), pp. 355-372. New York, 1980.

Hall 1962 H. Hall. "A Note on the Cattle Skull Excavated at Faras," *Kush* 10 (1962), pp. 58-61.

Hall 1986 R. Hall. *Egyptian Textiles*. Aylesbury, U.K., 1986.

Hamada 1938 A. Hamada. "A Stele from Manshiyet es-Sadr," Annales du Service de l'Egypte 38 (1938), pp. 217-230.

Hanelt 1972 P. Hanelt. "Die Infraspezifische Variabilität von *Vicia faba* und ihre Gliederung," *Kulturpflanze* 20 (1972) pp. 209-223.

Hanelt 1985 P. Hanelt. "Zur Taxonomie, Chronologie und Ökologie der Wildarten von *Allium* L. sect. *Cepa* (Mill.)," Prokh. *Flora, German Democratic Republic* 176 (1985), pp. 99-116.

Harer 1985 W. Harer. "Pharmacological and Biological Properties of the Egyptian Lotus," *Journal of the American Research Center in Egypt* 22 (1985), pp. 49-55.

Harlan 1967 J. Harlan. "A Wild Wheat Harvest in Turkey," *Archaeology* 20 (1967), pp. 197-201.

Harlan 1975 J. Harlan. *Crops and Man*. Madison, 1975.

Harlan 1976 J. Harlan. "Barley," *Evolution of Crop Plants*, N. Simmonds (ed), pp. 93-98. London, 1976.

Harlan 1977 J. Harlan. "The Origins of Cereal Agriculture in the Old World," *Origins of Agriculture*, C. Reed (ed), pp 357-383. The Hague, 1977.

Harlan 1986 J. Harlan. "Lettuce and the Sycamore: Sex and Romance in Ancient Egypt," *Economic Botany* 40 (1986), pp. 4-15.

Harlan and de Wet 1965 J. Harlan and J. de Wet. "Some Thoughts about Weeds," *Economic Botany* 19 (1965), pp. 16-24.

Harlan et al. 1976 J. Harlan, J. de Wet, and A. Stemler. "Plant Domestication and Idegenous African Agriculture," *Origins of African Plant Domestication*, J. Harlan, J. de Wet and A. Stemler (eds), pp. 2-22. The Hague, 1976.

Harlan and Zohary 1966 J. Harlan and D. Zohary. "Distribution of Wild Wheats and Barley," *Science* 153 (1966), pp. 1074-1080.

Hartman 1948 H. Hartman 1948. "The Olive Industry of California," *Economic Botany* 2 (1948), pp. 341-362.

Hartman and Oppeneheim 1950 L. Hartman and A. Oppeneheim. "On Beer and Brewing Techniques in Ancient Mesopotamia," *Journal of the American Oriental Society*, Supplement 10, 1950.

Hassan 1980 F. Hassan. "Prehistoric Settlements along the Main Nile," *The Sahara and the Nile*, M. Williams and H. Faure (eds.), pp. 421-450. Rotterdam, 1980.

Hassan 1981 F. Hassan. *The Predynastic of Egypt: Subsistence-Settlement Studies in the Nagada-Khattarra Region*. Final Report to NSF. (ms. in possesion of author).

Hassan 1984 F. Hassan. "Environment and Subsistence in Predynastic Egypt," *From Hunters to Farmers*, J. Clark and S. Brandt (eds), pp. 57-64. Berkeley, 1984.

Hassan 1985 F. Hassan. "Radio-carbon chronology of Neolithic and Predynastic Sites in Upper Egypt and the Delta." *The African Archaeological Review* 3 (1985), pp. 95-116.

Hassan 1986a F. Hassan. "Desert Environment and the Origins of Agriculture in Egypt," *Norwegian Archaeological Review* 19 (1986), pp. 63-76.

Hassan 1986b F. Hassan. "Holocene Lakes and Prehistoric Settlements of the Western Faiyum," *Journal of Archaeological Science* 13 (1986), pp. 483-501.

Hassan 1988 F. Hassan. "The Predynastic of Egypt," *Journal of World Prehistory* 2, (1988), pp. 135-185.

Hassan et al. 1980 F. Hassan, T. Hays, A. Hassan, J. Galagher, A. Gautier and W. Wetterstrom. "Agricultural Developments in the Nagada Region during the Predynastic Period," *Nyame Akuma* 17 (1980), pp. 28-33.

Hauck 1941 E. Hauck. *Die Hunderassen im Alten Ägypten*. Zeitschrift für Hundeforschung 16, Leipzig, 1941.

Hawkes 1969 J. Hawkes. "The Ecological Background of Plant Domestication," *The Domestication and Exploitation of Plants and Animals*, P. Ucko and G. Dimbleby (eds), pp. 17-30. Chicago, 1969.

Hayes 1951 W. Hayes. "Inscriptions from the Temple of Amenhotep III," *Journal of Near Eastern Studies* 10 (1951), pp. 82-112.

Hayes 1955 W. Hayes. *A Papyrus of the Late Middle Kingdom in the Brooklyn Museum*. Brooklyn, 1955.

Hayes 1964 W. Hayes. "Most Ancient Egypt," *Journal of Near Eastern Studies* 23 (1964), pp. 217-274.

Hecker 1982a H. Hecker. "Domestication Revisited: Its Implication for Faunal Analysis," *Journal of Field Archaeology* 9 (1982), pp. 217-236.

Hecker 1982b A. Hecker. "A Zooarchaeological Inquiry into Pork Consumption in Egypt from Prehistoric to New Kingdom Times," *Journal of the American Research Center in Egypt* 19 (1982), pp. 59-71.

Helbaek 1953 H. Helbaek. "Queen Ichete's Wheat. A Contribution to the Study of Early Dynastic Emmer of Egypt," *Det Kongelige Danske Videnskabernes Selskab Biologiske Meddeleser* 21 (1951), pp. 1-17.

Helbaek 1955 H. Helbaek. "Ancient Egyptian Wheats," *Proceedings of the Prehistoric Society* 21 (1955), pp. 94-95.

Helbaek 1959 "Domestication of Food Plants in the Old World," *Science* 130 (1959), pp 6-8.

Helck 1972 W. Helk. *Der Text des Nilhymnus*. Wiesbaden, 1972.

Helck 1975 W. Helck. Carnarvon Tablet 15-16, *Historisch Biographische Texte der 2. Zwischenzeit*. Wiesbaden, 1975.

Helck and Otto 1956 W. Helck and E. Otto. *Kleines Wörterbuch der Aegyptologie*. Wiesbaden, 1956.

Herre 1969 H. Herre. "The Science and History of Domestic Animals," *Science in Archaeology*, D. Brothwell and E. Higgs (eds), pp. 257-272. London, 1969.

Herre 1955 W. Herre. "Fragen und Ergebnisse der Domestikationsforschung am Hirn," *Verhandlungen der Deutschen Zoologischen Gesellschaft in Erlangen*, pp. 144-214. Leipzig, 1955.

Herre and Rohrs 1973 W. Herre and M. Rohrs. *Haustiere-zoologisch gesehen*. Stuttgart, 1973.

Hepper 1990 F. Hepper. *Pharoah's Flowers: The Botanical Treasures of Tutankhamum*. London, 1990.

Herodotus *The Histories*. A. de Sélincourt (trans.). London, 1972.

Herodotus *The History of Herodotus* II, G. Rawlinson (trans), New York, 1885.

Heussel 1981 L. Heussel. "Sahel-Ranching in Westafrika," *Die Nomaden in Geschichte und Gegenwart*, R. Krusche (ed), pp. 141-150. Berlin, 1973.

Higgs 1962 E.S. Higgs. "Fauna," Excavations at the Early Neolithic Site at Nea Nikomedeia, Greek Macedonia (1961 season), R. Rodden (ed), *Proceedings of the Prehistoric Society* 28 (1962), pp. 267-288.

Higgs 1967 E. Higgs. "Early Domesticated Animals in Libya," *Background to Evolution in Africa*, W. Bishop and J. Clark (eds), pp. 165-173. Chicago, 1967.

Higgs and Jarman 1972. E. Higgs and M. Jarman. "The Origins of Animal and Plant Husbandry," *Papers in Economic Prehistory*, E. Higgs (ed), pp. 3-13. Cambridge, 1972.

Hillman 1975 G. Hillman. "The Plant Remains from Tell Abu Hureyra: A Preliminary Report," *Proceedings of the Prehistoric Society* 41 (1975), pp. 70-73.

Hillman 1989 G. Hillman. "Late Paleolithic Plant Foods from Wadi Kubbaniya in Upper Egypt: Dietary Diversity, Infant Weaning and Seasonality in a Riverine Environment," *Foraging and Farming: the Evolution of Plant Exploitation*, D. Harris and G. Hillman (eds), pp. 207-239. London, 1989.

Hillman et al. 1989 G. Hillman, E. Madeyska and J. Hathor. "Wild Plant Foods and Diet at Late Paleolithic Wadi Kubbaniya: The Evidence from Charred Remains," *The Prehistory of Wadi Kubanniya II: Paleoeconomy, Environment and Stratigraphy*, F. Wendorf, R. Schild and A. Close (eds), pp. 159-242. Dallas, 1989.

Hilzheimer 1908 M Hilzheimer. "Beitrag zur Kenntnis der Nordafrikanischen Schakale," *Zoologica* 53, 20, 1908.

Hilzheimer 1926 M. Hilzheimer. *Natürliche Rassengeschichte der Haussaugetiere*. Berlin, 1926.

Hilzheimer 1932 M. Hilzheimer. "Dogs," *Antiquity* 6 (1932), pp. 411-419.

Hobbs 1989 J. Hobbs. *Bedouin Life in the Egyptian Wilderness*. Austin, 1989.

Hoch 1991 J. Hoch. *Foreign Words in Late Egyptian*. University of Toronto, Ph.D dissertation. Toronto, 1991.

Hodges 1964 H. Hodges. *Artifacts*. London, 1964.

Hoffman 1980 M. Hoffman. *Egypt Before the Pharaohs*. London, 1980.

Hole et al. 1965 F. Hole, K. Flannery, and J. Neely. "Early Agriculture and Animal Husbandry in Deh Luran," *Current Anthropology* 6 (1965), pp. 105-106.

Holmes 1989 D. Holmes. *The Predynastic Lithic Industries of Upper Egypt*, British Archaeological Reports, International Series 469, 1989.

Holy Bible O. May and B. Metzger (eds) *The New Oxford Annotated Bible*. New York, 1977.

Hopf 1983 M. Hopf. "Jericho Plant Remains," *Excavations of Jericho*. K. Kenyon and T. Holland (eds), pp. 576-621. British School of Archaeology in Jerusalem, London, 1983.

Houlihan 1986 P. Houlihan. *The Birds of Ancient Egypt*. Warminster, 1986.

Howard 1951 M. Howard. "*Dried Cats*." *Man* LI, (1951), pp. 149-151.

Hunt and Edgar 1932, 1934 A. Hunt and C. Edgar. *Select Papyri* I-II. Cambridge, 1932, 1934.

Iljin 1941 N. Iljin. "Wolf-dog Genetics," *Journal of Genetics* 42 (1941), pp. 359-414.

International Livestock Research Center 1978 (Bulletin) Winrock International Livestock Research Center. Morrilton, Arkansas, 1978.

Jacquet-Gordon 1962 H. Jacquet-Gordon. *Les Noms des Domains sous l'Ancien Empire Egyptien*. Cairo, 1962.

Jacob 1970 J. Jacob. *The Economy of Cities*. New York, 1970.

James 1984 T. James. *Pharoah's People*. Chicago, 1984.

James 1985 T. James. *Egyptian Painting and Drawing in the British Museum*. London, 1985.

Janssen 1975 J. Janssen. *Commodity Prices from the Ramesside Period*. Leiden, 1975.

Janssen and Janssen 1989 R. Janssen and J. Janssen. *Egyptian Household Animals*. Haverfordwest, 1989.

Jarman 1969 M. Jarman. "The Prehistory of Upper Pleistocene and Recent Cattle Part 1: East Mediterranean with Reference to Northwest Europe," *Proceedings of the Prehistoric Society* 35 (1969), pp. 236-266.

Jarman and Wilkinson 1972 M. Jarman and P. Wilkinson. "Criteria of Animal Domestication," *Papers in Economic Prehistory*, E.S. Higgs (ed), pp. 83-96. Cambridge, 1972.

Jeffrey 1980 C. Jeffrey. "A Review of Cucurbitaceae," *Botanical Journal of the Linean Society* 81 (1980), pp. 233-247.

Jenks and Ginsburg 1987 S. Jenks and B. Ginsburg. "Socio-sexual Dynamics in a Captive Wolf Pack," *Man and Wolf*, H. Frank (ed), pp. 375-399. Dordrecht, 1987.

Junker 1929 J. Junker. *Vorläufige Berichte über die Grabungen auf der Neolithischen Siedlung von Merimde-Benisalâma* 1. Kaiserliche der Akademie der Wissenschaften, Philosophische-Historische Klasse, Anzeiger, pp. 156-249. Vienna, 1929.

Kamal 1967 H. Kamal. *Dictionary of Pharaonic Medicine*. Cairo, 1967.

Kantor 1953 H. Kantor. "Prehistoric Egyptian Pottery in the Art Museum," *Princeton University Records of the Art Museum* 12 (1953), pp. 67-82.

Karper and Quinby 1947 R. Karper and J. Quinby. "Sorghum – Its Production, Utilization and Breeding," *Economic Botany* 1 (1947), pp. 355-371.

Kees 1977 H. Kees. *Ancient Egypt: A Cultural Topography*. Chicago, 1977.

Keimer 1924 L. Keimer. *Die Gartenpflanzen im alten Aegypten*. Hamburg, 1924.

Keimer 1929a L. Keimer. "Sur Quelques Petit Fruits en Faïence Emaillée Datant du Moyen Empire," *Bulletin de l'Institut Français d' Archéologie Orientale* 28 (1929), pp. 49-97.

Keimer 1929b L. Keimer. "Falcon Face," *Ancient Egypt* 14, 2 (1929), pp. 47-48.

Keimer 1933 L. Keimer. *Egyptian Religion I*, Hamburg, 1933.

Keimer 1939 L. Keimer. "Pavian und Dum-Palme," *Mitteilungen des Deutschen Institutes für Aegyptische Altertumskunde in Kairo* 8 (1939), pp. 42-45.

Kemp 1991 B. Kemp. *Ancient Egypt: Anatomy of a Civilization*. London, 1991.

Kilany 1939 M. El Kilany. *Flax in Egypt*. Ministry of Agriculture Egypt. Technical and Scientific Service Bulletin 204, 1939.

Kislev 1985 M. Kislev 1985. "Early Neolithic Horsebean from Yiftah'el, Israel," *Science* 228 (1985), pp. 319-320.

Klebs 1934 L. Klebs. *Die Reliefs und Malereien des Neuen Reiches*. Abhandlungen der Heidelberger Akademie der Wissenschaften, Philosophische-Historische Klasse 9. Heidelberg, 1934.

Knowles 1955 P. Knowles. "Safflower-Production, Processing and Utilization," *Economic Botany* 9 (1955), pp. 273-299.

Knowles 1967 P. Knowles. "Processing Seeds for Oil in Towns and Villages of Turkey, India and Egypt," *Economic Botany* 21 (1967), pp. 156-162.

Knowles 1976 P. Knowles. "Safflower," *Origins of Crop Plants*, N. Simmonds (ed), pp. 31-32. New York, 1976.

Kolenosky and Standfield 1975. G. Kolenosky and R. Standfield. "Morphological and Ecological Variation Among Gray Wolves (*L. lupus*) of Ontario, Canada," *The Wild Canids*, M. Fox (ed), pp. 62-77. New York, 1975.

Kuény 1950 G. Kuény. "Scènes Apicoles Dans L'Ancienne Egypte," *Journal of Near Eastern Studies* 9 (1950), pp. 84-93.

Kurten 1968 B. Kurten. *Pleistocene Mammals of Europe*. Chicago, 1968.

LaBarbara 1986 M. LaBarbara. "The Evolution and Ecology of Body Size," *Patterns and Processes in the History of Life*, D. Raup and D. Jablonski (eds), pp. 69-98, Berlin, 1986.

Ladizinsky 1975 G. Ladizinsky. "Seed Protein Electrophoresis of the Wild and Cultivated Species Selection of *Vicia faba*," *Euphytica* 24 (1975), pp. 785-788.

Ladizinsky 1987 G. Ladizinsky. "Pulse Domestication Before Cultivation," *Economic Botany* 41 (1987), pp. 60-65.

Ladizinsky et al. 1984 G. Ladizinsky, D. Braun, D. Goshen and F. Muehlbauer, "The Biological Species of the Genus *Lens* L.," *Botanical Gazette* 145 (1984), pp. 253-261.

Lange and Schäfer 1902-25 H. Lange and H. Schäfer. *Grab-und Denkstein des Mittleren Reiches* I-IV, #20181. Berlin, 1902-1925.

Lasota-Moskalewska 1977 A. Lasota-Moskalewska. "Ocena Morfologicza Kosci Bydlecynch z 'Gajowizny',". *Comentarzysko Kultury amfor Kultiotych w Zlotej Sandomierskiej*, J. Kowalczyk (ed), pp. 97-132. Wroclaw, 1977.

Lasota-Moskalewska 1980 A. Lasota-Moskalewska. "Morphological Changes of Domestic Cattle Skeletons from Neolithic Age to the Beginning of the Iron Age," *Wiadomosci Archeologiezne* 45 (1980), pp 119-163.

Lauer et al. 1951 J. Lauer, V. Täckholm, V. Laurent, E. Aberg. "Les Plantes Découvertes dans les Souterrains de l'Enceinte du Roi Zoser à Saqqara (IIIe Dynastie)," *Bulletin de l'Institut d' Egypte*, 32 (1951), pp. 121-157.

Lawes 1980 D. Lawes. "Recent Developments in Understanding, Improvement and Use of *Vica faba*," *Advances in Legume Science*, R. Summerfield and A. Bunting (eds), pp. 625-636. Richmond, U.K., 1980.

Lawerence and Bossert 1967 B. Lawerence and W. Bossert. "Multiple Character Analysis of *Canis lupus*, *latrans* and *familiaris*, with a Discussion of the Relationship of *Canis niger*," *American Zoologist* 7 (1967), pp. 223-332.

Lawrence 1967 B. Lawrence. "Early Domestic Dogs," *Zeitschrift für Saugetierkunde* 32 (1967), pp. 44-59.

Lawrence 1968 B. Lawrence. "Antiquity of Large Dogs in North America," *Tebiwa* 11 (1968), pp. 43-49.

Lee 1968 R. Lee. "What Hunters do for a Living, or How to Make out on Scarce Resources," *Man the Hunter*, R. Lee and I. Devore (eds), pp. 30-48. Chicago, 1968.

Lefébure 1906 E. Lefébure. "Le Chameau en Egypte," *Actes du Congrès International des Orientalistes, Alger Congress* XIV, 2 (1905), pp. 24-62.

Lefèbvre 1956 G. Lefèbvre. *Essai sur la Médecine Egyptienne de l'Epoque Pharaonique*. Paris, 1956.

Legge 1977 A. Legge. "The Origins of Agriculture in the Near East," *Hunters, Gatherers and First Farmers Beyond Europe*, J. Megaw (ed), pp. 51-67. Leicester, 1977.

Legge 1900 F. Legge. "The Carved Slates from Hierakonpolis and Elsewhere," *Proceedings, Society of Bibilical Archaeology* 22 (1900), pp. 125-139.

Legget 1945 W. Legget. *The Story of Linen*. Brooklyn, 1945.

Lehman et al. 1991 N. Lehman, A. Eisenhawer, K. Hansen, D. Mech, R. Peterson, P. Gogan, and R. Wayne. "Introgression of Coyote Mitochondrial DNA into Sympatric North American Gray Wolf Populations," *Evolution* 45 (1991), pp. 104-119.

Leidy 1846 J. Leidy. "Remarks on *Trichina*," *Proceedings of the Philadelphia Academy of Anatomical Sciences* 3 (1846), pp. 107-108.

Lesko 1977 L. Lesko. *King Tut's Wine Cellar*. Berkeley, 1977.

Lichtheim 1957 M. Lichtheim. *Demotic Ostraca from Medinet Habu*. University of Chicago Oriental Institute Publications 80. Chicago, 1957.

Lindsay 1966 J. Lindsay. *Leisure and Pleasure in Roman Egypt*. New York, 1966.

Littauer and Crouwel 1979 M. Littauer and J. Crouwel. *Wheeled Vehicles and Ridden Animals in the Ancient Near East*. Leiden, 1979.

Lorenz 1954 K. Lorenz. *Man Meets Dog*. London, 1954.

Loret 1892 V. Loret. *La Flore Pharaonique*. Paris, 1892.

Loret 1904 V. Loret. "L'ail chez les Anciens Egyptiens," *Sphinx* 8 (1904), pp. 135-147.

Lortet and Gaillard 1908 L. Lortet and C. Gaillard. *La Faune Momifiée de l'Ancienne Egypte* (série 4), Archives du Musée d'Histoire Naturelle de Lyon. Lyon, 1908.

Lovell 1993 N. Lovell. "Anemia in the Nile and Indus Valleys: Evidence and Interpretation," *Comparative and Intersocietal Perspectives: The Indus Valley, Mesopotamia and Egypt*, R. Wright (ed), 1993, (in press).

Lucas 1989 A. Lucas. *Ancient Egyptian Materials and Industries*. London, 1989.

Lumer 1940 H. Lumer. "Evolutionary Allometry in the Skeleton of the Domestic Dog," *American Naturalist* 74 (1940), pp. 439-467.

Lurker 1980 M. Lurker. *The Gods and Symbols of Ancient Egypt*. New York, 1980.

Lutz 1922 H. Lutz. *Viticulture and Brewing*. Leipzig, 1922.

Lyman 1987 R. Lyman. "On the Analysis of Vertebrate Mortality Profiles: Sample Size, Mortality Type and Hunting Pressure," *American Antiquity* 52 (1987), pp. 125-142.

MacDonald 1987 K. MacDonald. "Development and Stability of Personality Characteristics in Pre-Pubertal Wolves: Implications for Pack Organization and Behavior, *Man and Wolf*, H. Frank (ed), pp. 375-399. Dordrecht, 1987.

Mackworth-Praed and Grant 1952 C. Mackworth-Praed and C. Grant. *Birds of Eastern and North Africa* I. London, 1952.

Maesen 1972 L van der Maesen. *Cicer. A Monograph on the Genus with Special Reference to the Chickpea (Cicer arietinum), its Ecology and Cultivation*. Wageningen, 1972.

Malek 1993 J. Malek. *The Cat in Ancient Egypt*. London, 1993.

Manniche 1989 L. Manniche. *An Ancient Egyptian Herbal*. London, 1989.

Marcus 1982 J. Marcus. "The Plant World of the Sixteenth and Seventeenth Century Lowland Maya," *Maya Subsistence*, K. Flannery (ed), pp. 239-274. New York, 1982.

Martin 1971 G. Martin. *Egyptian Administrative and Private-Name Seals Principally of the Middle Kingdom and Second Intermediate Period*. Oxford, 1971.

Mason 1967 I. Mason. *Sheep Breeds of the Mediterranean*. Edinburgh, 1967.

Maspero 1901 G. Maspero. "The Dawn of Civilization," *Egypt and Chaldaea*. A. Sayce (ed), M. McClure (trans.). London, 1901.

Massoulard 1949 E. Massoulard. *Préhistoire et Protohistoire d'Egypte*. Paris, 1949.

Matthey 1954 R. Matthey. "Chromosomes et Systematiques des Canides," *Mammalia* 18, 3 (1954), pp 225-230.

Mayr 1982 E. Mayr. *The Growth of Biological Thought*. Cambridge, Mass., 1982.

McArdle 1982 J. McArdle. "Preliminary Report on the Predynastic Fauna of the Hierakonpolis Project," *Egyptian Studies Association* 1 (1982), pp. 116-121.

McCollum 1976 G. McCollum. "Onions and Allies," *Evolution of Crop Plants*, N. Simmonds (ed), pp. 186-190. London, 1976.

McCorriston and Hole 1991 J. McCorriston and F. Hole. "The Ecology of Season Stress and the Origins of Agriculture in the Near East," *American Anthropologist* 93 (1991), pp. 46-69.

McDonald 1982 M. McDonald. "Dakleh Oasis Project, Third Preliminary Report on the Lithic Industries in the Dakleh Oasis," *Journal of the Society of the Study of Egyptian Antiquities* 12 (1982), pp. 115-138.

McHugh 1971 W. McHugh. *Late Prehistoric Cultural Adaptation in the Southeastern Libyan Desert*. University of Wisconsin, Ph.D dissertation. Madison, 1971.

Meadow 1981 R. Meadow. "Early Animal Domestication in South Asia: A First Report of the Faunal Remains from Mehrgarh, Pakistan," *South Asian Archaeology*, H. Hartel (ed), pp. 143-179. Berlin, 1981.

Mech 1970 L. Mech. *The Wolf*. New York, 1970.

Meggers 1954 B. Meggers. "Environmental Limitations on the Development of Culture," *American Anthropologist* 56 (1954), pp. 801-824.

Mehra 1967 K. Mehra. "History of Sesame in India and its Cultural Significance," *Vishveshvaranand Indological Journal* 5 (1967), pp 93-107.

Meinertzhagen 1930 R. Meinertzhagen. *Nicoll's Birds of Egypt* I-II. London, 1930.

Mekhitarian 1954 A. Mekhitarian. *Egyptian Painting*. Geneva, 1954.

Menghin and Amer 1932 O. Menghin and M. Amer. *The Excavations of the Egyptian University in the Neolithic Site of Maadi. First Preliminary Report* 1930-31. Cairo, 1932.

Menu 1970 B. Menu. *Le Régime Juridique des Terres et du Personnel Attaché à la Terre dans le Paprus Wilbour*. Lille, 1970.

Menu 1982 B. Menu. *Recherches sur l'Histoire Juridique, Economique et Sociale de l'Ancienne Egypte*. Versailles, 1982.

Mertens 1936 R. Mertens. "Der Hund aus dem Senchenberg-Moor, ein Begleiter des Ur's," *Natur und Volk* 66 (1936), pp. 506-510.

Mikesell 1955 M. Mikesell. "Notes on the Dispersal of the Dromedary," *Southwestern Journal of Anthropology* 11, 3 (1955), pp. 231-245.

Miller 1992 N. Miller. "The Origin of Plant Cultivation in the Near East," *The Origins of Agriculture*, C. Cowan and P. Watson (eds), pp. 39-57. Washington, 1992.

Millet 1990 N. Millet. "The Narmer Macehead and Related Objects," *Journal of the American Research Center in Egypt* 27 (1990), pp. 53-60.

Moens and Wetterstrom 1988 M. Moens and W. Wetterstrom. "The Agricultural Economy of an Old Kingdom Town in Egypt's West Delta: Insights from the Plant Remains," *Journal of Near Eastern Studies* 3 (1988), pp. 159-173.

Mond et al. 1937 R. Mond, O. Myers, T. Baly, J. Cameron. A. Cave, S. Huzayyin, J. Jackson and D. O'Leary. *Cemeteries of Armant I*. London, 1937.

Montet 1910 P. Montet. "Les Scènes de Boucherie dans les Tombes de l'Ancien Empire," *Bulletin de l'Institut Français d'Archéologie Orientale* 7 (1910), pp. 41-65.

Montet 1925 P. Montet. *Vie Privée, Scènes de la Privée dans les Tombeaux Egyptiens de l' Ancien Empire*. Strasbourg, 1925.

Montet 1950 P. Montet. "Etudes sur Quelques Prêtres et Functionnaires du Dieu Min," *Journal of Near Eastern Studies* 9, pp. 18-27.

Montet 1985 P. Montet. *Everyday Life in Egypt in the Days of Ramesses the Great*. Philadelphia, 1985.

Morrison-Scott 1952 T. Morrison-Scott. "The Mummified Cats of Ancient Egypt," *Proceedings Zoological Society of London* 121, 4 (1952), pp. 861-867.

Moreau 1927 R. Moreau. "Quail," *Zoological Society of Egypt* 1 (1927), pp. 6-13.

Moreau 1966 R. Moreau. *The Bird Faunas of Africa and its Islands*. New York, 1966.

Morey 1990 D. Morey. *Cranial Allometry and the Evolution of the Domestic Dog*. University of Tennessee, Ph.D dissertation, Knoxville, 1990.

Mori 1965 F. Mori. *Tadrart Acacus. Arte Rupestre e Culture del Sahara Preistorico*. Torino, 1965.

Morley 1920 S. Morley. *The Inscriptions at Copan*. Carnegie Institute of Washington Publication 219, 1920.

Moustafa 1964 Y. Moustafa. "The Domesticated Animals of the Sekhemkhet Step Pyramid," *Annales du Service des Antiquités de l'Egypte* 58 (1964), pp. 225-265.

Müller 1903 R. Müller. *Studien und Beitrage zur Geographie der Wirtschaftstiere* I. Die Geographische Verbreitung der Wirtschaftstiere mit Besonderer Berücksichtigung der Tropenländer. Leipzig, 1903.

Muratova 1931 V. Muratova. "Common Beans (*Vicia faba*),". *Bulletin of Botanical Genetic Plant Breeding* supplement 50, pp. 248-295. Lenningrad, 1931 (English Summary).

Murie 1944 A. Murie. *The Wolves of Mount McKinley*. U.S. National Park Service, Faunal Series 5, 1944.

Murray 1967 G. Murray. *Dare Me to the Desert*. London, 1967.

Musil 1974 R. Musil. "Tiergesellschaft der Kniegrotte," *Die Kniegrotte, eine Magdalénian-Station in Thüringen*, R. Feustel (ed), pp. 30-72. Museum für Ur-und Frühgeschichte Thüringens 5, 1974.

Musil 1984 R. Musil. "The First Known Domestication of Wolves in Central Europe," *Animals and Archaeology 4: Husbandry in Europe*, C. Grigson and J. Clutton-Brock (eds), British Arcaheological Reports International Series 227 (1984), pp. 23-25.

Muthuri and Kinyamario 1989 F. Muthuri and J. Kinyamario. "Nutritive Value of Papyrus (*Cyperus papyrus*) a Tropical Emergent Macrophyte. *Economic Botany* 43 (1989), pp. 23-30.

Muzzolini 1980a A. Muzzolini. "L'Age des Peintures et Gravures du Djebel Ouenat et le Problème du *Bos brachyceros* au Sahara," *Travaux de l'Institut d'Art Préhistorique, Université de Toulouse* 12 (1980), pp. 347-371.

Muzzolini 1980b A. Muzzolini. "*Boeuf* (Préhistoire). (Extrait de l'Encyclopédie Berbère)," Laboratoire d'Anthropologie et de Préhistoire des Pays de la Méditerranée Occidentale, Université de Provence, Cahier 27 (1980), pp. 1-16.

Muzzolini 1981 A. Muzzolini. La datation de premiers boeufs domestiques sur les figurations rupestres au Sahara centrale. "La Période Bubaline," *Bulletin de l'Association Internationale pour l'Etude de la Préhistoire Egyptienne* III (1981), pp. 15-37.

Muzzonlini 1982 A. Muzzolini. "Le Vocabulaire zoologique Rélatif aux Boeufs en Egypte, au Maghreb et au Saharan durant l'Holocene," *Bulletin de l'Association Internationale pour l'Etude de la Prehistoire Egyptienne* IV (1982), pp. 21-39.

Nayer 1976 N. Nayer. "Sesame," *Evolution of Crop Plants*, N. Simmonds (ed.), pp. 231-233. London, 1976.

Netting 1986 R. Netting. *Cultural Ecology*. Prospect Heights, Illinois, 1986.

Newberry nd. P. Newberry. *El Bersheh* (part I), London, n.d.

Newberry 1889 P. Newberry. On the Vegetable Remains Discovered in the Cemetery of Hawara, *Hawara, Biahmu and Arsinoe*, W. Petrie (ed), pp. 46-53. London, 1889.

Newberry 1890 P. Newberry. "The Ancient Botany," *Kahun, Gurob, and Hawara*, W. Petrie (ed), pp. 46-50. London, 1890.

Newberry 1893 P. Newberry. *Beni Hasan* I-II. London, 1893.

Newberry 1900 P. Newberry. *The Life of Rekhmara*. Westminster, 1900.

Newberry 1928 P. Newberry. "The Pig and the Cult Animal of Set," *Journal of Egyptian Archaeology* 14 (1928), pp. 211-225.

Newsome et al. 1980 A. Newsome, L. Corbett and S. Carpenter. "The Identity of the Dingo: Morphological Discriminants of Dingo and Dog Skulls," *Australian Journal of Zoology* 28 (1980), pp. 615-625.

Nibbi 1979 A. Nibbi. "Some Remarks on Ass and Horse in Ancient Egypt and the Absence of the Mule," *Zeitschrift für Ägyptische Sprache und Altertumskunde* 106 (1979), pp. 148-168.

Nims 1958 C. Nims. "The Bread and Beer Problems of the Moscow Mathematical Papyrus," *Journal of Egyptian Archaeology* 44 (1958), pp 56-65.

Nixon 1951 R. Nixon. "The Date Palm-Tree of Life," *Economic Botany* 5 (1951), pp. 274-301.

Nobis 1971 G. Nobis. *Vom Wildpferd zum Hauspferd. Fundamenta Reihe* B, VI. 1971.

Nobis 1979 G. Nobis. *Der Älteste Haushunde Lebte vor 1400 Jahren. Umschau* 79, (1979), p. 610.

Nobis 1986 G. Nobis. "Die Wildsäugetiere in der Umwelt des Menschen von Oberkassel bei Bonn und das Domestikations-problem von Wölfen im Jungpaläolithikum," *Bonner Jahrbücher* 1986 (1986), pp. 367-376.

Nowak 1992. R. Nowak. "The Red Wolf is not a Hybrid," *Conservation Biology* 6 (1992), pp. 593-595.

Nowak et al. 1992 R. Nowak, M. Phillips, V. Henry. W. Hunter and R. Smith. "The Origin and Fate of the Red Wolf." Paper Presented at the 2nd North American Wolf Symposium. Edmonton Alberta, August 1992. (Paper in possession of author).

Olmo 1976 H. Olmo. "Grapes," *Evolution of Crop Plants*, N. Simmonds (ed), pp. 294-298. London, 1976.

Olsen 1985 J. Olsen. "Prehistoric Dogs in Mainland East Asia," *Origins of the Domestic Dog*, S. Olsen (ed.), pp. 47-70. Tucson, 1985.

Olsen 1985 S. Olsen. *Origins of the Domestic Dog*. Tuscon, 1985.

Orlov 1931 A. Orlov. The Most Important Agronomical and Botanical Forms of Barley (*Hordeum sativum* Jessen) *Bulletin of Applied Botany, Genetics and Plant Breeding* 27 (1931), pp. 329-381 (English Summary).

Osborn 1968 D. Osborn. "Notes on Medicinal and Other Uses of Plants in Egypt," *Economic Botany* 22 (1968), pp. 165-177.

Osborn and Helmy 1980 D. Osborn and I. Helmy. *The Contemporary Land Mammals of Egypt*. Fieldiana Zoology, new series 5.

Oudejans 1969 J. Oudejans. "Date palm *Phoenix dactylifera* L.," *Outlines of Perennial Crop Breeding in the Tropics*, F. Ferwerda and F. Wit (eds), pp. 243-257. Wageningen, 1969.

Parker 1989 "*Red Wolf Taxonomy. A Review*," U.S Fish and Wildlife Service Red Wolf Management Series, Report No. 5. 1989.

Paton 1925 D. Paton. *Animals of Ancient Egypt*. Princeton, 1925.

Peet and Woolley 1923. E. Peet and C. Woolley. *The City of Akhenaten* I. London, 1923.

Pellet 1946 F. Pellet. *The Development of Beekeeping: The Hive and the Honey Bee*. London, 1946.

Pendlebury 1951 J. Pendlebury. *The City of Akhenaten* III. London, 1951.

Percival 1921 J. Percival. *The Wheat Plant*. London

Percival 1936 J. Percival. "Cereals of Ancient Egypt and Mesopotamia," *Nature* 138 (1936), pp. 271-272.

Perkins 1964 D. Perkins. "Prehistoric Fauna from Shanidar, Iraq," *Science* 144 (1964), pp. 1565-1566.

Perkins 1965 D. Perkins. "Three Faunal Assemblages from Sudanese Nubia," *Kush* 13 (1969), pp. 56-61.

Perkins 1969 D. Perkins. "Fauna of Çatal Hüyük Evidence for early Cattle Domestication in Anatolia," *Science* 164 (1969), pp. 177-179.

Peters 1983 R. Peters. *The Ecological Implications of Body Size*. Cambridge, 1983.

Peterson 1965 R. Peterson. *Wheat*. New York

Peterson 1977 R. Peterson. *Wolf Ecology and Prey Relationships on Isle Royale*. U.S. National Park Service, Scientific Monograph Series II, 1977.

Petrie 1889 W. Petrie. *Hawara, Biahmu and Arsinoe*. London,1889.

Petrie 1890 W. Petrie. *Kahun, Gurob and Hawara*. London, 1890.

Petrie 1891 W. Petrie. *Illahun, Kahun and Gurob*. London, 1891.

Petrie 1892 W. Petrie. *Meidum*. London, 1892.

Petrie 1901 W. Petrie. *Royal Tombs II*. London, 1901.

Petrie 1907 W. Petrie. *Gizeh and Rifeh*. London, 1907.

Petrie 1920 W. Petrie. *Prehistoric Egypt*. London, 1920.

Petrie 1953 W. Petrie *Ceremonial Slate Palettes*. London, 1953.

Petrie and Quibell 1896 W. Petrie and J. Quibel. *Naqada and Ballas* I. London, 1896.

Petrie et al. 1903 W. Petrie, A. Weigall and F. Griffith. *Abydos* I-II. London, 1903.

Petrie et al. 1910 W. Petrie. E. McKay and G. Wainwright. *Meydum and Memphis*. London, 1910.

Phillips and Henry 1992 M. Phillips and V. Henry. "Comments on Red Wolf Taxonomy," *Conservation Biology* 6 (1992), pp. 596-597.

Pia 1942 J. Pia. Untersuchungen über die Rassenzugehörigkeit der Altägyptischen Hausziege. *Zeitschrift für Tierzüchtung und Züchtungsbiologie* 51, 1942.

Piankoff 1968 A. Piankoff. *The Pyramid Texts of Unas*. New York, 1968.

Pliny *Pliny: Natural History* I-VIII. H. Rackham and W. Jones (trans.). Cambridge, U.S.A., 1938-1956.

Plutarch. *Plutarch's Lives* I. B. Perrin (trans.), London, 1920.

Plutarch *Moralia* V (Isis and Osiris). F. Babbit (trans), Cambridge, U.S.A., 1936.

Porter 1965 P. Porter. "Environmental Potentials and Economic Oppportunites," *American Anthropoloigst* 67 (1965), pp. 409-420.

Portis 1907 A. Portis. *Di Alcani Avanzi Fossili di Grandi Ruminantia Principalmente della Provinzia di Roma*. Paleogeografica, Italia 13, 1907.

Posener 1962 G. Posener. *A Dictionary of Egyptian Civilization*. New York, 1962.

Prashad 1936 B. Prashad. *Animal Remains from Harappa*. Memoirs Archaeological Survey of India 51, 1931.

Przedziecki 1954 K. Przedziecki. "Le Lévrier en Afrique," *Bulletin de Liaison Saharienne* 17 (1954), pp. 89-101.

Pulliainen 1967a E. Pulliainen. "A Contribution to the Study of the Social Behavior of the Wolf," *American Zoologist* 7 (1967), pp. 313-317.

Pulliainen 1967b E. Pulliainen. "Wolf Ecology in Northern Europe," *The Wild Canids*, M. Fox (ed), pp. 292-299. New York, 1967.

Quibell 1908 J. Quibell. *Tomb of Yuan and Thuiu*. Cairo, 1908.

Quibell and Green 1900. J. Quibell and F. Green. *Hierakonpolis* IV. London, 1900.

Ramanujam 1976 S. Ramanujam. "Chickpea," *Evolution of Crop Plants*, N. Simmonds (ed), pp. 157-159. New York, 1976.

Randall-McIver and Mace 1902 D Randall-McIver and A. Mace. *El-Amrah and Abydos* 1899-1902. London, 1902.

Rawlinson 1885 G. Rawlinson. *The History of Herodotus*. New York, 1885.

Redding 1981 R. Redding. "The Faunal Remains," *An Early Town on the Deh-Luran Plain: Excavations at Tepe Farukhabad*, H. Wright (ed), pp 233-261. Museum of Anthropology, University of Michigan Memoir 13, 1981.

Redford 1988 D. Redford. *Akhenaten Temple Project: Rwd-Mnw and Inscriptions*. Toronto, 1988.

Redford 1990 D. Redford. *Egypt and Canaan in the New Kindgom*. Beer Seva, 1990.

Redman 1978 C. L. Redman. *The Rise of Civilization*. San Francisco, 1978.

Reed 1959 C. Reed. "Animal Domestication in the Prehistoric Near East," *Science* 130 (1959), pp. 1629-1639.

Reed 1960 C. Reed. "A Review of the Archaeological Evidence on Animal Domestication in the Prehistoric Near East," *Prehistoric Investigations in Iraqi Kurdistan*, R. Braidwood and B. Howe (eds), pp. 119-145. The Oriental Institute of the University of Chicago 31, 1960.

Reed 1969 C. Reed. "The Pattern of Animal Domestication in the Prehistoric Near East," *The Domestication and Exploitation of Plants and Animals*, P. Ucko and G. Dimbleby (eds), pp. 361-380. Chicago, 1969.

Reed 1977 C. Reed (ed). *Origins of Agriculture*. The Hauge, 1977.

Reed 1984 C. Reed. The Beginnings of Animal Domestication," *Evolution of Domesticated Animals*, I. Mason (ed), pp. 1-6. London, 1984.

Reinhardt 1912 L. Reinhardt. *Kulturgeschichte der Nutztiere*. Munich, 1912.

Rheenen 1968a H. A. van Rheenen. "Natural Cross-Fertilization in Sesame (*Sesamum indicum* L.)," *Samaru Research Bulletin* 94 (1968), pp. 147-153.

Rheenen 1968b H. A. van Rheenen. "Harvesting of Shattering Sesame," *Tropical Science* 9 (1968), pp. 204-210.

von Ricke 1967 H. von Ricke. Der Grundriss des Amama Wohrhauses. *Ausgrabungen der Deutschen Orient-Gesellschaft in Tel el-Amarna* IV, Osnabruck. 1967

Ricketson and Ricketson 1937 O. Ricketson and E. Ricketson. *Uaxactun Guatemala, Group E*, 1926-1931. Camegie Institute of Washington Publication 477. Washington, D. C., 1937.

Rosenweig 1966 M. Rosenweig. "Community Structure in Sympatric Carnivora," *Journal of Mammalogy* 47 (1966), pp. 602-612.

Rosman and Rubel 1989 A. Rosman and P. Rubel. "Stalking the Wild Pig: Hunting and Horticulture in Papua New Guinea," *Farmers as Hunters: Implications of Sedimentism*. S. Kent (ed), pp 27-36. Cambridge, 1989.

Ruffer 1919. M. Ruffer *Food in Egypt*. Mémoire Présenté à l'Institut Egyptien 1. Cairo, 1919.

Ryder and Whitaker 1976 E. Ryder and T. Whitaker. "Lettuce," *Evolution of Crop Plants*, N. Simmonds (ed), pp. 39-41. New York, 1976.

Ryder 1984. M. Ryder. "Sheep Representations, Written Records and Wool Measurements," *Animals in Archaeology 3: Early Herders and Their Flocks*. J. Clutton-Brock and C. Grigson (eds), pp. 69-82. British Archaeological Reports, International Series 202, 1984.

Saad 1951 Z. Saad. *Royal Excavations at Helwan* 1945-1947. Imprimerie de l'Institut Français d'Archéologie Orientale, 1951.

Sabloff and Willey 1967 J. Sabloff and G. Willey. "The Collapse of the Maya Civilization in the Southern Lowlands: A Consideration of History and Process," *Southwestern Journal of Anthropology* 23 (1967), pp. 311-336.

Sanford 1934 K. Sanford. *Paleolithic Man and the Nile Valley in Upper Middle Egypt. A Study of the Region During Pliocene and Pleistocene Times*. Part III. Oriental Institute Publication 18. Chicago, 1934.

Säve-Söderbergh 1957 T. Säve-Söderbergh. *Four Eighteenth Dynasty Tombs*. Oxford, 1957.

Schäfer 1973 H. Schäfer. "Zur Taxonomie der *Vicia narbonensis* Gruppe," *Kulturpflanze* 21 (1973), pp. 211-273.

Schäme 1922 R. Schäme. *Die Grundformen des Haushundschädels*. Jahrbuch der Jagdkunde 6, 1922.

Scharff 1957 A. Scharff. *Die Archäologischen Ergebnisse des Vorgeschichtlichen Grabenfelder von Abusir el Melaq, nach den Aufgezeichnungen, G. Muller*. Leipzig, 1957.

Schenkel 1967 R. Schenkel. "Submission: Its Features and Functions in the Wolf and Dog," *American Zoologist* 7 (1967), pp. 319-330.

Schmidtz-Nielson 1964 K. Schmidtz-Nielsen. *Desert Animals: Physiological Problems of Heat and Water*. Oxford, 1964.

Schmitz and Lavigne 1987 O. Schmitz and D. Lavigne. "Factors Affecting Body Size in Sympatric Ontario *Canis*," *Journal of Mammalogy* 68 (1987), pp. 92-99.

Schotté and Ginsburg 1987 C. Schotté and G. Ginsburg. "Development of Social Organization and Mating in a Captive Wolf Pack," *Man and Wolf*, H. Frank (ed), pp. 439-474. Dordrecht, 1987.

Schweinfurth 1885 G. Schweinfurth. "Notice sur le Restes de Végétaux de l'Ancienne Egypte Contenus dans une Armoire du Musée de Boulaq," *Bulletin de l'Institut Egyptien Année 1884*, 5 (1885), pp. 3-10.

Schweinfurth 1886 G. Schweinfurth. "Les Dernières Découvertes Botaniques dans les Anciens Tombeaux de l'Egypte," *Bulletin de l'Institut Egyptien Année 1885*, 6 (1885), pp. 256-283.

Schweinfurth 1912 G. Schweinfurth. *Alte Tierbilder und Felsinschriften bei Assuan*. Zeitschrift für Ethnologie 44. 1912.

Scott 1950 J. Scott. "The Social Behavior of Dogs and Wolves: an Illustration of Sociobiological Systematics," *Annals of the New York Academy of Sciences* 51 (1950), pp. 1009-1021.

Scott 1968 J. Scott. "Evolution and Domestication of the Dog," *Evolutionary Biology* II. T. Dobzhansky, M. Hecht and W. Steere (eds), pp. 243-275. New York, 1968.

Scott and Fuller 1965 J. Scott and J. Fuller. *Genetics and Social Behavior of the Dog*. Chicago, 1965.

Selim 1938 H Selim. *Excavations at Giza* IV 38. Cairo, 1938.

Serpell 1989 J. Serpell. "Pet-keeping and Animal Domestication: A Reappraisal," *The Walking Larder*, J. Clutton-Brock (ed), pp 10-21. London, 1989.

Sethe 1906 K. Sethe. *Urkunden der 18 Dynastie*. Fac. 1-22. Leipzig, 1906.

Sethe 1932 K. Sethe. *Urkunden des Alten Reiches* I. Leipzig, 1932.

Sheets 1982 P. Sheets. "Prehistoric Agricultural Systems in El-Salvador," *Maya Subsistence*, K. Flannery (ed), pp. 99-118. New York, 1982.

Sickenberger 1901 E. Sickenberger. "Contribution à la Flore d'Egypte," *Mémoire de l'Institut Egyptien* IV (1901), pp. 167-335.

Simonsen 1976 V. Simonsen. "Electrophoretic Studies on Blood Proteins of Domestic Dogs and Other Canidae," *Hereditas* 82 (1976), pp. 7-18.

Simmonds 1976 N. Simmonds. "Olive," *Evolution of Crop Plants*, S. Simmonds (ed), pp. 219-221. London, 1976.

Simoons 1961 F. Simoons. *Eat Not this Flesh: Food Avoidance in the Old World*. Madison, 1961.

Singh 1976 D. Singh. "Castor," *Evolution of Crop Plants*, S. Simmonds (ed), pp. 84-86. New York, 1976.

Singh et al. 1960 G. Singh, K. Gill and N. Rana. "Effect of Selfing and Sibbing on Certain Characters in Sesamum," *Indian Oilseeds Journal* 4 (1960), pp. 271-275.

Skaggs 1946 O. Skaggs. "A Study of the Dog Skeletons from Indian Knoll with Special Reference to the Coyote as a Progenitor," *Indian Knoll*, W. Webb (ed), pp. 341-355. University of Kentucky Reports in Anthropology and Archaeology 4. Lexington, 1946.

Smith 1984 A. Smith. "The Origins of Food Production in Northeast Africa," *Palaeoecology of Africa* 16 (1984), pp. 317-324.

Smith 1969 H. Smith. "Animal Domestication and Animal Cults in Dynastic Egypt," *The Domestication and Exploitation of Plants and Animals*. P. Ucko and G. Dimbleby (eds), pp. 307-314. London, 1969.

Smith 1976 P. Smith. "Minor Crops," *Evolution of Crop Plants*, N. Simmonds (ed), pp. 301-324. New York, 1976.

Spencer 1965 P. Spencer. *The Samburu*, London, 1965.

Sponsel 1989 L. Sponsel. "Farming and Foraging: A Necessary Complementarity in Amazonia," *Farmers and Hunters:The Implication of Sedentism*, S. Kent (ed), pp. 37-45. Cambridge, 1989.

Stager 1985 E. Stager. "First Fruits of Civilization," *Palestine in the Bronze and Iron Age: Papers in Honor of Olga Tufnell*, J. Tubb (ed), pp. 172-187. London, 1985.

Stager 1992 E. Stager. "The Periodization of Palestine from Neolothic through Early Bronze Times," *Chronologies in Old World Archaeology*, R. Erlich (ed), pp. 22-39, Chicago, 1992.

Stampfli 1966 H. Stampfli. The Fauna of the Prehistoric Archaeological Sites of Jarmo, Maturrah, Karim Shahir and the Amoq in South-Western Asia. (cited in C. Reed, *Animal Domestication in the Near East.*)

Stearn 1978 W. Stearn. "European Species of Allium and Allied Genera of Alliaceae: a Synonymic Enumeration," *Annales. Musei. Goulandris* 4. (1978), pp. 83-198.

Stemler 1980 A. Stemler. "Origins of Plant Domestication in the Sahara and the Nile Valley," *The Sahara and the Nile*, M. Williams and H. Faure (eds), pp. 503-26. Rotterdam, 1980.

Stemler and Falk 1980 A. Stemler and R. Falk. "A Scanning Electron Microscope Study of Cereal Grains from Nabta Playa," *Prehistory of the Eastern Sahara*, F. Wendorf and R. Schild (eds), pp. 397-400. New York, 1980.

Stockard 1941 C. Stockard. *The Genetic and Endocrine Basis for Differences in Form and Behavior.* American Anatomical Memoir 19. 1941.

Stockhaus 1965 K. Stockhaus. Metrische Untersuchungen an Schädeln von Wölfen und Hunden. *Zeitschrift für Zoologische Systematik und Evolutionsforschung* 3 (1965), pp 157-258.

Storey 1976 W. Storey. "Fig," *Evolution of Crop Plants.* N. Simmonds (ed), pp. 205-208. London, 1976.

Strabo *The Geography of Strabo* I-VIII. H. Jones (trans). New York, 1917-1932.

Strebel 1905 R. Strebel. *Die Deutschen Hunde.* Frankfurt, 1905.

Strekalovsky 1949 N. Strekalovsky. *Shooting and Fishing in Egypt.* Cairo, 1949.

Struever 1971 S. Struever (ed). *Prehistoric Agriculture.* New York, 1971.

Sturdy 1975 D. 1975. "Some Reindeer Economies in Prehistoric Europe," *Palaeoeconomy*, E. Higgs (ed), pp. 55-95. Cambridge, 1975.

Sullivan 1978 J. Sullivan. "Variability in the Wolf, a Group Hunter," *Wolf and Man: Evolution in Parallel*, R. Hall and H. Sharp (eds), pp. 31-40. New York, 1978.

Sweet 1965 L. Sweet. "Camel Pastoralism in North Arabia and the Minimal Camping Unit," *Man, Culture and Animals*, A. Leeds and A. Vayda (eds), pp. 129-152. Washington, 1965.

Täckholm 1961 V. Täckholm. *Le Monastère de Phoebammon dans la Thébaide III: Botanical Identification of the Plants Found at the Monastery of Phoebammon.* Cairo, 1961.

Täckholm 1974 V. Täckholm. *Student's Flora of Egypt.* Beirut, 1974.

Täckholm and Täckholm 1941 V. Täckholm and G. Täckholm. *Flora of Egypt* I. Bulletin of the Faculty of Science 17. Cario, 1941.

Täckholm and Drar 1950. V. Täckholm and M. Drar. *Flora of Egypt* II. Bulletin of the Faculty of Science 28. Cairo, 1950.

Täckholm and Drar 1954 V. Täckholm and M. Drar. *Flora of Egypt* III. Bulletin of the Faculty of Science 30. Cairo, 1954.

Talbot 1960 L. Talbot. "A Look at Threatened Species," *Oryx* 5 (1960), pp. 153-293.

Tannahil 1973 R. Tannahil. *Food in History.* New York, 1977.

Theophrastus *Enquiry Into Plants and Minor Works of Odours and Weather Signals* I, II. A. Hort (trans), New York, 1980.

Thiselton-Dyer 1875 W. Thiselton-Dyer. *The Papyrus.* Gardner's Chronicle 1. London, 1875.

Tobler 1950 A. Tobler. *Excavations at Tepe Gawra* II. University of Pennsylvania, Museum Monographs. Philadelphia, 1950.

Todd 1977 N. Todd. "Cats and Commerce," *Scientific American* 237/5 (1977), pp. 100-107.

Trigger 1968 B. Trigger. *Beyond History: The Methods of Prehistory.* New York, 1968.

Turnbull and Reed 1974 P. Turnbull and C. Reed. "The Fauna from the Terminal Pleistocene of Palegawra Cave, a Zarzian Occupation Site in Northeastern Iraq," *Fieldiana: Anthropology* 63 (1974), pp. 81-146.

Tylor and Griffith 1895 J. Tylor and Ll. Griffith. *The Tomb of Paheri at El-Kab.* London, 1895.

Uerpmann 1979 H. P. Uerpmann. *Probleme der Neolithisierung des Mittelmeerraumes.* Beihefte zum Tübinger Atlas des Vorderen Orients, Reihe B, 28. Wiesbaden, 1979.

Uerpmann 1987 H. P. Uerpmann. *The Ancient Distribution of Ungulate Mammals in the Middle East*, Beihefte zum Tübinger Atlas des Vorderen Orients. Reihe A, (Naturwissenschaften) 27. Wiesbaden, 1987.

van de Walle and Vergote 1943 B. Van de Walle and J. Vergote. "Traduction des Hieroglyphica d'Horapollen," *Chronique d'Egypte* 35 (1943), pp. 39-89.

van den Brink. 1988 E van den Brink. *The Archaeology of the Nile Delta, Egypt: Problems and Priorities.* Amsterdam, 1988.

Vandier 1952 J. Vandier. *Manuel d'Archéologie Egyptienne* V. Paris, 1952.

Vickers 1989 W. T. Vickers. "Patterns of Foraging and Gardening in a Semi-Sedentary Amazonian Community," *Farmers and Hunters: Implications of Sedentism*, S. Kent (ed), pp. 46-59. Cambridge, 1989.

Wahby 1938 A. Wahby. *Veterinary Hygiene.* Cairo, 1938.

Waines 1975 J. Waines. "The Biosystematics and Domestication of Peas, (*Pisum* L.)," *Bulletin of the Torrey Botanical Club* 102, 6 (1975), pp. 1975.

Wallert 1962 I. Wallert. *Die Palmer im Alten Ägypten.* Berlin, 1962.

Warden 1864 A. Warden. *The Linen Trade: Ancient and Modern.* London, 1864.

Watkins 1976 R. Watkins. "Apple and Pear," *Evolution of Crop Plants*, N. Simmonds (eds), pp. 247-250. New York, 1976.

Watkins 1981 R. Watkins. "Apples (genus *Malus*), Pears (genus *Pyrus*) and Plums, Apricots, Almonds, Peaches, Cherries (genus *Prunus*)," *The Oxford Encyclopedia of Trees of the World*, B. Hora (ed), pp. 187-201. Oxford, 1981.

Wayne 1986 R. Wayne. "Cranial Morphology of Domestic and Wild Canids: The Influence of Development on Morphological Change," *Evolution* 40 (1986), pp. 243-261.

Wayne 1992 R. Wayne. "On the Use of Morphologic and Molecular Genetic Characters to Investigate Species Status," *Conservation Biology* 6 (1992), pp. 590-592.

Wayne and Jenks 1991 R. Wayne and S. Jenks. "Mitochondrial DNA Analysis Implying Extensive Hybridization of the Endangered Red Wolf, *Canis rufus*," *Nature* 351 (1991), pp. 565-568.

Wayne and O'Brien 1987 R. Wayne and S. O'Brien. "Allozyme Divergence Within the Canidae," *Systematic Zoology* 36 (1987), pp. 339-355.

Weibel 1948 R. Weibel. "The Castor-Oil Plant in the United States," *Economic Botany* 2 (1948), pp. 273-283.

Wendorf 1968 F. Wendorf. "Late Paleolithic Sites in Egyptian Nubia," *Prehistory of Nubia*, F. Wendorf (ed), pp. 791-953. Dallas, 1968.

Wendorf and Schild 1976 F. Wendorf and R. Schild (eds), *Prehistory of the River Nile.* New York, 1976.

Wendorf and Schild 1980 F. Wendorf and R. Schild (eds), *Prehistory of the Eastern Sahara.* New York, 1980.

Wendorf et al 1970 F. Wendorf, R. Schild, and R. Said. "Egyptian Prehistory: Some New Concepts," *Science* 169 (1970), pp. 1161-1171.

Wendorf et al. 1979 F. Wendorf, R. Schild, N. el-Hadidi, A. Close, M. Kobusiewicz, H. Wieckowska, B. Issawi and H. Hans. "The Use of Barley in the Egyptian Late Paleolithic," *Science* 205 (1979), pp. 1341-1347.

Wendorf et al. 1984 F. Wendorf, R. Schild and A. Close. *Cattle-Keepers of the Eastern Sahara: the Neolithic of Bir Kiseiba.* New Delhi, 1984.

Wendorf et al. 1992 F. Wendorf, A. Close, R. Schild, K. Wasylikowa, R. Housley, J. Harlan and H. Królik. "Saharan Exploitation of Plants 8000 BP," *Nature* 359 (1992), pp. 721-724.

Wenke and Brewer 1993 R. Wenke and D. Brewer. "The Archaic and Old Kingdom Delta: The Evidence from Mendes and Kom el-Hisn," *House and Palace in Ancient Egypt*, M. Bietak (ed), Austrian Archaeological Institute. Cairo, 1993 (in press).

Wenke et al. 1983 R. Wenke, P. Buck, M. Lane, J. Long, and R. Redding. "The Fayum Archaeological Project: Preliminary Report of the 1981 Season," *American Research Center in Egypt, Newsletter* 122 (1983), pp. 25-34.

Wenke et al. 1988. R. Wenke, P. Buck, H. Hamroush, M. Kobusiewicz, K. Kroeper, and R. Redding. "Kom el-Hisn: Excavation of an Old Kingdom Settlement in the Egyptian Delta," *Journal of the American Research Center in Egypt* 25 (1988), pp. 5-34.

Werner and Gilliam 1984 E. Werner and J. Gilliam. "The Ontogenetic Niche and Species Interactions in Size-Structured Populations," *Annual Review of Ecology and Systematics* 15 (1984), pp. 393-425.

Werth 1944 E. Werth. "Die Primitiven Hunde und die Abstammungsfrage des Haushundes," *Zeitschrift für Tierzüchtung und Züchtungsbiologie* 56 (1944), pp. 216-260.

de Wet and Harlan 1971 J. de Wet and J. Harlan. "The Origin and Domestication of *Sorghum bicolor*," *Economic Botany* 25 (1971), pp. 128-135.

de Wet and Harlan 1975 J. De Wet and J Harlan. "Weeds and Domesticates: Evolution in the Man-made Habitat," *Economic Botany* 29 (1975), pp. 99-107.

Wetterstrom 1981 W. Wetterstrom. "Plant Remains," *The Predynastic of Egypt, Subsistence-Settlement Studies: The Nagada-Khattara Region*. Final Report to NSF, F. Hassan (ed), pp. 19-26. Pullman, 1981 (ms in possession of author).

Wetterstrom 1984 W. Wetterstrom. "The Plant Remains," *Archaeological Investigations at El-Hibeh 1980: Preliminary Report*. R. Wenke (ed), pp. 50-79. Malibu, 1984.

Wetterstrom 1993 W. Wetterstrom. "Foraging and Farming in Egypt: The Transition from Hunting and Gathering to Horticulture in the Nile Valley," *The Archaeology of Africa: Food, Metals and Towns*, T. Shaw, P. Sinclair, B. Anhah, and A. Okpoki (eds), pp. 165-225. London, 1993.

Whittaker and Bemis 1976 T. Whitaker and W. Bemis. "Cucurbits," *Evolution of Crop Plants*, N. Simmonds (ed), pp. 64-69. New York, 1976.

Wiesner 1939 J. Wiesner. *Fahren und Reiten in Alteuropa und im Alten Orient*. Der Alte Orient 38. Leipzig, 1939.

Wilkinson 1854 J. Wilkinson. *A Popular Account of the Ancient Egyptians* I-II. New York, 1854.

Wilkinson 1878 J. Wilkinson. *Manners and Customs of the Ancient Egyptians* I-III. London, 1878.

Willey and Shimkin 1971 G.R. Willey and D.B. Shimkin. "The Collapse of Classic Maya Civilization in the Southern Lowlands: A Symposium Summary Statement," *Southeastern Journal of Anthropology* 27 (1971), pp. 1-18.

Williams 1993 E. Williams. *Some Architectural Features Characteristic of Animal Enclosures*. Toronto, 1993 (ms. in possession of author).

Williams 1966 G. Williams. *Adaptation and Natural Selection*. Princeton, 1966.

Williams 1967 J. Williams. *A Field Guide to the Birds of East and Central Africa*. London, 1967.

Wilson 1975 E. Wilson. *Sociobiology*. Cambridge, Mass. 1975.

Winkler 1948 A. Winkler. "Grapes and Wine," *Economic Botany* 3 (1948), pp. 46-70.

Winkler 1938 H. Winkler. *Rock-Drawings of Southern Upper Egypt* I-II. Oxford, 1938.

Winlock 1955 H. Winlock. *Models of Daily Life in Ancient Egypt*. Cambridge, U.S.A., 1955.

Wolfgram 1894 A. Wolfgram. Die Einwirkung der Gefangenschaft auf die Gestaltung des Wolfsschädels. *Zoologische Jahrbucher*, 3 (1894), pp. 773-882.

Woolpy and Ginsburg 1967 J. Woolpy and B. Ginsburg. "Wolf Socialization, a Study of Temperament in a Wild Social Species," *American Zoologist* 7 (1967), pp. 357-363.

Wreszinski 1909 W. Wreszinski. *Der Grosse Medizinische Papyrus des Berliner Museums (pap. Berlin 3038) mit Uebersetzung, Kommentar und Glossar*. Leipzig, 1909.

Wreszinski 1912 W. Wreszinski. *Der Londoner Medizinische Papyrus (British Museum nr. 10059) und der Papyrus Hearst in Transkription, Uebersetzung und Kommentar*. Leipzig, 1912.

Wright 1971 G. Wright. "Orgins of Food Production in Southwest Asia: A Survey of Ideas," *Current Anthropology* 12 (1971), pp. 447-477.

Zander 1941 E. Zander. *Beitrage zur Herkunfstbestimmung bei Hönig III, II Tiel, Versuch der Pollenanalyse eines um 1350 v. Chr. einer aegyptische Mumie in der Nähe von Thebe Beigegeben Hönigs*. Leipzig, 1941.

Zarins 1976 J. Zarins. *The Domestication of Equidae in the Third Millennium BC Mesopotamia*. Phd Dissertation, University of Chicago, 1976.

Zeder 1986 M. Zeder. "The Equid Remains from Tal-el Malyan, Southern Iran, *Equids in the Ancient World*, R. Meadow and H. Uerpmann (eds), pp. 365-412. Weisbaden, 1986.

van Zeist 1970 W. van Zeist. "The Oriental Institute Excavations at Mureybit, Syria: Preliminary Report on the 1965 Campaign, Part III: Palaeobotany," *Journal of Near Eastern Studies* 29 (1970), pp. 167-176.

van Zeist 1980 W. van Zeist. "Aperçu sur la Diffusion des Végétaux Cultivés dans la Région Méditerranéenne," *Colloque sur la Mise en Place, l'Évolution et la Caractérisation de la Flore et la Végétation Circumméditerranéenne*. (Fundation L. Emberger) Naturalia Monspeliensia, Special Volume 1980, Montpellier (1980), pp. 129-145.

van Zeist 1983 W. van Zeist. "Fruit in Foundation Deposits of Two Temples," *Journal of Archaeological Science* 10 (1983), pp. 351-354.

Zeuner 1958 F. Zeuner. "Dog and Cat in the Neolithic of Jericho," *Palestine Exploration Quarterly*, London 1958, 1, pp 52-55.

Zeuner 1963 F. Zeuner. *A History of Domesticated Animals*. New York, 1963

Zeven 1967 A. Zeven. *The Semi-Wild Oil Palm and its Industry in Africa*. Agricultural Research Report 689. Wageningen, 1967.

Zimen 1975 E. Zimen. "Social Dynamics of the Wolf Pack," *The Wild Canids*, M. Fox (ed), pp. 336-362. New York, 1975.

Zohary 1969 D. Zohary. "The Progenitors of Wheat and Barley in Relation to Domestication and Agricultural Dispersion in the Old World," *The Domestication and Exploitation of Plants and Animals*, P. J. Ucko and G. W. Dimbleby (eds), pp. 47-66. Chicago, 1969.

Zohary 1971 D. Zohary. "Origins of South-West Asiatic Cereals: Wheats, Barley, Oats, Rye," *Plant Life of Southwest Asia*, P. Davis (ed), pp. 235-263. Edinburgh, 1971.

Zohary 1972 D. Zohary. "The Wild Progenitor and the Place of the Origin of the Cultivated Lentil, *Lens culinaris*," *Economic Botany* 26 (1972), pp. 326-332.

Zohary 1977 D. Zohary. "Comments on the Origin of Cultivated Broad Bean *Vicia faba* L.," *Israel Journal of Botany* 26 (1977), pp. 39-40.

Zohary 1989 D. Zohary. "Pulse Domestication and Cereal Domestication: How Different are They?," *Economic Botany* 43 (1989), pp. 31-34.

Zohary and Hopf 1973 D. Zohary and M. Hopf. "Domestication of Pulses in the Old World," *Science* 182 (1973), pp. 887-894.

Zohary et al. 1969. D. Zohary, J. Harlan, and A. Vardi. "The Wild Diploid Progenitors of Wheats and Their Breeding Value," *Eurphytica* 18 (1969), pp. 58-65.

Zohary and Hopf 1988 D. Zohary and M. Hopf. *Domestication of Plants in the Old World*. Oxford, 1988.

Zohary and Spiegel-Roy 1975 D. Zohary and P. Spiegel-Roy. "Beginnings of Fruit Growing in the Old World," *Science* 187 (1975), pp. 319-327.

Zohary 1973 M. Zohary. *Geobotanical Foundations of the Middle East* I-II. Stuttgart/Amsterdam, 1973.

Zohary 1976 M. Zohary. "Lentil," *Evolution of Crop Plants*, N. Simmonds (ed), pp. 163-164. New York, 1976.

Zohary 1983 M. Zohary. "Wild Genetic Resources of Crops in Israel," *Israel Journal of Botany* 32 (1983), pp. 97-127.

Zulficar 1937 M. Zulficar. "*Some Superstitions Relating to Plants,*" The Horticultural Review 24, 1937.

Index of Scientific and Common Names